Whiggish International Law

Legal History Library

VOLUME 29

Studies in the History of International Law

VOLUME 12

The titles published in this series are listed at *brill.com/shil*

Whiggish International Law

Elihu Root, the Monroe Doctrine, and International Law in the Americas

By

Christopher R. Rossi

BRILL
NIJHOFF

LEIDEN | BOSTON

Cover illustration: John Gast, *American Progress*, 1872. Oil on canvas. Autry Museum of the American West, Los Angeles; 92.126.1.

Library of Congress Cataloging-in-Publication Data

Names: Rossi, Christopher R., author.
Title: Whiggish international law / Elihu Root, the Monroe doctrine, and international law in the Americas / by Christopher R. Rossi.
Description: Leiden ; Boston : Brill Nijhoff, 2019. | Series: Legal history library ; volume 29 | Series: Studies in the history of international law ; volume 12 | Includes bibliographical references and index.
Identifiers: LCCN 2019002082 (print) | LCCN 2019004111 (ebook) | ISBN 9789004379510 (E-book) | ISBN 9789004389182 (hardback : alk. paper)
Subjects: LCSH: Latin America--International status--History--20th century. | International law--America--History--20th century. | United States--Foreign relations--Latin America--History--20th century. | Monroe doctrine--History--20th century. | Root, Elihu, 1845-1937--Influence. | International law--America--History--20th century--Historiography.
Classification: LCC KZ4116 (ebook) | LCC KZ4116 .R67 2019 (print) | DDC 341.098--dc23
LC record available at https://lccn.loc.gov/2019002082

Typeface for the Latin, Greek, and Cyrillic scripts: "Brill". See and download: brill.com/brill-typeface.

ISSN 1874-1793
ISBN 978-90-04-38918-2 (hardback)
ISBN 978-90-04-37951-0 (e-book)

This book is printed on acid-free paper and produced in a sustainable manner.

For Sigrid

Contents

Acknowledgments

This project began with an email to Nick Onuf. I had read a draft of his manuscript titled *Mightie Frame: Epochal Change and the Modern World* (2018), where he touched on historiography and discussed the post-Renaissance refreshment of history as veracity or storytelling. He got me thinking about the relevance of Herbert Butterfield's *Whig Interpretation of History* (1931). I thought it might be due for refreshment in the study of the international law and relations of the Americas. Nick noted Butterfield's work had become background knowledge in political theory, with periodic attempts by Skinnerians to foreground it. I thought it might be worthwhile to foreground it in the field of international law, and then I thought that Elihu Root unwittingly might have already done so. I thank Nick for stimulating my interest in the subject and for comments on an early draft, where I began to build my own frame.

I am grateful to Randall Lesaffer for adding this book to the Studies in the History of International Law series and to two anonymous readers for helpful comments. I am also grateful to my editor at Brill, Wendel Scholma, and to Kim Fiona Plas, for ably overseeing the production process.

I am indebted to Adrien Wing, the Bessie Dutton Murray Professor and Associate Dean for International and Comparative Law Programs, and John Reitz, the Edward Carmody Professor and Director of Graduate Programs and Visiting Scholars at the University of Iowa College of Law. They provided generous support for research assistance. I benefitted greatly from able research assistance provided by University of Iowa Law College students. I owe thanks to Antonio Martinez, Thais Fernandes Pereira, Waldemar Rodriquez, Rochelle Vazquez, and Charlotte Perez for their considerable efforts. Charlotte, especially, put her eyes to work in search of omissions and errors. Students in my advanced seminar on international law provided important feedback and criticism, and for their remarks I thank Douglas Hathaway, Bingqing He, Jung Min Kang, Derek LaBrie, Amanda Ndemo, Famatta Passawe, Matthew Roth, and Hyun Song.

From 1985 to 2014, Arthur Bonfield, now the Allan D. Vestal Professor Emeritus and Associate Dean Emeritus for Research at the Iowa Law College, turned a wonderful law library into one of the world's finest collections. All who enter Iowa's law library own tremendous thanks to him and the former deans and librarians who created and maintain this collection. Arthur, once again, cordially granted me access to his astounding private holdings of sixteenth and seventeenth century masterpieces of the age of discovery. His personal library is a sight to behold. Arthur's familiarity with these manuscripts, his proactive and insightful suggestions about which texts to review, and his generous personal attention to queries cannot be repaid. I am truly grateful for his help.

Portions of this work were presented at the Latin American conference on Rethinking and Renewing the Study of International Law, held at the universities de los Andes, del Rosario and the Externado de Colombia, with support from the History Section of the Latin American Society of International Law, Bogotá, September 26–28, 2017; the Latin America and International Law Conference, held at the Albrecht Mendelssohn Bartholdy Graduate School of Law, Universität Hamburg, February 8–9, 2018; the American Society of International Law Midwest Works-in-Progress Conference, Southern Illinois University College of Law, September 7–8, 2018; and the 2019 International Studies Association annual conference in Toronto. For helpful commentary, suggestions, and critique, I thank Ricardo Abello-Galvis, Walter Arevalo-Ramirez, José Manuel Barreto Soler, Edward Blumenthal, Stefano Cattelan, Theo Christov, Petra Gümplová, Andrei Mamolea, Liliana Obregón, Matthias Packeiser, Pedro Pizano, Ignacio de la Rasilla del Moral, Juan Pablo Scarfi, Joshua Simon, Frédéric Gilles Sourgens, Andreas Timmerman, and Guillermo Willard.

Marilyn Van Winkle and the curatorial staff at the Autry Museum of the American West in Los Angeles provided copyright clearance to reproduce on the book's cover John Gast's wonderfully whiggish chromolithographic allegory of American Progress (1872). Portions of Chapter 5 originally appeared or are reworked from "The Gulf of Fonseca and International Law: Condominium or Anti-Colonial Imperialism?" 3(1) *Jus Gentium, Journal of International Legal History* 115–153 (2018). Portions of Chapter 6 originally appeared in or are reworked from "Treaty of Tordesillas Syndrome: Sovereignty ad Absurdum and the South China Sea Arbitration." 50(1) Cornell International Law Journal 231–283 (2017).

I also thank and am grateful to Sigrid, Christian, Monica, and my father and brothers for providing company along the way.

Table of Cases and Treaties

1959 Antarctic Treaty, 1 December 1959, 402 U.N.T.S. 17; Treaty between Norway, The United States of America, Denmark, France, Italy, Japan, the Netherlands, Great Britain and Ireland and the British overseas Dominions and Sweden concerning Spitsbergen [Svalbard] signed in Paris 9th February 1920, http://www.sysselmannen.no/Documents/Sysselmannen_dok/English/Legacy/The_Svalbard_Treaty_9ssFy.pdf.

Agreement on the Delimitation of the Territorial Seas, Exclusive Economic Zones and Continental Shelves in the Beibu Gulf [Gulf of Tonkin] between the People's Republic of China and the Socialist Republic of Vietnam, Beijing, Dec. 25, 2000, entered into force June 30, 2004.

Agreement Governing the Activities of States on the Moon and Other Celestial Bodies, *opened for signature* December 18, 1979, 19 I.L.M. 1434.

Award in Regard to the Validity of the Treaty of Limits between Costa Rica and Nicaragua of 15 July 1858, Decision, 22 March 1888, 28 *Reports of International Arbitral Awards* 189-236 (2006).

Award on Jurisdiction and Admissibility. *In re* South China Sea Arbitration (Republic of the Phil. V. People's Republic of China) (Perm. Ct. Arb. 2016).

Boyd v. State of Nebraska, 143 U.S. 135 (1892).

Continental Shelf (Tunisia/Libyan Arab Jamahiriya), Judgment, 1982 I.C.J. Rep. 55.

Convention for the Establishment of a Central American Court of Justice, December 20, 1907, 2 American Journal of International Law (Suppl.) 231–243, 1908.

Costa Rica v. Nicaragua (1916) (C.A.C.J.).

Coyle v. Smith, 221 U.S. 559 (1911).

Declaration on the Maritime Zone Signed at Santiago on 18 August 1952, Chile, Ecuador, and Peru, Aug. 18, 1952, 1006 U.N.T.S 326.

El Salvador v. Nicaragua (1917) (C.A.C.J.).

Eritrea v. Yemen, (1998) (P.C.A.).

Final Transcript Day 1— Merits Hearing at 9, 77, *In re* South China Sea Arbitration (Republic of the Phil. V. People's Republic of China) (Perm. Ct. Arb. 2016).

Final Transcript Day 2—Merits Hearing at 156–58, 181–85, *In re* South China Sea Arbitration (Republic of the Phil. V. People's Republic of China) (Perm. Ct. Arb. 2016).

Fisheries Case (U.K. v Nor.) (1951) (I.C.J.).

Frontier Dispute (Burkina Faso/Mali) (1986) (I.C.J.).

Honduras v. Salvador and Guatemala, CACJ, Judgment, December 19, 1908. 3(3) *American Journal of International Law* 729–736, 1909.

Interoceanic Canal (Bryan-Chamorro Treaty), signed in Washington 5 Aug. 1915, 22 UST.

Island of Palmas (U.S. v. Neth.) (1928) (P.C.A.).

Land, Island and Maritime Frontier Dispute (El Salvador/Honduras: Nicaragua intervening), (1992) (I.C.J.).

North Sea Continental Shelf Cases (Den. v. F.R.G v. Den.; F.R.G. v. Neth.) (1969) (I.C.J.).

Pulp Mills on the River Uruguay (Argentina v. Uruguay) (2010) (I.C.J.).

R. v. Stevens, (2011) 106 O.R. 3d (Can. Ont. Sup. Ct. J.).

South China Sea Arbitration (Republic of the Phil. v. People's Republic of China) (2016) (P.C.A.).

Treaty between Norway, The United States of America, Denmark, France, Italy, Japan, the Netherlands, Great Britain and Ireland and the British Overseas Dominions and Sweden Concerning Spitsbergen Signed in Paris 9th February 1920.

Treaty of Peace, Amity, Navigation and Commerce with New Granada, Dec. 12, 1846 in Bevans, Charles I. *Treaties and Other International Agreements of the United States of America 1776–1949*. 1971.

"Treaty of Peace of Ancón, Chile-Peru, Oct. 20, 1883." In Obligation to Negotiate Access to the Pacific Ocean (Bol. v. Chile), Preliminary Objection, annex 1. July 15, 2014), http://www.icj-cij.org/files/case-related/153/18616.pdf (transcription and translation).

"Treaty of Peace and Amity between His Britannic Majesty and the United States of America." *Avalon Project*, http://avalon.law.yale.edu/19th_century/ghent.asp.

Treaty on Principles Governing the Activities of States in the Exploration and Use of Outer Space, including the Moon and Other Celestial Bodies, 610 U.N.T.S. 205 (1967).

CHAPTER 1

Reading International Law's Historiographic Turn in Latin America

The eighth annual meeting of the American Society of International Law convened at 8:00 p.m. on Wednesday, April 22, 1914 at the New Willard Hotel in Washington, D.C. Society president, Elihu Root (1845–1937), delivered opening remarks. He and Charles Francis Adams Jr. (1835–1915), grandson of statesman John Quincy Adams (1767–1848), who played a central role in creating the Monroe Doctrine, then delivered opening addresses on "The Real Monroe Doctrine" and "The Origin of the Monroe Doctrine," respectively.

Four sessions followed over the next three days. Each session dealt with the Monroe Doctrine, the 1823 Western Hemispheric message to Europe to steer clear of colonial intrusion. Adams later could hardly recall when he had "had such a solid dose of any subject."[1] Presentations canvassed its doctrinal offshoots, its misconceptions and limitations, its relevance as a domestic and international policy tool, and its role as a "gospel of peace."[2] Topics also included its influences in Latin America and Europe. Mindful of the "epidemic of discussion" swirling around the doctrine, the panel sessions concluded with George Blakeslee's paper on the question: "Should the Monroe Doctrine Continue to be a Policy of the United States?"[3]

Committing the entire substantive agenda to the Monroe Doctrine demonstrated both its central and controversial status in United States foreign policy. It had guided United States hemispheric policy for 91 years. However, Root wanted to dispel the notion that the doctrine had changed over time. He said the justification for his opening address "will be not because I say anything novel, but because there is occasion for restating well settled matters which seem to have been overlooked in some recent writings on the subject."[4]

In contrast to his stated intention, Root then reworked the Monroe Doctrine by overlooking what he had said less than a decade before. In a famous

1 Letter from Charles Francis Adams to Hiram Bingham (April 29, 1914) (on file with the Sterling Memorial Library, Yale University). The author thanks Andrei Mamolea for this information.

2 *See generally* 8 ASIL Proc. (1914).

3 George H. Blakeslee, *Should the Monroe Doctrine Continue to be a Policy of the United States?*, 8 ASIL Proc. 217, 217 (1914).

4 Elihu Root, *The Real Monroe Doctrine*, 8 ASIL Proc. 6, 6 (1914).

 | DOI:10.1163/9789004379510_002

speech delivered in Rio de Janeiro in 1906,[5] Root linked the Monroe Doctrine to hemispheric fraternal association and common cause.[6] His 1914 speech before the American Society of International Law emphasized the Monroe Doctrine's unilateralist, nonreciprocal character. "Since the Monroe Doctrine is a declaration based upon this nation's right of self-protection," said Root, "it cannot be transmuted into a joint common declaration by American states or any number of them." If Chile or Argentina or Brazil made such a declaration, it would affect their own individual safety, "not the safety of the United States.... Each nation would act for itself and in its own right."[7] Root then emphasized that a "false conception" of the Monroe Doctrine had "invaded the public press."[8] By "false conception," Root meant that the Monroe Doctrine had turned into an instrument justifying hegemonic intervention. The *real* Monroe Doctrine meant to counter "[g]randiose schemes of national expansion;" it opposed motives of compulsion against Central or South American countries, "clamors for national glory," "the essence of tyranny," and "interference in the internal affairs of all weaker nations in the New World."[9] In subtle ways, Root conflated incongruent messages with his reworking of the Monroe Doctrine in an attempt to balance its unilateralist and fraternal constructions while disassociating the doctrine from creeping interventionist criticisms. However, it was the doctrine's increasing association with intervention that may have provided the impetus for dissecting its meaning at the annual meeting.

Among the many issues discussed at the meeting, one leading concern related to whether the Monroe Doctrine had outlived its purpose. The central conditions present in 1823, when President James Monroe (1758–1831) announced the doctrine, no longer controlled modern affairs. The reconstituted European

5 *Address to the Third Conference of the American Republics, Rio de Janeiro* [July 31, 1906], *in* Latin America and the United States 10 (R. Bacon & J.B. Scott eds., 1917) [hereinafter *Address to the Third Conference*]. Root's South American tour included Brazil, Uruguay, Argentina, Chile Peru, Panama, and Colombia (he also visited Mexico). It was the first visit ever by a high-ranking United States official and Root's "first notable act as Secretary of State." *Biographies of the Secretaries of State: Elihu Root (1845–1937)*, Off. Historian, https://history.state.gov/departmenthistory/people/root-elihu.

6 The much-quoted portion of his speech, which became known as the Root Doctrine was as follows:

> We neither claim nor desire any rights or privileges or powers that we do not freely concede to every American republic.

Address to the Third Conference, *supra* note 5, at 10. *See also infra*, at 58.

7 *Id.* at 19.

8 *Id.* at 21.

9 *Id.* at 21–22.

order that then threatened the New World (the Holy Alliance), no longer existed. The United States had grown in power, influence, and prestige, and was less vulnerable to foreign demands. Blakeslee, who had polled international law and foreign policy professors around the country,[10] reported on the "dawning consciousness in the minds of the people of [the United States] that there exist strong, stable nations in South America, which no longer need the protection of this traditional foreign policy."[11] Root acknowledged that European monarchies no longer sought a revindication of their lost territories in the New World.[12] However, Root also noted the Monroe Doctrine had a continuing purpose, it "was intended to declare a general principle for the future."[13]

Beyond questions of its outdatedness, Monroe Doctrine criticisms had been mounting since the Venezuelan Boundary Dispute with Great Britain (1895–1898)[14] and the end of the Spanish-American War (1898), when victory secured for the United States control over Cuba, Guam, part of Samoa, Wake Island, Puerto Rico, the Philippines, and by annexation, Hawaii.[15] The United States "would never again acquire so much territory as it did during" the explosive period between 1898 and 1903.[16] William Graham Sumner (1840–1910), a leading Yale University social scientist, had published *Earth-Hunger* (1896), which attacked the "political dogmatizers" of the Cleveland and McKinley administrations

10 Blakeslee, *supra* note 3, at 218–19 (noting among 146 respondents that "a very large majority" concluded the doctrine was unsatisfactory, however "only nine wish[ed] to give up the policy entirely.").

11 *Id.* at 217–18.

12 Root, *supra* note 4, at 8.

13 *Id.*

14 A disputed western boundary with Venezuela, dating from Great Britain's 1841 acquisition of British Guiana from The Netherlands, prompted the United States to invoke the Monroe Doctrine against Great Britain. Following war talk, Britain agreed to arbitrate the dispute after the Cleveland administration received in 1895 Congressional authorization to establish a boundary commission. Venezuelan enthusiasm for the process waned given perceptions of the way its grievances were handled. *See* Charles Quince, Resistance to the Spanish-American and Philippine Wars: Anti-Imperialism and the Role of the Press, 1895–1902 (2017). *See also* George S. Boutwell, The Venezuelan Question and the Monroe Doctrine 13 (1896) (referring to the Monroe Doctrine as "an erroneous policy—a policy which will be burdensome to us and injurious to the states that shall rely upon us for protection. The Monroe doctrine is for us, and not for them.").

15 *See* Richard F. Hamilton, America's New Empire: The 1890s and Beyond 1 (2010).

16 Warren Zimmermann, First Great Triumph: How Five Americans Made Their Country a World Power 8 (2002).

and their bold defenses of the "Monroe fetish."[17] Thomas Jefferson's great-great grandson, Harvard history professor Archibald C. Coolidge (1866–1928), critically assessed the doctrine in his book, *United States as a World Power* (1908); and Yale University professor of international law, Theodore S. Woolsey (1879–1933), writing on the pages of *Scribner's Magazine* in 1909, cast doubt on its legal status as a principle of self-defense.[18] Moreover, Woolsey held that if the United States were to attempt to control the destinies of other hemispheric countries through its unilateral application, such an action "presupposes a power which [the United States] does not possess."[19] An Anti-Imperialist League formed in 1898.[20] Anti-expansionist movements spread across major United States campuses,[21] within the independent Mugwump faction of the Republican Party, in ethnic, Democratic Party, and religious camps, in the American Federation of Labor union under Samuel Gompers, within leftist communities, and among literary circles frequented by writers such as Mark Twain and Ambrose Bierce.[22] These criticisms most likely contributed to the reasons prompting Root's restatement of the unchanging nature of the doctrine.

One of the presenters at the meeting, Hiram Bingham (1875–1956), forcefully recounted these criticisms based on some polling of his own. He surveyed numerous hostile viewpoints from "trained observers," journalists, and Latin

17 William Graham Sumner, Earth-Hunger and Other Essays 58, 59 (Albert Galloway Keller ed., 1913).

18 *See* Thomas L. Karnes, *Hiram Bingham and his Obsolete Shibboleth*, 3 Dipl. Hist. 39, 43–44 (1979). Coolidge denied that the doctrine formed part of international law; he discussed elements that were no longer literal and out of date; he denied the doctrine was so full of altruism as Americans were inclined to think and he discussed obligations that could negatively impact United States foreign policy. *See* Archibald Cary Coolidge, The United States as a World Power 107–20 (Macmillan 1918) (1908); W.S. Ferguson, C.H. Haskins, E.F. Gay & R.B. Merriman, *Archibald Cary Coolidge (1866–1928)*, 64 Proc. Am. Acad. Arts & Sci. 514 (1930).

19 Theodore S. Woolsey, *An American Concert of the Powers*, XLV Scribner's Mag. 364, 366 (1909).

20 E. Berkeley Tompkins, Anti-Imperialism in the United States: The Great Debate 1890–1920, at 126 (1970) (noting the specific date as November 19, 1898).

21 *Id.* at 142–43 (noting protests and leaders at the University of Chicago (Prof. Hermann E. Von Holst); Columbia University (Prof. Felix Adler); Yale (Prof. William Graham Sumner); Northwestern University (Pres. Henry W.R. Rogers); Indiana University and Stanford University (Pres. David Starr Jordan)).

22 *See* Quince, *supra* note 14, at 28–63. For a compendium of newspaper accounts detailing the rise of the Anti-Imperialist League as well anti-imperialism's rise in United States labor, ethnic, and middle class circles, see generally 1 The Anti-Imperialist Reader: A Documentary History of Anti-Imperialism in the United States: From the Mexican War to the Election of 1900 (Philip S. Foner & Richard C. Winchester eds., 1984).

American leaders.[23] By this time the Monroe Doctrine already had achieved its own fractured status in South American legal circles.[24] Bingham mixed no words: "'Monroeism' … has come to mean to the Latin American mind interference, intervention, tutelage, and patronizing insolence."[25]

Bingham was an adventurer, a serious but informally trained anthropologist, an early Latin Americanist, and a future Governor of Connecticut and United States Senator. He taught the history of Latin America at Yale University from 1907 to 1915,[26] represented the United States at the First Pan-American Scientific Congress in Santiago in 1908,[27] and gained fame in 1911 by "finding" Machu Picchu.[28]

Bingham first went to South America as "a firm believer in the Monroe Doctrine;" over time he concluded it was an obsolete shibboleth for "American Intervention."[29] Following his American Society of International Law presentation, one discussant from the floor interpreted his words as a doctrinal death sentence for the Monroe Doctrine and declined to join Bingham's

---

23 Hiram Bingham, *The Latin American Attitude Toward the Monroe Doctrine*, 8 ASIL Proc. 180, 181 (1914).

24 *See, e.g.*, Pedro M. Benevenutto Murrieta, La Doctrina Monroe. Sus Antecedentes Históricos. Principales Aplicaciones 636 (1935) (describing *Monroísmo* as "*han formado una leyenda dorada y una leyenda negra*").

25 *Id.* at 186.

26 *See Hiram Bingham III*, Yale Peabody Museum Nat. Hist., http://peabody.yale.edu/collections/archives/biography/hiram-bingham-iii.

27 Three Latin American Scientific Congresses had taken place, in Buenos Aires (1898), Montevideo (1901), and Rio de Janeiro (1905). Bingham attended the fourth congress, renamed, in response to Secretary of State Elihu Root's suggestion that United States representatives should attend. Pioneering professors of Latin American studies, such as Archibald C. Coolidge (Harvard), Bernard Moses (California), W.R. Shepard (Colombia), Paul Reinsch (Wisconsin) and Leo S. Rowe (Pennsylvania) also attended as "Government Delegates." *See* Karnes, *supra* note 18, at 41 (1979). Hiram Bingham, Across South America: An Account of a Journey from Buenos Aires to Lima by way of Potosí with notes on Brazil, Argentina, Bolivia, Chile, and Peru, at vii (1911).

28 While pursuing lost Incan civilizations, he met a local Quechua-speaking muleteer, Melchor Arteaga, who knew of "very good ruins" nearby. Arteaga led him up a mountain, stopped after some hours to gossip with two mountain dwellers, and because he was tired and had been up the mountain once before, arranged for a small, nameless boy to show him the rest of the way. The boy guided him to the royal Incan ruins of Machu Picchu, which Bingham then reintroduced to the world. Despite the book's title, the ruins, obviously, were never lost to the locals. *See* Hiram Bingham, Lost City of the Incas: The Story of Machu Picchu and its Builders 159–67 (1948).

29 Bingham, *supra* note 23, at 195. *See also* Hiram Bingham, The Monroe Doctrine: An Obsolete Shibboleth, at vii (1913) [hereinafter Bingham, The Monroe Doctrine].

funeral procession.[30] However, Bingham would have been qualified to lead it. He had intimate knowledge of Latin American opinion-makers, and included the views of three former Latin American heads of state in his survey. He knew the region well and had ventured on four journeys across the Southern continent.[31] He had traveled extensively along the *caminos reales*, the myriad commercial and communication arteries over which conquistadors had portaged gold, silver, slaves, and the first hemispheric pandemic—smallpox.[32] In 1906–1907, he traced Símon Bolívar's 1819 march across Venezuela and Colombia; and in 1908 he trekked the fabled route from Buenos Aires to Lima via Potosi, chronicling along the way the stories of the Incas, Pizarro, the Spanish conqueror, and Bolívar and Sucre y Alcalá, leaders of the South American independence movement.[33] Root had used his good offices as Secretary of State to assist Bingham in his journey.[34]

In his presentation before the society, Bingham canvassed the historical animus produced by the Monroe Doctrine and reviewed current critiques in the Latin American press. Previously, he had acknowledged Root's 1906 journey as "partially successful," noting however that Root's trip did not disperse the logic of the situation that required it.[35] His conclusion represented one of the objectionable writings that Root claimed overlooked the doctrine's real meaning.[36] Ironically, among all conference participants, Root may have been most guilty of overlooking an occasion to revisit the meaning of the Monroe Doctrine. The day before the annual meeting opened, United States marines and Navy bluejackets from the Atlantic Fleet had stormed the port of Veracruz, the economic engine of the Mexican state.[37] Root gaveled to order the American Society of

30 Charles Herrick, *Statement*, 8 ASIL Proc. 196, 196 (1914).

31 Bingham, The Monroe Doctrine, *supra* note 29, at vii.

32 *See generally* Alfred W. Crosby, *Conquistador y Pestilencia: The First New World Pandemic and the Fall of the Great Indian Empires*, 47 Hisp. Am. Hist. Rev. 321 (1967).

33 *See* Bingham, The Monroe Doctrine, *supra* note 29, at vii–viii.

34 Bingham acknowledged Root's assistance in the preface to Across South America: An Account of a Journey from Buenos Aires to Lima by way of Potosí with notes on Brazil, Argentina, Bolivia, Chile, and Peru. *See id.* at viii. *See also Biographical/Historical Sketch*, Section of *Guide to the Bingham Family Papers*, Yale U. Libr., http://drs.library.yale.edu/HLTransformer/HLTransServlet?stylename=yul.ead2002.xhtml.xsl&pid=mssa:ms.0081&query=&clear-stylesheet-cache=yes&hlon=yes&big=&adv=&filter=&hitPageStart=&sortFields=&view=all.

35 Bingham, The Monroe Doctrine, *supra* note 29, at 53.

36 *See* Karnes, *supra* note 18, at 48 ("The most scholarly and analytical attack upon Bingham's works came from Senator and former Secretary of State Elihu Root," citing to Root's article, *The Real Monroe Doctrine*).

37 Robert E. Quirk, An Affair of Honor: Woodrow Wilson and the Occupation of Veracruz 82 (1962).

International Law meeting on the "real" meaning of the Monroe Doctrine as the Wilson administration was invading Mexico.

1 A Small Matter of Honor: The Incident at Tampico

The cause of the invasion seems "picayune."[38] Eight United States sailors and a paymaster mistakenly entered a sensitive Mexican military area that protected a strategic bridge, docking at a wharf in a small whaleboat from the *USS Dolphin*.[39] Mexico, governed at this time by General Victoriano Huerta (1845–1916), was in the throes of a civil war led by rival rebellious forces of the conservative generals Venustiano Carranza (1859–1920) and Álvaro Obregón (1880–1928), and the Southern and Northern peasant insurrectionists, Emiliano Zapata (1879–1919) and Pancho Villa (1878–1923). Government troops had set up a defensive perimeter around the town to guard against rebel attack.[40] United States warships had been ordered to anchor off Tampico Bay to protect American property and citizens doing business in this commercial center of Mexico.[41] Seven of the nine sailors went ashore to provision canisters of gasoline, but due to language confusion and the general commotion attending the unexpected arrival of a military party proximate to the strategic bridge, they were arrested. Importantly, Mexican soldiers also ordered ashore the two Bluejackets stationed in the vessel, which was flying United States flags fore and aft. Mexico's military governor happened on the procession of prisoners, interceded, and issued an immediate apology. All personnel were released within an hour and a half.[42] His apology did not suffice, nor did Huerta's expression of regret.[43] The commander of the Atlantic Fleet's 4th Division, Rear Admiral Henry T. Mayo (1856–1937), claimed the incident violated international law, noting that the sailors in the whaleboat had been abducted from United States soil. The Wilson administration demanded satisfaction and would settle

38 *Id.* at 1.

39 *See generally* Woodrow Wilson, *Address to a Joint Session of Congress on the Tampico Incident (Apr. 20, 1914)*, *reprinted in* Am. Presidency Project, http://www.presidency.ucsb.edu/ws/?pid=65376.

40 *See* Howard Jones, Crucible of Power: A History of U.S. Foreign Relations Since 1897, at 62 (2001).

41 *See Diplomatic Failure at Tampico: The "Dolphin Incident,"* Libr. Congress http://www.loc.gov/exhibits/mexican-revolution-and-the-united-states/wilson-to-veracruz.html#obj011.

42 51 Cong. Rec. 6949 (1914); *See also* Jack Sweetman, *Take Veracruz At Once*, 28 Naval Hist. Mag. 34 (2014).

43 *See* 51 Cong. Rec., *supra* note 42, at 6949.

for nothing less than a formal naval military salute to the flag. This protocol required that Mexico hoist the United States flag on its soil and offer a 21-gun salute, a gesture that the United States promised to acknowledge immediately.[44] Mexico refused to oblige the demands,[45] and for the next twelve days, diplomats fruitlessly labored to break the impasse.

This small matter of honor provided more pretext for Wilson's destabilization of Huerta's unpopular government,[46] which would crumble by July. The United States already refused to recognize it because it had come to power in a *coup d'état*.[47] Wilson later told the British ambassador the incident provided an opportunity to "teach the South American republics to elect good men."[48] However, Wilson seriously underestimated Mexican outrage, which even provoked Huerta's domestic enemies.[49] Wilson's response to the perceived snub, known as the Tampico Incident, targeted the customs house. Its seizure, however, sparked a spontaneous counter-insurgency, resulting in the need to pacify all of Veracruz. Root wrote to Admiral Mahan several days later fearing that a second war with Mexico was "inevitable."[50] The occupation resulted in the deaths of 193 Mexicans and 19 United States marines,[51] numerous injuries on both sides, and a seven month takeover of Veracruz by more than 6,000 United States troops.[52] It produced condemnations across Europe[53] and protests across South America, as well. Stunned by the reaction and loss of life, Wilson

44 *Id. See also Mexico Must Wipe Out Insult to Flag*, Photograph reprint in *Henry T. Mayo Papers* (1836–1937), Libr. Congress, http://www.loc.gov/exhibits/mexican-revolution-and-the-united-states/wilson-to-veracruz.html#obj010.

45 *See* Quirk, *supra* note 37, at 23, Ch. 2 (on the unmet demand of a military salute of apology).

46 *See id.* at 1–2.

47 *See Woodrow Wilson's Non-recognition*, Libr. Congress, http://www.loc.gov/exhibits/mexican-revolution-and-the-united-states/wilson-to-veracruz.html#obj004.

48 James M. Lindsay, *TWE Remembers: The U.S. Invasion of Veracruz Mexico, Council on Foreign Relations*, Council Foreign Rel.: The Water's Edge (Apr. 21, 2014), https://www.cfr.org/blog/twe-remembers-us-invasion-veracruz-mexico.

49 *See* Jones, *supra* note 40, at 63.

50 2 Philip Jessup, Elihu Root 260 (1938) (quoting Root's April 27, 1914 letter to Mahan).

51 *See* Enrique Krauze, *The April Invasion of Veracruz*, N.Y. Times: Opinion (Apr. 20, 2014), https://www.nytimes.com/2014/04/21/opinion/krauze-the-april-invasion-of-veracruz.html.

52 *See* Quirk, *supra* note 37, at 102.

53 *See* Jones, *supra* note 40, at 63 (citing the *London Economist* view that "the points of punctilio raised by [Washington's] admirals" mad it "a bad day for civilization."). *See also* Lindsay, *supra* note 48 ("Foreign capitals were virtually unanimous in condemning U.S. aggression.").

ultimately secured a diplomatic solution through a Canadian peace process mediated by Argentina, Brazil, and Chile.[54]

•••

All eyes settled on the breaking news of hostilities in Veracruz at the American Society of International Law meeting. Former United States Secretary of State John W. Foster (1836–1917) apologized for having no time to amend his presentation to account for the unfolding event.[55] Root, who at this time represented New York State in the United States Senate, had participated in a late night Senate debate that would belatedly confer Congressional approval on Wilson's belligerent actions.[56] Along with Henry Cabot Lodge (1850–1924) and other Republican senators, Root vainly worked on a more limited substitute proposal approving of the use of force in Mexico, but only to protect United States citizens' lives and property.[57] Speaking in the Senate Chamber, Root argued that the row represented more than bickering about the form and ceremony of a salute. "Lying behind it is a condition of anarchy in Mexico which makes it impossible to secure, by diplomatic means, protection for American life and property. ...The real object to be obtained ... is not the gratification of personal pride; it is not the satisfaction of an admiral or a Government. It is the preservation of the power of the United States to protect its citizens."[58] However, he remained deeply troubled about the possibility of a general war with Mexico given serious reservations about the justness of Wilson's taking of Veracruz.[59]

---

54 *See* Lindsay, *supra* note 48 (citing press reports describing Wilson as "prenaturally pale, almost parchmenty" over the immediate reports of U.S. loss of life and noting the Niagara Falls Peace Conference in Canada).

55 *See* John W. Foster, *Misconceptions and Limitations of the Monroe Doctrine*, 8 ASIL Proc. 119, 119 (1914) ("The paper which I am about to read was written several days ago, before the occurrence of the events of the last few days in Mexico.").

56 Wilson spoke before a joint session of Congress on April 20, 1914, asking to use armed force "in such ways and to such an extent as may be necessary to obtain from General Huerta ... the fullest recognition of the rights and dignity of the United States." Wilson, *supra* note 39. The House quickly approved Wilson's request. Senate approval took two days, thus providing support after the initiation of hostilities. Wilson's quick actions were motivated in part to interrupt a German shipment of armaments, which U.S. authorities feared "would strengthen Huerta's forces in Mexico's civil war and possibly be used against any invading U.S. force." Lindsay, *supra* note 48.

57 *See* Quirk, *supra* note 37, at 76.

58 53 Cong. Rec. 2821 (1916) (reprinting Root's speech).

59 Jessup, *supra* note 50, at 260 (quoting a letter by Root to Admiral Mahan on April 27, 1914: "I am feeling very unhappy about the whole business. It seems to me that while there might have been an international justification ... [it] did not furnish a just cause for war.").

He intimated as much a few days later at the annual banquet concluding the American Society of International Law meeting. The capstone event provided an esteemed audience for Root to address the unraveling relations with Mexico in terms of his framing of the Monroe Doctrine's false and future applications. Founded in 1906, the society quickly evolved into one of the United States' premier communities. The society's vice presidents and executive officers alone comprised the country's political elite. They included appellate judges and Supreme Court justices, a former president, six former and future Secretaries of State, ambassadors to Britain, France, China, and the Ottoman Empire, senators, leading university academicians and administrators, and internationalists and industrialists, including the rail and steel tycoon, Andrew Carnegie. Although pledging full patriotic support for Wilson's actions, his speech "shook with emotion," according to his official biographer, Philip Jessup (1897–1986).[60] He could no longer overlook the unfolding events. Root admitted to "feeling very unhappy" about the affair in Mexico. "Our people do not want anything that is unjust," he said, "But no side is always right."[61]

Writing to Bingham a few days after the meeting, Charles Francis Adams Jr. reflected on the American Society of International Law dramatics, trying to "boil down" "what it all amounted to." He concluded: "Mr. Root, John W. Foster and others dwelt at length and in much detail upon the Monroe Doctrine, as they called it—that is, in what it originated and what strictly pertaining to it. With all due respect, I am forced to say that their conclusions did not impress me with a sense of weight."[62] To Adams, over the course of the Polk, McKinley, Cleveland, and Roosevelt administrations, the Monroe Doctrine was turned into "a vague doctrine of 'America for the Americans' and the requirements of what they are pleased to term 'Self-defence.' ...the Monroe Doctrine is to-day, and will continue to be, just what the representatives of a party may pronounce it or find it convenient to construe it to be, provided only such pronunciamento or construction concurs at the moment with concurrent popular purpose, including the desire of acquisition."[63]

In addition to its political treatments in various administrations, doctrinal diffusion had blurred the meaning of the Monroe Doctrine before the Tampico Incident. Latin American skepticism sparked after the Mexican-American War (1848), when Chilean diplomat and lawyer, Francisco Bilbao (1823–1865) began reviving proposals for a "Latin American" union to counter

60 *Id.* at 260 (claiming Root's annual banquet speech "shook with emotion" and was delivered with "tears running down his cheeks.").

61 *See* Elihu Root, *Annual Banquet*, 8 ASIL Proc. 325, 326 (1914).

62 Letter from Charles Francis Adams to Hiram Bingham, *supra* note 1.

63 *Id.*

the rising United States threat.[64] The Argentine jurist, Carlos Calvo (1824–1906) incorporated "the term in the title of his 1862 Spanish American treaty compilation in defen[s]e of the region's sovereignty."[65] The Colombian diplomat José María Torres-Caicedo (1830–1889) specifically employed it in opposition to U.S. imperialism,[66] and his fellow intellectual, José María Samper (1828–1888) promoted its usage as validation of the region's European-inspired standard of civilization.[67] Already, draft expression of support had failed to pass at the Fourth Pan-American Congress in Buenos Aires in 1910. Even the staunch Pan-Americanist, Alejandro Álvarez (1868–1960), discerned there that a vote of approval "might sanction with it many acts of hegemony committed by the United States."[68] In the history of the Monroe Doctrine, and coinciding with the decades bookending the turn of the twentieth century, the meaning of the Monroe Doctrine indeed had changed dramatically.

2 Root and Whiggish International Law

Root did not always seek to articulate a future meaning of the Monroe Doctrine. His earlier message in Rio did not explicitly constitute a doctrine, in the sense of presenting a future-oriented foreign policy objective, but it did have a clarifying purpose. United States diplomat, Henry Stimson (1867–1950) claimed it presented a fraternal "policy of reassurance."[69] This reassurance was framed retrospectively as a legitimating reconstruction of hemispheric relations recently roiled by perceived imperial impulses in addition to the Tampico Incident—principally the taking of Panama from Colombia (1903), the overtaking of Dominican Republic finances by United States surety agents (1904), the proclamation of Cuba as a protectorate of the United States (the Platt Amendment, 1901), and an array of interventions—in Mexico (1905), Honduras (1905, 1907), Cuba (1906, 1912), Panama (1908), and Nicaragua (1909, 1910, 1912). Root's superimposition of the Monroe Doctrine onto the turmoil

64 Liliana Obregón, *Identity Formation, Theorization and Decline of a Latin American International Law*, *in* Latin America and the International Court of Justice: Contributions to International Law 3, 9 (Paula Wojcikiewicz Almeida & Jean-Marc Sorel eds., 2017) (in an 1853 lecture before the diplomatic community in Paris).

65 *Id.* at 10 (referencing 5 Carlos Calvo, Annales historiques de la revolution de l'Amérique latine (1864), as part of 16 C. Calvo, Recuel Complet des Traités (1862)).

66 *See id.* at 9.

67 *See id.* at 10.

68 Joseph Wheless, *What Countries Benefit by the Monroe Doctrine?*, 8 ASIL Proc. 171, 174 (1914) (quoting Álvarez).

69 *Address by Col. Henry L. Stimson*, *in* Elihu Root: President of the Century Association, 1918–1927, at 19, 30 (1937).

of the immediate past amounted to an attempt to anachronistically restore a progressive narrative to Monroe's message. It amounted to an implicit act of presentism—the framing of the past in terms of the present.[70] Historian Herbert Butterfield (1900–1979) would later brand this patchwork use of history *The Whig Interpretation of History* (1931).

Butterfield had nothing of Root in mind. He described his thin book as a "psychology of historians."[71] However, his polemic would grow to apply to all purpose-oriented recreations of the past. Butterfield's characteristically imprecise usage of the phrase suggested applications in "an extended sense."[72] Root is an exemplar of this historiographical complaint as extended to the methodology of international law in Latin America and the contested recreations of its past.

This book refreshes Butterfield's influential idea of whiggish thinking. Reduced to its elementary form, whiggish international law represents the anachronistic and ideological culling of historical events to bolster a presentist vision of circumstances as the triumphal manifestation of past events. This book employs the dominant narrative of the Monroe Doctrine to evaluate the tendency of historians and practitioners of international law to construct and legitimize teleological understandings of international law based on abridgments of history.

No modern treatment of international law in the Americas can escape the omnipresent significance of the Monroe Doctrine. Carl Schmitt even extended its significance to the world stage as the epochal replacement for his much-admired *Jus Publicum Europaeum*. The Monroe Doctrine is now often treated as a simulacrum for imperialism, however its hemispheric history is more complex than the simulacrum suggests. Elihu Root played a key role in this history, and also in ways more complex than the simulacrum suggests. He is employed here as a vehicle to note the historical application of Butterfield's admonishment against inappropriate and unwitting contextual shortcuts through history. Setting this discussion within a temporal framework dominated by Root's mindset and the sway he and his kind had over the evolution of international law provides valuable insight in itself in order to refresh international law in historical hemispheric perspective.

However, contemporary lessons obtain as well. Butterfield's concern about the whiggish disregard for historical context affects dominant contemporary liberal and critical post-colonial perspectives. Elihu Root conjectured during his famous 1906 tour of Latin America that international law's narrative would one day be written by Latin Americans. He opined that perhaps the twentieth century would bear out this point. Perhaps we glean a measure by which he was

70 Ernst Mayr, *When is Historiography Whiggish?*, 51 J. Hist. Ideas 301, 302 (1990).
71 C.T. McIntire, Herbert Butterfield: Historian as Dissenter 56 (2004).
72 *Id.* at 58.

not too far off, with emergent and notable twenty-first century commentaries about international law's turn not only to history, but to Latin America. As international law's historiographic turn to Latin America develops, important, if not abridged reconstructions of the Monroe Doctrine present worthy topics for revisitation and refreshment. This turn invites reconsideration of factors that seemingly have been occluded but never completely discarded given the heavy-handed imperial implications of the Monroe Doctrine's twentieth century trajectory in the Americas. Also embedded within the Monroe Doctrine were fragments of common colonial heritage, the fear of hemispheric encirclement and European revanchism, the dual gap-inducing and gap-closing problems of *uti possidetis*, the problematic idea of the standard of civilization, and the underappreciated and enduring hemispheric dream of republican virtue and federation. Butterfield's lament about whiggish thinking reduces to a lament about complexity, and how temporalized and politicized uses of history weed out history's complexity for purposes of reinforcing a contemporary perspective that is neither true to its time nor to the past. Latin America's emerging turn to history could benefit from a primer on Butterfield's unhearalded contributions to international law.

Historiography involves the historical study of history and how it is recorded and retold. Root attempted to rhetorically and temporally periodize the Monroe Doctrine based on an embedded vocabulary relating to the doctrine that, even in its original formulation, carried forth multiple and diachronic meanings. The genealogy of intellectual ideas is, of course, supremely important to historians like Butterfield. Root, however, was a practitioner of international law, a consummate diplomat, a student of foreign policy and a member of the emerging society of internationalists. Butterfield's whiggish critique has a crossover appeal here. His treatment of whiggishness traverses the realms of historiography, intellectual history, and international law, and encounters frequent visitations and contributions from diplomatic practice. Whiggishness presents practical problems and conceptual problems, and Butterfield's contributions should be read by practitioners and theorists of international relations and international law. If the heuristic overlap between the fields of international law and international relations comprises the arena of foreign policy, then Butterfield's idea of history suggests an underappreciated whiggishess to professional discourse pertaining to these three disciplines. Root has arisen recently as a convenient means for launching an investigation into the connectedness of these sets in the practice of international law and relations during a formative period of United States-Latin American relations.[73] His very presence in these

73 Root's role in the formation of international law in Latin America at the turn of the twentieth century has been a focal point of renewed academic attention at recent international

fields reminds us of the problem of compartmentalizing world politics into insular faculties of law, political science, and international relations.

Butterfield's critique has much unappreciated application to the history of United States relations with Latin America, and to the Monroe Doctrine. By implication, his *Whig Interpretation of History* also has relevance to international law and the problem of periodization that infiltrates arguments pertaining to contested sovereignties, most notably in the search for and application of factual evidence (*effectivités*) to settle such disputes by international courts and tribunals. Reviving Butterfield's sensitivity to whiggish thinking better informs the hemispheric understanding of international law, not only because it is undergoing its own historiographic revisitation, but because Butterfield's whiggish thinking argument imparts valuable lessons for international judges. They often must engage in the periodization and reconstruction of historical events to settle boundary and territorial disputes. If scholars and historians fall prey to whiggish tendencies, why should we think differently about international judges and arbitrators?

Root was an important figure in his time.[74] Surprisingly, his legacy today does not stretch much beyond United States international legal circles.[75]

---

conferences. *See generally* Jonathan Zasloff, *Law and the Shaping of American Foreign Policy: From the Gilded Age to the New Era*, 78 N.Y.U.L. Rev. 239 (2003); *Repensando y renovando el studio del Derecho internacional dentro, desde y sobre América Latina*, held in conjunction with the Latin American Society of International Law and the Universidad de los Andes, Universidad del Rosario and Universidad Externado, Bogotá, Colombia (Sept. 26–28, 2017); the Latin America and International Law Conference sponsored by the Albrecht Mendelssohn Bartholdy Graduate School of Law, University of Hamburg (Feb. 8–9, 2018).

74 Secretary of War (1899–1904); member, Alaskan Boundary Commission (1903); temporary chair, Republican National Convention (1903); Secretary of State (1905–1909); president, American Society of International Law (1906–1937); U.S. Senator (1909–1915); counsel for the U.S., North Atlantic Fisheries Arbitration (1910); member, Permanent Court of Arbitration (1910); president, Carnegie Endowment for International Peace (1910–1925); recipient, Nobel Peace Prize (1912); president, Hague Tribunal of Arbitration between Great Britain, France, Spain, and Portugal concerning church property (1913); chairman of the board of trustees, Carnegie Institute of Washington (1913–1937); president, American Bar Association (1915); ambassador extraordinary, special diplomatic mission to Russia (1917); member, Commission of International Jurists to create the Statute for the Permanent Court of International Justice (1920–1921); commissioner plenipotentiary for the U.S., International Conference on Limitation of Armament and on Far Eastern and Pacific Questions (1921); member, League of Nations Committee of Experts to revise the World Court Statute (1928–1929). For more discussion, see *infra*, Ch. 3. *See also* Zasloff, *supra* note 73, at 244 (calling Root the "most prominent American lawyer from 1890–1920 and the leading foreign policy thinker in the Republican Party.").

75 *See generally The Forgotten Senator, Statesman, and Nobel Laureate Elihu Root, with Charles Laderman* (Aug. 11, 2016), Libr. Congress: John W. Kluge Ctr., http://www.loc.gov/loc/kluge/podcasts/laderman.html.

Nevertheless, he embodied a complex mix of law, politics, diplomacy, and ideology that shapes foreign policy, international law, and international relations. His impress across these intersecting fields helps to contextualize the forces that framed United States-Latin American relations during the turbulent *fin de siècle* atmosphere and its nearby twentieth century history.

Such contextualization is not intended to straighten out disheveled historical facts. The suggestion here is that Butterfield's complaint about historiography has relevance beyond history's domain and within the extended and fragmented methodology and juridical practices of international law. Butterfield's perspective and complaint about historiography add to the coloration imparted by emerging treatments of the Monroe Doctrine and international law's recent turn to history.[76] Recalling and reframing his perspective, borrowing from the teachings of the so-called English School to which he subscribed, provides a deeper and richer hue to standard and postcolonial treatments of the Monroe Doctrine and Latin America. As new hemispheric voices emerge in telling the stories of international law's engagement in the Americas, the nuances and complexities imparted to the interwoven fabric of this historiographic turn should develop freshly reminded of international law's potential as an intrinsically whiggish discourse. Whiggish interpretations of history abound, however Butterfield's legacy reminds us against simplistic and unexamined habits of historical chronicling—the ultimate yardstick by which to measure whiggishness.

3 The Brackish Age of Legalist Empire

Root appeared in a brackish age, where the receding waters of the Old World Order, which legitimated war as a legal means of politics by another name, intermixed and yet began to recede against the tidal pull of internationalism that would give way to the post World War II New World Order.[77] Carl Landauer

76 *See generally* Ignacio de la Rasilla del Moral, *A Propósito del giro historiográfico en Derecho internacional, in* La idea de América en el pensamiento *ius* internacionalista del siglo XXI, at 33–42 (Yoland Gamarra Chopo ed., 2010). Many scholars associate publication of Martti Koskenniemi's The Gentle Civilizer of Nations: The Rise and Fall of International Law 1870–1960 with the spike in scholarly attention to the history of international law. *See, e.g.*, Samuel Moyn, *Martti Koskenniemi and the Historiography of International Law in the Age of the War on Terror, in* The Law of International Lawyers: Reading Martti Koskenniemi 340 (Wouter Werner, Marieke de Hoon & Alexis Galán eds., 2017).

77 *See* Oona A. Hathaway & Scott J. Shapiro, The Internationalists: How a Radical Plan to Outlaw War Remade the World, at xv–xvii (2017) (referencing in part Carl von Clausewitz's On War—"War is simply the continuation of politics by other means.").

noted an overlay of ambivalences that fostered a clash between a traditional American exceptionalism imperiled by imperialism and an exceptionalism that boasted of ingenuity, energy, commercial expansion, and territorial aggrandizement.[78] Both perspectives sustained an emerging tradition of United States international law that could be equally genteel and formalistic.[79] Root embodied both qualities. Benjamin Allen Coates likened this age to the ascending *legalist empire* ushered in by the rise of the United States as a global power.[80] This new empire relied on lawyer-officials (Coates named among others Root, William Howard Taft (1857–1930), John Bassett Moore (1860–1947), and James Brown Scott (1866–1943)),[81] who "projected the ethical attitude that holds moral conduct to be a matter of rule following."[82] Coates maintained that the outcome of this project, which he time-sliced as between 1898 and 1919, expressed a heterodoxy of legalist views that nevertheless revealed a close association between the professionalizing mindset of international law and empire—concepts erroneously viewed as mutually contradictory.[83] The lessons learned, however, speak to the need, which historians have always emphasized, of understanding the limits, pitfalls, and importance of contextualization. After all, who wants to be whiggish?

---

78 *See* Carl Landauer, *The Ambivalences of Power: Launching the American Journal of International Law in an Era of Empire and Globalization*, 20 Leiden J. Int'l L. 325, 329–30 (2007).

79 *See generally id.*

80 *See generally* Benjamin Allen Coates, Legalist Empire: International Law and American Foreign Relations in the Early Twentieth Century (2016).

81 *See id.* at 2. *See also* Tuomas Lihr, *Elihu Root and International Legalism: Legalist Remarks on Collective Security and American Realism*, 1 Helsinki L. Rev. 63, 64–65 (2014) (describing Root as a paragon of the legalist era and a stout supporter of legal institutionalism). Other notable lawyer-statesmen of this era included Philander Knox (1853–1921), Joseph H. Choate (1832–1917), LeBaron Colt (1846–1924), Nicholas Murray Butler (1862–1947), Henry L. Stimson, and Frank B. Kellogg (1856–1937). *See* Zasloff, *supra* note 73, at 250 n.44.

82 *Id.* at 3 (quoting Judith Shklar).

83 *Id.* at 4–5. Regarding the heterodoxy of legalist views, Coates noted "There was no single school" of American legalists, that they held "different views about" international law's "sources, content, and future," that they were not always lawyers, but that their views converged around "a commitment to expanding the use of legal techniques and institutions to resolve international problems." *Id.* at 3. Zasloff pointed out that the United States practice of world politics in this period preceding the "New Era" [the 1920s] could not depend on a professionalized diplomatic corps, which only came into being after passage of the Rogers Act in 1924. *See* Zasloff, *supra* note 73, at 250 n.43.

4 The Whig Interpretation of History

Butterfield focused on the objectionable English tendency of writing constitutional history "on the side of Protestants and Whigs to praise revolutions provided they have been successful, to emphasize certain principles of progress in the past and to produce a story which is the ratification if not the glorification of the present."[84] His major historiographical achievement extended Leopold von Ranke's (1795–1886) nineteenth century development of primary-source-based history. Butterfield restored to the study of history an autonomous identity, rejecting the use of history as a means of subordinating its lessons to the manipulations of the present.[85] Whiggishness is now "commonly used as a pejorative description of present-centered historical explanation."[86]

Within its specific British context, *The Whig Interpretation of History* involved the long seventeenth century conflict between the Crown and the Church against the Parliament, with the forward-leaning orientation of eighteenth century Whigs and their proto-Victorian agenda of religious and political freedom pitted against the Tories and the long-arm pull of the Stuart monarchy. At stake was the retrograde supremacy of Catholic autocracy, as personified by James II (reign: 1685–1688) and the dispute over his right of succession.[87] The Whig interpretation adopted the perspective of its preferred

84 Herbert Butterfield, The Whig Interpretation of History, at v (1931).

85 Kenneth B. McIntyre, Herbert Butterfield: History, Providence, and Skeptical Politics 47–48 (2011).

86 *Id.* at 46 n.117.

87 This is the fundamental theme of Thomas Babington Macaulay's influential *History of England*, which centers around the Glorious Revolution of 1688, the overthrow of James II and the conferral of the crown on William of Orange:

> This progress, having continued during many ages, became at length, about the middle of the eighteenth century, portentiously rapid, and has proceeded, during the nineteenth, with accelerated velocity. In consequence partly of our geographical and partly of our moral position, we have, during several generations, been exempt from evils which have elsewhere impeded the efforts and destroyed the fruits of industry ... While revolutions have taken place all around us, our government has never once been subverted by violence. During more than a hundred years there has been in our island no tumult of sufficient importance to be called an insurrection; nor has the law been once borne down either by public fury or by regal tyranny: public credit has been held credit: the administration of justice has been pure: even in times which might by Englishmen be justly called evil times, we have enjoyed what almost every other nation in the world would have considered as an ample measure of civil and religious freedom. Every man has felt entire confidence that the state would protect him in the possession of what had been earned by his diligence and hoarded by his self[-]denial.

subjects, the presumed "great patriarchs of history-writing."[88] It cast them as progressive and forward-looking recorders of truth who continuously struggled against backward-looking conservative perspectives.[89] The Whig method smugly supported the unexamined status quo, unwittingly and selectively spotlighted prior events, and moralized and ratified what is right in the present by opposing what is envisaged as wrong in the past. It subtly associated progress with liberty and liberalism and cast as regressive historical treatments oriented toward reactionary conclusions,[90] or in the broader sense, preordained conclusions that support a contemporary cause. Friedrich Nietzsche (1844–1900) forewarned of the problem of unwitting historical dissimilation, and the tendency to monumentalize the present in terms of past glorifications: "we must know the right time to forget as well as the right time to remember."[91]

Elements of political conservatism and Christian transcendentalism attached to Butterfield's critique of whiggish thinking.[92] While his personal beliefs are not relevant,[93] Christianity's connection to international law's

---

> Under the benignant influence of peace and liberty, science has flourished, and has been applied to practical purposes on a scale never before known. The consequence is that a change to which the history of the old world furnishes no parallel has taken place in our country. Thomas Babington Macaulay, History of England 220–21 (1967).

88 Butterfield, *supra* note 84, at 4.

89 *See* Mayr, *supra* note 70, at 301. On the persistence of the Whig/Progressive distinction in United States legal history, see Robert W. Gordon, *Historicism in Legal Scholarship*, 90 Yale L.J. 1037–45 (1980–1981).

90 Keith C. Sewell, Herbert Butterfield and the Interpretation of History 30–31 (2005).

91 Friedrich Nietzsche, The Use and Abuse of History 8 (Adrian Collins trans., 1980) (1874).

92 *See* Cornelia Navari, *The Concept of Practice in the English School*, 17 Eur. J. Int'l Rel. 611, 612 (2010) (noting "Butterfield, for example, considered international society as a historical development out of the religious stand-off of the Reformation, and an outgrowth of an emerging practice of liberal toleration"). On his Methodist identity, see McIntire, *supra* note 71, at 358–60; Kenneth Thompson, *Butterfield and the Theory of International Politics*, *in* Herbert Butterfield: The Ethics of History and Politics 41 (Kenneth Thompson ed., 1980) (noting "Butterfield … never wavered from a fundamental Augustinian theology that included belief in the infinite worth of human personality, the reality of sin, the sovereignty of God, the limitations of human nature, and the fragmentary character of human existence.").

93 Others place more emphasis on Butterfield's Christian historical consciousness, pinpointing it as the "natural antidote to whig history," rather than recovering from history themes of individual or national righteousness. Nicolas Guilhot, *Portrait of the Realist as a Historian: On Anti-Whiggism in the History of International Relations*, 21 Eur. J. Int'l L. 10 (2015). Guilhot also noted that Butterfield's political orientation—neo-traditionalist and antiliberal—generated a conciliatory type of political quietism in the face of fascism's rise, which "cast a dark shadow over his intellectual legacy." *Id.*

construction as a civilizing influence arise in his general thesis, which is relevant to Latin America's story involving the Monroe Doctrine.[94] Additionally, his broader formulation of historical abridgment, his textured concern for anachronistic thinking, which can better inform reconstructions of the Monroe Doctrine in the literature of international law and international relations (as well as the study of diplomacy), and his construction of context, make his whig formulation worthy of refreshment in terms of Latin American international legal history and in terms of the general problem of historical proofs, which are used to buttress contested claims of sovereignty.

Butterfield's whiggish idea emphasized a wary regard for the triumphalisms of liberal historiography, however his more lasting contribution extends beyond the personalities and perspectives of this critique. Here, Butterfield's idea is remodeled, extended, and applied to other, sometimes critical superimpositions of ideological perspectives on not-so-neatly conforming interpretations of the past. Whiggish international law retains significance regardless of presentist assertions that support the glorification or progressive development of international law.

Tim Dunne read Butterfield as firing a warning shot across historians' bow, cautioning them to dispense with their infused narratives of progressivism and write like recording angels rather than hanging judges.[95] This comment was perhaps in reference to one of the few Whig patriarchs identified by Butterfield—Lord Acton (1834–1902). To Butterfield, Lord Acton was "the person who most personified the historian as judge and avenger, the dispenser of moral judgments in history."[96] However, Butterfield intended that historians serve as expert witnesses rather than as factual stenographers or avengers.[97] He did not believe the recording of history could be separated completely from the telling of history. He consciously noted that historians could "never entirely abstract [themselves] from [their] own age."[98] The scholarly pursuit of the

94 *See, e.g.*, Geneviève Dorais, *Missionary Critiques of Empire, 1920–1932: Between Interventionism and Anti-Imperialism*, 39 Int'l Hist. Rev. 337 (2016); Liliana Obregón, *Between Civilization and Barbarism: Creole Interventions in International Law*, 27 Third World Q. 815 (2006).

95 *See* Tim Dunne, Inventing International Society: A History of the English School 73 (Eugene Rogan ed., 1998).

96 McIntire, *supra* note 71, at 414 (the "prince of amateurs" among historians, according to G.R Elton. *See* G.R. Elton, The Practice of History 17 (1967)).

97 Likening the historian to neither judge nor juror (nor stenographer), Butterfield regarded historians' courtroom role as a person called upon to give evidence—"one of those 'expert witnesses.'" Butterfield, *supra* note 84, at 131.

98 *Id.* at 16 (noting historians' proper sense of awareness as opposed to whig historians' lack thereof).

past "steps into a world of partial judgments" and "personal appreciations" and requires that one *recognizes* the problem of "speaking *ex cathedra*."[99]

Hans-Georg Gadamer noted the need for self-awareness in the writing of conceptual history (*Begriffsgeschichte*) but framed the art of historical understanding in terms of the "conscious assimilation of one's own fore-meanings and prejudices."[100] Reinhart Koselleck recognized "contemporary conceptual boundaries" as part of the self-awareness needed to interpret past speakers and writers.[101] Quentin Skinner interpreted this theme as forwarding the "salutary reminder about the need to be aware of our inevitable tendency towards pre-judgment and the fitting of evidence into pre-existing patterns of interpretation and explanation."[102] If eradicating prejudice presented the sublime ideal when piecing together the past, the awareness of the limitations inherent in that endeavor promoted circumspection—a heightened regard that *unknown* pieces of what Geoffrey Elton called history's "dead reality" may remain missing from the historical jigsaw puzzle.[103] In common with his contemporaries, R.G. Collingwood (1889–1943) and Michael Oakeshott (1901–1990), Butterfield's circumspection interjected an appreciation for sympathetic and empathetic treatments of the subject matter based on the belief that the historical past is somehow distinctive from merely practical accounts of the past.[104]

5 Whiggism's Straight-Line Thinking and Disregard of Context

Butterfield emphasized that the whiggish hanging judge perspective lacked a proper regard for context, which could only be approached by more textured regard for the piecemeal compilation of documentary artifacts. He recognized that the study of history presented a scattered debris field that could never be mapped with complete assurance. To Butterfield, whiggish thinkers drew strait lines through history's graveyard. They employed cartographic

99 *Id.* at 2 n.2.

100 Hans-Georg Gadamer, Truth and Method 238 (1975).

101 Reinhart Koselleck, Futures Past: On the Semantics of Historical Time 80 (Keith Tribe trans., 2004).

102 1 Quentin Skinner, Visions of Politics: Regarding Method 15 (2002).

103 Elton, *supra* note 96, at 53.

104 McIntyre, *supra* note 85, at 6–7. *See also* William Bain, *The English School and the Activity of Being an Historian, in* Theorising International Society: English School Methods 152 (Cornelia Navari ed., 2009) (noting the importance Butterfield placed on sympathetic understanding of historical writing).

shortcuts[105] and yet lacked awareness of the abbreviated turns they took and the historical tombstones they knocked over with their remote sensing. They constructed the uncareful diachronic "line of causation" across the "whole historical story." They produced the "scheme of general history [meta-narrative] which is bound to converge beautifully upon the present" while "demonstrating throughout the ages the workings of an obvious principle of progress."[106] However, the mythical linear path of convergence embodied twists and turns to Butterfield, even perversions that take anything but the straight track to its goal while often going astray.[107]

6 "Time is Out of Joint"

According to Butterfield, whiggish thinking produced abridged, less sensitive, and oversimplified treatments that themselves reflected anachronistic thinking. Put forth almost as an axiom, Butterfield wrote: "All history must tend to become more whig in proportion as it becomes more abridged."[108] Skinner, who was intellectually connected to Butterfield, defined anachronism as the parochial outcome of looking at the past from modernity's window.[109] Skinner warned that when we contaminate the review of the past through unconscious paradigms that are essentially inapplicable, we create historical anachronism.[110] Anachronism arises when scholars commit the sin of lifting subjects and concepts out of their own time and place, where "[t]he proper standards on which a historical work should be evaluated must be taken from the period

105 Butterfield, *supra* note 84, at 22 ("The fallacy of the whig historian lies in the way in which he takes his shortcut through this complexity.").

106 Butterfield, *supra* note 84, at 12.

107 *Id.* at 23 ("...what our history contributes is not evolution but rather the realization of how crooked and perverse the ways of progress are, with what willfulness and waste it twists and turns, and takes anything but the straight track to its goal, and how often it seems to go astray"). Simon elsewhere noted that American independence movements, although distinct in settings and results, "were animated by strikingly similar ideas. Patriotic political theorists throughout the Americas offered analogous critiques of imperial rule..., designed comparable constitutions immediately after independence..., and expressed common ambitions for their new nations' future relations with one another and the rest of the world." Joshua Simon, The Ideology of Creole Revolution: Imperialism and Independence in American and Latin American Political Thought 1 (2017).

108 Butterfield, *supra* note 84, at 7.

109 *See* Christopher R. Rossi, Sovereignty and Territorial Temptation: The Grotian Tendency 21 (2017) [hereinafter Rossi, Sovereignty and Territorial Temptation].

110 *See* Quentin Skinner, *Meaning and Understanding in the History of Ideas*, 8 Hist. & Theory 3, 7 (1969).

in which that work was produced."[111] This view governs the work of historians. John Sutherland and Cedric Thomas Watts framed the problem succinctly with their book title: *Henry v, War Criminal?* (2000).[112] The association of such a contemporary concept to Shakespeare's martial king "seems scandalously presentist."[113] Indeed, the Bard may have best crystallized the notion of anachronism: "Time is out of joint."[114]

7 A Nod from Science

The history of science maintains high regard for Butterfield's formulation, holding that careful treatments of scientific advancement and discovery result from numerous failed hypotheses and cold fusion perversions.[115] Crooked turns make impossible the paradigmatic desideratum of unilinear progress.[116] In scientific fields, the power of the whig epithet prompted critical assessments of developmental approaches, promoting something of a scientific backlash to remove any taint of social construction to the modern hindsight of historical sequencing. In answer to an earlier question, "Nobody wants to be whiggish," wrote Wilson and Ashplant.[117]

---

111 Martti Koskenniemi, *Vitoria and Us*, 22 J. Max Planck Inst. Eur. Legal Hist. 119, at 122 (2014) (summarizing the standard view of anachronism but not agreeing that the standard is proper).

112 John Sutherland & Cedric Thomas Watts, Henry v, War Criminal?: And Other Shakespeare Puzzles (2000).

113 Christopher N. Warren, *Henry v, Anachronism, and the History of International Law*, *in* The Oxford Handbook to English Law and Literature, 1500 1700, 710, 710 (Lorna Hutson ed., 2017).

114 William Shakespeare, Hamlet, act. 1, sc. 5, line 188 (2003) (stated by Hamlet after meeting the ghost of his father). Critical theory has made much of this notion in response to liberalism's triumphant claim of outdistancing Marxism. On the "hauntology" of Marxism and its coming back, see generally Jacques Derrida, Specters of Marx: The State of the Debt, the Work of Mourning, and the New International (1994). On liberalism's triumphant claim, see generally Francis Fukuyama, The End of History and the Last Man (1992).

115 Cold fusion is the scientific synonym for a 1989 claim by two electrochemists that asserted the achievement of nuclear fusion using a simple benchtop electrolysis device. The claim momentarily galvanized the scientific world, which then summarily condemned it as junk science. *See* Stephen K. Ritter, *Cold Fusion Died 25 Years Ago, but the Research Lives On*, 94 Chemical & Engineering News 33 (2016).

116 *See generally* Thomas S. Kuhn, The Structure of Scientific Revolutions (1962) (discussing the power and problems of paradigms).

117 Adrian Wilson & T.G. Ashplant, *Whig History and Present-Centered History*, 31 Hist. J. 1 (1988).

Ernst Mayr, one of the leading evolutionary biologists of the twentieth century, noted the skittish avoidance of the whig label by some historians of science who "decided it was better not to make any interpretation or evaluation of the past than to be called a whig." The result, according to Mayr was "a return to 'the Baconian inductive method, which attempts to investigate phenomena with an observant but empty mind.'"[118] Mayr's point, unlike some of the critics he noted, was not to rid historiography of its interpretive element, but to point out the fallacy of "strictly horizontal historiography." Such linear thinking may attempt to report in "loving detail the happenings of only a single moment in time," but its product is "singularly unrevealing" for failing to communicate or even recognize the needs of historical comparisons and selection. Mayr knew of no good presentation of developmental history that skirted intellectual and cultural context.[119] From historians' perspective, going astray often involves mindlessly shuffling the sequence of historical events, a problem that reduces, again, to anachronism.

8 "All Other Sins Can Be Forgiven"

Summarizing historians' governing view on anachronism, Constantine Fasolt wrote, "All other sins can be forgiven," except the sin of chronological pollution.[120] "No one who violates that great taboo may claim to be a true historian."[121] However, Fasolt noted the simple and natural division of time into past and present is not as elementary as it seems.[122] No universal office of chronology exists to provide temporal safekeeping for history's lost and found artifacts; "discreet contextual packages" do not emerge; contexts do not arrive in conveniently tailored suits.[123] "History does not permit us to step outside the realm of time."[124] Some form of pollution inheres in the process of historical review. His point also cautioned against the false ritualization of doing history as an ideological justification for validating the supremacy of the state, which his subject, the Commentator, Bartolus of Sassoferrato (c. 1313/14–1357), purportedly

118 Mayr, *supra* note 70, at 301 (quoting E. Harrison's *Whigs, Prigs and Historians of Science*' article in Nature (1987)).

119 *Id.* at 308.

120 Constantine Fasolt, The Limits of History 6 (2004) (claiming also that "Anachronism is the sin against the holy spirit of history.").

121 *Id.*

122 *See id.* at 4.

123 *Id.* at 11.

124 *Id.* at 231.

attempted in defense of the living legacy of Roman law's *Corpus Iuris Civilis*, and the supremacy of the Roman-German emperor. Butterfield made a substantially similar point about the nineteenth century Whig historians.

Butterfield's condemnation of using history as a false ideological justification for misperceived historical sequences reverberated profoundly. And he provided reasons for historical anachronism's scholarly appeal. It promoted simplicity in the face of complex problems; it had an elective affinity for certain historical projects or outcomes, such as the promotion of liberalism in the Anglophone context; and it fostered the construction of general historical narratives[125] as opposed to more narrowly framed historical pursuits. Skinner argued that ideology commonly sustained appeals to the past.[126]

Although not mindful of the historian's concern, or Butterfield's whiggish formulation, Root's close associate—in many ways his almost worshipful acolyte[127]—James Brown Scott fell prey to these sharp methodological critiques.[128] During the mid-1930s, Scott launched on a "self-imposed" academic mission to secure the name and place of the Dominican friar and Prima Professor of Sacred Theology, Francisco de Vitoria (c. 1483–1546) as the founder of international law.[129] Viewed as quaintly anachronistic today,[130] international law's paternity provoked an intense originary debate in the first part of the twentieth century,[131] perhaps prompted by international law's late nineteenth

125 *See* Marshall Poe, *Butterfield's Sociology of Whig History: A Contribution to the Study of Anachronism in Modern Historical Thought*, 25 Clio: J. Literature, Hist., & Phil. Hist. 345, 346 (1996). Poe noted "the propensity to accept anachronism was not evenly distributed in the scholarly community." Historians in pursuit of narrow topics tended to reject the whig technique as compared to historians working on general surveys. *Id.*

126 3 Quentin Skinner, *History and Ideology in the English Revolution*, *in* Visions of Politics: Hobbes and Civil Science, 238 (2002).

127 Root's two biographers describe Scott's "worshipful" relation to Root. *See* Christopher R. Rossi, Broken Chain of Being: James Brown Scott and the Origins of Modern International Law 6 (1998) [hereinafter Rossi, Broken Chain of Being].

128 Along with Root, he co-founded the American Society of International Law (Root served as its first president) and served as the founder and first editor in chief of the *American Journal of International Law*. *See* David J. Bederman, *Appraising a Century of Scholarship in the American Journal of International Law*, 100 Am. J. Int'l L. 20, 21 (2006). *See also* George A. Finch, *James Brown Scott, 1866–1943*, 38 Am. J. Int'l L. 183 (1944).

129 Papers of James Brown Scott, box 52(4), Lauinger Library, Georgetown University, Washington, D.C.

130 *See* Helen Kinsella, The Image Before the Weapon: A Critical History of the Distinction Between Combatant and Civilian 55 (2011).

131 For a partial review of scholars involved in the debate, see Randall Lesaffer, *International Law and its History: The Story of An Unrequited Love*, *in* Time, History and International Law 27, at 31 nn.16–19 (Matthew Craven, Malgosia Fitzmaurice & Maria Vogiatzi eds., 2006) [hereinafter Lesaffer, *International Law and its History*]. *See also* Peter Haggenmacher, *La place de Francisco de Vitoria parmi les fondateurs du droit international*, *in* Actualité de la

century coalescence as a discipline and its concomitant search for validating sources of legitimacy.[132] Scott drew a straight line through history to source international law's progenitor, along the way crediting Vitoria with framing the doctrine of citizenship for the Americas.[133] Scott argued that Vitoria's name and legacy had been wrongly superceded by the Hollander, Hugo Grotius (1583–1645) and his positivist followers, who nurtured his rule-oriented agenda that legitimated recourse to war.[134]

Critics roundly attacked Scott's whiggish treatment of Vitoria (and, by implication, Grotius). Yasuaki Onuma claimed Scott attempted to "deify[]" the Scholastic master.[135] Arthur Nussbaum's derision seemed almost personal.[136] Katherine Topulos accused him of bias.[137] However, Scott's triumphal vision, at least as related to the classical publicists of the law of nations, has company. Charles Alexandrowicz marveled at "how some of the classic writers anticipated the progress of the Family of Nations which (aside from the 19th century interlude of colonialism) went steadily ahead with endowing all its member communities with statehood and sovereignty."[138] Aside from his parenthetical abridgement of colonialism, concepts of statehood and sovereignty did not arrive as developmentally packaged as Alexandrowicz and others suggest. Contrary to Richard Falk's well received view, the appearance of the *Grotian Moment* in 1648, which suddenly announced the arrival of the sovereign state

---

pensée juridique de Francisco de Vitoria 27, 35 (Antonio Truyol Serra, Henry Mechoulan, Peter Haggenmacher, Antonio Ortiz-Arce, Primitivo Marino & Joe Verhoeven eds., 1998) (detailing the series of essays on the subject of *Les fondateurs du droit international* initiated and edited by Antoine Pillet in 1904).

132 *See* Arnulf Becker Lorca, *Universal International Law: Nineteenth-Century Histories of Imposition and Appropriation*, 51 Harv. Int'l L.J. 475, 476 (2010) (noting the nineteenth century global expansion of European international law but differing from standard accounts of its emergence).

133 1 James Brown Scott, Law, the State, and the International Community 319 (1939) (crediting Vitoria with the *jus soli* doctrine of nationality).

134 *See* Rossi, Broken Chain of Being, *supra* note 127, at 75 (noting "Scott would have been better advised to place Vitoria and Grotius in an intellectual continuum offset by the enervating influences of Hobbes."). *See also* Pablo Zapatero, *Legal Imagination in Vitoria. The Power of Ideas*, 11 J. Hist. Int'l L. 221, 230 (2009) (noting sensitivities regarding the "who was first" issue).

135 Yasuaki Onuma, *Introduction*, *in* A Normative Approach to War: Peace, War, and Justice in Hugo Grotius 1, 1 n.2 (Yasuaki Onuma ed., 1993).

136 *See* Arthur Nussbaum, A Concise History of the Law of Nations (1954) (labeling Scott's views "deprecating," "extreme," "uncritical," "repellant").

137 Katherine Topulos, *Book Review*, 28 Int'l J. Leg. Info. 150 (2000) ("To a certain degree, Scott had a bias in favour of the Catholic view of the world").

138 Charles H. Alexandrowicz, *Introduction*, *in* Alberico Gentili and the Development of International Law: His Life, Work, and Times viii (Gesina H.J. van der Molen ed., 1968).

and served as modern international law's birth certificate,[139] did not emerge rapidly out of the "shadow land" of Europe's Thirty Years' War. Modern sovereignty's ideological perturbation transmuted over a three hundred year period before the peace treaties of Westphalia and Onasbrück and years thereafter once European principalities internalized the idea of autonomy.[140] This internalization relocated authority in the form of the abstract state as opposed to the *majestas* of the personal ruler.[141] Encapsulating sovereignty's expression as the epiphenomenon of Westphalia is an example of modern whiggishness. This abridgment of sovereignty's genealogy has been extensively discussed in international relations scholarship.[142] Nothing in Nicholas Onuf's reading of the Westphalian treaties "reconceptualized authority as exclusive control over homogenized territory, much less launch a new European order based on any such idea." It was not an "epochal moment in launching modern international relations, but indeed a myth." At best it served as the somewhat arbitrary but convenient "mid-point in a centuries-long sequence of normatively freighted developments."[143]

---

139 Richard Falk coined the popular phrase in *Some Thoughts on the Decline of International Law and Future Prospects*, 9 Hofstra L. Rev. 399, 408 (1980). The idea caught on in academic and diplomatic circles. *See* Michael P. Scharf, Customary International Law in Times of Fundamental Change: Recognizing Grotian Moments (2013); Melana Sterio, *A Grotian Moment: Changes in the Legal Theory of Statehood*, 39 Denv. J. Int'l L. & Pol'y 209 (2010–2011); Christopher Weeramantry, *The Grotius Lecture Series: Opening Tribute to Hugo Grotius*, 14 Am. U. Int'l L. Rev. 1516, 1518 (1999); Boutrous Boutrous-Ghali, *The Role of International Law in the Twenty-First Century: A Grotian Moment*, 18 Fordham Int'l L.J. 1609, 1612 (1995).

140 *See* Derek Croxton, *The Peace of Westphalia of 1648 and the Origins of Sovereignty*, 21 Int'l Hist. Rev. 569, 573 (1999).

141 *See* Friedrich Kratochwil, *Sovereignty as Dominium: Is There a Right of Humanitarian Intervention?*, *in* Beyond Westphalia? State Sovereignty and International Intervention 21, 22–23 (Gene M. Lyons & Michael Mastanduno eds., 1995).

142 *See* Rossi, Sovereignty and Territorial Temptation, *supra* note 109, at 16–24; Jens Bartelson, Sovereignty as Symbolic Form (2014); Hent Kalmo & Quentin Skinner eds., Sovereignty in Fragments: The Past, Present and Future of a Contested Concept (2010); Randall Lesaffer, *Law and History: Law between Past and Present*, *in* Law and Method 133–52 (Bart Van Klink & Sanne Taekema eds., 2011); Stephen D. Krasner, Sovereignty: Organized Hypocrisy (1999); Daniel Philpott, *Ideas and the Evolution of Sovereignty*, *in* State Sovereignty: Change and Persistence in International Relations 15 (Sohail H. Hashmi ed., 1997); Thomas J. Biersteker & Cynthia Weber eds., State Sovereignty as Social Construct 3 (1996); Jens Bartelson, A Genealogy of Sovereignty (1995); Beyond Westphalia: State Sovereignty and International Intervention (Gene M. Lyons & Michael Mastanduno eds., 1995); Nicholas Greenwood Onuf, *Sovereignty: Outline of a Conceptual History*, 16 Alternatives 425 (1991).

143 Nicholas Greenwood Onuf, "The Mightie Frame": Epochal Change and the Modern World 85–86 (2018). *See also* Lesaffer, *Law and History: Law between Past and Present*, *supra* note 142, 8–17 (on the Westphalian myth).

As with Scott, Root was involved in the construction of a general historical narrative, although specifically relating to the Monroe Doctrine. Abridgments and shortcuts involving Latin American-United States history forestalled his earnest attempt to enlarge international society and to conform it to the rule of law. Ignacio de la Rasilla del Moral noted a variant of the whiggish invocation of Vitoria's name. Fascists coopted Vitoria's name to legitimize General Franco's *coup d'état* against the democratically elected Spanish Republican government during the Spanish Civil War (1936–1939). This ideological glorification of Vitoria and the Salamancan School's chief representative presented a strategic attempt to portray Franco's regime as the "last international bastion of Catholic values after [World War II]."[144] The resurrection of Vitoria's name indicated a recording of history with fascism's ideological eyes focused predominantly on the present.

9 Postcolonialism and the Historiographic Turn

Postcolonial perspectives present their own critique of anachronism that differs from standard historiographical practice, while unnecessarily implicating Butterfield's whig critique. They advance new perspectives to standard narrations about international law's history and teaching in Latin America.[145] The anachronistic retelling of international legal histories also motivates the recent historiographic turn in international law.[146] Mark Toufayan described the

144 Ignacio de la Rasilla del Moral, In the Shadow of Vitoria: A History of International Law in Spain (1770–1953) 5 (2018).

145 *See generally* 38 Revista Derecho del Estado (2017) (presenting postcolonial perspectives on REDIAL. REDIAL is acronym for a postcolonial movement focused on "rethinking education in international law in Latin America" [*Repensando la Educación en Derecho Internacional en América Latina*]). *See* Paola Andrea Acosta Alvarado, *REDIAL e Imperialismo y derecho internacional. Oportunidad para la reflexión*, 39 Revista Derecho del Estado 3, 4 n.2 (2017). The movement developed in tandem with the publication of Spanish translations of articles by Antony Anghie, Martti Koskenniemi, and Anne Orford (with an additional contribution by Luis Eslava, Liliana Obregón and René Ureña) titled, Imperialismo y Derecho Internacional (2016) and the international conference, *Repensando y renovando el estudio del derecho internacional dentro, desde y sobre la América Latina*, sponsored by the Universidad de los Andes, Universidad del Rosario, and Universidad Externado de Colombia, Bogotá, Sept. 27–28, 2017.

146 *See generally* Umut Özsu, Formalizing Displacement: International Law and Population Transfers (2015); Arnulf Becker Lorca, Mestizo International Law: A Global Intellectual History 1842–1933 (2014); Turan Kayaoğlu, Legal Imperialism: Sovereignty and Extraterritoriality in Japan, the Ottoman Empire, and China (2010); Martti Koskenniemi, The Gentle Civilizer of Nations: The Rise and Fall of International Law 1870–1960 (2001) [hereinafter

postcolonial project as "increasingly influencing the study of international law in ways that seek to decentre traditional disciplinary narratives to illuminate the heterodoxy" of the "international legal order."[147] Thomas Skouteris noted the turn unearths narratives that critically challenge "foundational doctrines and controlling argumentative forms of the discipline."[148] José-Manuel Barreto pointed out this rethinking revealed the imperial "geopolitics of knowledge" embedded in controlling liberal historical accounts.[149] Root's opening address before the 1914 assembly of American international lawyers sparks appropriate criticism of a whiggish attempt to re-center the traditional foreign policy narrative around a homogenous portrait of hemispheric unity. The jarring dislocation of hemispheric amity caused by the Tampico Incident reduced the dependably stolid Root to tears days later during his benedictory address, testing his rhetorical abilities to craft a credible defense of the Monroe Doctrine. However, this turn also contains twists. Some scholars have focused on shifting vocabularies of international law, or on perpetual themes, macro conversations, and the evolutionary narrative of classical intellectual history.[150] Critical interpretations, however, view the turn as a corrective for improper historical decodings. Can some of these decodings be whiggish, too?

10 Whiggish Uses of Vitoria

Much contemporary discussion about Latin American international law's turn to history traces to Antony Anghie's confrontation with Vitoria's influences on international law,[151] an assessment widely supported in the postcolonial

Koskenniemi, The Gentle Civilizer]. The historiographic turn has been summarized as the "constant and growing need on the part of international lawyers to review (even to confirm) the history of international law and to establish links between the past and the present situation." George Rodrigo Bandeira Galindo, *Martti Koskenniemi and the Historiographical Turn in International Law*, 16 Eur. J. Int'l L. 539, 541 (2005). *See also* Koskenniemi, *Vitoria and Us*, *supra* note 111.

147 Mark Toufayan, *"Suffering" the Paradox of Rights? Critical Subaltern Historiography and the Genealogy of Empathy*, *in* Critical International Law: Postrealism, Postcolonialism, and Transnationalism 167, 171 (Prabhakar Singh & Benoît Mayer eds., 2014).

148 Thomas Skouteris, The Notion of Progress in International Law Discourse 27 (2009).

149 José-Manuel Barreto, *Imperialism and Decolonization as Scenarios of Human Rights History*, *in* Human Rights from a Third World Perspective: Critique, History, and International Law 140, 143 (José-Manuel Barreto ed., 2013).

150 *See* Koskenniemi, Gentle Civilizer *supra* note 146, at 22–23.

151 *See generally* Antony Anghie, Imperialism, Sovereignty and the Making of International Law (2004) [hereinafter Anghie]. *See also* Koskenniemi, *Vitoria and Us*, *supra* note 111; José

literature.[152] Scott found it symbolically significant that the great Spanish scholastic was born exactly one century before Grotius[153]—a convenient proof of his paternity thesis concerning international law's proper founding father. While acknowledging that Vitoria was a "brave champion" of the rights of aborigines in the New World, Anghie claimed his sixteenth century employment of "the language of liberality and even equality" "could also be read as a particularly insidious justification of their conquest."[154] While characterizing asymmetries and differences posed by the Spanish encounter with New World aborigines, Vitoria allegedly developed a structure of imperialism (employing constructs of culture and sovereignty) that would persistently stain the discipline of international law for centuries.[155] The significance of Vitoria inhered in his development of the "'set of concepts' that ever since has been deployed by western powers in their suppression of the non-western."[156] Leslye Obiora read Anghie as "depict[ing] the chameleonic persistence of Vitorian epochs" that "engendered juridical techniques ... appropriated as license to live by

---

Mariá Beneyto & Justo Corti Varela eds., At the Origins of Modernity: Francisco de Vitoria and the Discovery of International Law (2017).

152 Koskenniemi, *Vitoria and Us*, *supra* note 111, at 122 (citing, among others, James Thuo Gathii, Enrique Dassel, Luigi Nuzzo, and Robert A. Williams, Jr.). According to Koskenniemi: "It is perhaps above all the person of Franciso Vitoria ... whose role and significance for the history of international law has been the object of the greatest recent interest." *Id.* at 121. *See also* de la Rasilla del Moral, *supra* note 144, at 7; Martti Koskenniemi, *Expanding Histories of International Law*, 56 Am. J. Legal Hist. 104 (2016); Thomas Duve, *European Legal History—Concepts, Methods, Challenges, in* Entanglements in Legal History: Conceptual Approaches 29, 49–50 (Thomas Duve ed., 2014).

153 James Brown Scott, The Spanish Origin of International Law 288 (1934). Vitoria's year of birth is not certain, with recordings of 1480, 1483, or 1486. Scott, however, found it "particularly pleasing to the international lawyer for sentimental and historical reasons" to found the date in 1483, "because, if adopted, we have the two great figures of international law, Vitoria and Grotius, separated by the span of exactly one century." *Id.* at 70. *See also* Rossi, *supra* note 127, at 45 n.1 and corresponding text. Antonio Truyol Serra located his birth between 1480 and 1486, but noted distinguished authorities who supported his birth year as 1493. *See* Antonia Truyol Serra, *Les principals étapes de la vie de Vitoria, in* Actualité de la pensée juridique de Francisco de Vitoria 1, 1 (Antonio Truyol Serra, Henry Mechoulan, Peter Haggenmacher, Antonio Ortiz-Arce, Primitivo Marino & Joe Verhoeven eds., 1988). Truyol Serra claimed, however, he came from Burgos, not Vitoria. *See id.* ("La question du lieu de sa naissance et de sa famililie ... entre les partisans de Vitoria et de Burgos ayant été résolue définitivement en faveur de Burgos.").

154 Anghie, *supra* note 151, at 28. *See also* Antony Anghie, *The Evolution of International Law: Colonial and Postcolonial Realities* 27 Third World Q. 739, 742 (2006) [hereinafter Anghie, *The Evolution of International Law*].

155 Anghie, *The Evolution of International Law*, *supra* note 154, 742–43.

156 Brett Bowden, *The Colonial Origins of International Law. European Expansion and the Classical Standard of Civilization*, 7 J. Hist. Int'l L. 1, 22–23 (2005).

plunder,"[157] and reread international law as a "useful corrective to conventional perspectives that normalize subjugation."[158] Adumbrating this essentialist view, Robert Williams Jr. claimed Vitoria "inaugurated the first critical steps toward a totalizing jurisprudence of international order—a Law of Nations intended to regulate all aspects of the relationships between independent states."[159]

For these postcolonialists, modernity's imperial turn traced directly back in time to this Salamancan. Accordingly, Vitoria's "singular innovation …initiated the process by which the European state system's legal discourse was ultimately liberated from its stultifying, expressly theocratic, medievalized moorings and was adopted to the rationalizing demands of Renaissance Europe's secularized will to empire."[160] James Anaya imputed an ambivalence to Vitoria on Indian land administration that nevertheless served as "a precursor to the trusteeship doctrine later adopted and acted upon by nineteenth-century states."[161] Accompanying this "backdrop of Eurocentric bias" were Vitoria's pejorative measurements of cultural expression and social organization that comported with "European forms of civilization with which Vitoria was familiar."[162] Henry Mechoulan admired Vitoria's ability to camouflage Spaniards' domination behind a rubric of charity or guardianship.[163] It seems some postcolonial literature has served as James Brown Scott's accomplice in elevating Vitoria's name to a position of historical primacy, however for reasons that Scott would abhor.

However, Anghie's attribution of the presentist language of liberality, equality, and sovereignty to adjudge the teachings of Vitoria's sixteenth century mindset embeds elements of anachronistic thinking, or whiggish hanging

157 Leslye Obiora, *Book review, Antony Anghie, Imperialism, Sovereignty and the Making of International Law*, 40 Law & Soc'y Rev. 729 (2006).

158 *Id.* at 731.

159 Robert A. Williams, Jr. The American Indian in Western Legal Thought: The Discourses of Conquest 96 (1990).

160 *Id.* at 96–97.

161 S. James Anaya, Indigenous Peoples in International Law 12 (1996).

162 *Id.*

163 *See* Henry Mechoulan, *Vitoria, père du droit international?*, *in* Actualité de la pensée juridique de Francisco de Vitoria 11, 16 (Antonio Truyol Serra, Henry Mechoulan, Peter Haggenmacher, Antonio Ortiz-Arce, Primitivo Marino & Joe Verhoeven eds., 1988) ("Et un peu plus loin, Vitoria, toujours soucieux de camoufler l'affirmation, écrit, à propos de la condition inférieure et infantile des barbares. Puis le 'père du droit international' fait une habile comparaison entre orphelins et barbares qui s'achève par la justification de la tutelle sur les Indiens au nom de l'amour: la charité robore le droit à la colonization et le droit international deviant un droit d'entr'aide international. Mais toute tutelle se termine à la majorité des bénéficiaires, or les barbares, même convertis, sont incapables d'accéder au statut d'adultes autonomes.").

judge narration.[164] At the same time, he forwards the idea that Vitoria, not Grotius, was international law's first purveyor of whiggish thinking. Perhaps both classical publicists were proto-Whigs centuries before coinage of the term. Butterfield's admonishment about the retrospective tendency toward pre-judgment and the selective and moralizing ratification of what is right in the present attaches to these postcolonial complaints—with one exception. The postcolonial project depicts what is *wrong* in the present. It constructs an antitriumphal meta-narrative. However, postcolonialism's critique still may produce selectively infused narratives with unconscious fore-meanings, making postcolonial historiography susceptible to whiggish infection as well. All narrative history runs this risk.

Georg Cavallar complained that Anghie made "fanciful connections" alien to Vitoria's natural law mindset and took "daring jumps" in order to construct a totalizing meta-narrative of Western legal discourse.[165] Anthony Pagden cautioned against the loss of specificity and temporal sequence by "re-describing the battles of the early modern world in modern terms," for instance making Vitoria "the remote ancestor of the United Nations Charter or the Bill of Rights."[166] Pablo Zapatero Miguel noted the artificiality of the postmodern approach, done to mould his ideas to the postcolonial view, thereby fueling "a new artificial north-south divide."[167] "Drawing on an array of contextual-historical studies," Ian Hunter cast doubt on the postcolonial critique of the early modern *jus naturae et gentium* by suggesting a general whiggishness in that its premises "are themselves European-specific" and "accessible only to those iteratively trained in an array of regional university-based European intellectual cultures."[168]

164 *See also* Balakrishnan Rajagopal, International Law from Below: Development, Social Movements and Third World Resistance 24 (2003) (positing the beginnings of a cultural divide between Christians and infidels in arguments "that became central in the founding texts of international law, such as those by Francisco de Vitoria, that have deeply influenced the evolution of the doctrine of sovereignty.").

165 Georg Cavallar, *Vitoria, Grotius, Pufendorf, Wolff and Vattel: Accomplices of European Colonialism and Exploitation or True Cosmopolitans?* 10 J. Hist. Int'l L. 181, 207–08 (2008).

166 Anthony Pagden, The Uncertainties of Empire: Essays in Iberian and Ibero-American History x (1994). *See also* Anthony Pagden, The Fall of Natural Man: The American Indian and the Origins of Comparative Ethnology 7 (1982) (on "general theoretical errors" regarding acontextual readings of Vitoria).

167 Pablo Zapatero Miguel, *Francisco de Vitoria and the Postmodern Grand Critique of International Law*, *in* At the Origins of Modernity: Francisco de Vitoria and the Discovery of International Law 177, 193 (José María Beneyto & Justo Corti Varela eds., 2017).

168 Ian Hunter, *Global Justice and Regional Metaphysics: On the Critical History of the Law of Nature and Nations*, *in* Law and Politics in British Colonial Thought: Transpositions of Empire 11, 12, 13 (Shannaugh Dorsett & Ian Hunter eds., 2010). *See also* Amitav Archarya

The postcolonial critique embraces Fasolt's attack against treating the past as sacred and the present as profane. For Fasolt, the past should be construed as a foreign country and "[h]istorians are just as active in invading that foreign country, conquering its inhabitants, subjecting them to their discipline and annexing their territories ... as any imperialist who ever sought to impose his power on colonies abroad."[169] Advancing this point, Martti Koskenniemi argued that treating the past as "'another country' whose mores and thinking can only be uncovered" but not submitted to present day standards of criticism "... is to attack both the progressivist narratives of the traditionalists as well as the postcolonial critiques of international law's involvement with empire."[170] The postcolonial project in Latin America seeks to dissolve international law's annexation, uproot its hidden history, and invigorate its trodden down living legacy.[171]

Butterfield, too, nuanced false distinctions between past and present, directing his greatest concern to the tendency of certain scholars to write with *both eyes in the present*, rather than with *one eye on the past*. Wilson and Ashplant argued that this distinction exemplified the condition of present-centeredness, which captured "the fundamental epistemological point" of whig history.[172]

International legal historian, Randall Lesaffer, regretted the functional orientation of current scholarship, concluding that it was "dictated by current needs" that spawned a presentism "rarely born out of a curiosity of the past itself."[173] He argued that the need "to better understand current issues and trends" has impaired the discipline of international law.[174] It has preferenced a kind of historiography that "sins against the most basic rules of historical methodology" [principally to understand the past] by reversing genealogical history [therefore moving from present to past] to give current "practices roots

& Barry Buzan, *Why Is There No Non-Western International Relations Theory? An Introduction*, 7 Int'l Rel. Asia-Pac. 307 (2007); and Arlene B. Tichner, *Seeing IR Differently: Notes from the Third World*, 32 Millennium 317 (2003).

169 Fasolt, *supra* note 120, at xviii. The phrase derives from the first line of L.P. Hartley's, The Go-Between (1953) ("The past is a foreign country; they do things differently there.").

170 Martti Koskenniemi, *Histories of International Law: Significance and Problems for a Critical View*, 27 Temp. Int'l & Comp. L.J. 215, 229 (2013) [hereinafter Koskenniemi, *Histories of International Law*].

171 The point is suggested but not necessarily part of the project implied by the title of Juan Pablo Scarfi's book, The Hidden History of International Law in the Americas: Empire and Legal Networks (2017).

172 Wilson & Ashplant, *supra* note 117, at 10–11.

173 Lesaffer, *International Law and its History*, *supra* note 131, at 29.

174 *Id.* at 33.

in the distant past"—"and the results are deplorable."[175] His self-evident reminder remains forever true: "*The clock always runs forwards*."[176] His point did not denigrate the scholarship or dogmatically insist that international lawyers must work according to historical protocols ignorant of the way international law operates,[177] but noted that its value derives from another purpose than reconstructing the past. This entire conversation, with its twists and turns, testifies to the continuing significance of Butterfield's lament about whiggish (mis) uses of history and historiography.

Lesaffer's criticism sparked a reaction among some postcolonial scholars, who continue to resist "strictly chronological compartmentalizations" of legal history.[178] Their perspective carries forth the important reminder that historiography may result in, or unwittingly express, embedded manipulations of disciplinary approach and historical explanation. While these outcomes may reflect an irredeemable problem of historiography, inculpating their own methodology as well, these postcolonialists maintain that the search for context should result in a legitimating quest for contemporary action. They emphasize the limits of contextual emphasis while deconstructing the geopolitics of legitimacy.

Anne Orford revisited the historiographic problem of context, which she thought served as a barrier to dealing with the living legacy of international law's imperial past. She pinpointed Skinner's contextualist approach to history as the culprit of chronological compartmentalization, noting that its policing of canonical texts resulted in the unrealistic demarcation between past and present, between history and politics, and the belief that "historical research requires that everything must be placed in the context of its time," with no anachronistic present-day comparisons to "distort our interpretation of past events."[179] Koskenniemi, as well, voiced concern about the contextualists' historical relativism and suppression "of patterns in history that might account for today's experiences of domination and injustice."[180] Focusing more on

175 *Id.* at 34. *Cf.* Zapatero, *supra* note 134, at 271 (noting "some standards of historiographical analysis have been abandoned.").

176 Lesaffer, *Law and History: Law between Past and Present*, *supra* note 142, at 26.

177 *Compare* Anne Orford, *International Law and the Limits of History*, *in* The Law of International Lawyers: Reading Martti Koskenniemi 297, 305 (Wouter Werner, Marieke de Hoon & Alexis Galán eds., 2017), *with* Paolo Amorosa, The American Project and the Politics of History: James Brown Scott and the Origins of International Law 9 (Apr. 14, 2018) (Doctoral dissertation, University of Helsinki) [hereinafter Amorosa, *The American Project*] (noting problems with stretching Skinner's approach too far).

178 Koskenniemi, *Vitoria and Us*, *supra* note 111, at 123 (agreeing with Anne Orford).

179 Anne Orford, *On International Legal Method*, 1 London Rev. Int'l L. 166, 171 (2013).

180 Koskenniemi, *Vitoria and Us*, *supra* note 111, at 124.

unnamed followers of Skinner and Koselleck, he questioned the partitioning of their views due to the aloof institutions and traditions of academic life.[181] Koskenniemi should know—he began his career as a diplomat and participated in the profane machinations of statecraft before entering academia's *sanctum sanctorum*.[182]

Orford argued that international legal methodology differed from historical methodology. In her view, "international legal scholarship is necessarily anachronistic because the operation of modern law is not governed solely by a chronological sense of time."[183] Anghie doubtless would agree, given his usages of liberality and equality to summarize Vitoria's views (which Vitoria never recorded himself). Orford viewed Skinner's policing of anachronism as a major response to critical histories of international law,[184] and a hindrance to "the art of making meaning move across time."[185] In this view, the healthy use of anachronism forces a contemporary consideration of the past and an "overt engagement with contemporary politics,"[186] rather than the needless devotion to "the neatness of chronological progression."[187] Anachronic uses of history stand as a reminder to critical theorists that the liberal penchant to move beyond international law's European heritage toward projects of universalizing law is premature, that the structural forces of empire endure, and that contemplation of decolonization and its living legacy are incomplete and far from anachronistic.

And yet Orford's reading of Vitoria imparted its own sense of whiggish preordination. It included the straight-lining of meaning through time, which itself selectively avoided the neatness of chronological progression. Her result emitted an almost desultory present-centeredness. James Brown Scott undertook as general editor to publish the "monumental"[188] twenty-two titles contained in the Carnegie *Classis of International Law* series (1911–1950) (including in 1917

181 *Id.* at 124.

182 *See* Martti Koskenniemi, *Diplomats, Professors, and Then Some: Notes for a History of International Law in 20th Century Finland*, 85 Nordic J. Int'l L. 322, 332 (2016) (noting his years of service with the Finnish Foreign Ministry before assuming Bengt Broms' vacated position at the University of Helsinki in 1995).

183 Orford, *On International Legal Method*, *supra* note 179, at 175.

184 *Id.* at 171.

185 *Id.* at 172.

186 *Id.* at 174.

187 *Id.*

188 Monumental in the sense that they were "ensconced ... in a suitable mausoleum: the monumental Carnegie 'Classics of International Law Series' ... reproducing and translating any work of any conceivable relevance to the field's origins ... provid[ing] the field with a canon that is uncontested because it is substantially unread." Nicholas Onuf,

Vitoria's two *relectiones*, *De Indis* and *De Jure Belli*). For Orford, it would provide "the ideological justification for the universal law of the American century."[189] She, like Anghie, sequenced Scott's focus on Vitoria, which led to the "the Berlin Conference, mandates, the Bretton Woods institutions, [and] the invasion of Iraq." Scott's "humanitarian critique of Spanish empire offered ideological innovators a means of rationalizing the form of empire that would triumph in the twentieth century."[190]

By focusing "[a]ttention to the 'context' in which Vitoria was reclaimed for modern (American) international law," Anghie, with elucidations of his work by Orford, "is not ... trying and failing to create a false connection between Vitoria and seventeenth or eighteenth century European colonialism, but instead creating a new context.... That context is the American century of free trade, liberalized economies, informal empire, and benevolent humanitarianism."[191] If so, their analysis seems to include an *unnecessarily* anachronistic treatment of free trade, conflating Scott's Carnegie Series project with countervailing constructions.[192] Scott launched his series (pejoratively, it would seem to Orford, because Scott's reclamation of Vitoria's name to Americanize Vitoria "arrived between the covers of a book emblazoned with the name of one of the richest industrialists of the nineteenth century [Andrew Carnegie])."[193] decades before the imposition of mercantilist, isolationist, and protectionist trade policy of the Hoover administration's Tariff Act of 1930 (the Smoot-Hawley Act) at

---

"Tainted by Contingency": Retelling the Story of International Law, *in* International Legal Theory: Essays and Engagements, 1966–2006, 259, 361 (2008).

189 Anne Orford, *The Past as Law or History? The Relevance of Imperialism for Modern International Law* 17 (History & Theory of Int'l Law Series, IILJ Working Paper 2012/2, 2012) [hereinafter Orford, *The Past as Law or History?*].

190 *Id.* at 15.

191 *Id.* at 16.

192 Despite assigning to Scott and his Carnegie Endowment for International Peace associates "a vague notion" of free trade, one "equated to just and peaceful relations," Amarosa argued the "basic thinking behind the CEIP program" followed Scott's blueprint whereby twentieth-century free trade ideology stood for conditional measures that have turned human rights language into imposed economic practices of the World Bank and the International Monetary Fund. Amarosa, *The American Project*, *supra* note 177, at 342. "Too often concepts like rule of law, democracy, equality and human rights act as thought-stoppers rather than rallying points for discussing inclusive, pluralistic and transformative politics. Scott's Spanish origin has contributed to this phenomenon by turning those concepts into unquestionable moral truths inscribed into international law centuries ago by the founding figure of Francisco de Vitoria." *Id.* at 343.

193 *Id.* at 17.

the start of the Great Depression.[194] The revolutionary 1934 Reciprocal Trade Agreements Act ushered in by Franklin Delano Roosevelt rescinded that disastrous legislation.[195] The history of free trade, as an idea attached to United States liberalism, transformed dramatically after 1934,[196] suggesting that the free trade idea achieved more ontological expression than certain postcolonial perspectives admit. Butterfield attempted to restore an autonomous identity to the study of history, not to deny its movement through time, but to resist the subordination of its lessons to parochial manipulations. Here, postcolonialists and liberals may selectively employ the history of free trade as an ideological justification for the American century, alternatively construed. However, it is the straight-line causation and cherry-picking of historical events that allow these opposing perspectives of the Hoover and Roosevelt administrations to methodologically converge around an abridged rubric—free trade. Perhaps we could blame Grotius for this discussion's whiggish treatment of the free trade idea. The full title of his pamphlet, *Mare Liberum* (1609) as translated in the Carnegie Series, is: *The Freedom of the Seas or the Right Which Belongs to the Dutch to take part in the East Indian Trade*.[197] This title suggested the Dutch East India Company had a right of unimpeded trade in Portuguese-controlled Asian waters—except Grotius was a mercantilist, and his usage of the right to trade idea predated David Ricardo's (1772–1823) articulation of the concept of comparative advantage, on which the modern notion of free trade is based, by 210 years. Moreover, Grotius' freedom of the seas concept meant to subvert Luso-Spanish interests (as well as indigenous sultanate interferences[198])

---

194 *See* Tariff Act of 1930, 19 U.S.C. § 1654 (1930). The Smoot-Hawley Act reinforced the idea of protectionism that Alexander Hamilton, the first United States Treasury Secretary, first gave sophisticated expression to in his *Report of the Secretary of the Treasury on the Subject of Manufactures* (Dec. 5, 1791), https://www.gilderlehrman.org/sites/default/files/inline-pdfs/T-00891_excerpts.pdf.

195 *See* Reciprocal Tariff Act, 19 U.S.C. § 1351 (1934).

196 *See* Michael J. Hiscox, *The Magic Bullet? The RTAA, Institutional Reform, and Trade Liberalization*, 53 Int'l Org. 669, 669 (1999) (noting the Act "has long been heralded as a simple institutional reform with revolutionary consequences.").

197 Translated from the original in Latin: *Mare Liberum, sive de iure quod Batavis competit ad indicana commercia dissertatio. See* Hugo Grotius, The Freedom of the Seas, or the Right Which Belongs to the Dutch to take part in the East Indian Trade (Ralph Van Deman Magoffin trans., 1916) (1609).

198 Grotius crafted a defense of Just War doctrine on the final pages of *Mare Liberum*, arguing that auxiliaries could make recourse to the doctrine against a person who "prevents … or in any way hinders another in the use of something which is his by common right" absent recourse to judicial administration. *See* Hugo Grotius, Mare Liberum 1609–2009, 153 (Robert Feenstra ed. & trans., 2009). For discussion of how the Dutch East India Company employed this right of self-help against indigenous populations, see Femme S. Gaastra,

to promote the Dutch East India Company's exclusive access to Asian emporia, not to secure open access. Ideas such as free trade and freedom of the sea, like victims put to the iron bed of Greek mythology, get stretched or shortened to conform to the ideological uses of their Procrustean handler.

Perhaps we might direct criticism to Hersch Lauterpacht, for his influential yet gloriously whiggish encomium to Grotius, *The Grotian Tradition in International Law*.[199] There, Lauterpacht credited Grotius' worldview with subjecting the totality of international relations to the rule of law, for recognizing the essential identity of states and individuals, for rejecting reason of state, for distinguishing just and unjust wars, for putting international law on the path of peace, idealism and progress, *and more*. How necessarily anachronistic should international legal historiography be?

Samuel Moyn noted Skinner's conventional antiquarianism and his pursuit of writing history to collect facts cut off from present considerations.[200] Koskenniemi argued the mortal sin of anachronism befell a majority of Anglo-American historians,[201] that contextualism has its own limits in that it may rely on uncritical patterns in history that may suppress "experiences of domination and injustice."[202] United States scholar and statesman Daniel Patrick Moynihan foreshadowed this complaint in foreign policy terms. In the era between the 1970s and 1990s, which was framed by the degeneration in relations between the United States and Central America (the invasion of Grenada (1983), the mining of Nicaragua's harbors (circa 1984), the invasion of Panama (1989), and the Iran-Contra "arms for hostages" scandal (1985–1987)), Moynihan deplored rampant historical amnesia in the making and recollection of United States foreign policy. "[A] practice of deception mutated into a policy

War, Competition and Collaboration: Relations between the English and Dutch East India Company in the Seventeenth and Eighteenth Centuries, *in* The Worlds of the East India Company 52 (H.V. Bowen et al., eds., 2002) (noting Dutch "injustice, perfidy, and cruelty" over its control of Asian waters); 2 Victor Lieberman, Strange Parallels, Mainland Mirrors: Europe, Japan, China, South Asia, and the Islands 845–57 (2009) (on Dutch practices in Ache, Johor, Banten, Makasar, Maluku, and Mataram).

199 *See* Hersch Lauterpacht, *The Grotian Tradition in International Law*, 23 Brit. Y.B. Int'l L. 1–53 (1946) (discussing 11 features of the Grotian Tradition). For commentary, see Rossi, Sovereignty and Territorial Temptation, *supra* note 109, at 48 n.145 and accompanying text (referring to Lauterpacht as glib and unwitting); Lesaffer, *Law and History: Law between Past and Present*, *supra* note 142, at 27–28 n.34 (noting Lauterpacht's intellectual masterpiece is nevertheless a good example of ahistorical reasoning).

200 Samuel Moyn, *Bonfire of the Humanities*, Nation (Jan. 21, 2015), https://www.thenation.com/article/bonfire-humanities/.

201 Koskenniemi, *Histories of International Law*, *supra* note 170, at 227.

202 *Id.*

of deceit,"[203] where lies were repeated enough to be believed, and where, in the end, "[t]he idea of international law *had* faded."[204] "In the annals of forgetfulness," he wrote, "there is nothing quite to compare with the fading of the American mind of the idea of the law of nations."[205]

John Fabian Witt termed this type of disregard for international law's history as "declension theory," thus indicating a whiggish-like abridgment leading to a moral deterioration in the historical understanding of international law.[206] To Witt, who framed his analysis around the history of norms that shaped warfare, contextualism retained an important meaning because it "entail[ed] more than merely understanding the status of ... norms: whether they were believed in, respected, perceived as legitimate, etc. It entail[ed] understanding their social significance and making sense of the social logics in which such norms took part."[207]

Witt's point is well taken, indicating that perhaps a whiggish gloss is at play. The work of Butterfield, the English School, and the Cambridge contextualists, or for that matter the majority of Anglo-American historians, need not reduce to a snap shot-like devotion to historical facts in ways that detract from an understanding of their movement across time. There is no need to force such a false dichotomy. Even the postcolonial school is broad enough to embrace this point.

In his book, *Provincializing Europe* (2000), Dipesh Chakrabarty elegantly reframed the postcolonial narrative on anachronistic history. Mindful of the crowding-out effect of the analytic western narrative (and its privileged treatment inside academia[208]), his project attempted to situate the thematics of post-Enlightenment Eurocentrism—secularism, objectivity, modernity, linear and stagist development (complicated and promoted by Marx's Eurocentric myopia[209])—within a complex relationship that included the hermeneutic tradition. This tradition produced "a loving grasp of detail in search of an understanding of the diversity of human life-worlds," and what he called "affective

203 Daniel Patrick Moynihan, On the Law of Nations 5 (1990).

204 *Id.* at 7.

205 *Id.* at 99.

206 John Fabian Witt, *The Dismal History of the Laws of War*, 1 U.C. Irvine L. Rev. 895, 897 (2011).

207 *Id.* at 903.

208 "[T]he so-called European intellectual tradition is the only one alive in the social science departments of most, if not all, modern universities." Dipesh Chakrabarty, Provincializing Europe: Postcolonial Thought and Historical Difference 5 (2000).

209 *See id.* Ch. 2 (criticizing Marx's analytic construction of labor and capital as underdeveloped and asserted universal principles received outside Europe differently than Marx would have imagined). Marx' myopia extended to his bewilderment over the Asiatic mode of production, which appears fleetingly in his *oeuvre*.

histories."[210] His point was to engage a conversation between the universal and Enlightenment rationalism of the western tradition and the "not always self-evident" subaltern study of affective histories. "'Modernity' is not the work of Europeans alone;" wrote Chakrabarty, "third-world nationalisms, as modernizing ideologies par excellence, have been equal partners in the process." Nothing in his argument supported straight-line caricatures or recognition of the need to be even a little bit anachronistic. "The idea is to write into the history of modernity the ambivalences, contradictions, the use of force, and the tragedies and ironies that attend it."[211]

Similarly, Walter Mignolo emphasized the tendency of international law to unwittingly tell only "half the story." As a semiotician, he uncovered "political blind spots" that hide international law's *coloniality* within a cosmology of modernity that emphasizes *excellence*, *innovation*, and *efficiency*.[212] Disciplinary formations embedded Eurocentric understandings of these terms, making international relations a local project and a local discipline that its own practitioners, including *évolués*, then projected over an interstate system.[213] His project of decoloniality, or de-linking from the colonial matrix of power,[214] involved a present-centerdness, but required a returned to the sixteenth century to investigate the historical foundations of the ethno-class that created the nation-state and international law, which he recognized formed "without intent to be what they will become."[215]

The problem with abject devotion to contextualism has long been understood by scholars interested in the English School and other problems of historiography. As noted by Dunne, contextualism "imputes causality to the world, relegating theory to an effect of changes 'out there.'"[216] Butterfield's lament was that Whig history forwarded thin causal connections because it "studies

210 *Id.* at 18.

211 *Id.* at 43.

212 Walter D. Mignolo, *The Making and Closing of Eurocentric International Law: The Opening of a Multipolar World Order*, 36 Comparative Studies of South Asia, Africa and the Middle East 182, 184 (2016). Mignolo credits scholars such as Siba N. Grovogui as attempting to tell the missing half of the story. *Id.* at 184. *See generally* Siba N. Grovogui, *Regimes of Sovereignty: Rethinking International Morality and the African Condition*, 8 J. Int'l Rel. 315–38 (2002); Siba N'zatioula Grovogui, Sovereigns, Quasi Sovereigns, and Africans: Race and Self-Determination in International Law (1996).

213 *Id.* at 185.

214 *See Interview—Walter D. Mignolo*, E-Int'l Rel. (June 1, 2017), http://www.e-ir.info/2017/06/01/interview-walter-d-mignolo/ (defining decoloniality in terms of de-linking from the colonial matrix of power).

215 *See* Mignolo, *supra* note 212, at 187.

216 Dunne, *supra* note 95, at 2.

the past with reference to the present,"[217] when the rightful approach "is the elucidation of the *unlikenesses* between past and present."[218] Investigating the unlikenesses of the past requires sensitive awareness of both past and present. Butterfield's subtle distinction need not provoke postcolonial critique, which would doubtless emphasize the hidden *likenesses* or connections between international law's universalizing present-day project and its deeply imperial past. For Butterfield, historical discontinuity—the recognition of "how much other ages differed from our own"—framed "the first condition of historical enquiry,"[219] but did not amount to its sum total. According to Dunne, "[Butterfield] railed against the presumption that history unfolds according to a grand master-plan, with a mythical origin and a triumphant *telos*."[220] This triumphal retelling of history constituted the attributes of presentism and progressivism fit for the moral absolutism of nineteenth century liberal historians such as Lord Acton, T.B. Macaulay, H.T. Buckle, and W.E.H. Lecky.[221] However, to Butterfield such portrayers of Whig fallacies diminished if not short-circuited application of contemporary critique. Indeed, Butterfield thought a chief aim of the historian was to "disillusion[] us concerning something in the past which we had assumed to be too like something in the present."[222]

This idea of historical discontinuity also informed the work of Michel Foucault, whose approach in the *Archeology of Knowledge* (1972) acknowledged, if not embraced, the disruptive challenges to historiography and the problem that time is forever out of joint:

217 Butterfield, *supra* note 84, at 11.

218 *Id.* at 10.

219 *Id.* at 36.

220 Dunne, *supra* note 95, at 73. *See also* Butterfield, *supra* note 84, at 10 ("for the chief aim of the historian is the elucidation of the unlikenesses between past and present … When [the historian] shows us that Magna Carta is a feudal document in a feudal setting, with implications different from those we had taken for granted, he is disillusioning us concerning something in the past which we had assumed to be too like something in the present.").

221 *See* George H. Smith, *Lord Acton and the History of Liberty, Part 2*, Libertarianism.org (Mar. 12, 2013), https://www.libertarianism.org/publications/essays/lord-acton-history-liberty-part-2. Smith noted that "[o]ther than a few names mentioned in passing, the only historian that Butterfield discussed was Lord Acton." Indeed, Butterfield pinpointed Acton as achieving the "highest consciousness" of the whig historian. Butterfield, *supra* note 84, at 109, who idealized history "to the extremity of its logical conclusion." *Id.* at 114. Dunne acknowledged the importance of Butterfield's *Whig Interpretation* but criticized his contextualism as well, agreeing with Geoffrey Elton's view that Butterfield's recourse to substance was "really perilously thin." Dunne, *supra* note 95, at 85 n.16.

222 Butterfield, *supra* note 84, at 10.

> Beneath the great continuities of thought … the solid homogenous manifestations of … a collective mentality … beneath the persistence of a particular genre, form, discipline, or theoretical activity … [there are interruptions] … they suspend the continuous accumulation of knowledge, interrupt its slow development; …they direct historical analysis away from the search for silent beginnings, and the never-ending tracing-back to the original precursors…; they show that the history of a concept is not wholly and entirely that of its progressive refinement, its continuously increasing rationality, its abstraction gradient, but that of its various fields of constitution and validity, that of its successive rules of use, that of the many theoretical contexts in which it developed and matured.[223]

Foucault's philosophical treatment inspires critical perspectives of international law's turn to history.[224] And yet, Skinner's critics associate Skinner's method of with the myth of history's underlying coherence.[225]

A closer reading of the problem of historical discontinuity, with its suggested twists and turns, gently informs of the point of contact between postcolonial and contextual concerns. This convergence of thought has been obscured, perhaps, by a discussion among intellectual historians about the treatment of context, writ large. This treatment indicated to Butterfield's student, J.G.A. Pocock, that the interpretation of history involved the situation of ideas within the conceptual vocabularies of a particular time.[226] Here was the distillation of an emerging method to treat intellectual history as "a multiplicity of language acts performed by language users in historical contexts."[227] This injunction

223 Michel Foucault, The Archaeology of Knowledge 4 (A.M. Sheridan Smith trans., 1972). The work first appeared in French in 1969.

224 *See, e.g.*, Rajagopal, *supra* note 164, 13–15; Ben Golder, *Foucault and the Incompletion of Law*, 21 Leiden J. Int'l L. 747 (2008); Leonard M. Hammer, A Foucauldian Approach to International Law: Descriptive Thoughts for Normative Issues (2007); B.S. Chimni, *The Self, Modern Civilization, and International Law: Learning from Mohandas Karamchand Gandhi's Hind Swaraj or Indian Home Rule*, 23 EJIL 1159 (2012). *See also* Janne E. Nijman, Seeking Change by Doing History 6 (2018) (crediting Foucault and post-colonial critic Edward Said with shifting our thinking about doing history to discontinuities and contestations).

225 Robert Lamb, *Quentin Skinner's Revised Historical Contextualism: A Critique*, 22 Hist. Human Sci. 51, 59 (2009) [hereinafter Lamb, *Skinner's Revised Historical Contextualism*].

226 *See* J.G.A. Pocock, The Machiavellian Moment: Florentine Political Thought and the Atlantic Republican Tradition 3 (2016).

227 Richard Whatmore, *Introduction to the New Princeton Classics Edition* to The Machiavellian Moment: Florentine Political Thought and the Atlantic Republican Tradition viii (2016).

would spread across disciplines and pinpoint language as the focal point of study, most forcefully framed by Ludwig Wittgenstein's philosophically reductionist summary: "The limits of my language are the limits of my world."[228]

Skinner's concern for method attempted to respond to the tendency to "create caricatures out of past thinkers," to assess them according to contemporary standards of moral argument, and to render intellectual history a "pack of tricks we play on the dead."[229] His point remains sound notwithstanding the argumentative nature of his theoretical view. He seems to have generated heated postcolonial criticism with his contention that political texts cannot be read as contributions to perennial debates.[230] Instead, they must be understood as particularistic, ideological speech acts (which he called linguistic contextualism);[231] that they "can only be understood correctly by locating them within their intellectual context, and in turn, that this intellectual context can only be properly understood in terms of the language available to individual authors."[232] Mark Bevir, a critic of Skinner's approach, nevertheless differentiated hard linguistic contextualists, "who argue that the meaning of a text derives from the paradigm to which that text belongs," and soft linguistic contextualists, who "situate that text within its contemporaneous linguistic conventions."[233] Orford makes no such distinction with her broad claim that "Skinner's approach to thinking about 'ideas in context' has been adopted largely without question by those who seek to stamp out anachronism in international legal scholarship, but their adoption ignores the criticisms to and challenges of his method."[234]

Fitzmaurice noted these complaints overstate the English School's detachment from contemporary problems, much as Mayr denounced linear attempts

---

228 Ludwig Wittgenstein, Tractatus Logico-Philosophicus 149 (1951) (1921). *See also* Andrew Fitzmaurice, *Context in the History of International Law*, 20 J. Hist. Int'l L. 5, 8 (2018) (noting Wittgenstein's impact on contextual approaches).

229 Robert Lamb, *Feature Book Review: Quentin Skinner's "Post-modern" History of Ideas*, 89 History 424, 425 (2004) (quoting Skinner's 1 Vision of Politics: Regarding Method). The epigram belongs to Voltaire: "History is a pack of lies we play on the dead."

230 *See generally* Lamb, *Skinner's Revised Historical Contextualism*, *supra* note 225, at 51 (arguing there is nothing wrong with appropriate treatments of past texts to recurring philosophical debates and maintaining Skinner's own arguments do not support the contextualism he defends).

231 Skinner, *supra* note 102.

232 Lamb, *supra* note 225, at 55.

233 Mark Bevir, *The Errors of Linguistic Contextualism*, 31 Hist. & Theory 276, 277 (1992).

234 Orford, *On International Legal Method*, *supra* note 179, at 173.

to scrub the history of science of its intellectual context.[235] Fitzmaurice knew of no "historians coming from the so-called 'Cambridge School' of intellectual history who would subscribe to such methodological notions."[236] Brunello Vigezzi's detailed forensic analysis of the English School's meetings noted an undergirding regard for historical sensitivity,[237] not the abject rejection of historiography's concern for contemporary problems.

To Butterfield, contextualism stood for the proposition "that judgements about right and wrong should be dispensed in accordance with our own standards."[238] Fitzmaurice critiqued Koskenniemi's reading of contextualists' political disengagement, arguing that a steady stream of adherents avowedly employed history as an instrument to understand the present.[239] However, Butterfield thought the magnetic pull of whiggish historical fallacy dismissed careful self-critical awareness.[240] Some critical scholars seem to condemn the ability of historians to break free from their contemporary inertial bonds because historians are ensnared in a contemporary structural trap of their own making. Koskenniemi claimed this ensnarement encouraged a kind of historical relativism that unavoidably suppressed discovery of the patterns of history.[241] However, Butterfield understood this point, as well, and realized that historians could "never entirely abstract" themselves from their own age. However, "he was not really concerned with the temporal logic that makes anachronism inevitable."[242] Butterfield treated anachronism as an aspect of

235 *See* Mayr, *supra* note 70, at 301.

236 Andrew Fitzmaurice, *The Problem of Eurocentrism in the Thought of Francisco de Vitoria*, *in* At the Origins of Modernity: Francisco de Vitoria and the Discovery of International Law 77, 88 (José María Beneyto & Justo Corti Varela eds., 2017).

237 *See* Brunello Vigezzi, The British Committee on the Theory of International Politics (1954–1985): The Rediscovery of History 173 (2005) (on the English School's "faith in detailed investigations and in 'history'"). *See also* William Bain, *The English School and the Activity of Being an Historian*, *in* Theorising International Society: English School Methods 148, 148 (Cornelia Navari ed., 2009) (on history's "pride of place" in English School thought).

238 Dunne, *supra* note 95, at 73.

239 Fitzmaurice, *supra* note 236, 89–90 (citing Anthony Pagden, Richard Tuck, James Tully, Istvan Hont, and more recent Cambridge-inspired intellectual historians such as David Armitage, Jennifer Pitts, himself, and Duncan Bell.).

240 Butterfield, *supra* note 84, at 7.

241 Koskenniemi, *supra* note 111, at 124 (noting that the intermingling of the object of historical research and the researcher's own context requires the critical awareness of such intermingling).

242 Poe, *supra* note 125, at 354.

historiography, and only as a problem when it became an unexamined habit of the historian's mind.[243]

The rethinking of international law's historiography has generated interest in global perspectives,[244] alternative and new methods of international law,[245] critical evaluations of the international law's close association with empire,[246] and the emergence or distinctness of American or Latin American narratives of international law.[247] Janne Nijman claimed "a discontent with orthodox

243 *Id.* at 345–346.

244 *See generally* The Oxford Handbook of the History of International Law (Bardo Fassbender & Anne Peters eds., 2013).

245 *See, e.g.* Lucie Delabie, *Les nouvelles approaches du droit international*, Revue Québécoise de droit int'l 57 (2016); 31 Hélène Ruiz-Fabri, Mark Toufayan & Emmanuelle Tourme-Jouannet, Droit international et nouvelles approaches sur le tiers-monde: entre repetition et renouveau/International Law and New Approaches to the Third World: Between Repitition and Renewal (2013); New Approaches to International Law: The European and The American Experiences (José María Beneyto & David Kennedy eds., 2012); Obiora Chinedu Okafor, *Critical Third World Approaches to International Law (TWAIL): Theory, Methodology, or Both?* 10 Int'l Community L. Rev. 371 (2008); B.S. Chimni, *Third World Approaches to International Law: A Manifesto*, 8 Int'l Community L. Rev. 3 (2006); International Law and its Others (Anne Orford ed., 2006); Antony Anghie & B.S. Chimni, *Third World Approaches to International Law and Individual Responsibility in Internal Conflicts*, 2 Chinese J. Int'l L. 77 (2003); Makau Mutua, *What Is TWAIL?*, 94 ASIL Proc. 31 (2000); Orford, *The Past as Law or History?*, *supra* note 189, at 6.

246 *See e.g.*, International Law and Empire: Historical Explorations (Martti Koskenniemi, Walter Rech & Manuel Jiménez Fonseca eds., 2017); Coates, *supra* note 80; Critical International Law: Postrealism, Postcolonialism, and Transnationalism (Prabhakar Singh & Benoît Mayer eds., 2014); Emmanuelle Jouannet, *Universalism and Imperialism: The True-False Paradox of International Law?*, 18 Eur. J Int'l L. 379 (2007); Anghie, *supra* note 151; Yasuaki Onuma, *When Was the Law of International Society Born? An Inquiry of the History of International Law from an Intercivilisation Perspective*, 2 J. Hist. Int'l L. 1 (2000).

247 *See, e.g.*, Ricardo Abello-Galvis & Walter Arévalo-Ramírez, *The Influence of the Latin American Doctrine on International Law: The Rise of Latin American Doctrines at The Hague Academy During the Early Twentieth Century*, *in* Latin America and the International Court of Justice: Contributions to International Law 15–28 (Paula Wojcikiewicz Almeida & Jean-Marc Sorel eds., 2016); Becker Lorca, *supra* note 146; Liliana Obregón, *Construyendo la region Americana: Andrés Bello y el Derecho Internacional*, *in* Andrés Bello y los Estudios Latinoamericanos 189–218 (Beatriz González Stephan & Juan Poblete eds., 2009); Liliana Obregón, *Latin American International Law*, *in* Routledge Handbook of International Law 154–64 (David Armstrong ed., 2009); Barreto, *supra* note 148. Focusing on center-periphery dynamics in international law, the *Leiden Journal of International Law* launched its periphery series with articles dedicated to the international legal scholarship of Alejandro Álvarez, which played an important role in rejuvenating attention on Latin American international law. *See* Fleur Johns, Thomas Skouteris & Wouter Werner, *Editors' Introduction: Alejandro Álvarez and the Launch of the Periphery Series*, 19 Leiden Int'l L.J. 875 (2006). *See also* Anne-Marie Slaughter, *An American Vision of International Law?* 97 ASIL Proc. 125 (2003); Philip Allot, *International Law and the American Mind*, 97 ASIL Proc. 129 (2003).

teleological, Eurocentric and hagiographic histories of international law" accounted for the emergence of new orientations.[248] Reshaping the contours of hemispheric historiography requires the construction of transnational narratives to displace the traditional national storylines. Ezra Manela noted "the influence of the transnational turn is now clearly pervasive" in the study of United States history, notwithstanding the incomplete recasting of national histories within the transnational frame.[249] This turn prompts consideration of the sometimes tense relationship between international lawyers and historians of international law and the relationship between that combined camp and international relations scholars,[250] opening up more generalized debates on context, formalism, and interdisciplinarity.[251] Elihu Root and the Monroe Doctrine are fast becoming unexamined habits of the emerging postcolonial discussion on international law's turn toward Latin America.

From the postcolonial perspective, the standard historical reconstruction of international law in Latin America either expresses an intellectual map of the present based on a reading back of contemporary events in search of triumphant historical clues that promote hagiography and pre-ordain such contemporary conclusions, or, it is used to delegitimate competing approaches, possibly to inform some polemical version of what current consensus should be.[252]

---

248 Nijman, *supra* note 224, at 6 (seeking change by doing history).

249 Ezra Manela, *The United States in the World, in* American History Now 202, 203 (Eric Foner & Lisa McGirr ed. 2011).

250 *See* Lesaffer, *International Law and its History, supra* note 131, at 29. Lesaffer discusses the interest in historiography of international law between international lawyers and legal historians in the text. Important contributions to the history of international law by diplomatic historians and international relation theorists are also noted. *See id.* at 30 n.13, 33. *See also* Fitzmaurice, *supra* note 228, at 6 (noting the methodological friction produced by scholars from different disciplinary backgrounds working on the same material); Or ford, *International Law and the Limits of History, supra* note 177, at 301 (quoting historians who "sternly cautioned international lawyers for making 'fanciful' connections"). *See also* Brian C. Schmidt, The Political Discourse of Anarchy: A Disciplinary History of International Relations (1998) (arguing for the need of international relations specialists to better grasp the historiography of their own field).

251 *See generally* Tanja Aalberts & Ingo Venzke, *Moving Beyond Interdisciplinary Wars: Towards an Understanding of International Law as Practice, in* International Law as a Profession 287 (Jean d'Aspremont et al., eds., 2017); *see also* Jean d'Aspremont, Epistemic Forces in International Law: Foundational Doctrines and Techniques of International Legal Argumentation 189–91 (2015); Martti Koskenniemi, *The Mystery of Legal Obligation*, 3 Int'l Theory 319 (2011); Jan Klabbers, *The Relative Autonomy of International Law and the Forgotten Politics of Interdisciplinarity*, 1 J. Int'l L. & Int'l Rel. 35 (2004); Gerry Simpson, *Duelling Agendas: International Relations and International Law (Again)*, 1 J. Int'l L. & Int'l Rel. 61 (2004).

252 John S. Dryzek & Stephen T. Leonard, *History and Discipline in Political Science*, 82 Am. Pol. Sci. Rev. 1245, 1247 (1988).

Postcolonialists interpret the contextual approach as the dominant methodological tradition in Anglophone intellectual history,[253] and regard it as a polemic against the postcolonial turn to history by international relations and international legal scholars. This contextual perspective impliedly views the English School's core propositions as contributing to problems of historicism when not reducing its tenets to nothing more than a restatement of the nineteenth and early twentieth century positivistic and statist formalities that gave first expression to the critique.[254] The English School's methodology has been attacked generally for a lack of cohesion and empirical emphasis,[255] for its complicity in liberalism's promotion of empire,[256] as "a Trojan horse for [R]ealism,"[257] and for its anachronistic concentration on main characters in a world supplanted by "systems, networks, bureaucratic structures" and faceless governance.[258] However, the English School's connection to the problem of context remains central to the postcolonial critique—and to the recovery of a more textured reading of the Monroe Doctrine and Elihu Root as the vehicle closely associated with its defense and projection into the twentieth century.

11 Why Butterfield Matters to International Law and Its Turn to Latin America

Butterfield's prominence due to *The Whig Interpretation of History* later helped launch the English School of international relations.[259] The English School

253 *See* ESIL Lecture Series, *Anne Orford-Histories of International Law and Empire*, YouTube, 4:43 (Jan. 23, 2013), https://www.youtube.com/watch?v=b5UzlTLEMko.

254 *See* Peter Wilson, *The English School's Approach to International Law*, in Theorising International Society: English School Methods 167 (Cornelia Navari ed., 2009); Koskenniemi, *Histories of International Law: Significance and Problems for a Critical View, supra* note 170, 229 (noting contextualism "tends to rely on a 'positivist' separation between the past and the present that encourages historical relativism").

255 *See* Jennifer Sterling-Folker, *English School Approaches, in* Making Sense of International Relations Theory 303, 303–04 (Jennifer Sterling-Folker ed., 2006).

256 *See* Anghie, *supra* note 151; Uday Mehta, Liberalism and Empire: A Study in Nineteenth-Century British Liberal Thought (1999); Jennifer Pitts, A Turn to Empire: The Rise of Imperial Liberalism in Britain and France (2006).

257 Dunne, *supra* note 95, at 5 ("Certain writers on the radical wing of the discipline treat the English School as a Trojan horse for realism, a way of smuggling in power politics in a language of community.").

258 Orford, *On International Legal Method, supra* note 179, at 167.

259 Butterfield and Wight would edit a "key" text of the English School. *See* Herbert Butterfield & Martin Wight, Diplomatic Investigations: Essays in the Theory of International Politics (1968); Daniel M. Green, *Introduction to the English School in International Studies, in* Guide to the English School in International Studies 1, 8 (Cornelia Navari & Daniel

focuses on the political life and formation of international society,[260] less so questions of historiography for which Butterfield is better known.[261] With his co-organizer, Martin Wight, Butterfield founded a salon of international relations scholars in 1958 called the British Committee on the Theory of International Politics.[262] It would include among its first generation of associates Charles Manning, Martin Wight, Hedley Bull, Alan James, R.J. Vincent, and Adam Watson.[263] With its regard for ethical questions, the role of international

Green eds., 2014). Awareness of the network of English School scholars grew against this background "in the late 1970s." *Id.* at 9.

260 *See* Richard Little, *Reassessing "The Expansion of International Society,"* E-Int'l Rel. (Jan. 28, 2016), http://www.e-ir.info/2016/01/28/reassessing-the-expansion-of-international-society/; Green, *supra* note 259, at 1.

261 *See* McIntyre, *supra* note 85, at 99 ("Most commentators of the English School have neglected to place Butterfield's work in the context of his ideas about the nature of political life and the character of human activity.").

262 *See* Paul Sharp, *Herbert Butterfield, The English School, and the Civilizing Virtues of Diplomacy*, 79 Int'l Aff. 855, 855 (2003) (noting he did much to get the committee "up and running"). On the formation of the British Committee in 1958, see Dunne, *supra* note 95, at 4. Roger Epp regarded Wight's role as "crucial" in launching with Butterfield. *See* Roger Epp, *The British Committee on the Theory of International Politics and Its Central Figures*, *in* Guide to the English School in International Studies, *supra* note 259, at 25, 26. Brunello Vigezzi indicated the birth of the British Committee among a "handful of friends" began between 1954 and 1958 and ended in 1985 with the publication of Bull & Watson's The Expansion of International Society, the death of Bull, Watson's "mounting commitments" in the United States "and the general dispersal of the other members." Vigezzi, *supra* note 237, at vii. Tim Dunne dated the English School's emergence as a self-conscious research program to the writings of early post-war theorists in leading UK universities. *See generally*, Tim Dunne, *The English School*, *in* The Oxford Handbook of Political Science 730 (Robert E. Goodin ed., 2011). An anonymous reviewer noted as well the primacy of the London School of Economics, Oxford University, and the Royal Institute of International Affairs in the development of the English School.

263 *See* Andrew Linklater & Hidemi Suganami, The English School of International Relations: A Contemporary Reassessment 41 (2006). Leading texts of the first wave of English School scholars include: C.A.W. Manning, The Nature of International Society (1962), Herbert Butterfield & Martin Wight, Diplomatic Investigations (1966), R.J. Vincent, Nonintervention and International Order (1974), Hedley Bull, The Anarchical Society: A Study of Order in World Politics (1977), Martin Wight, Systems of States (1977), Adam Watson, Diplomacy: The Dialogue Between States (1982), and Alan James, Sovereign Statehood: Basis of International Society (1986). The second wave of English School scholars include: David Armstrong, Barry Buzan, Bruce Cronin, Tim Dunne, Andrew Hurrell, Robert Jackson, Andrew Linklater, Richard Little, James Mayall, Cornelia Navari, Ioannis Stivachtis, Hidemi Suganami, John William, and Yongjin Zhang. A revival of interest in the English School began with the arrival of the third wave of scholars in 1999. They include: William Bain, Alex Bellamy, Molly Cochran, Edward Keene, John Pella Christian Reus-Smit, Laust Schouenborg, Richard Shapcott, Paul Sharp, Shogo Suzuki, and John Williams. *See* Green, *supra* note 259, at 2.

law, the centricity of historical knowledge to the study of international relations, and emphasis on diplomacy and motives, its adherents would oppose supervening waves of behavioralist and social science methods entering the field from the United States while also critiquing idealist interwar forms of internationalism.[264] It would also forge important (sometimes contested) convergences with constructivism.[265] The English School suggested a transnational approach to the study of world politics decades before international law's turn to history. These fields were precisely the fields cross-fertilized by the significant influence of Elihu Root.

At the same university to which the English School of international relations was born, "there [later] emerged an undertaking spearheaded by Cambridge historians to write the history of the past in terms of the ideas that animated it."[266] The bridge connecting the two schools buttressed the focus on contextualism. Kenneth B. McIntyre noted "[t]he methodological writings of the Cambridge School retain without substantive revision almost all of Butterfield's historiographical injunctions."[267] Along with Peter Laslett and later associates of the Cambridge School, principally Anthony Wrigley, Pocock, Skinner, John Dunn, and Duncan Forbes,[268] Butterfield modeled his critique of

264 For a general historiographic review, see Brian C. Schmidt, *The Historiography of Academic International Relations*, 20 Rev. Int'l Stud. 349 (1994). On the English School's united acknowledgment of the importance of historical knowledge to the study of international relations, see Green, *supra* note 259, at 18–21; Suganami, *The Historical Development of the English School*, *supra* note 259, at 7, 19 (noting the English School's treatment of the study of international relations as intrinsically historical). On the English School's focus on diplomacy and motives, see Watson, *supra* note 81; Andrew Linklater & Hidemi Suganami, The English School of International Relations: A Contemporary Reassessment 107 (2006); Schouenborg, *The English School and Institutions: British Institutionalists?*, *supra* note 259, 77 (on the importance placed on diplomacy as an institution); Hedley Bull, *The State's Positive Role in World Affairs*, 108 Daedalus 111, 115–16 (1979) (noting state cooperation in evolving the "rules of the road" and developing international law and the diplomatic system).

265 Christian Reus-Smit, *Imagining Society: Constructivism and the English School*, 4 Brit. J. Pol. & I.R. 487, 487–88 (2002). Reus-Smit noted as well that "[c]onstructivism and the English School are often said to bear striking family resemblances." *Id.* at 489.

266 Iver B. Neumann, *The English School on Diplomacy: Scholarly Promise Unfulfilled*, 17 Int'l Rel. 341, 356 (2003).

267 McIntyre, *supra* note 85, at 46.

268 *See generally* Peter Laslett, The World We Have Lost (1965); E.A. Wrigley, Industrial Growth and Population Change: A Regional Study of the Coalfield Areas of North-West Europe in the Later Nineteenth Century (1961); J.G.A. Pocock, Politics, Language, and Time: Essays on Political Thought and History (1971); Skinner, *supra* note 102; John Dunn, *The Identity of the History of Ideas*, 43 Phil. 85 (1968); and Duncan Forbes, The Liberal Anglican Idea of History (1952).

Anglophone history around the idea that the retelling of history must not submit to the temptation of acontextual or anticontextual storytelling. Michael Bentley wrote that Butterfield "lacked the intellectual vocabulary of this latter generation associated with Quentin Skinner and his contemporaries," however he "showed none the less a sensitivity to issues of context and *Zeitgeist* and foreshadowed significant developments in the history of political thought."[269] Predominant examples or contested claims of impaired storytelling in the history of international law include Scott's flawed reclamation of Vitoria's name, Julián Juderías' Black Legend (*leyenda negra*) complaint of calumnies against Spain since the early modern period,[270] Alejandro Álvarez' promotion of a hemispheric law known to him as American International Law and to others as a hollow simulacrum for United States international lawmaking,[271] and critical treatments of Hugo Grotius' "tactical re-deployment" of anti-Habsburg propaganda to bolster seventeenth century Dutch trade practices in the East Indies.[272] If Grotius was the putative father of international law, despite Scott's

---

269 Michael Bentley, The Life and Thought of Herbert Butterfield: History, Science and God 150–51 (2011).

270 *See generally* Julián Juderías, La leyenda negra: estudios acerca del concepto de España en el extranjero (1917[?]). Similar to Butterfield, Juderías' complaint focused on Protestant historiography, which he claimed tended to emphasize misappropriations of history, although unlike Butterfield, Juderías emphasized the intentionality behind the historiographic damage to Spain's reputation. Juderías reduced its meaning as follows: "En una palabra, entendemos por leyenda negra, la leyenda de la España inquisitorial, ignorante, fanática, incapaz de figurar entre los pueblos cultos lo mismo ahora que antes, dispuesta siempre a las represiones violentas; enemiga del progreso y de las innovaciones; o, en otros términos, la leyenda que habiendo empezado a difundirse en el siglo xvi, a raíz de la reforma, no ha dejado de utilizarse en contra nuestra desde entonces y más especialmente en momentos críticos de nuestra vida nacional." *Id.* at 20.

271 *See, e.g.*, Andrei Mamolea, The Myth of Legalism in US Foreign Relations (doctoral dissertation, Graduate Institute of International and Development Studies, Geneva, 2018).

272 Erich Michael Wilson, The Savage Republic: De Indis of Hugo Grotius, Republicanism and Dutch Hegemony within the Early Modern World-System (c. 1600–1619), 470–71 (2008). *See generally* Rossi, Sovereignty and Territorial Temptation, *supra* note 109; José-Manuel Barreto, *Cerberus: Rethinking Grotius and the Westphalian System, in* International Law and Empire: Historical Explorations 149, 154 (Martti Koskenniemi, Walter Rech & Manuel Jiménez Fonseca eds., 2017); Peter Borschberg, Hugo Grotius, the Portuguese and Free Trade in the East Indies (2011); Martine Julia van Ittersum, Profit and Principle: Hugo Grotius, Natural Rights Theories and the Rise of Dutch Power in the East Indies, 1595–1615, Ch. 2 (2006) (on the Black Legend). Arthur Weststeijn detected irony (opposable to himself, as well) in presentations of Grotius as the mouthpiece of Dutch imperialism in that these interpretations "enact[] a dramatic play of global interaction where the European attitude dominates the stage" and "risks maintaining the imperial structure of cetre and periphery that Grotius himself helped to create." Arthur Weststeijn, *Provincializing Grotius: International Law and Empire in a Seventeenth-Century Malay Mirror, in*

best efforts to discredit this claim, he then must have been its first whiggish purveyor, as well. Dutch practices, couched in terms of forwarding the freedom of the seas, amounted to a type of freebooting, or piracy indistinguishable from the practices of the Portuguese *Fidalgos* (noblemen) and their attempt to secure their empire in Asia, the *Estado da Índia*.[273]

Butterfield centrally influenced Cambridge School historians.[274] Pocock served as his research assistant and published his first book, *The Ancient Constitution and the Feudal Law* (1957) which grew out of the 1952 dissertation Butterfield's supervised.[275] Skinner's critique of contextualism—which included the conflation of moral and historical judgment and the autonomy of historical explanation (free of subordinating political influences)—"retain[s] much of the flavor of Butterfield's critique of the Whig historians."[276] Skinner produced "a number of sparkling polemical articles in the 1960s, attacking ahistorical and 'whig' treatments of the canon of political thinkers."[277]

"There is a tendency for all history to veer over into whig history," wrote Butterfield.[278] His epithet has powerfully informed the political and religious histories to which Butterfield first applied it,[279] and has entered into the everyday language of historians and perhaps he even embodied the "insularity it was designed to criticize."[280] Nevertheless, re-reading Butterfield refreshes the concept of whiggish thinking and the ways it has entered into the fields of diplomacy and international law using Elihu Root's multiple identities as politician, international lawyer, diplomat, and scion of Lotos Club high society.[281] Root is the vehicle for restating the persistent whig problem through his

International Law and Empire: Historical Explorations 21, 22 (Martti Koskenniemi, Walter Rech & Manuel Jiménez Fonseca eds., 2017).

273 *See* C.G. Roelofsen, *Grotius and International Law, in* Grotius Reader: A Reader for Students of International Law and Legal History 3 (L.E. van Holk & C.G. Roelofsen eds., 1983).

274 McIntyre, *supra* note 85, at 157, 187 n.118, and corresponding text.

275 *Id. See also* Whatmore, *supra* note 227, at viii.

276 McIntyre, *supra* note 85, at 46.

277 John Burrow, A History of Histories: Epics, Chronicles, Romances and Inquiries from Herodotus and Thucydides to the Twentieth Century 465 (2008) (citing Skinner's Vision of Politics, Vol. 1); *see generally* Skinner, *supra* note 102.

278 Butterfield, *supra* note 84, at 6.

279 *See* Wilson & Ashplant, *supra* note 117, at 2.

280 *See id.* at 3.

281 *See* Speeches at the Lotos Club 137–39 (John Elderkin, Chester Sanders Lord & Horatio Nelson Fraser eds., 1901) (reprinting Root's after dinner speech honoring Charles A. Dana, Jan. 16, 1896). The Lotos Club was the grandest of the fourteen high society clubs in Manhattan. It was formed to promote social intercourse among elite and professional gentlemen who "would naturally be attracted by such a club." John Elderkin, A Brief History of The Lotos Club 8–9 (1895). Theodore Roosevelt received the Nobel Peace Prize in 1906 for

magnetizing attempt to pull the Monroe Doctrine into a direction that alters the bearings of the whole subject and its subaltern complexities.[282] However, the doctrine expressed multiple identities, as well, and embraced various, sometime simultaneous, usages across time that whiggish straight-liners ignore. Was it a rational trope for liberal internationalism and economic integration, a critical manifestation of imperial anticolonialism, a geospatial border construct to secure hemispheric security, a geospatial reordering construct to alter transisthmian politics, a regional springboard for worldwide expansion, an idealized expression of hemispheric union, an expression of United States exceptionalism, or a vehicle for redefining or refining a unique Latin American standard of civilization?

Standard and postcolonial narratives have impaired the understanding of the doctrine precisely because of their straight-line whiggish abridgments that support Butterfield's reasons for anachronism's appeal: simplicity, the promotion of ideology, and general narration. Whiggish thinking obscures deeper histories of international law, not simply hidden histories.

Butterfield's capacious usage of the term whiggish now applies to all oversimplified narratives of progress that seek moral clarity by interpreting past events in light of present politics.[283] Such staged, pro-establishment or anti-imperial narratives seek, like Procrustes, to retrofit new circumstances "into the old story even when the research in detail has altered the bearings of the whole subject."[284] As Ian Hall has written: Butterfield's "coruscating short book … lamented the tendency of … liberal historians to let their moral values intrude into their historiography and to relate the past as a kind of drama of good versus evil, in which the good eventually and inexorably prevailed."[285]

---

facilitating an end to the Russo-Japanese war, which purportedly reached agreement at the Lotos' bar. *See* Moynihan, *supra* note 203, at 23. Zimmermann noted the interlocking network of social relations that made many leading figures of early twentieth century United States expansion intimate friends and frequenters of the same clubs, adding the Metropolitan Club in Washington, D.C. and the Union League Club and Century Association in New York. Zimmermann, First Great Triumph, *supra* note 16, at 10, 133.

282 *See* Butterfield, *supra* note 84, at 6 (alluding to the magnet metaphor).

283 William Cronon, *Two Cheers for the Whig Interpretation of History*. Persp. on Hist. (Sept. 2012) https://www.historians.org/publications-and-directories/perspectives-on-history/september-2012/two-cheers-for-the-whig-interpretation-of-history; Franz Samelson, *Whig and Anti-Whig Histories-And Other Curiosities of Social Psychology*, 36 J. Hist. Behav. Sci. 499 (2000); Charles Lilley, *American-East Asian Relations in the Heroic and Whig Modes*, 18 Diplomatic Hist. 135 (1994); A. Rupert Hall, *On Whiggism*, 21 Hist. Sci. 45 (1983).

284 Butterfield, *supra* note 84, at 6. *See also* Sewell, *supra* note 90, at 30 (on the anachronistic staging of narratives).

285 Ian Hall, *Martin Wight, Western Values, and the Whig Tradition of International Thought*, 36 Int'l Hist. Rev. 961, 970 (2014).

John Dryzek and Stephen Leonard underscored the goal-oriented project of whiggish historiography: "Whigs write the history of the discipline as though it were teleological, culminating in some correct current understanding or, more usually, some bright imminent future in which past difficulties are resolved."[286] Dryzek and Leonard noted the irony: to whiggish historians "the past has little intrinsic value."[287] Whiggish thinkers may seek to "liberate the discipline from the dead weight of past errors and illusions,"[288] however Butterfield claimed they forwarded their own wishful version of history. His point underscored that historiography's inherent construction of history needed to treat critically developmental assumptions and received truths of disciplinary approach.

Notwithstanding the sensitivities presented by the postcolonial critique and by the discursive treatments on problems of contextualism, international law's turn to history in Latin America (and elsewhere[289]) presses onward. Much of this project attempts to uproot more of international law's hidden history during this seminal period in western hemispheric history,[290] a period marked by the rise of the legalist empire of Elihu Root and his associates. And new narratives arise.

Already, international law encounters mestizo[291] and creole[292] influences and the discrete emergence of a Latin American consciousness of international law.[293] This narrative asserts a mimetic engagement with traditional European ideas of international law and its accompanying standard of civilization. Becker Lorca argued, however, these ideas were internalized in ways that ultimately, but imperfectly as we shall see,[294] contributed to a reordering of the rules to carve out a progressive voice for marginalized perspectives during the

286 Dryzek & Leonard, *supra* note 252, at 1253.

287 *Id.*

288 *Id.*

289 *See* Anthea Roberts et al., *Comparative International Law: Framing the Field*, 109 Am. J. Int'l L. 467, 467 n.3 (2015) (canvassing French, Chinese, Russian, regional, Asian, Italian, transcivilizational, in addition to various Latin American traditions of international law).

290 *See generally* Scarfi, *supra* note 171; Latin America and the International Court of Justice: Contributions to International Law, *supra* note 247 (with essays on the historical contribution of Latin America to the development of international law through Hague Peace Conference II of 1907, international courts and tribunals, procedural codification, the Central American Court of Justice, and the Permanent Court of International Justice).

291 *See* Becker Lorca, *supra* note 146.

292 *See* Obregón, *supra* note 94.

293 *See* Obregón, *Identity Formation, supra* note 64; Arnulf Becker Lorca, *International Law in Latin America or Latin America International Law—Rise, Fall, and Retrieval of a Tradition of Legal Thinking and Political Imagination*, 47 Harv. Int'l L.J. 283 (2006).

294 *See infra* Ch. 5 on 1914 CACJ case.

eventful early part of the twentieth century.[295] Matthias Packeiser noted that a constellation of economic and political insecurities foisted a condition of Latin American dependency on foreign capital, making practical if not necessary the embrace of European value standards to achieve diplomatic status and acceptance as sovereign equals.[296] Krausist philosophy, with its organic construction of society, its commitment to ethics, education, and its harmonization of traditional Catholic social rights emphases with the dictates of liberalism (*racionalismo armónico*), tremendously influenced Spanish cultural and political thought.[297] It spread throughout Latin America in the late nineteenth and early twentieth centuries.[298] Argentina's two-time president Hipólito Yrigoyen (1850–1933; terms 1916–1922; 1928–1930), became a strong advocate, as did Uruguay's president, José Batlle (term: 1921–1923), and Cuban nationalist, José Martí.[299] It particularly influenced the international legal views of Rafael Altimira y Crevea (1866–1951), the Americanist who served on the Permanent Court of International Justice.[300] He aimed at the "the renewal of the discourse

295 *See generally* Becker Lorca, *supra* note 146.

296 *See* Matthias Packeiser, Full Sovereign Equality: A Historical Study of Latin American Countries Under International Law 4–5. Paper presented at the *Repensando y renovando el derecho internacional dentro, desde y sobra la América Latina* conference, sponsored by the Latin American Society of International Law, the Universidad de los Andes, Universidad del Rosario, and Universidad Externado, Bogotá, Colombia (Sept. 26–28, 2017) (on file with author).

297 *See generally* Juan López Morillas, El krausismo español: Perfil de una aventura intelectual (1956). Morillas dated its appearance in Spanish cultural life to the mid-nineteenth century. *Id.* at 7 ("A mediados del siglo pasado se esboza en la vida cultural de España la fase inicial de una trasvaluación ideológica"). The second edition first published in English titled the book as The Krausist Movement and Ideological Change in Spain, 1854–1874 (1981); Thomas Neuner, Karl Krause (1781–1832) in der Spanischsprachigen Welt: Spanien, Argentinien, Kuba (2004) (noting particularly its influence on the socio-reformist theory (*Die gesellschaftsreformistische Konzeption*) of Francisco Giner de los Ríos (1883–1915), professor of international law and jurisprudence at the University of Madrid).

298 *See* Neuner, *supra* note 297, at 55; O. Carlos Stoetzer, Karl Christian Friedrich Krause and His Influence in the Hispanic World (1998). Dierksmeier noted distinct Krausist influences in Mexico, Brazil, Guatemala, Ecuador, and Peru in addition to its influences on constitutionalism and politics in Argentina and Uruguay. *See* Claus Dierksmeier, *Krausism, in* A Companion to Latin American Philosophy 110, 120 (Susana Nuccetelli, Ofelia Schutte & Otávio Bueno eds., 2009). *See also* Richard Gott, Karl Krause and the Ideological Origins of the Cuban Revolution (Occasional Paper No. 28, University of London Institute of Latin American Studies, 2002).

299 *See* Neuner, *supra* note 297, at 114–21; Cintio Vitier & Daisaku Ikeda, José Martí, Cuban Apostle: A Dialogue 117 (2013) (noting Vitier's conclusion that Krause "undoubtedly influenced" Martí).

300 *See* Yolanda Gamarra, *Rafael Altamira y Crevea (1866–1951). The International Judge as "Gentle Civilizer,"* 14 J. Hist. Int'l L. 1, 13–15 (2012) (on Altimira and Krausism).

of what he saw as the Spanish history of civilization by drawing on the legacy of Francisco de Vitoria and his successors."[301] Krausism's contribution to the distinct idea of a Latin American approach to international law only now is emerging from German and Spanish language circles.[302] The work of Alejandro Álvarez, the well-known Pan-American advocate and promoter of a distinctly American idea of international law,[303] already has received undivided attention on the pages of the *Leiden Journal of International Law*.[304] Some of this emphasis has shifted in focus toward postmodern or critical constructions of hemispheric *Nouvelles Courant* (New Stream) perspectives bubbling up from Cambridge (Massachusetts) scholars and associates.[305] However, contributions of other lost South American perspectives are again surfacing.

Ricardo Abello and Walter Arévalo recently revived the contributions of Colombian international lawyer, regional integrationist, delegate to the League of Nations Assembly and signatory of the United Nations Charter, Jesús María Yepes (1892–1962).[306] Along with luminaries such as Roberto Ago (1907–1995) and Hans Kelsen (1881–1973), Yepes lectured three times at The Hague Academy and was "among the first ... to demonstrate the influence of Latin American doctrine."[307] What started out as a project to reacquaint a new generation of

301 *Id.* at 1.

302 *See* Andreas Timmermann, Hipólito Yrigoyen (1850–1933): "Krausism" and International Understanding 23–25. Paper presented at the Latin America and International Law Conference, Albrecht Mendelssohn Bartholdy Graduate School of Law, University of Hamburg, (Feb. 8–9, 2018) (on file with author) (noting Krausist influences on Yrigoyen to advocate inter-Hiberian dialogue, Pan-Americanism, a new international law separate from entanglements with emerging United States foreign policy, and German and Spanish language sources of Krause's hemispheric influence).

303 *See generally* Alejandro Álvarez, Le droit international américain (1910).

304 *See generally* the special edition, 19 Leiden J. Int'l L. (2006), *supra* note 247 (with treatments by Fleur Johns, Thomas Skouteris, Wouter Werner, Arnulf Becker Lorca, Jorge L. Esquirol, Carl Landauer, Liliana Obregón, and Katharina Zobel).

305 *See* Lucie Delabie, Approaches Américaines du droit international: Entre unite et diversité 342–71 (2011) (discussing the divergence in methodological approaches between (mostly) United States critical scholarship and Europe). Much of her attention regarding the wellspring of the "new current" of the American approach to international law traces to David Kennedy's International Legal Structures (1987), along with formative contributions by Roberto Unger, Duncan Kennedy, Mark G. Kelman, Hilary Charlesworth, and Christine Chinkin, among others.

306 Ricardo Abello-Galvis & Walter Arévalo-Ramírez, *Jesús María Yepes (1892–1962)*, Société française pour le droit international (2017), http://www.sfdi.org/internationalistes/yepes/.

307 Abello-Galvis & Arévalo-Ramírez, *supra* note 247, at 16. *See generally* J.M. Yepes, *La contribution de l'Amérique latine au développement du droit international public et privé*, 32 Recueil des Cours 691 (1930); J.-M. Yepes, *Les problèmes fondamentaux du droit des gens en Amérique*, 47 Recueil des Cours 1 (1934); J.M. Yepes, *Les accords régionaux et le droit*

scholars with his work turned into a much broader investigation for Abello and Arévalo.[308] They reclaimed the work of Brazilian, Raul Fernandes (1877–1968), who proposed acceptable language that led to the creation of the optional clause now contained in Article 36(2) of the ICJ Statute.[309] They also highlighted The Hague Academy lecture of Mexican foreign relations minister, Francisco León de La Barra (1863–1939), who influentially shaped the course of dispute resolution discussions that led to the Pact of Bogotá,[310] and Guatemala's José Matos's retelling of the hemispheric contributions in support of the League of Nations.[311]

As much as empire's legacy affects the scholarship of today, the recovery of distinct Latin American voices retraces subaltern themes of intervention, union, and ideals that deepen the complexities associated with this legacy. The Colombian jurist and member of the *Institut de droit internacional*, F.J. Urrutia, drew inspiration for the codification of American international law from the French *philosophes* and American Enlightenment.[312] Similarly, Albert Guani, Uruguay's representative on the League of Nations Council focused on the longstanding hemispheric appeal of confederation.[313] Yepes, in 1930, recounted the allure of federation, which forms a connective tissue weaving throughout hemispheric relations from the time of Henry Clay (1777–1852) and Simón Bolívar's call for the 1826 Congress of Panama to Secretary of State James Blaine's idea in 1889 to form the International Union of American Republics, which resulted in the Pan-American Union and now the Organization of American States.[314] Rodrigo Octavio returned to the fundamental problem

international, 71 Recueil des Cours 227 (1947). *See also* Inés Yepes de Uprimny, Jesús María Yepes y el derecho internacional americano (1980).

308 C. Alihusain, *Interview: A Historical Look at Latin American Contributions in the early Years of The Hague Academy*, Peace Palace Libr. (Aug. 30, 2017), https://www.peacepalacelibrary.nl/2017/08/interview-a-historical-look-at-latin-american-contributions-in-the-early-years-of-the-hague-academy/.

309 *See id.*

310 Fr[ancisco] León de la Barra, *La mediation et la conciliation internals*, 1 Recueil des Cours 553 (1923).

311 *See* José Matos, *L'Amérique et la Société des Nations*, 28 Recueil des Cours 1 (1929).

312 *See* F.J. Urrutia, *La codification du droit international en Amérique*, 22 Recueil des Cours 81, 85–89 (1928).

313 Albert Guani, *La solidarité international dans l'Amérique Latine*, 8 Recueil des Cours 203 (1925).

314 J.M. Yepes, *La contribution de l'Amérique latine au développement du droit international public et privé*, *supra* note 307, at 709. *See also* Yepes de Uprimny, *supra* note 307, at 118–20 (on *El pensamiento de Henry Clay*), & 122–38 (on *El pensamiento del Libertador Simón Bolívar*).

of the discovery of aborigines within the Biblical context that seemingly denied their humanity.[315] Much of these conversations were framed with the Monroe Doctrine and Elihu Root as backdrops. Prompted by consideration of the Venezuelan Boundary Dispute, Yepes devoted a chapter of his 1934 Hague lecture to hemispheric problems of intervention;[316] Venezuela's Minister to Lisbon, Simón Planas-Suárez, devoted his entire Hague Lecture to the Monroe Doctrine.[317]

12 Conclusion

These voices intersect with an unending story about international law's engagement with the Americas. Depictions of descendent Europe and ascendant United States factor into history's explanatory equation during the critical inflection point at the beginning of the twentieth century. Encountering international law's turn to Latin American history invites reconsideration of its fuller history, occluded in large part by the crowding out of complexities owing to present-centered imperial and postcolonial policing of narratives. The project should move forward, however, freshly aware of the problems of historiographic straight-lining and simplistic coloration, aware of the false triumphalisms of liberal hagiographers and postcolonial Procrusteans, and respectful of the dislikenesses and discontinuities of historical narration that inevitably rendezvous with Butterfield's admonition against using international legal history as a present-centered hostage to ideology.

Uprooting more of the hidden history of the Monroe Doctrine during a seminal period in western hemispheric history adds texture to international law's

315 Rodrigo Octavio, *Les sauvages américains devant le droit*, 31 Recueil des Cours 177, 185 (1930 I) ("Colomb affirmait que la découverte des terres nouvelles fournirait à la domination du people conquérant un formidable contingent de nouveaux sujets. On accueillit cette affirmation comme une hérésie. Elle s'opposait à la paternité exclusive que l'on attribuait officiellement à Adam. Si les fils de Noé, ses descendants disait-on, les seuls exemplaires du genre humain qui avaient échappé au Déluge, n'avaient peuplé que des terres connues, on ne pouvait admettre qu'il existât des hommes dans des region qui ne présentaient avec celles-là acun rapport.").

316 Yepes, *Les problèmes fondamentaux du droit des gens en amérique*, *supra* note 307, Ch. 3 (*Le problème de l'intervention*).

317 Simón Planas-Suárez, *L'extension de la doctrine de Monroe en Amérique du Sud*, 5 Recueil des Cours 267 (1924).

continuing turn to the history of the Americas, chips away at caricatures that play games on the dead, and acknowledges the ever-present pitfall of whiggishness that inheres in the weavings of Spain's sixteenth century presence in the New World, extending its not-so-dead hand into the twentieth century and beyond by the likes of Elihu Root.

CHAPTER 2

The Birth of the Root Doctrine

United States Secretary of State Elihu Root toured South America in 1906,[1] proclaiming good will, mutual respect, sovereign equality, and according to his close associate James Brown Scott, and to his successor as United States Secretary of State Robert Bacon, a new doctrine – the Root Doctrine.[2] Root presented its core components in a speech in Rio de Janeiro at the Third Conference of American Republics:

> We wish for no victories but those of peace; for no territory except for our own; for no sovereignty except the sovereignty over ourselves. We deem the independence and equal rights of the smallest and weakest member of the family of nations entitled to as much respect as those of the greatest empire; and we deem the observance of that respect the chief guaranty of the weak against the oppression of the strong. We neither claim nor desire any rights or privileges or powers that we do not freely concede to every American republic.[3]

More loosely conceived than a set of instructions or edicts, and only informally received into the canon of doctrines that have framed United States foreign policy,[4] Root's formulation nevertheless galvanized South America officials.

---

1 Root's South American visits included Brazil, Uruguay, Argentina, Chile, Peru, Panama, and Colombia. The capital cities of Paraguay, Bolivia, and Ecuador were too distant from the seaboard to accommodate a visit given the time at his disposal. Theodore Roosevelt, *Sixth Annual Message to the Senate and House of Representatives* (Dec. 3, 1906), *reprinted in* Am. Presidency Project, http://www.presidency.ucsb.edu/ws/index.php?pid=29547. Root then accepted Mexican President Porfirio Díaz' invitation to visit Mexico, which he did in 1907.

2 J.B. Scott & R. Bacon, *Introductory Note* to Latin America and the United States: Addresses by Elihu Root (R. Bacon & J.B. Scott eds., 1917). They did not coin the term, however, as South Americans began referring to his speech in such terms during his tour. *See, e.g.*, Ruy [Rui] Barbosa, *Speech of Senator Ruy Barbosa* (Aug. 2, 1906), *in* Latin America and the United States: Addresses by Elihu Root 19, 27 (R. Bacon & J.B. Scott eds., 1917).

3 Elihu Root, *Address to the Third Conference of the American Republics* (July 31, 1906), *in* Latin America and the United States: Addresses by Elihu Root 10 (R. Bacon & J.B. Scott eds., 1917). The conference is also referred to as the Third Pan-American Conference. For documents associated with the conference, see James Brown Scott, The International Conferences of American States, 1889–1928, at 111–50 (1931).

4 *See* James Curtis Ballagh, Book Review, *The Monroe Doctrine: An Interpretation*, 12 Am. J. Int'l L. 214 (1918).

 | DOI:10.1163/9789004379510_003

He greeted the "elder sisters in the civilization of America," noting the forces of progress moved in a continental, not exceptional direction;[5] he spoke of the American republics engaged in the "same great task, inspired by the same purpose, and professing the same principles"; and he counterbalanced the "all-American" project of unity against the limited and militarized Old World frontiers of Europe.[6] In Uruguay, Root said: "The great declaration of Monroe, made in the infancy of Latin American liberty, was an assertion to all the world of the competency of Latin Americans to govern themselves. That assertion my country has always maintained; and my presence here is, in part, for the purpose of giving evidence of her belief that the truth of the assertion has been demonstrated."[7]

Peruvian diplomat and scholar, Francisco García Calderón (1834–1905), referred to the speech as "the noble words of a modern stoic."[8] Peru's foreign minister interpreted Root's message as part of the United States' guarantee of independence for all American countries.[9] Brazil's ambassador to the United States and conference president, Joaquim Nabuco (1849–1910), a devoted Pan-Americanist with whom Root had originally conceived of the conference,[10] expressed the widespread sentiment that Root's presence "assuredly means that America forms a political system separate from that of Europe—a constellation with its own distinct orbit."[11] Luis Drago, the eminent Argentine jurist, who started a hemispheric movement in 1902 to prevent states from resorting to war to recover debt,[12] referenced Root's "eloquent expression" as constituting "a separate political factor, a new and vast theater ... which will serve as a counterpoise" to the "other hemisphere."[13] Drago's own delegation, along with

---

5 *See* Root, *supra* note 3, at 8.

6 *Id.* at 11 ("armaments as are massed behind the frontiers of Europe"); *id.* at 6 ("limitations of the Old World").

7 *Reply of Mr. Root (Montevideo, Aug. 10, 1906), in* Latin America and the United States: Addresses by Elihu Root 58–59 (R. Bacon & J.B. Scott eds., 1917).

8 Francisco García Calderón, *A Latin-American Criticism of the Monroe Doctrine*, 29 Current Hist. 548, 549 (1929).

9 Javier Prado y Ugarteche, *Speech of His Excellency Javier Prado y Ugarteche (Sept. 11, 1906), in* Latin America and the United States: Addresses by Elihu Root 116–17 (R. Bacon & J.B. Scott eds., 1917).

10 *See* Juan Pablo Scarfi, The Hidden History of International Law in the Americas: Empire and Legal Networks 14–15 (2017).

11 Joaquim Nabuco, *Speech of His Excellency Joaquim Nabuco (July 30 1906), in* Latin America and the United States: Addresses by Elihu Root 3, 4 (R. Bacon & J.B. Scott eds., 1917).

12 *See generally* Luis M. Drago & H. Edward Nettles, *The Drago Doctrine in International Law and Politics*, 8 Hisp. Am. Hist. Rev. 204 (1928).

13 Luis M. Drago, *Speech of Dr. Luis M. Drago (Aug. 17, 1906), in* Latin America and the United States: Addresses by Elihu Root 93, 95 (R. Bacon & J.B. Scott eds., 1917).

Root, would undercut his hemispheric initiative by conditioning and then transposing his proposal onto the landscape of general international law,[14] intentionally "denaturing" its regional tenor and impact by removing it from the Rio agenda onto the international Hague Conference platform, scheduled for the following year.[15] There, under the rubric of the so-called Porter Convention, named after the United States delegate, General Horace Porter, it was further denatured by focusing on contract debt rather than public debt and ultimately preserving the recourse to war if arbitration efforts failed.[16] Lars Schoultz claimed Root's South American tour had sped ahead of Roosevelt's position, which "was not prepared for an unequivocal prohibition on the use of force" given problems caused in Venezuela under the rule of Cipriano Castro (1858–1924) and the recent blockading of that country by European powers, which almost erupted in hemispheric war.[17] Drago resigned his appointment as a member of the Argentine delegation in protest,[18] however he also praised Root as "the highest and most eloquent representative of American solidarity,"[19] a disciple of hemispheric independence and fraternity in the tradition of the Pan-Americanist, United States politician, Henry Clay.[20] Drago,

14 Arthur P. Whitaker, The Western Hemisphere Idea: Its Rise and Decline 100–01 (1954).

15 *Id.* at 101, 102. *See also Programme for the Third International American Conference*, art. IV, *in* The International Conferences of American States, 1889–1928, art. IV, at 114 (James Brown Scott ed., 1931) ("Public Debts: A resolution recommending that the Second Peace Conference at The Hague be requested to consider whether and if at all, to what extent, the use of force for the collection of public debts is admissible.").

16 *See Convention II Respecting the Limitation of the Employment of Force for Recovery of Contract Debts, Oct. 18, 1907, in* The Hague Conventions and Declarations of 1899 and 1907, art. 1, at 89 (James Brown Scott ed., 1915) ("The Contracting Parties agree not to have recourse to armed force for the recovery of contract debts claimed from the Government of one country by the Government of another country as being due to its nations. This undertaking is, however, not applicable when the Debtor State refuses or neglects to reply to an offer of arbitration, or, after accepting the offer, prevents any *compromise* from being agreed on, or, after the arbitration, fails to submit to the award."). *See also* Carsten-Andreas Schulz, *Accidental Activists: Latin American Status-Seeking at The Hague*, 61 Int'l Stud. Q. 617 (2017).

17 Lars Schoultz, Beneath the United States: A History of U.S. Policy Toward Latin America 195 (1988).

18 Whitaker, *supra* note 14, at 102 ("resigned when he read his instructions, in which his successor as head of the Argentine foreign office opposed the hemispheric character of the Drago Doctrine").

19 Drago, *supra* note 13, at 93–97.

20 *See id.* at 94 (referring to Clay as a defender of independence and solidarity among the Americas).

as well as Nabuco[21] associated Root's words with the "traditional policy of the United States, which, without accentuating superiority or seeking preponderance, condemned the oppression of the nations of this part of the world and the control of their destinies by the great powers of Europe."[22]

Latin American historian Arthur Whitaker found it unsurprising "that Root was able to keep Drago happy while playing ducks and drakes with his doctrine," noting "Root was remarkably successful in winning the friendship and confidence of the Latin Americans" during this 1906 tour.[23] And with good reason. Drago served as the president of the reception committee, which welcomed Root to the Buenos Aires Opera House during the Argentine leg of his tour. There, Root delivered an assertive speech that embraced much of Drago's concerns regarding the forceful collection of debt:

> The United States of America has never deemed it to be suitable that she should use her army and navy for the collection of ordinary contract debts of foreign governments to her citizens. ...[this] has become the settled policy of our country. We deem it to be inconsistent with that respect for the sovereignty of weaker powers which is essential to their protection against the aggression of the strong. We deem the use of force for the collection of ordinary contract debts to be an invitation to abuses, in their necessary results far worse, far more baleful to humanity that the debts contracted by any nation should go unpaid. We consider that the use of the army and navy of a great power to compel a weaker power to answer to a contract with a private individual, is both an invitation to speculation upon the necessities of weak and struggling countries and an infringement upon the sovereignty of those countries, and we are now, as we always have been, opposed to it[.][24]

Root aimed to promote international arbitration as the formalistic means of insuring debt repayment.[25] In addition to these words, Root's very presence in Latin America symbolized a new and significant development. Root's

21 *See* Scarfi, *supra* note 10, at 14 ("[Nabuco] was very supportive of the Monroe Doctrine as a legitimate continental principle to protect the region from European interventions. He also emphasized the beneficial role of United States supremacy on the continent.").

22 Drago, *supra* note 13, at 96.

23 Whitaker, *supra* note 14, at 103.

24 *Reply of Mr. Root* [August 17, 1906], *in* Latin America and the United States: Addresses by Elihu Root 96 (R. Bacon & J.B. Scott eds., 1917).

25 *See* Richard H. Collin, Theodore Roosevelt's Caribbean: The Panama Canal, the Monroe Doctrine, and the Latin American Context 496 (1990).

predecessor as Secretary of State, James Blaine (1881–1881; 1889–1892), had helped to establish in Washington, D.C., the International Union of American Republics, which formed in 1890 to harden hemispheric dispute settlement mechanisms and improve commercial ties. Root extended Blaine's initiative first by elevating legations to embassy status in Central American Republics,[26] and then by personally venturing to South America. It was the first visit by a high-ranking United States official, indeed, his "first notable act as Secretary of State,"[27] and Latin American leaders thanked him profusely for "exploring political seas never navigated before."[28] His tour was a "spectacular diplomatic success" and it marked the transitional character in the meeting of the two Americas as equals.[29] He worked to ensure that Latin American countries would be invited to the 1907 Hague Peace Conference, a greatly appreciated gesture.[30] Only Mexico had been invited to attend the first Hague Conference in 1899.[31] Moreover, he presided over the Rio Conference agenda-setting activities, which had been organized by the Bureau of the American Republics.[32] It set out an ambitious program of hemispheric integration, presenting resolutions affirming arbitration as a means of regional dispute settlement, promoting public and private international law development, enhancing commercial integration, harmonizing intellectual property and customs regulations, reaffirming the intent to construct a Pan-American railway,

---

26 *See* Frederick W. Marks III, Velvet on Iron: The Diplomacy of Theodore Roosevelt 188 (1979).

27 *Biographies of the Secretaries of State: Elihu Root (1845–1937)*, Off. Historian, https://history.state.gov/departmenthistory/people/root-elihu.

28 Nabuco, *supra* note 11, at 6. Additionally, Root had worked to guarantee the success of the Rio Conference by petitioning Russia to postpone the Second Hague Peace Conference to avoid a scheduling conflict. *See* Collin, *supra* note 25, at 497.

29 Collin, *supra* note 25, at 491 ("spectacular success"), 492 (transitional character).

30 Schoultz, *supra* note 17, at 195 (noting Root's inclusiveness of Latin American countries was "the secret of his success.").

31 *See* A.G. de Lapradelle & Ellery C. Stowell, *Latin America at The Hague Conference*, 17 Yale L.J. 270, 270 (1908) (calling the presence of South and Central American states "[p]erhaps the most salient feature of the Second Peace Conference."). On the motion of the United States, the Latin American countries not represented at the first Hague Peace Conference were permitted to adhere to the proceedings of the first conference, thereby allowing participation at the second conference. James L. Tryon, *The Hague Conferences*, 20 Yale L.J. 470, 478 (1911).

32 *See Invitation to the Conference, The Brazilian Ambassador to the United States to the Secretary of State, Mr. Elihu Root* (Apr. 25, 1906), *in* The International Conferences of American States, 1889–1928, at 113 (James Brown Scott ed., 1931) (inviting the United States to the conference and acknowledging that the conference program had been organized by the Bureau of the American Republics under Root's presidency).

coordinating the control of infectious disease by means of a sanitary convention, and strengthening learned societies and education exchanges.[33] Listed first among these undertakings was the proposal to reform the International Bureau of the American Republics into a permanent structure for hemispheric administration. The proposal resulted in the renamed Pan-American Union, and the construction of its headquarters in Washington, D.C., funded as an American Temple of Peace by the Scottish-American industrialist and philanthropist, Andrew Carnegie.[34] At the dedication ceremony in 1910, Carnegie credited Root as chiefly responsible for its creation.[35]

1 A Tendentious Subtext

There was more to the Rio agenda. A tendentious subtext involving deteriorating hemispheric relations prompted a call to action. United States President Theodore Roosevelt (term of office: 1901–1909) later claimed he sent Root to Latin America to shore up United States support.[36] Officially, the United States delegation operated under the same set of instructions Roosevelt had provided to his contingent at the Second International American Conference in Mexico City in 1901: promote the "safety and permanence of the political system" underlying the common existence of American republics, and reinforce that "the United States should be understood to be the friend of all the Latin American republics and the enemy of none."[37] However, the United States' rise as a world power cast conspicuous hemispheric shadows over its foreign policy, principally given recent dealings in Panama, Cuba, and the Philippines,[38] a

33 *See Programme for the Third International American Conference*, *supra* note 15, arts. I–XIV, at 113 16.

34 *Id.* at 113. *See also* Scarfi, *supra* note 10, at 27 (on Carnegie's $950,000 financial contribution to construct the permanent "Temple of Peace"); Randall Lesaffer, *The Temple of Peace: The Hague Peace Conferences, Andrew Carnegie and the Building of the Peace Palace (1898–1913)*, 140 Mededelingen van de Koninklijke Nederlandse Vereniging voor Internationaal Recht 1 (2013).

35 *See* John Barrett, The Pan American Union: Peace, Friendship, Commerce 230 (1911) (reprinting Carnegie's dedication comments and crediting Root, "to whom we chiefly owe this beautiful structure.").

36 Joseph Byrne Lockey, Pan-Americanism: Its Beginnings 6–7 (1920).

37 *Id.* (quoting the 1901 instructions to the Mexico City conference). According to Lockey, the 1906 delegates "were provided with a copy of the instructions of 1901" and "instructions indicated no occasion for changing them except in some minor details." *Id.* at 7.

38 *See, e.g.*, Hiram Bingham, *The Latin American Attitude Toward the Monroe Doctrine*, 8 ASIL Proc. 180, 191 (1914) (noting former Honduran president Policarpo Bonilla's concern that United States territorial conquests following the Spanish American war, "done while

far-flung former holding of the Spanish empire that became the United States' first major military engagement of the twentieth century.[39] Root instructed the delegation to focus on the community of interests that forged functional, non-controversial cooperative ventures.[40] His objective, with his signature speech in Rio and throughout his tour, intended to shine a light on what he claimed were his country's true and unchanging objectives.

To accomplish this task, Root attempted to reframe the rhetoric surrounding United States hemispheric foreign policy, which revolved around the Monroe Doctrine—the traditional policy to which Drago referred. That doctrine asserted two key points: non-colonization, in the sense that the Americas, henceforth, were not to be considered as subjects for future colonization by any European powers; and non-interference, meaning that any attempt to oppress or control the destiny of newly independent nations of the hemisphere would endanger "*our* peace and safety." The Monroe Doctrine originally focused on the United States' peace and safety *vis-à-vis* Europe. Cast in this light, it amounted to a defensive doctrine. In furtherance of this interpretation, the Root Doctrine emphasized sovereign equality, suggesting added dimensions of interest to hemispheric counterparts. The United States sought no hemispheric entitlements other than those it accorded to others. To Root this policy underscored the importance of reciprocity. His emphasis on equality and independence among all American states, weak or strong, also implied equal standing.

To Latin Americans, these ideas suggested more than the traditional Monroe Doctrine freedoms *from* foreign subjugation and interference. They suggested strengthened hemispheric integration in the form of greater political

---

invoking the Monroe Doctrine," has menaced the dignity and vital interests of Latin America).

39 The McKinley administration committed 20,000 United States troops to the war (1899–1902). It was the first of Asian venture, which included the annexation of Hawaii (1898), the ceding of Guam and the Philippines by Spain (1899), the partitioning of Samoa with Germany (1899), and the commencement of the Open Door policy to secure equal trading privileges with China, prompting the Boxer Rebellion and invasion of North China by 4,000 United States troops and other forces. *See* Michael H. Hunt, The American Ascendancy: How the United States Gained and Wielded Global Dominance 47–48 (2007). The three year war resulted in over 4,200 American and over 20,000 Filipino combat deaths; "[a]s many as 200,000 Filipino civilians died from violence, famine, and disease." *The Philippine-American War, 1899–1902*, Off. Historian, https://history.state.gov/milestones/1899-1913/war.

40 Lockey, *supra* note 36, at 7. ("The delegates...were reminded by Mr. Root ... that 'The true function of such a conference is to deal with matters of common interests which are not really subjects of controversy'").

and economic coordination, perhaps even a loose hemispheric federation. These elements of cooperation, along with the proposal to establish a permanent hub for hemispheric administration, lent support to Latin America's enthusiastic embrace of Root's chosen words of solidarity in Rio.

Latin American historian Greg Grandin noted the United States' underexplored connection to South and Central America, and the emergence of a normative ideal of a republican America that "would give substance to Jefferson's vision."[41] He noted that the relationship was at times antagonistic,[42] imperfectly formed around competing constructions of an American international law,[43] and sometimes similarly reflective of the generative tension between ideology and practice that produced brutal "nineteenth-century western settlement and land entitlement" in North America and "expansionist, Indian-killing" displays of absolute sovereignty in Latin America. "It turns out that the United States' 'imperial anticolonialism,' to use William Appleman Williams' description of the nation's motivational creed, was not so unique."[44] Even so, the "region's intellectuals, jurists, and politicians" worked to "bridge[] the chasm separating their universalizing ideal of 'America' from their territorial fundamentalism by laying out the legal foundation of multi-lateral cooperation. Based on principles of non-aggression, international arbitration, and economic justice, they developed a sovereignty-social rights complex" that Grandin claimed "would revolutionize the interstate system."[45] Even though short-lived, Grandin noted Latin America's consequential "success in helping to socialize hemispheric liberalism and diplomacy."[46]

To critics, such as the Argentine essayist and diplomat, Manuel Ugarte (1875–1951), Root's words reflected a bias among Latin American defenders of the Monroe Doctrine, who naively overlooked the troublesome "Minotaur of Mythology" presented by defensive characterizations of the doctrine.[47] He sounded deep suspicious of North American capital penetrations into Latin

41 Greg Grandin, *The Liberal Traditions in the Americas: Rights, Sovereignty, and the Origins of Liberal Multilateralism*, 117 Am. Hist. Rev. 68, 70 (2012).

42 *Id.*

43 *Id.* ("Put crudely, Spanish Americans and Brazilians came to hold individual rights relative to the establishment of the public common good and territorial sovereignty as absolute. In the United States, the terms were reversed; U.S. politicians defined individual rights as inherent and inalienable, and qualified state sovereignty on responsible public administration that could protect those rights.").

44 *Id.* at 71.

45 *Id.* at 72.

46 *Id.*

47 Scarfi, *supra* note 10, at 26 (quoting Ugarte).

America,[48] and would be among the ardent "impugners" of the intentions of the Monroe Doctrine,[49] and advocates of Latin American union.[50] However, Root's arrival in Latin America coincided with a turbulent period of state-building and modernization, where "democracy was neither consolidated, nor well-structured."[51] His broader words of integration, reinforced by the Rio agenda, provided welcome support for this democratization project. They "had a profound and lasting impact on Latin American jurists and politicians"[52] not simply because they were ripe for the time, but because they were expressive of a federation ideal launched by the decolonization movement in North America one century earlier. Whiggish anti-triumphal treatments of the Monroe Doctrine tend to gloss over the historical connection to federal union, much as they also underreport "the fact that Spanish-American diplomats and politicians did no object to" the doctrine excepting Latin America from European intrusion.[53]

2 "Regions of Futurity": Federation, Frontier Mentality, Fear of Retrocession

The federation concept had longstanding appeal across the Americas during the nineteenth century. It first arose due to inherent deficiencies in the Articles of Confederation and within the domestic context of western expansion in the United States at the end of the eighteenth century.

The newborn country had trouble honoring its peace treaty commitments that ended the Revolutionary War. Article v of that treaty (the Paris Peace Treaty, 1783) proved particularly problematic. The legislatures of the respective states imperfectly respected the obligation "to provide for the restitution of all estates, rights, and properties, which have been confiscated belonging to real

48 *See* Manuel Ugarte, La Nación Latinoamericana 6 (1987) (reprinting his 1901 opinion piece, *La Defensa Latina*).

49 *Id.* at 85 (in *La Doctrina de Monroe, 1919*: "La doctrina de Monroe … empieza a encontrar impugnadores, no ya entre los internacionalistas independientes, sino entre los mismos jefes de Estado.").

50 *See* Henry Gil, *The Point of View of Latin-America on the Inter-American Policy of the United States*, 6 Am. Pol. Sci. Rev. 164, 165 (1912) (discussing Ugarte's advocacy of Latin American confederation to offset North American rule).

51 Scarfi, *supra* note 10, at 20.

52 *Id.* at 23.

53 Grandin, *supra* note 41, at 84 ("Rarely discussed in all the considerable scholarship on the doctrine is the fact that Spanish-American diplomats and politicians did not object to Monroe's declaration").

British subjects." Congress' inability to force the actions of states in respect of this principle (*pacta sunt servanda*) impinged on commercial relations and diminished the United States' international standing. Alexander Hamilton (1757–1804) wrote with alarm in *Federalist Paper No. 22* that even the "most superficial view" demanded federal superintendency here:

> No nation acquainted with the nature of our political association would be unwise enough to enter into stipulations with the United States, by which they conceded privileges of any importance to them, while they were apprised that the engagements on the part of the Union might at any moment be violated by its members.[54]

In North America, territory west of the Appalachian Mountains, north of the Ohio River, south of the Great Lakes, and east of the Mississippi River formed a new federal domain ceded by Britain from France to the United States.[55] The Confederation Congress (1781–1789) transposed into federation not only to form a more perfect union—to correct structural deficiencies due to a lack of central leadership—but to quiet states' overlapping interests involving western expansion. Many of these overlapping claims originated from royal charters granted by king James I in 1609 to trading companies,[56] a practice similar to the establishment of the Dutch East India Company, thereby enabling its worldwide presence.

Additionally, a widespread "Empire of Liberty" presented at once an open agrarian landscape fit for Jeffersonian Republicans, a resource-rich industrial habitat attractive to Hamiltonian Federalists,[57] a revenue generator or land

54 Alexander Hamilton, *Federalist Paper No. 22, Dec. 14, 1787*, *reprinted in* Avalon Project, http://avalon.law.yale.edu/18th_century/fed22.asp.

55 *See generally* Andrew R.L. Cayton, The Frontier Republic: Ideology and Politics in the Ohio Country, 1780–1825 (1987). France ceded ownership of continental North American territory east of the Mississippi River following conclusion of the French and Indian War. British king George III then issued the Proclamation of 1763, which, with exceptions, precluded American settlers from venturing over the Appalachian Mountains. After conclusion of the Revolutionary War with the Treaty of Paris (1783), Great Britain ceded the land stretching from the Appalachians to the Mississippi to the United States.

56 *See Motion Regarding the Western Lands,* [*6 September*] *1780*, Nat'l Archives: Founders Online, https://founders.archives.gov/documents/Madison/01-02-02-0051. Claims of the Old Dominion of Virginia far exceeded any other state's claims, which were ceded by deed to Congress, thus creating "for the first time a national domain." Robert F. Berkhofer, Jr., *Jefferson, the Ordinance of 1784, and the Origins of the American Territorial System*, 29 Wm. & Mary Q. 231, 232 (1972).

57 *See* Cayton, *supra* note 55, at 2–13. Thomas Jefferson introduced the term, "Empire of Liberty" in a letter to George Rogers Clark. *See From Thomas Jefferson to George Rogers Clark,*

warrant exchange system for the deeply indebted post-Revolutionary War confederation of states,[58] and open ground for extending the Southern slave system.[59] The revolutionaries' natural rights orientation required a charter or organic act to manage western expansion, and the Confederation Congress' Northwest Ordinance (1787) served that purpose.[60] It put an end to the idea of colonies or second-class states in the expanding United States.[61] The Ordinance and the Enabling Act (1802) created the compact that allowed for expansion, admitting new states "on an equal footing with the original states."[62] Fearful of

---

25 December 1780, Nat'l Archives: Founders Online, https://founders.archives.gov/documents/Jefferson/01-04-02-0295 ("we shall form to the American union a barrier against the dangerous extension of the British Province of Canada and add to the Empire of liberty an extensive and fertile Country thereby converting dangerous Enemies into valuable friends.").

58 For details of the cash-strapped Continental Congress, see U.S. *Debt and Foreign Loans, 1775–1795*, Off. Historian, https://history.state.gov/milestones/1784-1800/loans. For a discussion of the Western World as a new source of wealth and income for states, see, *e.g.*, Eric Hinderaker, Elusive Empires: Constructing Colonialism in the Ohio Valley, 1673–1800, at 202–04 (1997). Important examples of colonial interests extending into the Ohio Country, some later sold or exchanged through land warrants issued in lieu of Revolutionary War soldier pay, included the Connecticut Western Reserve on the southern littoral of Lake Erie (Greater Cleveland), the Virginia Military Tract founded at Chillicothe, the Miami Purchase, on the accessible and water rich plains north of Cincinnati, and the Ohio Company Purchase founded by Bay Staters, an off shoot of Seven Ranges, the first area surveyed by the United States government as part of the Northwest Territory (demarcated by the "Initial Point of Beginning" near the tri-point intersection of Ohio, Pennsylvania, and the northern tip of West Virginia running 42 miles westward and bounded to the south by the Ohio River.) *See generally* Robert Brewer, *The Ohio Country*, Map, *in* The Frontier Republic: Ideology and Politics in the Ohio Country, 1780–1825 [unnumbered] (1986).

59 *See* Paul Finkelman, *Jefferson and Slavery: "Treason Against the Hopes of the World"*, *in* Jeffersonian Legacies 181, 199 (Peter S. Onuf ed., 1993) (noting Jefferson's 1783 "Plan of Government for the Western Territory," which would have banned slavery after 1800, already had been compromised by the arrival of the slave system in what became Indiana and Illinois).

60 *See* Paul Finkelman, *The Northwest Ordinance: A Constitution for an Empire of Liberty*, *in* Pathways to the Old Northwest: An Observance of the Bicentennial of the Northwest Ordinance 1, 6–10 (Lloyd A. Hunter ed., 1988).

61 *See* Warren Zimmermann, First Great Triumph: How Five Americans Made Their Country a World Power 21 (2002).

62 *An Ordinance for the Government of the Territory of the United States North-West of the River Ohio* § 13, July 13, 1787, *reprinted in* Our Documents, https://www.ourdocuments.gov/doc.php?flash=true&doc=8; *Enabling Act of 1802 (Transcript)* § 1, *reprinted in* Ohio Hist. Ctr., http://www.ohiohistorycentral.org/w/Enabling_Act_of_1802_ (Transcript) (enabling the people of the eastern division of the territory northwest of the Ohio River to be admitted into the Union "upon the same footing with the original States in all respects whatever.").

creating a template that would diminish the power of established states, the Constitution's drafters initially rejected admission "on the same terms with the original States," as proposed in the draft text of the Constitution.[63] The Constitution's "admissions clause" crafted a neutral solution, which allowed for new state admissions but prevented the subdivision or joining of established states without the consent of all parties, including Congress.[64]

The Ordinance presented a novel procedure of internal colonization that balanced competing state and western interests.[65] Although adapted to the peculiar spatial and political landscape of North America, it offered the beginnings of a conceptual template that would have hemispheric appeal. Specifically, it operationalized admission while prohibiting slavery in the new territories "whenever any of the said States shall have sixty thousand free inhabitants therein."[66] However, ambiguities and disputes "undercut its constitutional force."[67]

The Ordinance derived its authority from Congress but did not apply to Congress, and "could be altered at will."[68] It served as a blueprint for territorial expansion and state accession[69] but encountered rapid deconstitutionalization challenges once territories gained states' rights protections under the

---

63 By a vote of 9-2. *See* 2 Records of the Federal Convention of 1781, at 454 (Max Farrand ed., 1911) ("Mr. Govr. Morris [New York] moved to strike out the ...sentences...—He did not wish to bind down the Legislature to admit Western States on the terms here stated. ... [he] did not mean to discourage the growth of the Western Country. He knew that to be impossible. He did not wish however to throw the power into their hands."). James Madison opposed the motion, "insisting that the Western States neither would nor ought to submit to a Union which degraded them from an equal rank with the other States." *Id.*

64 U.S. Const. art. IV, §3, cl. 1 ("New States may be admitted by the Congress into this Union; but no new state shall be formed or erected within the jurisdiction of any other state; nor any state be formed by the junction of two or more states, or parts of states, without the consent of the legislatures of the states concerned as well as of the Congress"). *See also* Coyle v. Smith, 221 U.S. 559 (1911). Once in effect, Congress admitted Vermont and Kentucky on terms equal to extant states, formalizing adoption of a policy of equal status for newly admitted states. *See New States Clause*, Heritage Guide Const., https://www.heritage.org/constitution/#!/articles/4/essays/125/new-states-clause.

65 *See* Robert F. Berkhofer, Jr. *Americans versus Indians: The Northwest Ordinance, Territory Making, and Native Americans*, 84 Ind. Mag. Hist. 90 (1988).

66 *Northwest Ordinance, July 13, 1787*, art. 5, *reprinted in* Avalon Project, http://avalon.law.yale.edu/18th_century/nworder.asp.

67 Peter S. Onuf, Statehood and Union: A History of the Northwest Ordinance at xiv (1987). Although conceived under the Continental Congress, the Northwest Ordinance was reenacted under the first new United States Congress in 1789 with minor changes.

68 *Id.* at 134.

69 Andrew R.L. Cayton, *The Northwest Ordinance from the Perspective of the Frontier, in* The Northwest Ordinance 1787: A Bicentennial Handbook 1, 3 (Robert M. Taylor, Jr. ed., 1987)

Tenth Amendment.[70] Upsetting a balance of power between slaveholding and free states deadlocked Missouri's admission to the union. Missouri formed part of the Louisiana Territory, land situated farther west than the Old Northwest. On December 29, 1819, it applied for admission to the republic as a slave state.[71] The ensuing dispute produced the Missouri Compromise (1821), which admitted Missouri to the union as a slave state, Maine as a free state, and prohibited slavery north of the 36 degree 30 minute parallel that formed Missouri's southern border. However, boundary claims disputes in the trans-Ohio territory, directly affected by the Ordinance, also embroiled interests in Wisconsin and Michigan,[72] further complicating the idea of union and undercutting the cohesion of western expansion. Competing visions of political economy challenged at the outset the founders' vision of union.[73] The Ordinance presented the geospatial framework for the expression and development of the nation's nascent individualism and nationalism, and its nascent virtue and power.[74] Paul Finkelman labeled this settlement story a "microcosm of America's history."[75]

"[S]peculators, squatters and other adventurers" already had begun settling beyond the Appalachians.[76] These frontiersmen exhibited dangerous tendencies to "take matters into their own hands."[77] Displaced West Virginians and Pennsylvanians protested their distant legislatures. Kentucky harbored western separatists. North Carolinians in the Western World, as it was sometimes called, attempted to form their own state of Franklin.[78] George Washington feared frontiersmen would fall "prey to the blandishments of British

---

(calling the Ordinance "more a blueprint of political and social conquest than a blueprint for the peaceful expansion of a stable republican empire.").

70 *See* Boyd v. State of Nebraska, 143 U.S. 135 (1892) ("Admission on an equal footing with the original states, in all respects whatever, involves equality of constitutional right and power, which cannot thereafterwards be controlled").

71 *Application of Missouri for Admission into the Union as a State* (*Dec. 29, 1819*), Lib. Cong.: Am. State Papers 557, https://memory.loc.gov/cgi-bin/ampage?collId=llsp&fileName=038/llsp038.db&recNum=570. Applicant states had to submit a state constitution, reviewable for ratification by Congress. Missouri's application recognized the right to hold slave property. *See* 1 Kenneth L. Lyftogt, Iowa and the Civil War: Free Child of the Missouri Compromise 1850–1862, at 3 (2018).

72 *See* Onuf, *supra* note 67, at 135.

73 *Id.* at xiv.

74 *See generally* John Kane, Between Virtue and Power: The Persistent Moral Dilemma of U.S. Foreign Policy (2008).

75 Finkelman, *supra* note 60, at 1.

76 Onuf, *supra* note 67, at xiii.

77 Ray Allen Billington & Martin Ridge, Westward Expansion: A History of the American Frontier 215 (1949).

78 *Id.*

and Spanish agents and become involved in separatist movements"; indeed, squatters in the Ohio Valley resisted Congressional authority for nearly one decade.[79] Federation harnessed disparate political perspectives by favoring no competing state or western migratory interest. Expanding and settling the frontier required an orderly process and union became the necessary solution. Federation suggested a ready-made political pathway for reorganizing a continent emerging from three hundred years of colonial rule.

As the freewheeling frontier mentality suggested, abridging for the moment the problem of indigenous peoples, the Western World presented a *terra nullius*, a political void of verdant, water-rich terrain waiting to be claimed. United States patriarchs understood the unfolding temptations of this landscape, and indeed acted on such temptations. "[F]uture leaders of the independent republic"—George Washington (1732–1799), Benjamin Franklin (1706–1790), Patrick Henry (1736–1799), and Thomas Jefferson (1743–1826)—had "direct, personal interests" in the fertile lands of the Ohio Valley.[80] Competition over the western expanse and complex land acquisition schemes of benefit to individual families and speculators intensified by the mid-eighteenth century.[81] These personal interests overlapped with French and British imperial interests and territorial enlargement schemes by the original North American colonies.[82]

From a foreign policy perspective, the basis for the Monroe Doctrine reduced to the "real danger ... that Britain or France might take territory in Spanish America before the United States was in a position to do so."[83] Spain's retrocession of Louisiana to France in 1800 fed these anxieties,[84] evidencing protean elements of *raison d'état* within the early United States mindset, notwithstanding Jefferson's rejection of this Old World guiding principle.[85] Control over the

---

79 Cayton, *supra* note 55, at 13.

80 Robert Kagan, Dangerous Nation 17–18 (2006).

81 *See* John R. Van Atta, Securing the West: Politics, Public Lands, and the Fate of the Old Republic, 1785–1850, at 11–12 (2014) (discussing private schemes and speculative colonial frontier land grants from the British Crown dating to before the mid-eighteenth century).

82 Kagan, *supra* note 80, at 17 (noting colonial competitions beyond the Allegheny Mountains, the creation of joint-stock companies, and inducements by George II to exchange land grants for pro-British encampments to parry French interests).

83 Robert W. Tucker & David C. Hendrickson, Empire of Liberty: The Statecraft of Thomas Jefferson 29–30 (1990).

84 Anglo-French competition in North America began with the French and Indian War in 1754. The Seven Years War followed beginning in 1756. At the conclusion of that war in 1763, France transferred its disputed title-by-discovery claims to Spain and England. Land west of the Mississippi River went to Spain, which Spain retroceded to France in 1800. Land east of the Mississippi River, including Canada, went to England.

85 *See* Francis D. Cogliano, Thomas Jefferson: Reputation and Legacy 239 (2006).

port of New Orleans, including its gateway access along the Gulf coast of West Florida, presented a grave concern. The loss of this access could impinge on United States commercial and navigation interests involving the entire Mississippi Valley, effectively encircling or cutting off evolving western designs. To complicate matters, Russia had issued an 1821 decree (*ukase*) over exclusive fishing and navigation rights off the northwest coast of North American from the Behring Straits to the 51st parallel north,[86] presenting impingement concerns by another power from yet another direction. More complicated than the idea of simple territorial aggrandizement, early American expansionism embedded an "aversion to balance-of-power politics" emerging on its peripheries.[87] In 1803, Jefferson dispatched James Monroe to join Robert R. Livingston, United States Minister to France, who was already seeking out a solution with Napoleón.[88] Preoccupied by an impending war with Great Britain, and a Caribbean policy that had bogged down in Saint Domingue (Haiti), Napoleón surprisingly offered to sell the entire Louisiana territory for an agreed on price of $15 million[89]—pennies an acre.[90] Jefferson's strict construction of the Constitution granted no enumerated power to the executive to purchase foreign land. While he sensed such a land deal with France required a constitutional amendment,[91] timing presented a problem. Jefferson's treasury secretary, Albert Gallatin (1761–1849), constructed a permissible constitutional basis for the deal under the theory of implied treaty-making power.[92] However, Jefferson likened the

86 *See* Charles E. Hughes, *Observations on the Monroe Doctrine*, 17 Am. J. Int'l L. 611, 613 (1923).

87 Willem Theo Oosterveld, The Law of Nations in Early American Foreign Policy: Theory and Practice from the Revolution to the Monroe Doctrine 237 (2015).

88 *See* Stephanie P. Newbold, *Statesmanship and Ethics: The Case of Thomas Jefferson's Dirty Hands*, 65 Pub. Admin. Rev. 669, 670 (2005) (on Jefferson's appointment of Monroe as special envoy to assist Livingston).

89 3 Julian Hawthorne, History of the United States from 1492 to 1910, at 52 (2012) ($15 million).

90 The deal involved the purchase of 530,000,000 acres for $15 million, or approximately 35 cents per acre. *See Louisiana Purchase, 1803*, Off. Historian, https://history.state.gov/milestones/1801-1829/louisiana-purchase.

91 *See Letter from Thomas Jefferson to John Dickinson, August 9, 1803, reprinted in* Envisaging the West: Thomas Jefferson and the Roots of Lewis and Clark, http://jeffersonswest.unl.edu/archive/view_doc.php?id=jef.00004 ("...there is a difficulty in this acquisition which presents a handle to the malcontents among us .... The general government has no powers but such as the constitution has given it; and it has not given it a power of holding foreign territory, & still less of incorporating it into the Union. An amendment of the Constitution seems necessary for this.").

92 Albert Gallatin, *To Thomas Jefferson from Albert Gallatin, Jan. 13, 1803, reprinted in* Nat'l Archives: Founders Online, https://founders.archives.gov/documents/Jefferson/01-39-02-0281 ("That whenever that acquisition is by treaty, the same constituted authorities in

purchase absent an amendment to principles of guardianship, which aligned with primordial interests of the state: "It is the case of a guardian, investing the money of his ward in purchasing an important adjacent territory; and saying to him when of age, I did this for your good."[93] The extraconstitutional means employed to secure Louisiana may have adroitly avoided war with France, however, according to Robert Tucker and David Hendrickson, it "could be justified only on the basis of constitutional doctrine in direct contradiction to prohibitions that Jefferson had long held inviolable."[94]

3 Guardianship and Encirclement

This element of guardianship—based on the need to parry encirclement—offset contradictions and crosscutting domestic competitions over western expansion. It reinforced the crusader's impulse to apply the Old World principle of *raison d'état*, notwithstanding the ideal that the United States statecraft "stood for something new under the sun."[95] The idea that "we did this for your good"—a sentiment directed by republican leadership to its newborn citizenry—presented the first and recurrent tension that would seep into the emerging lexicon of hemispheric and international relations. It would help instrumentalize the law of nations as a flexible and pragmatic tool to address concrete problems interwoven in a landscape informed by politics, economics, and security questions.[96] Dilemmas prompted by geography and necessity would produce an exceptionalist mythology. They would expose core dualities in United States foreign policy discourse that revolved around an overarching theme. This theme contrasted realist and idealist perspectives[97]—policy

---

whom the treaty-making power is vested have a constitutional right to sanction the acquisition of territory").

93 Thomas Jefferson, *To John C. Breckinridge, Monticello, Aug. 12, 1803*, *reprinted in* Am. Hist., http://www.let.rug.nl/usa/presidents/thomas-jefferson/letters-of-thomas-jefferson/jefl159.php.

94 Tucker & Hendrickson, *supra* note 83, at 94.

95 *Id.* at 11.

96 According to Lucie Delabie, these are the values that marked international law's divergent development and normative flexibility in the United States, as opposed to its more autonomous treatment in Europe. *See generally* Lucie Delabie, Approaches américaines du droit international: Entre unité et diversité (2011).

97 *See, e.g.*, Robert Osgood, Ideals and Self-Interest in America's Foreign Policy (1953); Joseph S. Nye, Jr., The Paradox of American Power (2002); Niall Ferguson, Colossus: The Rise and Fall of American Power (2004); David Milne, Worldmaking: The Art and Science of American Diplomacy (2015).

encryptions that counterbalanced national interests and principles. Variations take the form of debates between unilateralism and universalism, power and virtue, reason of state and humanitarian intervention, and imperialism and democracy. These stylized counter positions obscure contextual shadings and complexities and highlight contradictions and paradoxes.[98] Although deeply embedded in the national psyche, this dualism debate could not eclipse accompanying sentiments of hemispheric federation or union, however diffusely or inchoately expressed. Root would carry this complex mix of sentiment around South America. It could not be unbundled or dismissed or simply categorized as stylized, as versions of United States foreign policy tend to suggest. The duality of United States foreign policy and the sentiment of federalism or some form of hemispheric coordination created a foreign policy symbiosis with pragmatic, post-colonial appeal.

4 Latin American Sentiment of Unity

The sentiment of unity resonated in South America, as well. In his exposition on the fate of Spanish America, the *Jamaica Letter* (1815),[99] Simón Bolívar (1783–1830)—*El Libertador*—imagined but rejected as impractical the grandiose idea "of consolidating the New World into a single nation, united by pacts into a single bond." He found more compelling the creation of a federated state across the isthmus: "How beautiful it would be if the Isthmus of Panama could be for us what the Isthmus of Corinth was for the Greeks!"[100] He conjectured it would control the world's emporium, establish a global capital, and create "a

98 Historian Walter LaFeber made this point in specific reference to Jefferson, who dramatically argued in favor of an alliance with Britain in 1823 "to protect the new Latin American revolutionary nations from the designs of the Holy Alliance." LaFeber noted the context within which Jefferson's view developed, highlighting the period between the 1790s and 1820s when "an agrarian republic first showed signs of becoming a quite different kind of society," including signs of becoming a continental empire and "modern presidency." Walter LaFeber, *Jefferson and an American Foreign Policy*, *in* Jeffersonian Legacies 370, 370–71 (Peter S. Onuf ed., 1993).

99 Simón Bolívar, *La "Carta de Jamaica": Contestación de un Americano meridional a un caballero de esta isla, el 6 de septiembre de 1815*, http://cw.routledge.com/textbooks/dawson/data/Carta_de_Jamaica_by_de_Simon_Bolivar.pdf.

100 Simón Bolívar, *Letter from Jamaica (1815)*, Mod. Latin Am., https://library.brown.edu/create/modernlatinamerica/chapters/chapter-2-the-colonial-foundations/primary-documents-with-accompanying-discussion-questions/document-2-simon-bolivar-letter-from-jamaica-september-6-1815/.

new Byzantium for the modern world."[101] Other voices across the Plata region, including Mariano Moreno (1778–1811), Bernardo de Monteagudo (1789–1825), along with Venezuelan Francisco de Miranda (1750–1816) already had expressed similar thoughts of a Latin American internationalism.[102] Their efforts would find expression with the establishment of the landmark Panama Congress in 1826, which attempted to foster greater hemispheric unity and cooperation. Territories of the former Captaincy-General of Guatemala attempted a union shortly after independence in 1821. The Federation of the Center of America (also known as the Central American Federation) modeled itself on the structure of the United States. The Monroe administration (1817–1825) recognized it in 1824 and established a legation at its government seat in Guatemala City in 1826.[103] However, its sweeping amalgam of thirteen ill-fitted provinces of the former Spanish crown (now comprising Guatemala, El Salvador, Honduras, Nicaragua, and Costa Rica)[104] could not hold together.[105] No less than seven attempts to re-create this union failed.[106] Whiggish history promotes triumphalism, not failure. However, these recurrent attempts tell a story of union's hemispheric appeal.

Other constructions of federation radiated across South America, inspired by the republican virtues represented by United States independence. Jefferson's attempt to secure the colonies' equal standing "among the powers of the earth" countered "metropolitan intransigence" against sovereign equality and spurred domestic political institutions and reforms, including written constitutions, bicameralism and the separation of powers, and charters of basic

---

101 Simón Bolívar, Doctrina del Libertador 82 (Manuel Pérez Vila ed., Fundación Biblioteca Ayacucho 3d ed. 2009).

102 *See* Whitaker, *supra* note 14, at 24.

103 *A Guide to the United States' History of Recognition, Diplomatic, and Consular Relations, by Country, since 1776: Central American Federation*, Off. Historian, https://history.state.gov/countries/central-american-federation.

104 The Captaincy-General of Guatemala operated nominally under the jurisdiction of the Viceroyalty of New Spain and spread from Costa Rica to the Chiapas and Soconusco provinces of Mexico. It included also Suchitepec, San Miguel, Vera Paz, Izaleos, Jerez de la Cholutec, Tegucigalpa, Honduras, San Salvador, Guatemala, and Nicaragua. *See* William F. Slade, *The Federation of Central America*, 8 J. Race Dev. 79, 82–83 (1917). After independence, the Federation of Central America formed with the five current states of Guatemala, El Salvador, Honduras, Nicaragua, and Costa Rica.

105 *See* Joshua Simon, *The Americas' More Perfect Unions: New Institutional Insights from Comparative Political Theory*, 12 Am. Pol. Sci. Ass'n. 808, 809 (2014).

106 *See* Manley O. Hudson, *The Central American Court of Justice*, 26 Am. J. Int'l L. 759, 759 (1932) (discussing failed attempts among Central American states to federate in 1835, 1842, 1847, 1852, 1889, 1895, and 1921).

rights.[107] These political markings of federal union, notwithstanding their complicated expression as a compound republic in the United States,[108] generated hemispheric appeal, particularly in light of the breakdown of the European balance of power system caused by the wars of the French Revolution.[109] Mariano Moreno, secretary of the junta of governing authorities for the newly independent Río de la Plata (*Secretario de la Junta de Gobierno Patrio*, Buenos Aires) openly admired Jefferson's federated government model[110] and wrote of "balance of power" government,[111] and constitutional governance.[112] In a letter to James Monroe, then Governor of Virginia, Jefferson noted "it is impossible not to look forward to distant times, when our rapid multiplication will expand itself beyond those limits, & cover the whole northern, if not the southern continent, with a people speaking the same language, governed in similar forms, & by similar laws."[113] Jefferson's private correspondence after his presidency (ending in March 1809) gave "even clearer and more forcible expression" to the American system idea.[114] In a letter to Alexander von Humboldt (1769–1859), he wrote: "America has a hemisphere to itself. It must have its separate system of

---

107 Simon, *supra* note 105, at 808. Simon elsewhere noted that American independence movements, although distinct in settings and results, "were animated by strikingly similar ideas. Patriotic political theorists throughout the Americas offered analogous critiques of imperial rule…, designed comparable constitutions immediately after independence…, and expressed common ambitions for their new nations' future relations with one another and the rest of the world." Joshua Simon, The Ideology of Creole Revolution: Imperialism and Independence in American and Latin American Political Thought 1 (2017).

108 James Madison introduced the term "compound government" in Federalist Paper No. 51, employing it to mean the double security system of checks and balances divided between and within the two distinct federal and state governments. *The Structure of the Government Must Furnish the Proper Checks and Balances Between the Different Departments, Federalist Paper No. 51, Feb. 8, 1788, reprinted in* Avalon Project, http://avalon.law.yale.edu/18th_century/fed51.asp (ascribing authorship to Hamilton or Madison).

109 *See generally* Peter Onuf & Nicholas Onuf, Federal Union, Modern World: The Law of Nations in an Age of Revolutions 1776–1814 (1993).

110 Mariano Moreno, Doctrina Democrática, at xx (Ricardo Rojas ed., 1915) ("Los pueblos modernos son los únicos que nos han dado un exacta idea del gobierno federativo, y aún entre los salvajes de América se ha encontrado practicado en términos que nunca conocieron los griegos. Oigamos a Mr. Jefferson. . . .").

111 Ellen Garwood, The Undying Flame: Mariano Moreno of Buenos Aires 187 (1986).

112 *See* Enrique De Gandía, Mariano Moreno Su Pensamiento Político Ch. XXIII (1968).

113 Thomas Jefferson, *To the Governor of Virginia (James Monroe) Washington, Nov. 24, 1801*, Am. Hist., http://www.let.rug.nl/usa/presidents/thomas-jefferson/letters-of-thomas-jefferson/jefl142.php.

114 Whitaker, *supra* note 14, at 27.

interests, which must not be subordinated to those of Europe."[115] Able Spanish American diplomats, none more admired than Manuel Torres (1762–1822),[116] congregated in Philadelphia, Baltimore, and New York City to promote hemispheric solidarity and learn of republican rule.[117] The Chilean, Juan Martínez de Rozas (1759–1813), proposed in 1810 "the formation of a single nation and a single state" with a Spanish American administrative system of local governments connecting to a to-be-determined coordinating hub.[118] His countryman Juan Egaña (1768–1836) petitioned for the establishment of a hemispheric *cortes*, or parliament principally to safeguard against the French.[119] Argentina's Domingo Faustino Sarmiento (1811–1888) openly admired the United States' federal system, lecturing that the defensive construction of the Monroe Doctrine would help to draw capital to Latin America and fortify the development of republicanism.[120] The Rio Conference's proposal that resulted in Carnegie's American Temple of Peace animated these century-old expressions to establish a Pan-American *cortes*, a kind of "human freedom league" envisioned by Henry Clay in 1820 to unite "all the nations from Hudson's Bay to Cape Horn."[121]

The idea of federation also served as a prophylaxis. A reconstituted European political order following the Napoleonic Wars in 1815, posed immediate hemispheric concerns. Austria, Prussia, Russia, and Britain reconstituted under a variety of names—the Concert of Europe, the Holy Alliance, the Confederation of Europe, the Quadruple Alliance, then, the Quintuple Alliance three years later.[122] The purpose of this reordering was partly restorative—to reclaim the old European equilibrium for continental monarchs, albeit through the employment of "new diplomacy" balance-of-power counterweights.[123] However, a new nomenclature of federalism, spurred by the American constitutional redesign and spreading sentiments across the Americas, even had its effect

---

115 Thomas Jefferson, *Letter to Alexander von Humboldt, December 6, 1813*, Am. Hist., http://www.let.rug.nl/usa/presidents/thomas-jefferson/letters-of-thomas-jefferson/jefl224.php.

116 *See* Charles H. Bowman Jr., *Manuel Torres, A Spanish Patriot in Philadelphia, 1796–1822*, 94 Pa. Mag. Hist. & Biography 26, 50 (1970).

117 *See generally id.*

118 Lockey, *supra* note 36, at 282.

119 *Id.* at 283.

120 *See generally* Domingo Faustino Sarmiento, North and South America: A Discourse Delivered Before the Rhode-Island Historical Society (1866).

121 Scott, *supra* note 3, at vii (quoting Clay).

122 The Quintuple Alliance formed with the addition of the rehabilitated Bourbon monarchy of France; Britain decamped in 1823, sparking Canning's overture to the United States.

123 *See* David C. Hendrickson, Union, Nation, or Empire; The American Debate over International Relations, 1791–1941, at 69 (2009).

in Europe. The Austrian secretary to the Congress of Vienna (1815), Friedrich von Gentz (1764–1832) proclaimed the reconstituted European order the "true federal system," as opposed to the universal monarchy of Bonaparte.[124] While Thomas Jefferson "took a far harsher view" of the "shuffling" of nations, noting it produced "no more moderation, forbearance, or even honesty ... than in that of Bonaparte,"[125] historian David C. Hendrickson labeled it "genuine." Although based on prescription and authority, and certainly comprised of a "repressive character," it did rest on a degree of unprecedented cooperation.[126] And its potential restoration of control over the New World created a real sense of alarm.

The Quintuple Alliance meeting and protocol following the Congress of Troppau in 1820 reinvigorated the suppression of revolutions—in Italy by Austria in 1821, and in Spain by France in 1823. That later intervention to assist Spanish Royalists generated concerns in the Americas that the reconstituted European powers would allow the reinstatement of the Spanish American empire. That fear would jeopardize United States interests, which included by that time Adams' central diplomatic achievement, the acquisition of Florida from Spain with the 1819 Transcontinental Treaty (the Adams-Onís Treaty).[127] Historian Worthington Chauncey Ford asserted that the Monroe Doctrine was framed and almost forced over "an unwilling and fearsome President and Cabinet," with gloomy concerns that the European powers "would turn their attention to the United States" after having subdued South America.[128]

Clay had warned against the intentions of the Holy Alliance as early as 1815.[129] Although he and Jefferson differed on estimates that Spanish American statehood would achieve United States-styled independence, both shared the opinion that South American governance would be "animated by an American feeling" and "obey the laws of the ... New World ... in contradistinction to that of Europe."[130] Clay spoke of creating an "American system," self-generating and independent of "the lead of the Holy Alliance."[131] He envisioned it as "a sort of counterpoise to the Holy Alliance" and composed of the two Americas, North

124 *Id.*

125 *Id.* at 73 (quoting Jefferson).

126 *Id.* at 75.

127 *See* Mark T. Gilderhus, *The Monroe Doctrine: Meanings and Implications*, 36 Presidential Stud. Q. 5, 6–7 (2006).

128 Worthington Chauncey Ford, *John Quincy Adams and the Monroe Doctrine*, 8 Am. Hist. Rev. 28, 52 (1902) ("fearsome"); *id.* at 44 ("gloomy").

129 Whitaker, *supra* note 14, at 31 (claiming Clay was the first leading statesman to do so, making his viewpoint known on return from negotiating the Treaty of Ghent (8 Stat. 218) ending the War of 1812 with Britain).

130 Hendrickson, *supra* note 123, at 94 (quoting Clay's 1818 Emancipation of the South American States speech).

131 Robert V. Remini, Henry Clay: Statesman for the Union 174 (1991) (quoting Clay).

and South.[132] He emphasized the stabilizing contribution of republican institutions, which "now make us free." "It is in our power to create a system which we shall be the centre, and in which all South America will act with us."[133] Jefferson, leery of South America's "priest-ridden" ability to maintain a free civil government, nevertheless asserted that in the end "they will be *American* governments," geographically and culturally insulated from the "never-ceasing broils of Europe ... America has a hemisphere to itself ... which must not be subordinated to those of Europe."[134]

Jefferson's expression forwarded the idea of American unity as a premise, not a goal.[135] He would reassert the idea of an American "cis-Atlantic" system, distinct from Europe and "peculiarly her own" in consultations that produced the Monroe Doctrine.[136] Alexander Hamilton imagined "regions of futurity" in *Federalist Paper No. 11*. These republican regions would "vindicate the honor of the human race," teach moderation to "arrogant" Europeans ("that assuming brother"), and hold out the prospect of union as the enabling device ("Union will enable us to do it [teach Europe]") to secure a future "great American system, superior to the control of all trans-atlantic force or influence, and able to dictate the terms of the connection between the old and the new world!"[137] John Quincy Adams (1767–1848) defended inter-American cooperation, arguing that such an association in no way conflicted with George Washington's Farewell Address (1796), "the most famous state paper in [United States] history."[138] Co-written by Hamilton,[139] the message underscored the "true" United States policy: "steer clear of permanent alliances."[140] Adams, arguing in favor of sending a United States delegation to the Panama Congress, noted: "Our distant and detached situation with reference to Europe remains the same." However, the

---

132 Samuel Flagg Bemis, John Quincy Adams and the Foundations of American Foreign Policy 356 (1949) (quoting Whitaker's summary of a Clay speech).

133 Remini, *supra* note 131, at 174 (quoting Clay).

134 Jefferson, *supra* note 115.

135 Whitaker, *supra* note 14, at 31.

136 Thomas Jefferson, *Letter to the President of the United States (James Monroe), Monticello, October 24, 1823, reprinted in* Am. Hist., http://www.let.rug.nl/usa/presidents/thomas-jefferson/letters-of-thomas-jefferson/jefl275.php.

137 Alexander Hamilton, *The Utility of the Union in Respect to Commercial Relations and a Navy for the Independent Journal, The Federalist Papers: No. 11, reprinted in* Avalon Project, http://avalon.law.yale.edu/18th_century/fed11.asp.

138 John Lamberton Harper, American Machiavelli: Alexander Hamilton and the Origins of U.S. Foreign Policy 171 (2004).

139 *Id.* at 171.

140 *Washington's Farewell Address 1796, reprinted in* Avalon Project, http://avalon.law.yale.edu/18th_century/washing.asp.

spread of republicanism across the hemisphere had created eight independent nations, "seven of them Republics like ourselves, with whom we have an immensely growing commercial [and political] connections." Far from conflicting with Washington's advice, Adams noted a strengthened inter-American policy was "directly deducible from and conformable to it."[141]

5 The Monroe Doctrine's Provocative and Defensive Assertiveness

Progenitors of the Monroe Doctrine took care to frame it as a defensive policy. It was also framed in the negative, informing about what the United States would oppose in the New World and avoid in the Old World while remaining artfully ambiguous on what would constitute intervention[142] or how "the views of other American states were to be taken into account."[143] Nevertheless, its provocative assertiveness could not be disguised. The boldness of Monroe's message created a guarded diplomatic stir, with particularly robust commentaries in the French press.[144] The conservative Austrian statesman, foreign minister, and host of the post-Napoleonic order created at the Congress of Vienna, Klemens von Metternich (1773–1859), penned the most vociferous complaint. In a private letter to Russian Chancellor Nesselrode (1780–1862), Metternich condemned the North Americans' message:

> In their indecent declarations they have cast blame and scorn on the institutions of Europe most worthy of respect. ...In permitting themselves these unprovoked attacks, in fostering revolutions wherever they show themselves, in regretting those which have failed, in extending a helping hand to those which seem to prosper, they lend new strength to the apostles of sedition and reanimate the courage of every conspirator.[145]

---

141 John Quincy Adams, *Special Message to the House of Representatives of the United States, March 15, 1826, reprinted in* Am. Presidency Project, http://www.presidency.ucsb.edu/ws/index.php?pid=66632.

142 *See* Alan Tzvika Nissel, A History of State Responsibility: The Struggle for International Standards (1870–1960), at 60 (Feb. 28, 2016) (unpublished LL.D. dissertation, University of Helsinki, Faculty of Law).

143 Patrick J. Garrity, *Debating the Monroe Doctrine*, CRB Digital (Aug. 15, 2012), http://www.claremont.org/crb/basicpage/debating-the-monroe-doctrine/.

144 William Spence Robertson, *The Monroe Doctrine Abroad in 1823–24*, 6 Am. Pol. Sci. Rev. 546, 553–55 (1912) (noting ensuing debates in *L'Etoile, Le Constitutionnel*, and *Le Courrier Française*).

145 1 David M. Kennedy & Thomas Bailey, The American Spirit: United States History as Seen by Contemporaries 276 (2009) (citing Prince Metternich's letter to Nesselrode on January 19, 1824).

Monroe's Secretary of War, John C. Calhoun (1782–1850), who partook in the internal Monroe Doctrine debates, feared it would provoke the British. He unsuccessfully lobbied in favor of British Foreign Minister George Canning's 1823 proposal that the two states issue a joint declaration deterring other powers from intervening in Central or Latin America.[146] An attempt to take the assertive edge off the doctrine resulted in its claim that the United Sates was proclaiming for itself nothing more than the same standard it had always accorded to others, a point Root again would emphasize on his 1906 tour. As Monroe proclaimed, "In the wars of the European powers in matters relating to themselves we have never taken any part, nor does it comport with our policy to do so."[147] In 1821, Adams also had stressed this point in opposing popularly-supported

146 Spanish military defeats in the New World in 1822 and 1823 opened up rivalries with Britain for influence among newly or soon-to-be recognized governments in Argentina (1823), Brazil (1824), Peru (1826), Chile (1823), Colombia (1822), and Mexico (1823). Secretary of State John Quincy Adams viewed suspiciously British Foreign Minister George Canning's 1823 proposal that the two states issue a joint declaration deterring other powers from intervening in Central or Latin America. *See* Ford, *supra* note 128, at 46–48 (reprinting Adams' November 20, 1823 letter to U. Envoy Extraordinary Richard Rush explaining the administration's response to Canning's initiative). (Canning made the proposal in the form of a letter to Rush in August, 1823.) Britain had not yet recognized the new states in Spanish America and Russia had issued an 1821 decree (*ukase*) over exclusive fishing and navigation rights off the northwest coast of North American from the Behring Straits to the fifty-first parallel north. *See* Hughes, *supra* note 86, at 613. Meanwhile, Britain continued to dispute colonization rights over the north-west territory of North America. *See* Robertson, *supra* note 144, at 549–50. Machinations following the end of the Napoleonic Wars in 1815 complicated the situation. Austria, Prussia, Russia, and Britain reconstituted under a variety of names—the Concert of Europe, the Holy Alliance, the Confederation of Europe, the Holy Alliance, or, the Quadruple Alliance, then as the Quintuple Alliance three years later (with the addition of the rehabilitated Bourbon monarchy of France; Britain decamped shortly thereafter, sparking Canning's overture to the U.S). The Quintuple Alliance meeting and protocol following the Congress of Troppau in 1820 reinvigorated the suppression of revolutions—in Italy by Austria in 1821, and in Spain by France in 1823. That later intervention to assist Spanish Royalists generated concerns in the Americas that the reconstituted European powers would allow the reinstatement of the Spanish American empire. That fear would jeopardize United States interests, which included by that time Adams' central diplomatic achievement, the acquisition of Florida from Spain with the 1819 Transcontinental Treaty (the Adams-Onís Treaty). *See* Gilderhus, *supra* note 127, at 6–7. Historian Worthington Chauncey Ford asserted that Adams prevailed in the rejection of Canning's proposal and framed the unilateral policy, almost forcing its acceptance over "an unwilling and fearsome President and Cabinet," principally Calhoun, who was filled with "gloomy apprehensions" that the European powers "would turn their attention to the United States" having subdued South America. Ford, *supra* note 128, at 52 ("fearsome"); *id.* at 44 ("gloomy").

147 *Monroe Doctrine; December 2, 1823, reprinted in* Avalon Project, http://avalon.law.yale.edu/19th_century/monroe.asp.

material aid for Greece's independence movement against the Ottoman Empire.[148] He most famously said: "[the United States] has, in the lapse of nearly half a century, without a single exception respected the independence of other nations, while asserting and maintaining her own. She has abstained from interference in the concerns of others, even when the conflict has been for principles to which she clings.... But she goes not abroad, in search of monsters to destroy."[149]

Patrick Garrity called Adams' aphorism "the epigrammatic departure for an entire strain of thought about American foreign policy."[150] The implicit principles of reciprocity and respect for sovereign equality meant to convey the benefits of European powers' approval, not that any European power feared an invasion from the Americas. If the doctrine embedded shadings of meaning that ultimately inverted its defensive orientation into a self-deputized right of intervention,[151] those shadings could not have been present at the creation of the doctrine. In 1823, when Monroe declared that future European meddling in the Americas presented a *casus belli* for the United States, few European states took serious notice.[152] A toothless element of the doctrine reinforced Calhoun's concern that British naval superiority held the key to the doctrine's hemispheric effectiveness. Simón Bolívar noted: "The whole of America together is not equal to a British fleet; the entire Holy Alliance is powerless against her liberal principles combined with immense resources."[153]

Don Juan Stoughton (1734–1820), Ferdinand VII's (1784–1833) counsel in New York reported to Madrid that the message was "a political maneuver ... to flatter the vanity of the American people."[154] Monroe's minister to the Spanish

---

148 *See* Kane, *supra* note 74.

149 John Quincy Adams, *July 4, 1821: Speech to the* U.S. *House of Representatives on Foreign Policy, reprinted in* Miller Ctr.: Presidential Speeches, https://millercenter.org/the-presidency/presidential-speeches/july-4-1821-speech-us-house-representatives-foreign-policy.

150 Patrick Garrity, *She Goes Not Abroad, In Search of Monsters to Destroy: The Dispute Between John Quincy Adams and Henry Clay Over the South American Revolutions*, Classics of Strategy 2 (Mar. 2009), http://www.classicsofstrategy.com/She%20Goes%20Not%20Abroad.pdf.

151 *See* Gilderhus, *supra* note 127, at 5.

152 Carl Schmitt, *Forms of Modern Imperialism in International Law*, *in* Spatiality, Sovereignty and Carl Schmitt: Geographies of the Nomos 31–32 (Stephen Legg ed., Matthew Hannah trans., 2011).

153 Jay Sexton, The Monroe Doctrine: Empire and Nation in Nineteenth-Century America 69 (2011) (quoting Bolívar).

154 Robertson, *supra* note 144, at 556–57 (quoting Stoughton). Stoughton served as Spanish consul for the entire district of New England from 1795–1820. *See* Sean Perrone, *Spanish Consuls and Trade Networks between Spain and the United States, 1795–1820*, 38 Bull. for Spanish & Portuguese Hist. Stud. 75 (2013).

Court first read of the doctrine from bits and pieces culled from the French press. When the full message appeared in the English language Parisian publication, *Galignani's Messenger*, he fully expected that Ferdinand's First Minister of State, Narcissio Heredia (the Count of Ofalia; 1775–1847), would address the matter in a scheduled meeting on January 15, 1824, but he "found the deportment of the Monarch and the Royal family in perfect harmony with their former behavior—precisely as if ... they had no knowledge of it."[155] More likely, the perception of indifference had a more *Realpolitik* explanation. As noted by Viscount Châteaubriand, Louis XVIII's minister of foreign affairs, "the American Government is wholly unable to enforce such pretensions."[156]

Indeed, members of the Holy Alliance had more to fear if Canning had committed British frigates, sloops, and bomb vessel warships to the cause of preventing renewed intervention in Spanish America. This was Calhoun's position in the internal Monroe Doctrine debates, which he could not sustain in the face of Adams' interest in forwarding a unilateral declaration. The U.S. Navy certainly had performed well in war against the British in 1812: one dozen open ocean victories against British cruisers, "spectacular" exploits of privateers,[157] Admiral Perry's (1794–1858) Lake Erie victory, the destruction of the British squadron at the Battle of Plattsburg on Lake Champlain, and the defense of New Orleans with the assistance of French pirates commanded by Jean Lafitte (c. 1780–c. 1823).[158] However, the afterglow of this performance occluded more direct assessments of the strategic insignificance of the naval operations, which in turn impeded the type of reforms needed to enforce credibly a hemispheric defense against Europe or to put seafaring strength into the Monroe Doctrine.[159]

Even so, Adams shrewdly understood that the United States could pursue a unilateral policy and adroitly avoid encumbrances demanded by Canning—specifically "a joint pledge prohibiting both states from the future annexation of territories in Spain's crumbling empire."[160] Such a pledge would cut off for the United States any future interest in Cuba or Texas while allowing Britain to

155 *Id.* at 557–58 (quoting U.S. minister to Spain, Hugh Nelson's dispatch of January 16, 1824).

156 *Id.* at 551 (quoting Châteaubriand's letter of January 24, 1824 to Sir Charles Stuart, English ambassador at Paris).

157 Harold H. Sprout & Margaret Sprout, The Rise of American Naval Power, 1776–1918, at 86 (1966).

158 *See id.*

159 *Id.* at 86–87, 185 (noting that passive defense doctrines were reinforced by the War of 1812, and the demand for the U.S. Navy to "put teeth into the Monroe Doctrine").

160 Sexton, *supra* note 153, at 52.

"take credit for protecting Spanish America from the Holy Allies" and extend financial interests already deeply established throughout the Americas.[161]

6 Heightened Ambivalence

Moreover, a deep ambivalence, in addition to the recognition of relatively weak military status, permeated the United States Congress at that time, making domestic support for Latin American independence less than an established fact.[162] Part of this ambivalence was racial, and part of it was religious. The enslaved black revolution against France in Saint Domingue (Haiti, 1791–1804) deeply threatened Jeffersonian notions of a generational, progressive republican emancipation process, which "had white Americans *declaring blacks* a 'free and independant [sic] people' through ... new state governments."[163] The proposition that "the enslaved would take their freedom rather than wait for whites to confer it" made the Caribbean island a troubling exemplar for the Jefferson administration and southern slave-holders that "what happened on the Caribbean island might happen in their state."[164] Concerns of South American fealty to priestly Roman influence fueled Protestant North America's skepticism "over the prospects for republican government in South America."[165] Perhaps it was far better not to incite the large black and mestizo populations with encouraging thoughts of self-rule.[166] Speaker of the House, Clay's 1818 initiative to recognize the revolutionary government in Buenos Aires and establish an embassy failed decidedly.[167] Delicate negotiations with Spain over

161 *Id.*

162 Maurice G. Baxter, Henry Clay and the American System 57 (1995).

163 Annette Gordon-Reed & Peter S. Onuf, "Most Blessed of the Patriarchs": Thomas Jefferson and the Empire of Imagination 284 (2016). *See also* Liliana Obregón, *The Non-Recognition of Haiti and the Cosmopolitan Imagination*, *in* Cosmopolitanisms in Enlightenment Europe and Beyond 159, 172 (Mónica García-Salmones & Pamela Slotte eds., 2013) (noting the nervousness in the United States of Haitian independence serving as precedent).

164 Gordon-Reed & Onuf, *supra* note 163, at 284.

165 Hendrickson, *supra* note 123, at 94.

166 *See* Tim Matthewson, *Jefferson and the Nonrecognition of Haiti*, 140 Proc. Am. Phil. Soc'y. 22, 23 (1996).

167 Clay made the case for recognition of the United Provinces of the Rio de la Plata in a remarkable articulation and defense of the declaratory principle of state recognition. Aligned with the Roman law principle of *ex factis jus non oritur*, Clay held that "We have constantly proceeded on the principle that the government *de facto* is that we can alone can notice." Furthermore: "We have invariably abstained from assuming a right to decide in favor of the sovereign *de jure*, and against the sovereign *de facto*. That is a question for the nation in which it arises to determine. And, so far as we are concerned, the sovereign

the purchase of Florida and the delimitation of the transcontinental border between the United States and New Spain (secured as noted in 1819 by the Adams-Onís Treaty) added to Congressional concerns about further complicating relations with Spain. A similar but discretionary resolution in support of Argentine independence passed the United States House of Representatives in 1821 by one vote,[168] and domestic divisions blocked a show of hemispheric solidarity in 1826, which precluded the United States delegation from participating in timely fashion at the Inter-American Congress in Panama.[169] Cosmopolitan North American voices attempted to counter these concerns. They underscored commercial and ideological points of contact.[170] The Adams administration thought that participation in the Congress would "cement[] good relations with the nation's southern neighbors" and might "facilitate the eventual purchase of Texas and smooth the way for an interoceanic canal through the Isthmus of Panama."[171]

More than 60 legislators debated United States participation in the Panama Congress, which dominated the agenda of the Nineteenth Congress,[172] and produced "one of the severest parliamentary battles" in the Adams administration's history.[173] Objections to United States participation ranged from implied entanglements fostered by presidential overreach to abject racial disparagement of Latin America as a "second-rate region."[174] Virginia Senator John Randolph (1773–1833) led the racial camp,[175] forewarning that associating with Latin America would undermine slavery interests in the South. Clay advocated on behalf of the American system, which presented with the Panama Congress an opportunity to cut "commercial and political fetters" to Europe and "become real and true Americans, and place ourselves at the head of the

---

de facto is the sovereign *de jure*." He argued the Buenos Aires seat satisfied all the factual conditions determining statehood, "morally and politically" requiring acknowledgment and recognition by the United Sates. Henry Clay, *On the Emancipation of South America*, *in* 1 The Life and Speeches of the Hon. Henry Clay 377, 391–92 (Daniel Mallory ed., 1854).

168 Bemis, *supra* note 132, at 345–46, 353.

169 Baxter, *supra* note 162, at 56.

170 *See* Andrew R.L. Cayton, *The Debate Over the Panama Congress and the Origins of the Second American Party System*, 47 Historian 219, 223 (1985).

171 Paul D. Naish, Slavery and Silence: Latin America and the U.S. Slave Debate 39 (2017).

172 *See id.* at 34.

173 Charles Wilson Hackett, *The Development of John Quincy Adams's Policy with Respect to an American Confederation and the Panama Congress, 1822–1825*, 8 Hisp. Am. Hist. Rev. 496, 526 (1928).

174 Naish, *supra* note 171, at 33.

175 *See id.* at 44 (noting Randolph's observation that should a U.S. delegation attend the Congress, "they might as well be seated 'beside the native African, or their American descendants, the mixed breeds, the Indians, and the half breeds.'").

American system."[176] "As to an American system," opined John Quincy Adams in 1821, "we have it; we constitute the whole of it; there is no community of interests or of principles between North and South America. Mr. Torres and Bolívar and [Chilean independence leader, Bernardo] O'Higgins [1778–1842] talk about an American system as much as the Abbé Correa [1750–1823], but there is no basis for any such system."[177] When Britain seized the Malvinas/Falkland Islands from Argentina in 1833 and claimed them for the British crown, the United States again displayed its ambivalence, or at least selective support of the doctrine. It rebuffed Argentine appeals to invoke the Monroe Doctrine, in part to protect fishing interests that had come into conflict with Argentine restrictions.[178]

Spanish military defeats in the New World in 1822 and 1823 opened up rivalries with Britain for influence among newly or soon-to-be recognized governments in Argentina (1823), Brazil (1824), Peru (1826), Chile (1823), Colombia (1822), and Mexico (1823). The internal debate rejecting Canning's 1823 proposal that the two states jointly deter other powers from intervening in Central or Latin America highlighted those suspicions. Further British inactions and actions augmented those concerns. Britain had not yet recognized the new states in Spanish America and it continued to dispute colonization rights over the Northwest Territory.[179]

From a South American perspective, historian Joshua Simon noted the interest in federalism arose not to "erase the differences in climate, demographics, and history that invested different parts of the Americas with divergent interests," but to "discourage member-states' resort to arms or to foreign alliances in their disagreements with other member-states."[180] The conquistadors' importation of administrative techniques to subdue peoples and reconfigure territory embedded a legacy of rivalrous ambition. Spatial divisions disrupted indigenous and mestizo populations, which creole post-colonialists could not easily dislodge. In one of his most famous Congressional speeches, Clay described in detail the administrative "language of menace" that allowed Spain to impede commerce and movement, and "lock[] up" Spanish America through

176 Cayton, *supra* note 170, at 224 (quoting Henry Clay).

177 5 John Quincy Adams, Memoirs of John Quincy Adams, Comprising Portions of his Diary from 1795–1848, at 176 (Charles Francis Adams ed., 1875).

178 Christian J. Maisch, *The Falkland/Malvinas Islands Clash of 1831–32:* U.S. *and British Diplomacy in the South Atlantic*, 24 Diplomatic Hist. 185, 192 (2000).

179 *See* Robertson, *supra* note 144, at 549–50.

180 Simon, *supra* note 105, at 809.

its network of viceroys and captaincies-general.[181] These legacies contributed to the defeat of Andrés de Santa Cruz' (1792–1865) short-lived confederation of Peru and Bolivia (1836–1839), which Chile and to a lesser extent, Argentina disrupted.[182] Other failed union attempts involved "the United Provinces of the Río de la Plata (comprising present-day Argentina, Uruguay, Paraguay, and Bolivia), Gran Colombia (comprising present-day Venezuela, Colombia, Ecuador, and Panama), and Mexico (originally comprising present-day Mexico, Guatemala, Honduras, El Salvador, Nicaragua, Costa Rica, and the western United States)."[183] Failed or forestalled, the idea retained significance and forged single political unions in Venezuela, Colombia, and Ecuador.[184] Brazil retained its monarchy until 1889. However, its leading jurist and diplomat, Rui Barbosa (1849–1923), referred to the United States system as the "model of actuality, a treasure of experience, a complete example of the political demands of the nineteenth century, and for the nations of this continent it is the great source of federative democracy."[185]

7 The Closing of the Frontier and *Uti Possidetis*

Unity against meddlesome Europe had been an incipient desire following Spain's retreat from the New World. It stood behind the Northwest Ordinance, the Louisiana Purchase, the Monroe Doctrine, and the appeal of hemispheric common cause. Hemispheric anxiety that European powers would retake lost imperial possessions periodically tested continental nerves and inexact or unsecured perimeters of the new republics sparked border clashes.

To reduce the fear of border clashes in post-colonial Latin America, international law made recourse to the private law of Rome. It adapted a praetorian-inspired procedure that eventually took on significance in property disputes, morphing in the early nineteenth century into a brutal principle of international law—*uti possidetis* (as you possess, so you may possess). This principle stitched together the imprecise borders of South American republics following Spain's imperial retreat. It mandated that sovereign states inherit the same

181 Clay, *supra* note 167, at 378 ("language of menace"); *id.* at 380–81 (describing Spain's administrative network of South American subjugation).

182 Lane Carter Kendall, *Andrés Santa Cruz and the Peru-Bolivian Confederation*, 16 Hisp. Am. Hist. R. 29, 40–41 (1936).

183 Simon, *supra* note 105, at 809.

184 *See* Kendall, *supra* note 182, at 29.

185 Jacob Dolinger, *The Influence of American Constitutional Law of the Brazilian Legal System*, 38 Am. J. Comp. L. 803, 807–08 (1990) (quoting Barbosa).

borders that their preceding dependent area had secured before the arrival of independence.[186] The principle gained support because it instantaneously quieted title and allowed succeeding authorities the ability to turn attention inwards for purposes of consolidating power. As historian Greg Grandin noted: "Rarely discussed in all the considerable scholarship on the [Monroe Doctrine] is the fact that Spanish-American diplomats and politicians did not object to Monroe's declaration. …Rather, they understood its prohibition against recolonization as an affiliate and affirmation of their antecedent *uti possidetis*, and moved to incorporate the Monroe Doctrine into their emerging multilateral framework."[187] However, it exacted a steep, post-colonial price, not in the least because it paid no attention to bisected human geographies. Moreover, its application could never seal borders to the degree demanded by state sovereignty. The Spanish viceroy system, which administered colonial possessions, hardly created any secure borders. It presided for three hundred years over an impossibly porous and overlapping landscape. Its spatial divisions could only imprecisely fabricate border demarcations throughout its New World imperium with holdings that stretched across deserts such as the Atacama, the Chihuahuan, the Sonora, and the Mojave, over mountain ranges from the Andes to the Rockies and Cascades, though the jungles of the Amazon, and into the vast, uncharted interiors connecting Tierra del Fuego to the California coast. In an age before the development of the global grid, precise determination of coordinates depended on often imprecise descriptions and cartographic representations. Nevertheless, the new republics of South America applied the principle extensively and it spread across the hemisphere, except in North America.

In the United States, the Jay Treaty (1794) had resolved through arbitration a lingering border dispute between Maine and Canada, and attempted, less successfully, solutions to pre-war debt and impressment issues.[188] These post-Revolutionary War disputes festered and included the refusal of Britain to vacate certain northwestern military posts, border tensions with Spain over the control of Florida, and Native American rebellion in the Ohio Valley, which ultimately brought the Shawnee Nation and Tecumseh's confederation of Native Americans into alliance with Britain.[189]

---

186 *See* Giuseppe Nesi, L'Uti Possidetis Iuris Nel Diritto Internazionale 25–26 (1996).

187 Grandin, *supra* note 41, at 84.

188 *See generally* Richard B. Lillich, *The Jay Treaty Commissions*, 37 St. John's L. Rev. 260 (1962–1963).

189 *See* Robert M. Owens, Red Dreams, White Nightmares: Pan-Indian Alliances in the Anglo-American Mind, 1763–1815, at 187 (2015) (noting the perception more than the reality until the Battle of Tippecanoe (Prophet's Town)).

Damaged by its inability to avoid "the vortex of European politics and perpetual war,"[190] caught between French and British bans on neutral trade, (resulting in the enactment of the disastrous Embargo Act, 1807; repealed 1809,[191] and the Non-Intercourse Acts, 1809[192]), and vexed by persistent impressment practices on the high seas, the Madison administration (1809–1817) declared war on Britain. The War of 1812's inconclusive result in 1815 restored disputed boundaries to the status quo ante bellum but merely forestalled territorial and hemispheric disputes involving western expansion. The war did, however, settle an important question regarding the interior. Article IX of the final peace treaty, the Treaty of Ghent (1814),[193] promised "forthwith to restore to [Native Americans] all the possessions, rights, and privileges which they may have enjoyed or been entitled to in [1811] previous to such hostilities." With Tecumseh's confederacy destroyed, and no concerted attempt to delineate the lands in question, the war "left the West effectively open to United States territorial expansion."[194] The British ambassador Henry Goulburn (1784–1856) wrote that until he came to the negotiations, he "had no idea of the fixed determination which there is in the heart of every American to extirpate the Indians and appropriate their territory."[195] The British attempted to formally negotiate the application of *uti possidetis*,[196] which would have allowed parties to keep territory captured in the war. British holdings, on war's cessation, included parts of Maine and northern New York, and ten million acres across what is now Ohio, Michigan, and Illinois.[197] A British attempt to set aside the entire Northwest Territory as a Native American barrier between Canada and the United States also failed to gain traction. United States negotiators rejected

---

190 Onuf & Onuf, *supra* note 109, at 178 (quoting U.S. Senator Robert Wright's Feb. 24, 1803 speech in Congress).

191 *See* Tucker & Hendrickson, *supra* note 83, Chs. 21–24.

192 *Id.*

193 *Treaty of Peace and Amity between His Britannic Majesty and the United States of America*, art. 9, *reprinted in* Avalon Project, http://avalon.law.yale.edu/19th_century/ghent.asp. The treaty took six weeks to reach the United States, where the United State Senate unanimously ratified it on February 16, 1815. *See The Senate Approves the Treaty of Ghent for Ratification, (Feb. 16, 1815)*, U.S. Senate, https://www.senate.gov/artandhistory/history/minute/Senate_Approves_Treaty_of_Ghent.htm.

194 Kane, *supra* note 74, at 91.

195 Carl Benn, The Iroquois in the War of 1812, at 175 (1998) (quoting Goulburn).

196 R.V. Remini, *The Treaty of Ghent: The American Perspective*, 44 Handeligen Der Maatschappij Voor Geschiedenis en Oudheidkunde te Gent 21, 31 (1990).

197 *Stalemate: Treaty of Ghent Ends War of 1812 in a Draw*, U.S. Naval Inst. (Dec. 24, 2014), https://www.usni.org/naval-history-blog/9644.

these solutions,[198] indicating their awareness of the rewards of territorial enrichment that only proximity could provide.

Enclosing the western frontier brought the United States into protracted difficulties with Britain and Mexico over the uneasy status of the Oregon Territory, control over the California coast, the annexation (1836) and later absorption of the Mexican state of Tejas (Texas, 1845) and Pacific ports southward. Border conflicts with Mexico would begin to color the intentions behind hemispheric common cause. During the Mexican-American War (1846–1848), which ultimately cost Mexico half of its territory,[199] the U.S. Navy seized key ports in the Gulf of Mexico's Yucatan Peninsula, including the port at Veracruz (as it would do again with the Tampico Incident in 1914). It also opened up a second-theater naval operation by seizing Mexican Pacific coast ports from Mazatlán up the California coast to Oregon. Britain's designs on California rather than grievances with Mexico per se, contributed to motivations behind this United States strategy.[200]

In 1848, Britain seized the port of San Juan del Norte on the Atlantic coast of Nicaragua in exercise of its protectorate of the Mosquito Nation,[201] in part to parry United States commercial dealings to secure a right of way across Panama through an agreement with New Granada (Colombia).[202] In 1862, with the United States enmeshed in civil war, British, French, and Spanish forces invaded Mexico to recover contractual debts, deeply shocking the entire hemisphere.[203] Napoleón III (1808–1873) deposed the Liberal reformist, Benito Juárez (1806–1872) and installed Habsburg Emperor Maximilian (1832–1867) as the Emperor of Mexico. He reigned until Juárez' reconstituted forces captured and executed him in 1867. In 1862, Britain declared its settlement in the Bay of Honduras a crown colony (British Honduras), and between 1864–1866, the quadruple alliance—Peru, Ecuador, Bolivia, and Chile—fought off Spain's attempt to seize Peru's guano (fertilizer)-rich Chincha Islands. At that time,

198 Hawthorne, *supra* note 89, at 480.

199 The Treaty of Guadalupe Hidalgo formally ended the war in 1848, with more than 500,000 sq. miles of formerly Mexican territory transferring to the United States. *See* Nissel, *supra* note 142, at 65.

200 *See* Karl Jack Bauer, The Mexican American War, 1846–1848, at 164–66 (1974); Christopher R. Rossi, *Jura Novit Curia? Condominium in the Gulf of Fonseca and the "Local Illusion" of a Pluri-State Bay*, 37 Hous. J. Int'l L. 793, 823 (2015).

201 George T. Weitzel, American Policy in Nicaragua 6 (1916).

202 *See Treaty of Peace, Amity, Navigation and Commerce with New Granada, Dec. 12, 1846, in* 6 Treaties and Other International Agreements of the United States of America 1776–1949, at 868–81 (Charles I. Bevans ed., 1971).

203 Robert N. Burr, By Reason or Force: Chile and the Balancing of Power in South America, 1830–1905, at 90 (1965).

guano was as valuable a commodity as oil is today.[204] Spain already had reentered the hemisphere by retaking Santo Domingo (in 1861) when it launched its Pacific campaign (with French and British backing) against the Chincha Islands.[205]

Concerns of European revanchism also involved surrogate economic intrusions. British capital heavily financed the Triple Alliance War (1864/5–1870; Paraguay v. Argentina, Brazil, and Uruguay)—the bloodiest conflict in Latin American history—which has been described as a confrontation between British imperialism and Paraguayan nationalism.[206] British financiers heavily backed Chile in its devastating War of the Pacific against Peru and Bolivia (1879–1883).[207] This war has sometimes been described more as a British war against Peru using Chile as its instrument.[208] Peru made peace with Chile in 1883,[209] but Bolivia's humiliation burns to this day.

A history of unsecured borders, the allure of federalism, fears of revanchism, the rhetoric and institutions of republicanism, the closing of the frontier—a process that took shape in Latin America as well through application of the legal principle of *uti possidetis*—and a century of political independence from the common denominator of colonialism stood behind Root's appearance in Rio. Whiggish interpretations of the Monroe Doctrine abridge these histories. Each of these elements contributed to an emerging Pan-American identity, which found rhetorical expression in support of informal and more formal ideas of union. With much hemispheric history supporting it, the Root Doctrine, articulated in support of the Monroe Doctrine, fell on attentive and

---

204 *See* Cara Giaimo, *When the Western World Ran on Guano*, Atlas Obscura (Oct. 14, 2015), https://www.atlasobscura.com/articles/when-the-western-world-ran-on-guano (referring to guano as "white gold"). For an account of guano's properties as a fertilizer, see Levi Bartlett, *Guano, Hen Manure, and some other Things*, *in* 6 Cultivator Ser. No. 3, 177, 177–78 (1858).

205 Cynthia R. Rush, *The War of the Pacific: The Empire Crushes Peru's American System Project*, EIR Hist. 56 (Feb. 3, 2013) http://www.larouchepub.com/eiw/public/2013/eirv40no6-20130208/54-60_4006.pdf.

206 Diego Abente, *The War of the Triple Alliance: Three Explanatory Models*, 22 Latin Am. Res. Rev. 47, 52 (1987) (noting but later discounting the explanation).

207 *See generally* Luis E. Vásquez Medina, La Verdad Detrás de la Guerra del Pacífico: el imperio Británico contra el sistema Americano de economía en Sudamérica (2012).

208 *See* Heraclio Bonilla, *The War of the Pacific and the National and Colonial Problem in Peru*, 81 Past & Present 92, 92–95 (1978).

209 *See Treaty of Peace of Ancón, Chile-Peru, Oct. 20, 1883, reprinted in* Obligation to Negotiate. Access to the Pacific Ocean (Bol. v. Chile), Preliminary Objection, Annex 1, at 71 (July 15, 2014), http://www.icj-cij.org/files/case-related/153/18616.pdf (transcription and translation).

receptive ears. However, incipient expressions of *raison d'état*, directed initially against Europe already had begun to involve contested sovereignties with Mexico, and Central and South America. Root's objective in commencing his 1906 tour bore conflicting raiments of progressivism, insecurity, and self-interest, forwarding an already established North American ambivalence that could not but cloud the success of his mission.

CHAPTER 3

Pan-Americanism and Rehabilitated Monroeism

Merely days after Root's Rio speech, Brazil's distinguished statesman Rui Barbosa had elevated it to the status of doctrine—the Root Doctrine.[1] Captious phrases already had attached to the Monroe Doctrine, producing an array of foreign policy off-shoots: the Olney Doctrine (1895), proclaiming the United States the sovereign of the continent; the Cleveland and Lodge Doctrines (1895), contesting the annexation of Hawaii; the Roosevelt Corollary (1904), ensuring that Latin America debtors honored debts to international creditors; and later the Lodge Corollary, forbidding foreign surrogates from acquiring control over hemispheric territory (1912), the American Doctrine (1913), the Wilson Doctrine (1915), as well as Latin American permutations such as the Drago Doctrine (1902) and the Meléndez Doctrine (1916).[2]

Now there was one more doctrine, however it emphasized amity and equality rather than hegemony and intervention. By numerous accounts during Root's tour, a burgeoning sense of unity held this emerging fraternal Pan-American orbit together. Alejandro Álvarez would refer to it as a triple bond of unity based on hemispheric colonization and emancipation, fear of re-conquest, and a new, twentieth century spirit of community. For Álvarez, it would produce a theoretically distinct, substantively mature addition to international law—American International Law.[3] He claimed it emerged at the end of the nineteenth century as distinct from the juridically scientific forms of Anglo-Saxon and continental law rule-orientation,[4] and he would devote considerable professional attention to codifying international law in the Americas. In 1912, he would co-found, along with James Brown Scott, the American Institute of International Law (AIIL) to promote hemispheric international

1 *See Speech of Senator Ruy* [*Rui*] *Barbosa* [2 Aug. 1906], *in* Latin America and the United States 19 (R. Bacon & J.B. Scott eds., 1917).

2 *See* Albert Bushnell Hart, The Monroe Doctrine: An Interpretation 101ff. (1916) (detailing doctrinal variations of the Monroe Doctrine). For more on the Meléndez Doctrine, see generally Salvador Rodríguez González, *Doctrina Meléndez, in* Las Tres Doctrinas: La Doctrina Monroe, La Doctrina Drago, La Doctrina Meléndez 106–14 (1949).

3 Alejandro Álvarez, *Latin America and International Law*, 3 Am. J. Int'l L. 269, 347 (1909). *See also* Liliana Obregón, *Noted for Dissent: The International Life of Alejandro Álvarez*, 19 Leiden J. Int'l L.983 (2006).

4 *See* Antony Anghie, Imperialism, Sovereignty and the Making of International Law 130 n.60 & accompanying text (2004) [hereinafter Anghie].

 | DOI:10.1163/9789004379510_004

legal development.[5] He, too, would regard the Monroe Doctrine as a defensive doctrine,[6] part of the "true gospel of the new continent."[7]

The Root Doctrine embraced much of this ethos. As Root explained in Montevideo, "I have been preaching for the past few weeks in many places and before many audiences the gospel of international fraternization."[8] In Cartagena and Santiago he discussed common features about sister republics and the hemispheric transitioning to a new age of commercial and economic integration.[9] In Uruguay, he underscored "the substantial similarity of interests and sympathies" throughout the Americas, noting that "[t]he great declaration of Monroe ... was an assertion to all the world of the competency of Latin Americans to govern themselves."[10]

He helped shape the Rio Conference and shortly thereafter became the ex-officio chair of the governing Board of the Bureau of American Republics, the precursor to the Pan-American Union. His participation paid multiple dividends. It ensured the conference's success, validated its significance, and set the stage for Latin American representation at the Second Hague Peace Conference in 1907, and the 1907 Central America Peace Conference in Washington, D.C. A spark of international institutionalism generated from the 1907 Central American conference. Although delegates deadlocked over proposals for regional international integration (juxtaposing a federal framework against creation of a pedagogical institute), consensus emerged to create the first international court, the Central American Court of Justice (CACJ). Andrew Carnegie donated $100,000 to build it in Costa Rica.[11]

The inclusion of Latin American states among the roster of invitees to the Second Hague Peace Conference reflected a substantial change in world

---

5 *See* Arnulf Becker Lorca, Mestizo International Law: A Global Intellectual History 1842–1933, at 327–34 (2014).

6 *See generally* Alejandro Álavarez, The Monroe Doctrine: Its Importance in the International Life of the States of the New World (1924).

7 G.L. Ulmen, *American Imperialism and International Law: Carl Schmitt on the US in World Affairs*, 72 Telos 43, 52 (1987) (quoting Álvarez).

8 *Reply of Mr. Root, in* Latin America and the United States 70 (R. Bacon & J.B. Scott eds., 1917).

9 *See Address of the Minister for Foreign Affairs, His Excellency Vásquez-Cobo, in* Latin America and the United States 154–55 (R. Bacon & J.B. Scott eds., 1917) (taking place in Cartagena); *Speech of His Excellency José Pardo y Barreda, in* Latin America and the United States 109–12 (R. Bacon & J.B. Scott eds., 1917) (taking place in Santiago).

10 *Reply of Mr. Root, supra* note 8, at 58–59 (R. Bacon & J.B. Scott eds., 1917) (commenting on remarks in Uruguay).

11 Benjamin Allen Coates, Legalist Empire: International Law and American Foreign Relations in the Early Twentieth Century 119 (2016).

affairs.[12] It reversed a longstanding practice of "legalized hegemony" emanating from the Great Power system established by the Congress of Vienna (1815).[13] The post-Napoleonic reformulation of state relations imposed hierarchies between the Great Powers and others, among the Great Powers, among small powers, and in relation to enemy states.[14] It reflected Europe's incomplete embrace of the Westphalian order, which had imperfectly supplanted the hierarchical arrangement of the Holy Roman Empire with a system of anarchy based on the equally imperfect expressions of state sovereignty and equality.[15] The Congress system affirmed not only the practice of inequality, but the practice of exclusion, which stoked insecurities among lesser powers about Europe's irredentist intentions, certainly in the Americas. France's invasion of Mexico, Spain's re-conquest of Santo Domingo, and embedded impressions of the *leyenda negra*, the Black Legend portrayal of Spain's Old World association with all that was clerical, feudal, bigoted, and backward, animated this insecurity.[16] It also promoted a cosmopolitan search for a western hemispheric counterbalance.

Argentina's activist-intellectual, Domingo Faustino Sarmiento, who became Argentina's president (1868–1874) openly admired ideas of republicanism and federalism and sought ways to strengthen connections to the United States. These connections were to import to Latin America those traditions and the attending North American capital and technology that would break the inertial bonds of nineteenth century *caudillo* misrule. *Caudilloism* emerged out of a strong-willed Spanish creole tradition.[17] It spread across the region in hundreds of patrimonial incarnations, forming localized personal rulerships and fealties based on charisma, patronage, patriotism, and private militia. Occasionally, it produced giant figures—Antonio López de Santa Anna (1794–1876) in Mexico, Justo José de Urquíza (1801–1970) in Argentina, Antonio Guzmán Blanco (1829–1899) in Venezuela, and Andrés Santa Cruz (1792–1865) in Bolivia and Peru. Whether grand or local, *caudilloism* arose to fill the vacuum caused by the

12 Gerry Simpson, Great Powers and Outlaw States: Unequal Sovereigns in the International Legal Order 93 (2004) (noting "The Second Hague Peace Conference represent[ed] the culmination of a series of defections from the congressional system of legalized hegemony ... enfranchise[ing] smaller states organized around a uniquely strong form of sovereign equality").

13 *Id.* at 94.

14 *See id.* at 102.

15 *See id.* at 103.

16 *See* Arthur P. Whitaker, The Western Hemisphere Idea: Its Rise and Decline 67–68 (1954).

17 1 Robert L. Scheina, Latin America's Wars: The Age of the Caudillo, 1791–1899, at xxvi (2003).

removal of the Spanish viceroyalty system's institutional authoritarianism,[18] which respected nobility and protected the landed gentry (*encomienderos*) who demanded and received tribute. It significantly forestalled democratic development and federalism,[19] contributed to Latin America's tradition of conservative authoritarianism, and fostered a hemispheric retrenchment against liberalism through the professionalization of officer corps that were meant to preserve the rule of the *caudillos* "against the likes of themselves."[20]

A material component attached to these rising revanchist concerns. Views across the Americas attributed Chile's devastating defeat of Peru and Bolivia in the War of the Pacific (1879–1883) to capital infusions by Britain on behalf of Chilean encroachments into the mineral rich Atacama Desert region of Bolivia.[21] Chile's growing power unsettled a large part of Latin America.[22] As the war progressed, a burgeoning sense of continentalism began to form. Against this backdrop, United States Secretary of State James G. Blaine invited North and South American states to the 1881 Washington Conference. Promoting a condition of equality, not counsellorship, he sought to discuss "on the same footing" means of preventing continental wars,[23] which increasing included European economic interests.[24] The assassination of President Garfield (1881) forestalled Blaine's initiative until 1889, when, under the new Harrison administration, Blaine returned to the same position and presided over an assembly of eighteen American states, the misnamed First International American Conference (it was hardly the first). Again, under the condition of absolute equality, Blaine pushed for strengthened economic integration in the form of

---

18 Hugh M. Hamill, *Introduction* to Caudillos: Dictators in Spanish America 6 (Hugh M. Hamill ed., 1967) (quoting Francisco José Moreno).

19 "*Caudilloism* has been the bane of Latin American democracy for almost 200 years," weakening the legitimacy of constitutionalism and republicanism and contributing to the explanation of Latin America's failure to replicate the United States example. Rodolfo Diaz, *Caudillos and Constitutions*, Harv. Int'l Rev. (Aug. 1, 2010), http://hir.harvard.edu/article/?a=2681.

20 Scheina, *supra* note 17, at xxvi–xxvii (conflict with federalism), 426 ("against the likes of themselves"), 427 (stagnating democratic evolution).

21 *See* Heraclio Bonilla, *The War of the Pacific and the National and Colonial Problem in Peru*, 81 Past & Present 92, 92–95 (1978) (summarizing various perspectives and the 1882 view of the U.S. Secretary of State, Frederick Frelinghuysen—"It is a British war against Peru using Chile as its instrument").

22 David Healy, James G. Blaine and Latin America 93 (2001).

23 *Letter of Mr. Blaine to Mr. Osborn*, 1 Foreign Rel. U.S. 13, 14 (1881) http://images.library.wisc.edu/FRUS/EFacs2/1881-82v01/reference/frus.frus188182v01.i0008.pdf.

24 J. Lloyd Mecham, The United States and Inter-American Security, 1889–1960, at 50 (1961).

an American *Zollverien* (customs union),[25] a subject to which somewhat suspicious delegates would return to at the Second International Conference of American States in Mexico City (1899). Historians have credited Blaine for embracing higher motivations favoring mediating inter-hemispheric conflicts,[26] however his rhetorical emphasis on Pan-Americanism never instilled complete support among Latin American delegates that Blaine meant something more than "merely the substitution of the United States for European economic intrusion into [Latin American] affairs."[27]

The rhetorical emphasis on equality intermixed with material interests of North and South American to keep at a distance European economic intrusions. The waning of the Concert of Europe system, which for internecine reasons revealed itself to be over even before the Crimean War (1853–1856), provided added incentives for western hemispheric countries to search for greater participation rights. Although loosened, the privileged status of inequality inhering to the advantage of Great Powers still prevailed by the time of the First Hague Peace Conference in 1899.[28]

The French jurist, Albert de Lapradelle (1871–1955) and the United States representative at the 1907 Hague Convention, Ellery Cory Stowell (1875–1958), credited the South and Central American presence at the Second Hague Peace Conference as its "most salient feature," expanding the profile of international law and bringing Europe "for the first time ... face-to-face with Latin

---

25 *See id.* at 52–53. *See also* Joseph Smith, *The First Conference of American States (1889–1890) and the Early Pan American Policy of the United States, in* Beyond the Ideal: Pan Americanism in Inter-American Affairs 19, 21 (David Sheinin ed., 2000) (emphasizing the commercial appeal of Pan-Americanism).

26 Lester D. Langley, America and the Americans: The United States in the Western Hemisphere 87 (2d ed. 2010); Healy, *supra* note 22, at 95 ("Blaine had a genuine commitment to the principle of arbitration").

27 Langley, *supra* note 26, at 88. *See also* David Sheinin, *Rethinking Pan Americanism: An Introduction, in* Beyond the Ideal: Pan Americanism in Inter-American Affairs 2 (David Sheinin ed., 2000) (noting Latin American concerns that Blaine's Pan-Americanism "seemed to be less focused on hemispheric cooperation than on the expansion of U.S. trade and financial interests.").

28 Matthias Packeiser, Full Sovereign Equality: A Historical Study of Latin American Countries Under International Law 5 (Paper presented at the *Repensando y renovando el derecho internacional dentro, desde y sobra la América Latina* conference, sponsored by the Latin American Society of International Law, the Universidad de Los Andes, Universidad del Rosario, and Universidad Externado, Bogotá, Colombia, Sept. 26–28, 2017) (on file with author).

America."[29] For his "splendid" work solidifying hemispheric understanding, the Nobel Committee awarded Root the 1912 Peace Prize.[30]

Juan Pablo Scarfi noted synergistic extensions and networks pertaining to this burgeoning Pan-American legal consciousness, including associates at the Carnegie Endowment for International Peace, the AIIL, the American Society of International Law, and later, the Pan-American Union and the Inter-American System.[31] Liliana Obregón framed this burgeoning ethos around an underlying story of regional sensibility, a *Criollo consciousness* that included international law as part of the legitimation and recognition process for hemispheric nation-building.[32] Arnulf Becker Lorca concentrated on the legal discourse promoted within semi-peripheral states that had enough "autonomy to insert themselves strategically into the [emerging] global economy" but not enough power to disrupt the legal discourse providing legitimacy and stability to the global order. The location of legal ideas to the global periphery, where they were reshaped and expanded, marked for Becker Lorca the beginning of modernity's encounter with *mestizo* international law.[33]

However, focusing on the common political denominator of sovereign equality, in addition to non-interference, presumed a shared understanding of these terms, which had undergone much nineteenth century interpretation under the rubric of the European standard of civilization. United States President Theodore Roosevelt (term of office: 1901–1909) bluntly invoked this standard with his assertive "Big Stick" policy, promising that the United States would not ignore its forceful application among those neighboring Western Hemispheric countries that chose to slight its significance through chronic wrongdoing or political impotence.[34] And Roosevelt was good to his word.

---

29 A.G. de Lapradelle & Ellery C. Stowell, *Latin America at the Hague Peace Conference*, 17 Yale L.J. 270, 270 (salient feature), 271 (face-to-face) (1908).

30 *Presentation Speech by Ragnvald Moe, Secretary of the Nobel Committee, on December 10, 1913*, Nobel Prize, https://www.nobelprize.org/nobel_prizes/peace/laureates/1912/press.html. Root was awarded the Nobel Peace Prize in 1912 but he received it in 1913 due to technicalities pertaining to nominations criteria. *See The Nobel Peace Prize 1912: Elihu Root*, Nobel Prize, https://www.nobelprize.org/nobel_prizes/peace/laureates/1912/summary/.

31 *See generally* Juan Pablo Scarfi, The Hidden History of International Law in the Americas: Empire and Legal Networks (2017).

32 *See* Liliana Obregón, *Between Civilization and Barbarism: Creole Interventions in International Law*, 27 Third World Q. 815 (2006).

33 *See* Becker Lorca, *supra* note 5, at 18 (strategic autonomy), 19 (not enough power), 354 (the location to the periphery).

34 Theodore Roosevelt, *Fourth Annual Message to the Senate and the House of Representatives, December 6, 1904, reprinted in* Am. Presidency Project, https://www.presidency.

The standard of civilization thesis, importantly informed by a memorandum from the former State Department official and Columbia University professor of international law, John Bassett Moore (1860–1947), provided Roosevelt with the moral and legal basis for taking Panama from Colombia and combating the Filipino revolutionary, Emilio Aguinaldo (1869–1964) following metropolitan Spain's loss of the Philippines.[35] Philip Jessup, Root's friend and official biographer,[36] noted deep hemispheric divisions on the eve of Root's South American tour. "The South Americans now hate us," wrote Root to a Senator, "largely because they think we despise them and try to bully them."[37] Although in fundamental agreement with Roosevelt, Root nevertheless set out to change this attitude.[38]

Roosevelt referenced the retrospective intent and remediation designs of Root's mission to South America in his 1906 State of the Union Message to Congress. He acknowledged that Root had been dispatched to South America to dispel unfounded impressions and clear up "much misunderstanding of the attitude and purposes of the United States toward the other American republics."[39] These attitudes pertained specifically to the Monroe Doctrine, and its spreading interpretation of North American superiority, superintendency, and designs to convert the aspirational Federation of Central American Republics into protectorates.

ucsb.edu/documents/fourth-annual-message-15 ("All that this country desires is to see the neighboring countries stable, orderly, and prosperous. ...Chronic wrongdoing, or an impotence which results in a general loosening of the ties of civilized society, may in America, as elsewhere, ultimately require intervention by some civilized nation, and in the Western Hemisphere the adherence of the United States to the Monroe Doctrine may force the United States, however reluctantly, in flagrant cases of such wrongdoing or impotence, to the exercise of an international police power.").

35 *See* Coates, *supra* note 11, at 49–55.

36 Root has had two principal biographers to date. Richard Leopold's biography published in 1954 noted the "unusual advantages" and access enjoyed by Philip Jessup, who published Root's "official" biography in two volumes in 1938. Jessup served as an assistant to Root and drafted much of the biography during Root's lifetime, with unusual access to Root's private papers and contemporaries. Leopold noted Root left Jessup "remarkably free to reach his own conclusions and interpretations," and "never asked to see what had been written." Richard W. Leopold, Elihu Root and the Conservative Tradition 199 (1954).

37 1 Philip C. Jessup, Elihu Root 469 (1938) (quoting Root's December 13, 1905 letter to Senator Tillman).

38 *Id.*

39 Theodore Roosevelt, *Sixth Annual Message to the Senate and the House of Representatives, December 3, 1906, reprinted in* Am. Presidency Project https://www.presidency.ucsb.edu/documents/sixth-annual-message-4.

1 Root's Whiggish Remediation of the Monroe Doctrine

Latin America weighed heavily on Roosevelt's mind in 1906. Construction of the Panama Canal dominated his foreign policy agenda, and in his opinion it amounted to "[b]y far the most important action" of his presidency.[40] He had recently returned from an inspection trip to the canal site and to Puerto Rico, making that trip the first official diplomatic tour for a United States president outside the country's continental boundaries.[41] His State of the Union address devoted twenty-one paragraphs to hemispheric relations, which had deteriorated due to Panama's 1903 secession from Colombia. Intense domestic opposition to Roosevelt's Caribbean policy and his "hasty"[42] recognition of the newly formed Republic of Panama required refinements of his foreign policy position. Oswald Garrison Villard (1872–1949), a leading reformer and editor of the *New York Evening Post*, labeled Roosevelt's actions "ignoble beyond words;" former Secretary of State Richard Olney claimed "For the first time in my life I am ashamed of my country;" the Daughters of the Confederacy "sarcastically endorsed Roosevelt's actions as a defense of the right of secession."[43] In his 1903 message to Congress, and again in a second message delivered in early 1904, Roosevelt attempted to explain the moral and legal foundation, relying on John Bassett Moore's construction of the idea that the taking of Panama and the United States' supervisory control over the canal's neutral status accomplished the "interests of collective civilization."[44] This separation put a definitive end to Bolívar's "dream republic" of Gran Colombia.[45] It exposed inherent weaknesses of the Colombian state to integrate the province and brought national shame over the strategic territorial loss and huge economic loss of the isthmus.[46] And it reflected a coming-into-its-own of international law and lawyers to sell a type of empire that William Appleman Williams (1921–1990) would later describe as imperial anticolonialism.[47] Roosevelt had

---

40 Theodore Roosevelt, An Autobiography 512 (1920) (1913).

41 Andrew Glass, *Theodore Roosevelt Embarks for Visit to Panama: Nov. 9, 1906*, Politico (Nov. 9, 2016), https://www.politico.com/story/2016/11/theodore-roosevelt-embarks-for-visit-to-panama-nov-9-1906-230890.

42 Coates, *supra* note 11, at 55.

43 *Id.*

44 *Id.* at 55–56.

45 Jorge L. Sarmiento, *Consolidating Power: The Making of Modern Colombia After the Panama Debacle*, 3 Ezra's Archives 93, 98 (2013).

46 *See generally id.* at 93–113.

47 On the emergence of international law as a means of "selling empire," between the period of 1898–1904, see Coates, *supra* note 11, Ch. 2. On the idea of imperial anticolonialism, see William Appleman Williams, The Tragedy of American Diplomacy Ch. 2 (1972) (1959).

dispatched United States warships to Panama City on the Pacific, and Colón on the Atlantic, to quiet Colombian opposition to Panama's secession. He took this action after Colombia's congress rejected financial terms of a treaty allowing the United States to construct the canal. If the Monroe Doctrine originally intended to allay latent concerns about European interference, the Root Doctrine intended to dispel rising anxieties about the emerging hemispheric and hegemonic proclivities of the United States.

Root's tour of Latin America in 1906 intended to restage the whiggish narrative of the Monroe Doctrine as a purely defensive, good "old story"—an enlightened and progressive statement of anti-imperialism. His mission attempted to capitalize on the fraternal good will common to all former colonies of the Americas and to allay concerns of a counter-narrative. "[T]hey think we despise them and try to bully them," wrote Root in December 1905,[48] "I want to show them distinguished consideration."[49]

2 The Counter-Narrative

However, a counter-narrative already had developed, beginning in the mid-nineteenth century and rising to a level of United States concern by the eve of Root's 1906 Latin American tour. This counter-narrative projected darker implications of the United States' hemispheric rise beginning with the annexation of Texas (1845), the Mexican-American War (1846–1848), which sparked the rise of Latin Americanism among critical factions of South America's intelligentsia, and the mid-nineteenth century competition with Great Britain over the control or neutral status of the isthmus (resulting in the Bidlack-Mallarino Treaty with Colombia (1846), and the Clayton-Bulwer Treaty with Great Britain (1850)). In Central America, the counter-narrative would influence a judgment of the CACJ that would attempt to reformat the language of international law as a prophylactic against the application of the Monroe Doctrine. In attempting to reshape international law, the CACJ ended up forwarding its own whiggish interpretation of international legal history.[50]

By 1906, more immediate events had cast doubt on the defensive and fraternal character of the Monroe Doctrine. At the 1889 First International Conference of American States, the United States had promoted mandatory

48 Jessup, *supra* note 37, at 469 (quoting Root's December 13, 1905 letter to Sen. Ben Tillman).

49 *Id.* at 469 (quoting Root's May 16, 1906 letter to Colonel [Henry] Watterson).

50 *See infra* Ch. 5.

arbitration of hemispheric disputes as a core objective. This idea sought to secure a new Magna Carta of the Americas.[51] The initiative launched in conjunction with the coining of a new term owing to the conference and efforts of Secretary of State Blaine—Pan-Americanism.[52] However, the United States imperfectly embraced the arbitration principle, at times undermining or ignoring it. An 1891 crisis with Chile (the *Baltimore* incident) bypassed arbitration. Instead, the United States demanded indemnity from Chile for the port-call stabbing deaths of two United States sailors.[53] Other veiled threats of satisfaction and a severance of diplomatic relations suggested a weak arbitral foundation for the creation of a new hemispheric Magna Carta.[54] In 1894, the United States Congress repudiated economic integration agreements that the Harrison administration (1889–1893) had "bullied" eight Latin American governments into signing.[55] In 1895, President Cleveland's Secretary of State, Richard Olney, invoked the Monroe Doctrine in defense of Venezuela's long-festering border dispute with Britain over British Guiana, but brokered an arbitration agreement that precluded territory settled by British subjects for more than fifty years. Venezuela had repeatedly opposed such an exemption and was never consulted about this basis for the deal, an act that "coldly rejected the spirit of hemispheric cooperation" that the Monroe Doctrine's invocation purportedly defended.[56] Already, the "redeemer nation" quality of Manifest Destiny had displayed "mercenary rather than messianic" motives with the pacification of the Philippines (1899–1902).[57] Indeed, merely days before the United States Senate ratified the Treaty of Paris with Spain (February 4, 1899), which ceded its colony of the Philippines to the United States, war broke out between United States occupiers and Filipino nationalists animated

51 Jay Sexton, The Monroe Doctrine: Empire and Nation in Nineteenth-Century America 193–96 (2011).

52 Latin American historian Arthur P. Whitaker dated first mention of the term "Pan-American" to a *New York Evening Post* article on June 27, 1882. Drawing influences from references to earlier Pan-Slav and Pan-Germanic movements, Whitaker noted "the term gained common currency during the inter-American conference at Washington in 1889–1890." Whitaker, *supra* note 16, 74 n.15 and accompanying text. *Cf.* Joseph Byrne Lockey, Pan-Americanism: Its Beginnings 1–2 (1920).

53 *See generally* Osgood Hardy, *The* Itata *Incident*, 5 Hisp. Am. Hist. Rev. 195 (1922) (describing the *Baltimore* incident and preceding events involving the Chilean vessel, *Itata*, which shipped insurgents' arms purchased in the United States to Chile, which United States customs officials later forced Chilean revolutionaries to hand over to the United States).

54 *Id.* at 197.

55 *Id.* at 196.

56 *Id.* at 209.

57 Ernest Lee Tuveson, Redeemer Nation: The Idea of America's Millennial Role 132 (1968).

by grievances that independence amounted to nothing more than a change in colonial governance. At the same time, political turmoil in Venezuela had revealed selective and "opportunis[tic]" components of United States policy. Venezuelan dictator Cipriano Castro's corrupt regime engendered great forbearance on the part of the Roosevelt administration, which came to its defense vis-à-vis belligerent threats by European creditors. Arbitration proved a resourceful if short-lived conclusion to the threatened European invasion[58]—a rupture in diplomatic relations would contribute to the United States' involvement in Castro's overthrow.[59] Nevertheless, the peaceful resolution of the dispute through the establishment of the Venezuelan Claims Commission and resulting arbitration did result in the important and often forgotten establishment of the first modern legal restriction on the previously unfettered right of states to resort to war.[60]

Roosevelt's Caribbean policy also bypassed arbitration to deal with Santo Domingo's insolvency. He invoked executive authority in 1905 to impose a financial protectorate over the island to confront European demands for satisfaction of debt. A hesitant if not reluctant Senate agreed to a treaty in 1907, affirming the interests of New York creditors, who reaped 55 percent of country's customs revenue; 45 percent returned to the Dominican government to manage state affairs and international debt.[61] While these events were taking place, Root and others successfully forestalled Luis Drago's hemispheric initiative to outlaw armed intervention to recover public debt.[62]

And yet important signs foretold of an emerging commitment to legalized dispute settlement techniques at this time. The Central American Conference, held in Washington, D.C. in 1907, undertook as its most notable achievement the creation of the CACJ. Composed of one judge from each of the five Central American republics, the states agreed to submit, without exception, all disputes not subject to diplomatic resolution. The Court's jurisdiction extended to citizens of Central America, and by special agreement, controversies between

---

58 *See generally* Jackson H. Ralson & W.T. Sherman Doyle, Venezuelan Arbitrations of 1903 (1904).

59 H.C. Hill, Roosevelt and the Caribbean 212 (1965).

60 *See Convention (II) Respecting the Limitation of the Employment of Force for the Recovery of Contract Debts, signed at The Hague, October 18, 1907, in* The Hague Conventions and Declarations of 1899 and 1907, at 89–95 (James Brown Scott ed., 3rd ed. 1918) (precluding in art. 1 "recourse to armed force for the recovery of contract debts" if a debtor state replies affirmatively to an offer of arbitration). For early commentary, see 1 James Brown Scott, The Hague Peace Conferences of 1899 and 1907, at 386–422 (1909).

61 *See* The American Presidency: Origins and Development, 1776–2014, at 242 (Sidney M. Milkis & Michael Nelson eds., 7th ed. 2016).

62 *See supra* Ch. 1.

a Central American state and a foreign government.[63] The Convention for the Pacific Settlement of Disputes, adopted at the 1907 Hague Peace Conference, recognized (but did not mandate) arbitration as the most effective means of settling questions of a legal nature.[64] Root, as Secretary of State, extended the spirit of third party dispute settlement in 1908 with a series bilateral agreements modeled after treaties negotiated with Mexico, Peru, El Salvador, Costa Rica, Ecuador, and Haiti.[65] The Fourth International Conference of American States in Buenos Aires (1910) reflected this piecemeal approach. The idea of promoting a general arbitration agreement was off the agenda and members of the United States delegation had instructions to keep it off the agenda.[66]

These progressive steps developed under the shadow of the Platt Amendment (1901), named after Connecticut Senator Orville Platt but substantially drafted by Root, then the Secretary of War, and efficiently supervised by Root's "loyal subordinate," Leonard Wood, the United States Military Governor of Cuba.[67] The Platt Amendment, introduced as a rider to the 1901 Army Appropriations Bill, granted Cuba independence following the United States' military occupation, which began in 1898 during the Spanish-American War. However, eight conditions attached to end the occupation. The conditions restricted Cuba from pursuing an independent foreign policy, incurring debt, revising or rescinding United States acts during its military occupancy, or unilaterally determining the fate of Cuba's second largest island. Furthermore, the conditions imposed health demands to protect commerce and southern ports of the United States, and enabled the United States to maintain its independence and defense through the establishment of the military base at Guantánamo. The Platt Amendment established these provisions in perpetuity, but most centrally, in Article III, it established Cuba as a protectorate by granting the United States a right of intervention in Cuban affairs.[68]

---

63 *See* Mecham, *supra* note 24, at 69.

64 *See* 1907 Convention for the Pacific Settlement of International Disputes art. 38, Oct. 18, 1907, https://pca-cpa.org/wp-content/uploads/sites/175/2016/01/1907-Convention-for-the-Pacific-Settlement-of-International-Disputes.pdf.

65 Mecham, *supra* note 24, at 71.

66 *Id.*

67 Isaac Frederick Marcosson, Leonard Wood: Prophet of Preparedness 45 (1917).

68 Article III read: "That the government of Cuba consents that the United States may exercise the right to intervene for the preservation of Cuban independence, the maintenance of a government adequate for the protection of life, property and individual liberty, and for discharging the obligations with respect to Cuba imposed by the treaty of Paris on the United States, now to be assumed and undertaken by the government of Cuba," *reprinted in* Jessup, *supra* note 37, at 312.

Article III essentially conditioned the United States' withdrawal from Cuba on a predetermined set of understandings relating to the nature of Cuba's new constitution, the political orientation of delegates to its constitutional convention, and the restoration of security conditions that would promote United States hemispheric security interests and investment opportunities. Wood and Root began coordinating these issues in 1900 when the terms of the Platt Amendment were initially conveyed to delegates.[69]

Standing in their way on the domestic front was the Teller Amendment (1898), a condition that Congress attached to the McKinley administration's war plan against Spain. It disclaimed "any disposition of intention to exercise sovereignty, jurisdiction or control over [Cuba]," and promised "to leave the government and control of the island to its people" once the war objective had been achieved.[70] The Teller Amendment expressed the stout and combined anti-imperial sentiments of isolationists, anti-imperialists, and burgeoning liberal internationalists. Root and Wood were determined to establish guarantees that Cuba would not compromise that independence in respect of foreign powers. Moreover, both believed the Cubans needed tutelage in the art of self-governance.[71] Root wrote to Wood that the United States had "a moral obligation" to ensure a "stable and adequate government in Cuba" and "a substantial interest in the maintenance of such a government ... for our own protection."[72] Wood acknowledged the Teller Amendment, professing "a government of and by the people of Cuba ... because we have promised it, but I do not believe in surrendering the present Government to adventurers," whom he did not believe competent to protect established United States interests.[73] Root had legal concerns about Cuban self rule, and based on his concern that the Monroe Doctrine did not have the character of a principle of general international law, he worked to mute the implications of the Teller Amendment by securing a right of United States intervention within Cuba's internal framework.

69 *See The United States, Cuba, and the Platt Amendment, 1901*, U.S. Dep't St. Archive, https://2001-2009.state.gov/r/pa/ho/time/ip/86557.htm.

70 1 Herman Hagedorn, Leonard Wood: A Biography 339 (1931). Similarly, the so-called Foraker Act (Organic Act of 1900) guaranteed civilian rule in Puerto Rico. *See* Foraker Act of 1900, Pub. L. 56-191, 31 Stat. 77–86.

71 Jack C. Lane, Armed Progressive: General Leonard Wood 103 (1978) ("Like Wood, Root believed that the Spanish had left the Cubans 'wholly ignorant of the art of self-government, and unless they were taught new methods and new ideas they would fail to achieve a stable government.'").

72 Hagedorn, *supra* note 70, at 338–339 (quoting Root's letter to Wood, Feb. 9, 1901).

73 Jack McCallum, Leonard Wood: Rough Rider, Surgeon, Architect of American Imperialism 183 (2006) (quoting Wood's letter to Root, Jan. 19, 1900).

In Root's formalistic opinion, leaving Cuba to the Cubans would terminate the United States' right of guardianship and protection, which international law recognized in accordance with the Paris Treaty (1898) that ended the Spanish-American War. Because the Europeans did not consider the Monroe Doctrine part of international law, no other recognized rule precluded European revanchism. "How soon some one of these nations may feel inclined to test the willingness of the United States to make war in support of her assertion of that doctrine, no one can tell. It would be quite unfortunate for Cuba if it should be tested there."[74] To protect United States interests, a legal right of intervention needed to be preserved, and that could only be accomplished by writing it into the Cuban constitution. Of course, an element of indeterminacy attached to this route. Cuban delegates would need to ratify such a right of intervention.[75]

According to historian Jack C. Lane, the process of molding Cuban life in the image of progressive middle-class America or restructuring Cuban economic political life "should [not] have been exceedingly complicated":

> The United States had pledged to help the Cubans establish an independent republican government and most Cubans seemed inclined to accept American aid. Many Cubans believed their island would greatly benefit from economic aid. All that seemed necessary was for the military government to give the Cubans an opportunity to draft a constitution, set up a government and then help them institute trade reciprocity arrangements with the United States. But as it happened, no such political-economic reconstruction was possible, mainly because the entire process was complicated by, and in a sense subordinated to, the needs of America's newly emerging empire.[76]

Recalcitrant Cuban sentiments stood in the way. Wood informed Root of concerns expressed by members of the Cuban Committee on Relations about the provisions dealing with the establishment of a military base and Article III.[77] Root instructed Wood to "state officially that in the view of the President the intervention described in the third clause of the Platt amendment is not synonymous with the intermeddling or interference with the affairs of the Cuban Government … based upon just and substantial grounds, for the preservation

74 Hagedorn, *supra* note 70, at 341 (quoting Root's letter to Wood, Jan. 9, 1901).

75 Jonathan Zasloff, *Law and the Shaping of American Foreign Policy: From the Gilded Age to the New Era*, 78 N.Y.U.L. Rev. 239, 289 (2003).

76 Lane, *supra* note 71, at 102.

77 Jessup, *supra* note 37, at 316.

of Cuban independence."[78] The concessionary interpretation did not convince the Cuban delegates, who attempted in vain to counter the intervention provision until essentially put to them as an ultimatum.[79] The newly elected Cuban Assembly delegates signed their constitution on February 21 to an abbreviated smattering of applause, no public notice or celebration, and no representative of the United States military occupying government.[80]

According to Root, Germany's increasing involvement in the Caribbean influenced the establishment of this right of intervention. "German designs on the Caribbean had been rumored in the United States press throughout the 1890s," with a specific concern that Germany would seize Venezuela's Margarita Island to gain influence over projected isthmian canal proposals in Nicaragua and Panama.[81] By this time, Germany had cultivated extensive trade relations throughout Latin America, "mainly as a counterweight to American aspirations" in South America.[82] Moreover, a fear arose "that a scramble for Latin America might develop alongside ... concurrent scrambles for Africa and Asia, imperiling hemispheric security."[83] In 1897, German warships appeared in the harbor of Port-au-Prince and secured by ultimatum the release of a Haitian-born son of a German national in addition to payment and a formal salute to the Prussian flag from a threatened and compliant Haiti leadership (the Lueders Incident).[84] The United States rebuffed a Haitian plea to invoke the Monroe Doctrine in this instance,[85] however anxiety grew over a possible trade of the Danish West Indies to Germany in exchange for the reestablishment of Danish control over Schleswig, Holstein, and Lauenburg—territories that Prussia pried from Denmark in the first Schleswig War (1848–1852).[86] James Brown

78 *Id.* at 317 (quoting Root telegraph to Wood, Apr. 2, 1901).

79 *See* McCallum, *supra* note 73, at 186–87.

80 *See id.* at 187.

81 Holger H. Herwig, Germany's Vision of Empire in Venezuela 1871–1914, at 151 (1986).

82 *Id.* at 19 (quoting Chancellor Leo von Caprivi in 1891). Germany's trade accords created customs unions (*Zollvereins*) with Argentina (1857), Paraguay (1859), Chile (1862), Peru (1863), Brazil and Mexico (1882), Dominican Republic (1885), Ecuador, Guatemala, Honduras, and Paraguay (1887), El Salvador (1888), and Uruguay (1892). *Id.* at 19. Venezuela (and Colombia) established extensive trade relations with Germany but not in accordance with a formal trade agreement (*Handelsvertrag*), which the two countries concluded in 1909, well after the blockade episode of 1902–1903. *Id.* at 20.

83 David C. Hendrickson, Union, Nation, or Empire: The American Debate over International Relations 1789–1941, at 262 (2009).

84 *See Haiti's Trouble with Germany*, 26 Chautauquan 439 (1898).

85 *See* Álvarez, *supra* note 3, at 319 (noting that "United Sates Secretary of State Sherman declared that the Monroe Doctrine did not compel the United States to be involved").

86 *See* James Brown Scott, *The Purchase of the Danish West Indies by the United States of America*, 10 Am. J. Int'l L. 853, 856 n.2 (1916). Danish Foreign Minister Baron Reedtz-Thott

Scott concluded: "The islands are comparatively valueless to Denmark, and they would only be a cause of war with the United States if they passed into other hands without the consent of the United States."[87] Senator Henry Cabot Lodge's report of the Senate Foreign Relations Committee concluded, "So long as these islands are in the market, there is always the danger that some European Power may purchase or try to purchase them. This would be an infraction of the Monroe Doctrine, and would at once involve the United States in a very serious difficulty with the European Power which sought possession of the islands."[88] The United States' attempt to purchase the Danish West Indies in 1902 fell through.[89] Jessup noted the United States concern that Germany may have "thwarted" the deal;[90] official Danish sources, however, point to the "violent public and political debate" fomented by "the more conservative and nationalistic" faction in its *Landsting*, the upper chamber of Danish Parliament.[91] Of greatest concern, perhaps, was the joint action taken by Great Britain, Italy, and Germany to blockade Venezuelan ports in 1902 to force the payment of debts incurred by European financiers of Venezuela's interior, railroad system, and Orinoco River Basin.[92] The events led Root later to summarize: "You cannot understand the Platt Amendment unless you know something about the

---

contacted the German Embassy in Copenhagen in February 1896, suggesting a swap, and the German Ambassador mentioned North Schleswig as "bait." Kaiser Wilhelm II opposed the deal. Herwig, *supra* note 81, at 152.

87 Scott, *The Purchase of the Danish West Indies by the United States of America*, *supra* note 86, at 859.

88 *Id.* (quoting Lodge's Senate Executive Report).

89 The Danish *Folketing* approved the sale 88-7, however the voted deadlocked (32-32) in the Landsting and failed ratification. *See The Sales Treaty of 1902*, Rigsarkivet, https://www.virgin-islands-history.org/en/history/sale-of-the-danish-west-indian-islands-to-the-usa/the-sales-treaty-1902/. An earlier United States attempt to purchase the islands took place in 1866–1867. A Danish referendum overwhelmingly supported the sale for $7.5 million, but the United States Senate balked at the deal in 1870. *See Negotiations with the U.S. on Sail Fail, The Danish West-Indies*, Rigsarkivet, https://www.virgin-islands-history.org/en/timeline/negotiations-with-the-u-s-on-sale-fail/. The United States acquired ownership of the U.S. Virgin Islands (St. Thomas, St. Jan [John], and St. Croix) from Denmark in 1917 for $25 million, again motivated out of concern that Denmark would come under the control of Germany. *See* Bruce Schoonover, *Acquisition of the Danish West Indies by the United States*, St. John Hist. Soc'y (Mar. 8, 2005), https://stjohnhistoricalsociety.org/vol-vi-no-5-march-2005-acquisition-of-the-danish-west-indies-by-the-united-states-by-bruce-schoonover/.

90 Jessup, *supra* note 37, at 315.

91 *New Sale Negotiations with the U.S., The Danish West-Indies*, Rigsarkivet, https://www.virgin-islands-history.org/en/timeline/new-sale-negotiations-with-the-us/.

92 *See* Albert H. Washburn, *The Legality of the Pacific Blockade III*, 21 Colum. L. Rev. 442, 452–59 (1921).

character of Kaiser Wilhelm the Second."[93] Following several failed attempts to reject or modify the terms, and fortified by a United States market guarantee for exports of Cuban sugar, the Cuban Constitutional Convention ratified the Platt Amendment, which would remain in force until canceled in 1934.[94]

The Platt Amendment would serve as the legal basis for United States interventions in Cuba in 1906, 1912, 1917, and 1920. As noted, the "taking" of Panama from Colombia in 1903 depended on the United States' military support of secession,[95] and between 1901—1916, protectorate schemes would envelop Nicaragua, Haiti, and Santo Domingo.[96] The movement to establish a new Magna Carta for the Americas, based on a reliance on third party dispute settlement approaches, harbored impediments from within, which began to generate noticeable conflict.

3 Root: The Logical Choice

Root was a logical and steady choice to reinforce the mixed messages of the new Magna Carta. According to Warren Zimmermann, a fastidious attention to formalism and legalism muted the moral contradictions that crossed his smooth career path, creating an ambivalence in his moral universe that "marked his entire career."[97]

---

93 Jessup, *supra* note 37, at 314 (quoting Root's letter to Jessup, Nov 19, 1929). For a discussion of other episodes causing United States anxiety about Germany's increasing presence in the Caribbean, see *id.* at 315.

94 The Cuban constitutional delegates ratified the Platt Amendment by a vote of 16-11 on June 12, 1901. *See The United States, Cuba, and the Platt Amendment, 1901, supra* note 69.

95 Roosevelt dispatched the warship, *USS Nashville* to Colón to interrupt the transit of Colombian troops to combat the rebellion. *See* Thomas M. Leonard, Panama, the Canal and the United States: A Guide to Issues and References 64 (1993). In securing Panama's independence from Colombia, the United States presented Panama with the Hay-Bunau-Varilla treaty establishing U.S. control over the Panama Canal Zone, promising to revoke its protection of the new republic if it did not ratify the treaty, which it did do on December 2, 1903. *See id.* At that time, the United States had close to 2,000 marines stationed strategically along rail lines and in the frontier province of Darién in the isthmus. *See* John Major, Prize Possession: The United States and the Panama Canal 1903–1979, at 51 (1993). Root reviewed a draft of the treaty informally sent to him by Hay, although "[t]here is no indication on the draft of what suggestions Root may have made." Jessup, Vol. 1, *supra* note 37, at 406. In a speech delivered at the University of California on March 23, 1911, Roosevelt boasted, "I took the Canal Zone." *See* Henry G. Granger, *The Stain on Our Flag*, 71 Independent 13 (Aug. 17, 1911) (excerpting Roosevelt's 1911 University of California speech).

96 10 Lectures on the Growth and Development of the United States 575 (Edwin Wiley & Irving E. Rines eds., 1916).

97 Warren Zimmermann, First Great Triumph: How Five Americans Made Their Country a World Power 148 (2002).

His name is closely associated with third party dispute settlement, paving the road for the creation of international institutions that his near contemporaries would support—names such as Salmon O. Levinson (1865–1941), Chandler P. Anderson (1866–1936), James T. Shotwell (1874–1965), Sumner Welles (1892–1961), and Dean Acheson (1893–1971). Zimmermann associated his name with another assortment of able upper-class New York lawyers or bankers who stood at the crossroad of United States economic enterprise and public service: Averell Harriman (1891–1986), Douglas Dillon (1909–2003), Cyrus Vance (1917–2002), Paul Nitze (1907–2004), and Robert Rubin.[98] Whiggish accounts of history tend to project contextual abridgments in the attempt to periodize a triumphal contemporary and ideological message. Efforts to recapture lost, forgotten, or uncovered historical circumstances, as suggested by the English School, revive the attribute of diplomacy in the telling of this story, mindful that contextual abridgments of history often result from human intercession in the personhood of the diplomat—as much as through historical recreations conformed by the historian's hand.

Root was a member of the 1903 Alaska Boundary Commission, which settled by arbitration an 1821 dispute between Russia and Britain over the border demarcation of Southeast Alaska, which the United States inherited when it purchased Alaska from Russia in 1867. As Secretary of State, he negotiated twenty-five bilateral arbitration pacts in 1908–1909,[99] an astonishing accomplishment in an age before the establishment of a professional diplomatic corps.[100] The treaties required specification of the question at issue and expired after twenty years.[101] He was counsel for the United States in the 1910 North Atlantic Fisheries Arbitration.[102] He served as a member of the Permanent Court of Arbitration in The Hague, and presided over the 1913 Hague Tribunal of Arbitration between Great Britain, France, Spain, and Portugal concerning church property. Toward the end of his distinguished career, he served as

98 *Id.* at 148.

99 The treaties were referred to as Root Treaties. Twenty-two of the 25 were ratified. *See The March of Arbitration and Conciliation*, 93 Advocate Peace Through Justice 235 (1931). *See also Arbitration and Peace Treaties*, 8 Am. J. Int'l L. 341 (1914).

100 The Rogers Act (1924) reformed United States diplomatic practice by establishing career service, unifying diplomatic and consular activity, establishing a competitive examination and merit-based promotion system, setting salaries rather than commissioning for service and leading the way toward the establishment in 1925 of the Foreign Service School. *See The Rogers Act*, Off. Historian, https://history.state.gov/departmenthistory/short-history/rogers.

101 L. Ethan Ellis, Frank B. Kellogg and American Foreign Relations, 1925–1929, at 222 (1961).

102 *See generally* North Atlantic Coast Fisheries Case (Gr. Brit. v. U.S.), Arbitral Award, 1910 XI R.I.A.A. 167–226 (Sept. 7).

commissioner plenipotentiary for the United States at the 1921 great power arms limitation and Far Eastern questions conference in Washington, D.C.[103]

He was the great conciliator of his age,[104] a title that seemingly passes generationally in American politics, and he was Roosevelt's trusted standard-bearer for the promotion of third party dispute settlement. Roosevelt referred to him as the man in his cabinet "on whom I most relied."[105] He traveled in circles that brought him an astonishing array of prominent friendships—from Wall Street and Washington, D.C., among industrial barons of the Gilded Age, within the Supreme Court and diplomatic circles, among academics and international societies. He occupied a key position in American and international life for decades,[106] a position of preeminence that strangely belies the waning of his memory.

Schoolmates recalled that he was "thoughtful, careful, industrious and modest," like his mathematician father and brother, both Orens (dubbed "Cube Root" and "Square Root").[107] He was the youngest graduate of his class at Hamilton College and its valedictorian, noted for his "deliberation and precision."[108] His personal papers, housed at the Library of Congress, reveal the mind of a lawyer rather than a politician. His letters emit occasional wit but little flair.[109] His orations seemed "logical instead of rhetorical, cultural rather than imaginative,"[110] and accompanied by a self-sensitive nasal pitch.[111] Jessup praised him for his "skillful" administration, resourceful mind, and adaptive abilities, but noted his style eschewed creativity and demonstrations of brilliance. He said of Theodore Roosevelt what Jessup thought best applied to Root, himself: "'He did not originate great new truths, but he drove old fundamental truths into the minds and hearts of his people … never straining for

---

103 *See generally* Charles E. Hughes, Henry Cabot Lodge, Oscar W. Underwood & Elihu Root, *Conference on the Limitation of Armament: Report of the American Delegation*, 16 Am. J. Int'l L. 159 (1922).

104 Leopold, *supra* note 36, at 195.

105 *Letter from Theodore Roosevelt to Andre Carnegie (Dec. 14, 1909)*, *in* 7 The Letters of Theodore Roosevelt 42 (Elting E. Morison ed., 1954).

106 *See* Zasloff, *supra* note 75, at 244 (calling Root "the Zelig of American politics from the Gilded Age to the New Era.").

107 James B. Morrow, *Life of Elihu Root, Statesman and Peace-Worker*, Wash. Herald (Jan. 11, 1914), http://chroniclingamerica.loc.gov/lccn/sn83045433/1914-01-11/ed-1/seq-32/.

108 *Id.*

109 *The Forgotten Senator, Statesman, and Nobel Laureate Elihu Root, with Charles Laderman*, Libr.Congress (Aug. 11, 2016), http://www.loc.gov/loc/kluge/podcasts/laderman.html.

110 Morrow, *supra* note 107.

111 *See Address by Dr. Nicholas Murray Butler*, *in* Addresses Made in Honor of Elihu Root 50 (1937).

novelty…, but always driving, driving, driving.'"[112] He was described as a loyal friend and a man without ambition or pretense.[113] "No anecdotes are told of Elihu Root," wrote *The Washington Herald* of Root's unassuming lifestyle, "[h]e is a grave man and his face is almost sad."[114]

His phlegmatic demeanor, selflessness, and quotidian attention to detail produced numerous allegiances and professional dividends. Like Franklin Roosevelt (1882–1945) and Henry Stimson (1867–1950), he launched his career from Wall Street. He co-founded Root & Clarke in 1868,[115] the "white shoe" Wall Street firm,[116] which attracted his great "friend and disciple,"[117] Henry Stimson, advisor to four U.S. presidents, and Stimson's admirer, future U.S. Supreme Court Justice Felix Frankfurter (1882–1965). In 1883 he served as U.S. Attorney for the Southern District of New York, where he mentored his clerk, future New York Governor, Secretary of State, and Supreme Court Chief Justice, Charles Evans Hughes. His administrative acumen propelled him to the leadership of the New York City Republican Party in 1886, chair of the Republican National Convention in 1912, and chair of the New York Republican State Conventions from 1908–1922. He became a close friend and strong ally of future president, Chester A. Arthur (term of office: 1881–1885) and counted another future president, William Howard Taft (term of office: 1909–1913), also among his

112 2 Philip C. Jessup, Elihu Root 473 (1938) [hereinafter Jessup, Vol. II].

113 Leopold, *supra* note 36, at 6, 14 (lack of pretense).

114 *See* Morrow, *supra* note 107. Notwithstanding his visage, many accounts laud Root for his tremendous sense of humor, dry wit, and personal, unassuming charm.

115 Edwin M. Yoder Jr., *A Gentleman and a Scholar*, Wash. Post (June 21, 1986), https://www.washingtonpost.com/archive/lifestyle/1986/06/21/a-gentleman-and-a-scholar/84870ef7-8382-4a58-9977-f2f7dc19b739/?utm_term=.ce0181eb5f54. *See* Gerald T. Dunne, Grenville Clark, Public Citizen (1986).

116 Oona A. Hathaway & Scott J. Shapiro, The Internationalists: How a Radical Plan to Outlaw War Remade the World 258 (2017) (noting the firm had been later been renamed, Winthrop, Stimson, Putnam and Roberts).

117 Joseph P. Lash, From the Diaries of Felix Frankfurter: With a Biographical Essay and Notes 5 (1974). Stimson gifted to Harvard Law School start up funds to endow a professorship in Root's name, but sufficient additional funds could not be raise, resulting in the establishment of the Root Room in 1939. *See* Lincoln Caplan, *The Root Room*, Harv. L. Bull. (Nov. 29, 2017), https://today.law.harvard.edu/feature/the-root-room/. Harvard had awarded Root an honorary degree of LL.D. in 1907. *See also* David F. Schmitz, Henry L. Stimson, The First Wise Man 5 (2001) (noting Stimson's association with Root & Clarke first as a clerk in 1891, then as partner in 1893). Frankfurter had a forty year association with Stimson, serving first as something of a personal assistant when Stimson was U.S. Attorney. *See* H.N. Hirsch, The Enigma of Felix Frankfurther 24–25 (1981) (discussing the beginnings of the relationship).

personal friends.[118] However, he supported reformists and directed Theodore Roosevelt's unsuccessful mayoral campaign in 1886. Roosevelt, as president, later appointed him Secretary of State (1905–1909). Immediately preceding that appointment, President William McKinley (term of office: 1897–1901) had enlisted him as Secretary of War (1899–1904) (having failed to recruit him in 1897 to negotiate the Cuba controversy with Spain in Madrid), where he presided over Leonard Wood's brutal pacification of the Philippines and the Moro Rebellion,[119] "strong-arming" the Ordinance Department into deploying the semi-automatic Colt .45 Double-Action (DA) "Philippine" revolver.[120] Claims of American military atrocities against noncombatants and members of the Filipino resistance resulted in Senate hearings in 1902, a three volume record, and subsequent allegations that Root participated in a cover up.[121]

Poet William Vaughn Moody encapsulated the rising anti-imperial sense that would attach to Root and others in his poem, *On a Soldier Fallen in the Philippines* (1900):

> Let him never dream that his bullet's scream went wide of its island mark;
> Home to the heart of his darling land where she stumbled and sinned in the dark.

In a remarkable address in Canton, Ohio on October 24, 1900, Root took it upon himself to target charges of imperialism lodged against McKinley by his democratic challenger, William Jennings Bryan. Root's attempt to delegitimize the Filipino resistance reduced to racial and civilization discourse,[122] concluding

118 Alton Earl Ingram, *The Root Mission to Russia, 1917*, LSU Hist. Dissertation & Theses 71 (1970).

119 Root also principally drafted the Philippine Commission's set of instructions to establish civil governance. *See* Ralph Eldin Minger, William Howard Taft and United States Foreign Policy: The Apprenticeship Years 1900–1908, at 23 (1975).

120 *The Legend of the Colt .45 Caliber Semi-Automatic Pistol and the Moros*, Morol & Hist., http://www.morolandhistory.com/related%20articles/legend%20of%20.45.htm. The .45-caliber Colt automatic pistol, adopted in 1911, "was to remain a mainstay of the Army" until 1985. 1 American Military History: The United States Army and the Forging of a Nation, 1775–1917, at 367 (Richard W. Steward ed., 2005).

121 *See* Louise Barnett, Atrocity and American Military Justice in Southeast Asia: Trial by Army 22 (2010) (discussing the hearings contained in Senate Document 331, which began January 31, 1902); Zimmermann, *supra* note 97, at 148 (claiming Root viewed it as his duty to cover up atrocities committed against the Philippine population).

122 Coates, *supra* note 11, at 50. Root claimed the "Philippine archipelago are incapable of self-government (p. 16),"; that they have "no common medium of communication" (p. 16); that "they never had a government except the arbitrary rule of Spain (p. 16)"; and that their revolutionary leader, Emilio Aguinaldo, was a "Chinese half-breed (p. 9)." *Id.*

that the Tagalog domination in Luzon marked "the worst evils of semi-civilised mis-government."[123] Regarding the practice of Gunboat Diplomacy, he wrote this course of action was "undoubtedly often necessary" to protect nationals against the general diffusion of intelligence among the practice of the semi-civilized, for example in China, Turkey, Central America, and the West Indies.[124]

One of the more subtle abridgments of history during this period of United States expansion assumes that all anti-imperialists held views antithetical to the illiberal racialisms of the newly forming large policy. Clearly many did in terms of the Enlightenment principles of the United States Constitution, and concerns over foreign and commercial entanglement. However, in important economic ways, anti-imperial and imperial viewpoints merged. Both perspectives reflected support of social Darwinism and the idea of the inherent inequality of races; both embedded views of Anglo-Saxon superiority; neither "quarrel[ed] with the idea of 'destiny'," or concerns associated with assimilation.[125] Elements of the anti-imperial mindset "resembled the expansionist rationale, against which it appeared to be a protest."[126] The discourse was national and international in scope. Gerrit Gong noted that civilization discourse solidified in the language of international law by 1905; Schwarzenberger claimed it crystallized into a rule customary international law by the mid-nineteenth century.[127] Root, with an insouciance that accorded with European acceptance of this view, referenced in one form or another the consciousness of civilized people 26 times in his Nobel laureate address.[128]

Although he disagreed with Wilson's neutrality policy,[129] supporting instead the Allied campaign from the outset, interests converged following Wilson's

123 *Speech by the Hon. Elihu Root, Secretary of War at Canton, Ohio, Oct. 24, 1900*, Libr. Congress 18, https://babel.hathitrust.org/cgi/pt?id=loc.ark:/13960/t12n60f0b;view=1up;seq=3.

124 *See* Elihu Root, *The Basis of Protection to Citizens Residing Abroad*, 4 ASIL Proc. 17, 20 (1910).

125 Christopher Lasch, *The Anti-imperialists and the Inequality of Man*, *in* American Expansion in the Late Nineteenth Century: Colonialist or Anticolonialist? 89, 90 (J. Rogers Hollingsworth ed., 1968).

126 *Id.* at 90.

127 Garrit Gong, The Standard of "Civilization" in International Society 14 (claiming its emergence by 1905 as an "explicit legal principle" and citing Schwarzenberger's Manual of International Law (6th ed. 1976) for its mid-nineteenth century expression as a customary rule).

128 Elihu Root, *Towards Making Peace Permanent*, Nobel Prize, https://www.nobelprize.org/nobel_prizes/peace/laureates/1912/root-lecture.html.

129 1 Spencer C. Tucker, *Elihu Root*, *in* A Global Chronology of Conflict: From the Ancient World to the Modern Middle East 1747 (Spencer C. Tucker ed., 2010).

War Message to Congress.[130] Wilson selected him in 1917 to head a nine-delegate diplomatic mission to Russia to assess the financial needs and political/military stability of the new, pre-Bolshevik, provisional government.[131] Assisted by James Brown Scott, the Wilson administration then sent Root to The Hague to join the 1920 Advisory Committee of Jurists group, which crafted the draft statute founding the Permanent Court of International Justice. As an aged statesman, President Harding (term: 1915–1921) appointed Root to serve as one of four U.S. delegates to the 1921 International Conference on Limitations of Armaments (Washington Naval Conference).[132]

Throughout his life he demonstrated exceptional organizational and administrative skills, which he applied to reconstitute governments in Cuba, Puerto Rico, and the Philippines. He reorganized the State Department, professionalized the Foreign Service and Consular Services, created the first Foreign Service Exam, reconfigured civilian-military relations, solidified the chief of staff hierarchy, and ushered in U.S. Army administrative reforms following scandals of the Spanish-American War that assisted preparedness for entry into WWI.[133]

He came of age in upstate New York during the United States Civil War. His maternal grandfather commanded revolutionary troops in the first fight of the Revolutionary War in 1775.[134] He excelled as corporate counselor to powerful individuals and "corporations that dominated American economic life after the Civil War."[135] He represented rail lines and mining companies, New York City aldermen and police commissioners.[136] He assisted the restructuring of the American Sugar Refining Company, which ended up controlling 98 percent of the national output despite monopolistic industrial policies that produced the 1890 Sherman Anti-Trust Act.[137] For thirteen years, he represented the Widener-Elkins-Dolan-Whitney-Ryan Traction Syndicate, an astonishing amalgam of five capitalists who acquired control of gas and electric utilities

130 Ingram, *supra* note 118, at 70 (noting Wilson's gratification upon receiving a "generous letter" of support from Root following Wilson's appeal for congressional authority to declare war). For Wilson's war request of Congress, see Woodrow Wilson, *War Messages*, S. Doc. No. 5-7264, 65th Cong., 1st Sess., at 3–8 (1917).

131 *See generally* Ingram, *supra* note 118.

132 Joining Secretary of State Hughes, and Senators Lodge and Underwood. *See* Jessup, Vol. II, *supra* note 112, at 447.

133 *See id.* On scandals of the Spanish-American War and Root's administrative reforms, see generally Leopold, *supra* note 36.

134 *See* Caplan, *supra* note 117 (quoting Root's claim of the battle for Concord bridge, April 19, 1775, Emerson's "shot heard round the world").

135 Leopold, *supra* note 36, at 6.

136 2 Great American Lawyers: An Encyclopedia 612, at 615–16 (John R. Vile ed., 2001).

137 Leopold, *supra* note 36, at 16.

and street railways (trolley cars) in more than one hundred cities and towns, including New York, Chicago, Philadelphia, and Pittsburgh. The united capitalization of the street railways under their control in 1908, impacting one-eighth of the population, amounted to one billion dollars.[138]

He served as junior defense counsel in the corruption trial of William M. "Boss" Tweed, controller of the Tammany Hall machine that dominated the politics of New York City and State in the nineteenth century. He seemed to prefer such law practice and service to the bar more than the politician's life and setting of D.C.[139] He chaired the New York Constitutional Convention in 1915, the same year he served as president of the American Bar Association. There, he led the special committee that recommended education reforms for admission to the bar and the establishment of a three year full-time course of study at law schools.[140] Between 1910–1925, he served as first president of the Carnegie Endowment for International Peace, and was also first honorary president of the Council on Foreign Relations, co-founder and for thirty-one years President of the American Society of International Law, and co-founder of the *American Journal of International Law*. In 1909, he became U.S. Senator only because he was asked by the Republican-controlled New York State legislature. In an age before the 17th Amendment to the U.S. Constitution (1913), Senators were not popularly elected, and not subject to the populist requirements of campaigning, which did not fit Root's temperament.

His diplomacy marked a similar avoidance of the spotlight. Often his accomplishments were marked by negative actions designed to keep the United States out of trouble.[141] Jonathan Zasloff associated this mindset with Root's "deep connection" to the inductive legal case method, anticipated by Root's mentor at New York University School of Law, John Norton Moore, and influentially introduced into American law schools in 1870 by Harvard Law Dean Christopher Columbus Langdell.[142] The clinical distillation and dispassionate application of established (but uncovered) principles, rationally and formally

138 Burton J. Hendrick, *Great American Fortunes and their Making*, McClure's Mag. 33, 33 (Nov. 1907). Zimmermann noted that Root had no difficulty biting this corporate hand that fed him, owing to his separation of what the law required from what the law should be. He backed the reform movement to conform street railway companies to fair labor standards and to bring them under city control. *See* Zimmermann, *supra* note 97, at 139.

139 *The Forgotten Senator, Statesman, and Nobel Laureate Elihu Root*, *supra* note 109.

140 Michael J. Powell, From Patrician to Professional Elite: The Transformation of the New York City Bar Association 36 (1988).

141 Leopold, *supra* note 36, at 68; Mary Ellen O'Connell, *Elihu Root and Crisis Prevention*, 95 ASIL Proc. 115, 115 (2001).

142 Zasloff, *supra* note 75, at 277 ("deep connection"), 253 (association with Moore and Langdell).

derived, revealed legal solutions that could harmonize opposing interests and avoid future conflict.[143] The Hague Conventions of 1899 and 1907, with its assorted refinements pertaining to the initiation but more so the conduct of war, supported this incremental, rationalist mindset.

He had a deep commitment to the rule of law and to its attendant international institutions. His isolationist sensibility separated him from Theodore Roosevelt's foreign policy assertiveness and from Woodrow Wilson's spirited liberalism and League of Nations ideal, but not from an understanding that the United States had a role to play as a global power.[144] Although that administration employed him as an emissary to Russia after the 1917 Russian Revolution (in a bid to keep Russia in the war), Wilson overlooked him as a delegate to Versailles.[145] Reasons for this omission included temperamental differences, Root's standing as a high-ranking Republican, and Wilson's general dislike of lawyers.[146] Jessup concluded the relationship between Root and Wilson lacked mutual confidence and admiration, elements that had made so successful Root's association with Roosevelt.[147] However, Root's omission from the Versailles delegation reflected ideological divisions about internationalism, as well. Root's idea about the development of international law required a kind of state consent based on formal machinery and practical juridical enforcement mechanisms. Wilson "rebuffed legalism and sanctionism" by putting forth a "looser organicist alternative" to international organizations.[148] Root

---

143 *Id.* at 340. Zasloff noted that the Langdellian idea of discovering by logical analysis the underlying principles awaiting discovery formed the basis for the American Law Institute's Restatement project. Root assumed the leading role in founding the ALI. *See id.* at 277. *See also* Paolo Amorosa, The American Project and the Politics of History: James Brown Scott and the Origins of International Law 75 (Apr. 14, 2018) (Doctoral dissertation, University of Helsinki) (noting that the Langdellian strain of formalism rendered "a legal obligation as neutral and just by definition," making it possible for American legalists to "mask the contradiction between democratic ideals and imperial uses of American power.").

144 Leopold, *supra* note 36, at 187. *See also* Martin David Dubin, *Elihu Root and the Advocacy of a League of Nations, 1914–1917*, 19 W. Pol.Q. 439 (1966) (noting Root's equivocal course in which he simultaneously professed support while leading Republican attacks on its Covenant).

145 *The Forgotten Senator, Statesman, and Nobel Laureate Elihu Root, supra* note 109.

146 O'Connell, *supra* note 141, at 116; Jessup, Vol. II, *supra* note 112, at 380 (Jessup noted American labor interests opposed Root's presence at Versailles. *Id.* at 379). *See also* Frederic L. Kirgis, Jr. The American Society of International Law's First Century: 1906–2006, at 59 (2006).

147 Jessup, Vol. II, *supra* note 112, at 380.

148 Stephen Wertheim, *The League That Wasn't: American Designs for a Legalist-Sanctionist League of Nations and the Intellectual Origins of International Organization*, 35 Diplomatic Hist. 798 (2011).

maintained an unyielding and lawyerly interest in committing the country only to promises that could and must be kept.[149]

Root forwarded a long-standing interest in securing United States participation in the World Court. In his last appointment of his distinguished career, he served in 1928–1929 as a member of the League of Nations committee of experts to revise the World Court Statute. Renewing interest in the 1908–1909 Root Treaties, Secretary of State Frank B. Kellogg enlisted the ailing elder statesman to renew the pragmatic "Root Formula," which attempted to make disputes more concrete in order to focus attention on specific interests at stake.[150] His attempt to secure United States participation in the World Court remained an important part of his life's work through succeeding presidencies leading up to World War II. Root had proposed a World Court at the Second Hague Peace Conference in 1907 and again that same year at the Central American Peace Conference,[151] and he had worked to craft a workable statute for the World Court, parrying (although in his mind ultimately unsuccessfully) Civil law lawyers' attempts to expand the bases of the proposed court's jurisdiction. During the proceedings of the Advisory Committee of Jurists, Root sought to limit the court's application of law solely to the "rules contained in conventions and positive international law."[152] He and Britain's representative, Lord Phillimore,

149 Root's adamancy about promise keeping was perhaps no better revealed than in the 1912–1914 Panama Canal tolls dispute between the United States and Great Britain. In view of the near completion of the project, Congress levied domestically popular toll charges on commercial passage through the canal that exempted ships engaged in *coastwise trade* (between the United States coasts). Tolls on commercial shipping were also set, but could not be less—"other than for vessels of the United States and its citizens"—than costs estimated for canal operation. *See* Peter F. Neary, *The Panama Canal Tolls Dispute 1912–1914*, 7 J. Transp. Hist. 173, 173 (1966). According to the British, the tolls exemption provisions favoring the United States violated the Hay-Pauncefort Treaty of 1901 guaranteeing equal treatment for all nations, thus triggering recourse to arbitration in accordance with a five year Arbitration Convention concluded in 1908. The Republican-controlled United States administration offered instead to create a commission of inquiry, although Root steadfastly maintained that the treaty terms were not debatable and introduced legislation to repeal the exemptions when the Wilson administration came to power. William S. Coker, *The Panama Canal Tolls Controversy: A Different Perspective* 55 J. Am. Hist. 555, 557 (1968). In a dinner speech before the New York Chamber of Commerce, Root maintained: "if we refuse to arbitrate…, we shall be in the position of the merchant who is known to all the world to be false to his promises." *Arbitration and the Panama Canal*, Outlook 739, 740 (Dec. 7, 1912), https://www.unz.com/print/Outlook-1912dec07-00740/ (quoting Root).

150 Ellis, *supra* note 101, at 230; Jessup, Vol. II, *supra* note 112, at 438.

151 *See* Jessup, Vol. II, *supra* note 112, at 373–74.

152 Procès-Verbaux of the Proceedings of the Committee, June 16th–July 24th 1920 with Annexes 294 (1920).

proposed more specific language that referenced judicial decisions and the opinion of writers as a concrete means "for the application and development of law," rather than relying on obscure "international jurisprudence."[153] Straying from the limits of his positivist perspective, that is, allowing international judicial rulemaking based on custom or an amorphous "legal conscience of civilized nations," (as originally proposed), invited confusion and distracted participants from the primary goal of the undertaking—creating a system based on compulsory jurisdiction. Root doubted that states would agree on the elements of international custom as a source to be applied by the court.[154] For Root, this fragmentation presented real political obstacles. Even before setting sail for The Hague Advisory Committee of Jurists' meetings, the United States Senate had rejected ratification of the League Covenant.[155] Although the Permanent Court of International Justice never officially served as organ of the League, Root's goal of bringing the United States into the court depended more than ever on pragmatic designs to woo reservationists and other political skeptics.

Root's regard for purposeful commitments led him to keep distant an association with the 1915 League to Enforce Peace, headed by former United States President Taft.[156] Andrew Carnegie had introduced the idea in 1905 and it gained traction in Europe and at the Second Hague Peace Conference, and indeed, originally with Root himself.[157] Although it promoted judicial settlement through international courts, a council of conciliation, and dedicated international meetings, signatories pledged to "use their economic and military forces against any member that goes to war before taking its case either to the court or council."[158] Root considered this sanctions element unacceptable,[159] notwithstanding his second-to-none significance in the development of the

---

153 *Id.* at 344.

154 *Id.* at 293.

155 *See* Jessup, Vol. II, *supra* note 112, at 418–19.

156 Jessup, Vol. II, *supra* note 112, at 376; Leopold, *supra* note 36, at 185 (holding Root regarded Taft as "hopelessly idealistic" in pursuing the League to Enforce Peace).

157 Hamilton Holt, *The League to Enforce Peace*, 7 Proc. Acad. Pol. Sci. City N.Y. 65, 66 (1917) (noting a 1906 proposal in Belgium by the President of the American Group of the Interparliamentary Union, a Uruguayan proposal at the Second Hague Conference, and Theodore Roosevelt's expression of interest in his 1910 Nobel Peace Prize address.).

158 *Id.* at 68. *See also Historical Light on the League To Enforce Peace, in* 6 World Peace Foundation Pamphlet Series, at i (1916).

159 Jessup, Vol. II, *supra* note 112, at 376.

League to Enforce Peace.[160] He also questioned the loose jurisdictional limits of the proposed organization, noting that the United States "would break forty treaties" rather than submit the legality of the Monroe Doctrine to a third party.[161] In a 1918 letter to Wilson's confidant, Colonel House,[162] which House and Wilson read together,[163] Root expressed concern about the creation of a future "league of peace or under whatever name should be contemplated."[164] "Nothing can be worse in international affairs than to make agreements and break them," he wrote.[165] Foremost on his mind was the "really crucial" notional change in sovereignty that President Wilson's League of Nations idea contemplated.[166] While the "Monroe Doctrine asserted a specific interest on the part of the United States in preventing certain gross breaches of the peace on the American Continent," Root asserted Wilson's idea enlarged the subject matter jurisdiction of war (thus limiting sovereignty) by "making every sovereign state subject to the superior right of a community of sovereign states."[167] Root likened sovereignty's traditional domain to the distinction in municipal law systems between civil responsibility (tort) and criminal law. "If I make a contract with you and break it, it is no business of our neighbor … if I assault and batter you, every neighbor has an interest in having me arrested and punished, because his own safety requires that violence shall be restrained."[168] However, he feared that rudimentary international institutions, for instance arbitral tribunals or commissions of enquiry as had been employed in the recent Dogger Bank incident,[169] operated according to individual national initiatives,

---

160 Ruhl J. Bartlett, The League to Enforce Peace 44 (1944) ("second to that of no other individual, although he was never a member of the organization.").

161 Dubin, *supra* note 144, at 447 (quoting Root).

162 *Letter from Senator Root to Colonel House, August 16, 1918, in* 4 The Intimate Papers of Colonel House 43 (Charles Seymour ed., 1928).

163 *Letter from Colonel House to Senator Root, August 23, 1918, in* 4 The Intimate Papers of Colonel House 47 (Charles Seymour ed., 1928) ("We read [your letter of August 16] together and discussed it in detail.").

164 *Letter from Senator Root to Colonel House, August 16, 1918, supra* note 162, at 46.

165 *Id.*

166 *Id.* at 44.

167 *Id.*

168 *Id.* at 43–44.

169 A 1904 incident, resolved by payment after an international commission of inquiry, following Russia's mistaken attack against British fishing trawlers on the Dogger Bank, sixty miles off the east coast of England. The Russian warships mistook the British commercial vessels for Japanese naval vessels during the Russo-Japanese War (1904–1905). *See Report of the Commissioners, Drawn Up in Accordance with Article VI if the Declaration of St. Petersburgh of the 12th (25th) November, 1904,* 2 Am J. Int'l L. 931 (1908).

and only inchoately expressed sentiments of an international community.[170] He intimated that the international system did not have the requisite capacity to channel multiple expressions of fragmented opinion.[171] "I do not think that system has so far developed that it is now practicable to make such an agreement."[172]

Root never bought in to Wilson's ethos of internationalism, concerned as were other Republican irreconcilables like Lodge and Philander Knox (1853–1921) "that collective security would make the United States the world's police, dragging it willy-nilly into dangerous conflicts in which it had no intrinsic stake."[173] While he ultimately "favored U.S. membership in Wilson's League," he argued the U.S. commitment should come with key reservations against unworkable features, for instance Article X of the League Covenant, which required signatories to "respect and preserve as against external aggression the territorial integrity and existing political independence of all members."[174] Despite his deep experience with negotiation and dispute settlement—he negotiated and successfully steered 24 arbitration treaties through the U.S. Senate, averted problems with Japan over Pacific relations and the Open Door policy in China (the Root-Takahira Agreement, 1908), and established the International Joint Commission with Canada[175]—Robert Lansing (1864–1928), not Elihu Root, made the trip in 1919 to the Paris Peace Conference. When Wilson's successor, Warren Harding overlooked Root's reinstatement as Secretary of State (1921), selecting Charles Evans Hughes instead, Root assumed the role of elder statesman.[176]

Richard Leopold, another of Root's biographers, referred to him in the early 1950s as "the ablest, most constructive conservative in American public life since 1900,"[177] outranked historically in terms of creative achievement by Alexander Hamilton and John Marshall but among the leviathans of conservatism.[178] However, he espoused a form of conservatism that blended gradational change with a commitment to internationalism unadorned by ideal sentiment.

170 *Letter from Senator Root to Colonel House, August 16, 1918*, *supra* note 162, at 45.

171 *Id.*

172 *Id.* at 47.

173 John Kane, Between Virtue and Power: The Persistent Moral Dilemma of U.S. Foreign Policy 158 (2008).

174 *See* O'Connell, *supra* note 141, at 117. *See also* Dubin, *supra* note 144, at 452 (1966) (noting Root's abhorrence of Article X based on the prospect the U.S. might default on its promise).

175 O'Connell, *supra* note 141, at 116.

176 Leopold, *supra* note 36, at 6.

177 *Id.* at 9.

178 *See id.* at 197.

His historical view focused on the linear exposition of pragmatic, rule-oriented positivism, which validated by its formality, transformed into an end in itself. According to Leopold, "He was a voice of caution in an era of change" and formulated an ill-fitted conservatism that "failed to fire the imagination" of his contemporaries.[179] He fell out of favor from both the left and the right of the conservative movement, and yet he embodied the ethos of an age and a profession committed to the discordant civilizing influences of international law.

---

179 *Id.* at 193 ("voice of caution"), 195 ("fire the imagination").

CHAPTER 4

The Monroe Doctrine and the Standard of Civilization

The Root Doctrine emphasized the hemispheric equality of American states. However, this equality reflected dispersive and problematic shadings of the dominant nineteenth century European international legal order. This order rationalized the inequality of states in parochially homogenous terms that evoked a particularly European standard of civilization. This standard forwarded a relativism that supplanted native institutions with a pervading sense of European paternalism.[1] John Stuart Mill (1806–1873) expressed a rationalized liberal variant of this nineteenth century mindset: "[T]he only purpose for which power can be rightfully exercised over any member of a civilized community, against his will, is to prevent harm to others." As for barbarians, however, "[d]espotism is a legitimate mode of government ... provided the end be their improvement, and the means justified by actually effecting that end."[2] Here again arose an expression of guardianship: To do it for another's own good.

This European mindset reflected hierarchical attitudes, which penetrated the institutional promotion of international law first through the establishment of the first professional international law journal in 1869,[3] then through the establishment in 1873 of an independent association of international legal professionals, the *Institut de droit international*.[4] The *Institut* consciously sought to codify "the juridical conscience of the civilized world."[5] This mindset, in its many presentations, drew straight lines through history that validated

1 *See* Martti Koskenniemi, The Gentle Civilizer of Nations: The Rise and Fall of International Law 1870–1960, at 130 (2001).

2 John Stuart Mill, On Liberty I.9 ("to prevent harm to others"), I.10 ("despotism") (1859).

3 The *Revue de Droit International et de Législation Comparée*. *See* Koskenniemi, *supra* note 1, 11–24 (2002).

4 *See* Les origins de l'institut de droit international 1873–1923 (1923), http://www.idi-iil.org/app/uploads/2018/04/Les-origines-de-lInstitut-de-Droit-international-Souvenirs-dun-t%C3%A9moin-par-le-Baron-Alb%C3%A9ric-Rolin-1873-1923.pdf. The organization first met in Ghent from September 8–11 and included Pascal Mancini (president), Emile de Laveleye, Tobie Michel Charles Asser, James Lorimer, Wladimir Besobrassof, Gustave Moynier, Jean Gaspar Bluntschli, Augusto Pierantoni, Charles Calvo, Gustave Rolin-Jaequemyns, and David Dudley Field.

5 *See* Koskenniemi, *supra* note 1, at 41 (quoting art. 1 of the *Institut's* statute).

 | DOI:10.1163/9789004379510_005

the humanitarian correctness of Europe's state and institution building project, making it an important component of whiggish international law.

Historian A.J.P. Taylor noted these attitudes coalesced at the Congress of Berlin (1884–1885), where 30 years of European concussions ended when rivalries temporarily diverted to the "less dangerous field of extra-European expansion."[6] By the time of the conference, European leaders knew that the major central African Atlantic deltas opened up to vast and navigable interiors. The Congo River's catchment alone drained an area larger than India, with a navigable main stretch covering one thousand miles.[7] Its resource-rich immensity awaited the European country capable of portaging around its rapids and steep drop to the ocean, which cuts a 100 mile-long canyon into the Atlantic Ocean floor, in places, four thousand feet deep.[8]

In the last quarter of the nineteenth century, atlasses of the Americas and Asia admitted of no *terrae nullius*. All land had been claimed. However, much of Africa remained wide open to European rule, spurring French and German incursions into the region, and stimulating thoughts of a "great African land rush."[9] In 1878, the International Red Cross president petitioned the *Institut de droit international* to turn immediate attention to the legal status of the Congo region, clearly out of concern for the coming land grab.[10] The organization's vice president, the Belgian international lawyer Emile De Laveley, proposed in 1883 the neutral status of the region, modeling his view on the example of the Danube River Commission (1856).[11] This idea would animate the neutrality status of Honduras, which stylistically became the Congo of Central America

6 A.J.P. Taylor, Germany's First Bid for Colonies 1 (1967). *See generally* No. 128-*Preamble* to General Act of the Conference of Berlin, relative to the Development of Trade and Civilization in Africa, the free Navigation of the Rivers Congo, Niger, &c., the Suppression of the Slave Trade by Sea and Land, the occupation of Territory on the African Coasts, &c. Signed at Berlin 26th Feburary 1885, *in* 2 The Map of Africa by Treaty 468 (E. Hertslet ed., 3rd ed. 1967).

7 Adam Hochschild, King Leopold's Ghost: A Story of Greed, Terror, and Heroism in Colonial Africa 8, 61 (as large as India), 63 (one thousand mile main stretch) (1998). The steep descent of the river to the Atlantic, complicated by impassable rapids, impenetrable surrounding terrain, and the problem of yellow fever, forestalled European movements inwards for several hundred years, until the development of portage routes and the introduction of steam-powered sidewheelers and sternwheelers. *Id.* at 90.

8 *See id.* at 8.

9 *Id.* at 84.

10 Andrew Fitzmaurice, *The Justification of King Leopold II's Congo Enterprise by Sir Travers Twiss, in* Law and Politics in British Colonial Thought: Transpositions of Empire 112–13 (Shaunnagh Dorsett & Ian Hunter eds., 2011).

11 *Id.* at 113.

once imperial attention turned toward carving a canyon across the isthmus to connect the two oceans.[12]

Richard Burton's and John Hanning Speke's 1857–1859 search for the source of the Nile River, underwritten by Britain's Royal Geographical Society, secured Britain's interest in Greater East Africa from Indian Ocean launching points. However, counterbalancing European encroachments inland from the Atlantic Ocean forewarned of collision. Lord Curzon, who oversaw the painful 1905 partitioning of Bengal as Viceroy of India, famously reflected on this turmoil, not that it dissuaded him from the idea: "Frontiers are indeed the razor's edge on which hang suspended the modern issues of war or peace, of life or death to nations."[13]

Achille Mbembe recounted that the protogenesis of this antagonism began incrementally, and centuries before, with the establishment of European trading posts on Africa's Atlantic seaboard. Here Europe's informal African empire began.[14] Portuguese explorer, Diogo Cão (b. 1450) erected an iron cross at the mouth of the Congo River in 1482. Priests and emissaries followed. Their "arrival marked the beginning of the first sustained encounter between Europeans and a black African nation."[15] Vasco Da Gama (d. 1524) would follow such West African entrepôts farther southward, enabling him to round the Cape of Good Hope (more precisely, Cape Agulhas) in 1488, where *fortuna* revealed the Roaring Forties westerlies that propelled him and the Portuguese empire to the Indian Ocean and Asia. Subsequent penetrations into the "vortex zones of colonial rivalry"—the Niger and Congo Basins—necessitated as among the Europeans the application of international law's effective occupation principles.[16] These principles meant to create a "visible infrastructure on the ground" to quiet title or at least lay the ground rules for "frontier marches" involving the "quintessentially competitive character of the partition dynamic."

German Chancellor Otto von Bismark (1815–1898) convened 15 states at the Berlin West Africa Conference to "obviate misunderstandings" over the European partitioning of almost ten million square miles (25,899,000 km^2) of

---

12 *See* Salvador Rodríguez González, *The Neutrality of Honduras and the Question of the Gulf of Fonseca*, 10 Am. J. Int'l L. 509 (1916).

13 Lord Curzon of Kedleston, *Frontiers*, *in* The Romanes Lectures 7 (1907).

14 Achille Mbembe, Sortir de la grande nuit: Essai sur l'Afrique décolonisée 174 (2013) (referring to the Berlin Conference and the subsequent partitioning of the continent: "Leur protogenèse remonte à l'époque de l'économie des comptoirs, lorsque les Européens implantèrent des factoreries sur les côtes et se mirent à traiter avec les autochtones.").

15 Hochschild, *supra* note 7, at 8.

16 Crawford Young, The African Colonial State in Comparative Perspective 96 (1994).

sub-Saharan Africa.[17] Its resulting General Act "remains a centerpiece of international law's close nineteenth-century association with imperialism."[18] Although focused on mapping the navigation signposts of the Niger and Congo watersheds by 1900, the conference necessarily turned attention to the informal ground rules for European continental conquest. The partitionment that resulted would look much like the Africa of 1960, when 17 African nations achieved independence. Its markings resemble the Africa of today.

The conference, through its amalgam of ancillary discussions, also served as a template for the regulation of another kind of tributary system—the divisible sovereignty system that subcontracted colonial government to private contractors or joint-stock companies and colonial chiefs, creating a comprador class of imperial functionaries—Western spatial *imaginaires*—who constructed space and territory along linear boundaries and put them to a European use as they spread across equatorial Africa and its Great Lakes region. These auxiliaries served as indirect agents of imperial power,[19] penetrating deeper into Africa's interior through the conclusion of treaties and concords neither allowed nor thought possible in Europe. The Dutch East India Company established this model in its seventeenth century rise to prominence in Asia. Its charter from the United Provinces granted it free reign to serve the state's security interests on the cheap. It could raise and maintain armies and navies, pursue war or sue for peace, and divert a portion of the receipts of its commercial monopoly to strengthen its military to claim more ground and expand the interests of its state suitor. The formula worked well, in terms of destroying the Spanish trading empire in the Mediterranean and the Portuguese *Fidalgos*' colonial control over Asia while delivering colonial rewards to the United Provinces as overseer of the commercial markets once ruled by the great sultanates of Indonesia and the Malay pennninsula.

In the late nineteenth century, Africa, Germany, France, and Britain again took up this territorializing model. Belgian king Leopold II already had

17 *See* Christopher R. Rossi, *The Migingo Island Dispute Between Kenya and Uganda*, 42 Brooklyn J. Int'l L. 659, 672 (2017) (citing Matthew Craven ["obviate misunderstandings"]); Saul David, *Slavery and the "Scramble for Africa,"* BBC (Feb.17, 2011), http://www.bbc.co.uk/history/british/abolition/scramble_for_africa_article_01.shtml ("[B]y 1900, European nations had added almost 10 million square miles of Africa—one-fifth of the land mass of the globe").

18 *Id.* at 673.

19 *See* Benjamin N. Lawrance et al., *African Intermediaries and the "Bargain" of Collaboration*, *in* Intermediaries, Interpreters, and Clerks: African Employees in the Making of Colonial Africa 3–4 (Benjamin N. Lawrance et al., eds., 2006) (noting these functionaries operated at key intersections of colonial power and authority; Nelson Mandela, as a youth, aspired to such a position as a clerk).

deployed his own secret plan to secure as much land as possible in the Congo Basin through use of his spectaculary effective and rutheless agent, Welsh-American, Henry Morton Stanley (1841–1904).[20] Leopold also quiety hired the eminent British legal scholar, Sir Travers Twiss (1809–1897), to buttress legal arguments empowering the king to perfect suzereignty through the treaty making capacities of his private company operating under Stanley's authority.[21]

Twiss' deployment on behalf of the Belgian king's personal desire for an African colony required an abridgment of international law's "long-held Vattelian attachment to the monopoly of sovereign states in international society."[22] In the Vattelian world of modern international law, divisible sovereignty existed as an idea, however as applied to the peripheral world, colonial enterprises required a nexus to a public authority. Private individuals and associations, such as Leopold's front organization, the International African Association, did not have standing or status as a sovereign state.[23]

Twiss' solution to normalizing the king's project first rejected neutrality as an option for the Congo region. That much he could argue in good faith. It comported with his long-held view that neutrality served as nothing more than a euphemism for anarchy in a world controlled by force.[24] However, Twiss' previous treatise on *The Oregon Territory* (1846) put him in a bind on the question of private actors establishing themselves as the sovereign authority.[25] Twiss had opposed this position in his earlier treatise. Competing United States and British claims to the territory, now formed by Oregon, Washington, Idaho, parts of Montana, Wyoming, and British Colombia, resulted in an uneasy joint occupation or condominium agreement (the Treaty of 1818; amended 1827)—which became a major diplomatic preoccupation in the first half of the nineteenth century. By 1844, expansionist-minded American settlers, motivated by

---

20 *See* Hochschild, *supra* note 7, at 70, 71 (detailing land deals negotiated from 450 chiefs).

21 *See id.* at 71. Twiss was indeed an eminent international legal authority, but he had a fall from grace. A personal humiliation involving previous activities of his wife forced him to resign his posts as vicar general to the archbishop, chancellor of the diocese of London, the queen's advocate general, and Regius professor. His secret employment by king Leopold marked his attempt at redemption and reintroduction to public life. *See* Fitzmaurice, *supra* note 10, at 112–13.

22 Fitzmaurice, *supra* note 10, at 109.

23 Leopold's formation of a private enterprise was done "to protect himself against the widespread feeling in Belgium that, for a small country, a colony would be a money-losing extravagance." Additionally, he "wanted to do nothing to alert any potential rivals for this appetizing slice of the African cake, expecially France." Hochschild, *supra* note 7, at 65.

24 Fitzmaurice, *supra* note 10, at 113.

25 *Id.* at 113–14.

the newly coined, quasi-theological justification for the Monroe Doctrine—"Manifest Destiny"[26]—had flooded into the region across the Oregon Trail. Claiming the territory on behalf of the activities of these private actors became an explosive political issue. Popular sentiment linked the territory's status with the southern fight to annex Texas, a coupling that would secure presidential victory for the unmatched xenophobe, James Polk,[27] over Henry Clay.

Twiss' service to Leopold forced him to argue against his published views. Root would be forced to do the same with the historical shortcuts he took to defend the unchanging nature of the Monroe Doctrine at the 1914 American Society of International Law. Both were in good company. Grotius, acting as diplomat during the Anglo-Dutch colonial conferences (London, 1613; The Hague, 1615), had his views on the freedom of the seas "constantly quoted against" his delegation's maritime monopoly policy of exclusion over the Spice Islands.[28]

In his treatise while referencing Vattel, Twiss had argued as "rash and ridiculous" that private actors could arrogate to themselves sovereignty rights to unoccupied territory. At best, they could only establish beneficial and possessory claims (*dominium utile*), not a right of sovereignty or eminent domain (*dominium eminens*).[29] He did not dispute the right of agency, holding that "[a] nation ... may delegate its sovereign authority to one or more of its members for the occupation of a vacant country." However, he stipulated that "colonists must be set forth *by the public authority of the nation*."[30] Twiss agreed that sovereignty could be delegated, but not divided. Without a nexus to sovereign authority, colonists lost their national character and became "a body of *emigrants*, who have abandoned their country."[31] The Belgian state had denied this licensure to Leopold. As Andrew Fitzmaurice summarized, convoluted references to medieval practice and colonial history in North America, and behind-the-scene maneuvering by Twiss at the Berlin Conference (where he not only managed to secure an invitation to attend but also ended up working for opposing sides in negotiations over the Congo's status), managed to secure the birth of the *État*

26 *See* Warren Zimmermann, First Great Triumph: How Five Americans Made their Country a World Power 33 (2002) (crediting journalist John O'Sullivan with coining the phrase. O'Sullivan wrote in 1839: "In its magnificent domain of space and time, the nation of many nations is destined to manifest to mankind the excellence of divine principles").

27 *Id.* at 19 (referring to Polk as "unmatched among American presidents in his xenophobic belligerence").

28 C.R. Boxer, The Dutch Seaborne Empire, 1600–1800, 102 (1965).

29 Travers Twiss, The Oregon Territory, Its History and Discovery 112 (1846).

30 *Id.*

31 *Id.*

Indépendant du Congo, the Congo Free State, on Leopold's terms. Although neither free nor a state,[32] the king's personal province was seventy-six times the size of Belgium.[33]

A competition between German and British trading companies produced sphere-of-influence agreements in 1886 and 1890. The 1890 agreement delimited the northern boundary of the German sphere of influence as "the point on the eastern side of Lake Victoria Nyanza." By 1895, German and British spheres became more defined, with Germany ceding influence north of the present Kenya-Tanzania border to the British Crown. Taking the form of a Euclidean-like administrative mindset, European expansion embedded a Christian ethos of superintendency, complete with its fractured exportation of denominationalism, and sectarianism.[34] In French colonial territories, expansion into the hinterland resulted in the creation of parallel systems of justice, one for French citizens, the other for African subjects. Although "totally ignorant of the local customs and languages ... under their control," the Governor General's office in Dakar, the capital of French West Africa, issued a decree in 1903 respecting the application of African customary law (*loi coutumier*) as long as the local customs "did not contradict the principles of French civilization."[35] Purportedly adapted to African traditions and cultures, the imposed system began operation in 1905 under a hierarchical structure of legal administration "imported virtually intact" from the metropolitan power.[36] Agents of the British East Africa Company, equipped with parcels of blank *pro forma*, dispersed across the frontier of the Great Rift Valley to perfect territorial acquisitions through the formalistic process of obtaining the inscription of an unwitting chief. To insure the legality of the transfer, the British Foreign Office required the signature of two witnesses.[37] The "Scramble for Africa" ensued,[38] once the conferees regulated "the procedures according to which the powers should be entitled

32 Fitzmaurice, *supra* note 10, at 114–18.

33 Hochschild, *supra* note 7, at 87.

34 Olayemi Akinwumi, *Polititcal or Spiritual Partition: The Impact of the 1884/85 Berlin Conference on Christian Missions in Africa, in* Christianity in Africa and the African Diaspora: The Appropriation of a Scattered Heritage 1, 10 (Afe Adogame et al., eds., 2008).

35 Ruth Ginio, *Negotiating Legal Authority in French West Africa: The Colonial Administration and African Assessors, 1903–1918, in* Intermediaries, Interpreters, and Clerks: African Employees in the Making of Colonial Africa 115, 117 (Benjamin N. Lawrance et al., eds., 2006).

36 *Id.* at 118.

37 D. Anthony Low & R. Cranford Pratt, Buganda and British Overrule: 1900–1955, Two Studies 3 (1960).

38 *See* Thomas Pakenham, The Scramble for Africa 1876–1912, at xix (noting the phrase first appeared in 1884 to embrace the hectic period of partitionment that historians inexactly date to the period between 1876–1912).

to claim formal control of colonial territories, in West Africa and elsewhere."[39] As Koskenniemi recounted, in 1885, "the *Institut de droit international* passed a resolution celebrating the philanthropy of king Leopold of the Belgians for having assumed the humanitarian task of administering the failed state of the Congo." Baron Édouard Descamps (1847–1933), who later helped draft the Statute of the Permanent Court of International Justice, "wrote a 600-page track *L'Afrique nouvelle* to celebrate the civilizing mission in the Congo."[40]

1 The European Standard of Civilization

The European standard of civilization spread across the non-European world, conspicuously turning large swaths of the Levant, Asia, and Africa into colonial dependencies.[41] The etymology of *civilization* indicates nuances in the way the term traveled through time.

The term derived from *civitas* and corresponding Greek derivatives associated with politic, also polite, and by the eighteenth century "attached to a set of formal behavioural characteristics, to what were called broadly 'manners.'"[42] Helen Kinsella noted that in the seventeenth century, the term arose within law to transform a criminal matter into a civil matter; to recognize civil authority, "to domesticate, tame and make moral." "Lacking any positive content of its own," she held, "the term … *to make civil* referred to a distinct yet related set of behavioral norms and a particular legal status"; … "to encode a complex set of regulative and productive strictures … making one a subject of the law."[43] Associating the term opposite the condition of barbarity or savagery arose in

39 Stig Förster, Wolfgang J. Mommsen & Ronald Robinson, Bismarck, Europe, and Africa: The Berlin Africa Conference 1884–1885 and the Onset of Partition, at v (Stig Förster et al., eds., 1988).

40 Martti Koskenniemi, *International Law in Europe: Between Tradition and Renewal*, 16 Eur. J. Int'l L. 113, 116 (2005). Descamps served as Senator and Belgian Minister of State when he presided over the proceedings of the Advisory Committee of Jurists, which drafted the Statute of the Permanent Court of International Justice between June 16 and July 24, 1920. Article 38 (1)(c) of the Statute recognized that the Court shall apply, in addition to international conventions and international custom, "the general principles of law recognized by civilized nations."

41 *See* Nicholas Onuf, *Henry Wheaton and the "Golden Age of International Law,"* 6 Int'l Legal Theory 2, 2–3 (2001).

42 Anthony Pagden, The Uncertainties of Empire: Essays in Iberian and Ibero-American Intellectual History Ch. XI 33. *See also* Nicholas Onuf & Peter Onuf, Nations, Markets, and War: Modern History and American Civil War 84 (2006).

43 Helen M. Kinsella, The Image Before the Weapon: A Critical History of the Distinction between Combatant and Civilian 56 (2011).

the eighteenth century, and found its way into legal taxonomy through Jeremy Bentham's importation of the term to international law.[44] The idea of civilization, distinguished from civility, indicated "the presence of an agent."[45]

The nineteenth century turn from a normative, natural law order to a rule-oriented, positivist order, transformed universal law into a regional European international law.[46] Anghie argued that positivism's late nineteenth century colonial encounter necessitated first Europe's postulation of a gap between civilized and uncivilized nations and then its articulation of international legal doctrines and techniques to bridge the gap.[47] Protectorate schemes, unequal treaties, bureaucratized cadres of compradors, and self-proclaimed universalist aspiration followed, contributing to international law's framework for "what became the first global international system in history."[48]

The nineteenth century logic of civilization justified displays of "power and caprice" against non-conforming non-Western peoples while establishing "codes of *noblesse oblige*" on the self-anointed overseers of civility.[49] Western international lawyers "deployed the idea of an exclusively European international law in order to justify the exclusion of non-European entities from the privileges of an international legal order based on sovereign equality."[50] United States international lawyers reflected the Christianizing influences of a community of nations projected from the writings of James Kent's four volume *Commentaries on American Law* (1826–1930) and Henry Wheaton's first English language treatise devoted to international law, his *Elements of International Law with a Sketch of the History of the Science* (1836).[51] Georg Schwarzenberger, whose general international legal *oeuvre* has not stood up well as against the test of time,[52] wrote that the "generation pre-1914 international lawyers was

44 *See id.* at 56–57.

45 Pagden, *supra* note 42, Ch. XI 35.

46 *See* C.H. Alexandrowicz, An Introduction to the History of the Nations in the East Indies (16th, 17th and 18th Centuries) 235 (1967) ("The nineteenth-century positivists banned the idea of universality of the law … and supplanted it by a purely European concept of international law.").

47 Antony Anghie, Imperialism, Sovereignty and the Making of International Law 36, 37 (2005).

48 Gerrit W. Gong, The Standard of "Civilization" in International Society 4 (1984).

49 *Id.* at 6.

50 Arnulf Becker Lorca, Mestizo International Law: A Global Intellectual History 1842–1933, at 46 (2014). *See generally* Koskenniemi, *supra* note 1.

51 *See* Mark Weston Janis, The American Tradition of International Law: Great Expectations 1789–1914 (2004) (esp. Ch. 2: "Jurists: The International Law of Christendom").

52 Robert McCorquodale & Jean-Pierre Gauci, British Influences on International Law, 1915–2015, at 461 (Robert McCorquodale & Jean-Pierre Gauci eds., 2016) (describing Schwarzenberger's intellectual output as "patchy," "excessively self-referential," "pedantic,"

fully justified in regarding international law as a powerful civilizing agency."[53] This contentious conclusion nevertheless incorporated a concern for its ethical dilution from its Christian foundation as it underwent a "process of formalization" to make international law "congenial to the needs of the industrial pioneer and capitalist investor."[54] Nicholas Onuf noted that "Europeans made the best of their tangled political arrangements by erecting them into a formal, universal standard of sovereign equality that other, ostensibly less civilized peoples were unlikely to meet."[55] Samuel Huntington labeled the concept of a universal civilization the "distinctive product of a Western civilization," benignly construed as a modern form of global integration by westerners and their "intellectual migrants," but denounced elsewhere as a nefarious threat.[56] His "clash of civilizations" thesis noted that "[t]he concept of a universal civilization is a distinct product of Western civilization," where "[t]he non-Wests see as Western what the West sees as universal."[57]

Mark Mazower noted that the European deployment of civilization was "riven with ambiguities. It was a claim to power as well as a justification for violence. It was a hypothetical basis for global order in a world of hierarchy. And it was a fitting irony of history that while Europe may have bestowed the conceptual architecture of an international order upon the world, it only managed this by tearing itself apart in the process."[58] Critical scholars, such as John M. Hobson, described the Eurocentric metanarrative as a multivalent, promiscuous discourse that advanced a "hyper-sovereignty" to Western states that either denied or conditioned sovereignty on satisfaction of civilized conditions.[59]

"repetitive," "antiquarian."). Schwarzenberger held the Chair of International Law at the University of London from 1963–1975. The university's board of advisers twice refused his appointment (in 1952 and 1957) given a number of career complications and feuds, principally with Hersch Lauterpacht. *See* Stephanie Steinle, *Georg Schwarzenberger (1980–1991)*, *in* Jurists Uprooted: German-Speaking Emigré Lawyers in Twentieth Century Britain 663, 672 (Jack Beatson & Reinhard Zimmermann eds., 2004).

53 Georg Schwarzenberger, The Standard of Civilization in International Law, Current Legal Problems 212, 222 (1955).

54 *Id.* at 220.

55 Onuf, *supra* note 41, at 2.

56 Samuel P. Huntington, The Clash of Civilizations and the Remaking of World Order 66 (1996).

57 *Id. See also* Martin Hall & Patrick Thaddeus Jackson, Civilizational Identity: The Production and Reproduction of "Civilizations" in International Relations (Martin Hall & Patrick Thaddeus Jackson eds., 2007).

58 Mark Mazower, *An International Civilization? Empire, Internationalism and the Crisis of the Mid-Twentieth Century*, 82 Int'l Aff. 553, 554 (2006).

59 John M. Hobson, The Eurocentric Conception of World Politics: Western International Theory, 1760–2010, at 3 (introducing the multivalent discourse), and 19 (hyper-sovereignty) (2012).

Brett Bowden interpreted the civilizational confrontation as a redemptive project whereby European juridical techniques and institutional management provided to the colonial world the sovereignty Europeans thought it lacked.[60] Koskenniemi referred to its cosmopolitan pretense as a false universal, a tribal generalization of ideological preference that produced fragmentation and messianic arguments rather than convergence around liberal principles.[61]

Other critical scholars have attached Christian narratives of salvation or sacrifice to western international law's messianism,[62] perhaps fueled by notable Christian influences in the writings of Butterfield and Martin Wight.[63] Carl Schmitt's (1888–1985) problematic authoritarian and Christian world view construed the civilizing influence of western international law reverentially until the early twentieth century collapse of its European spatial container (the *Jus Publicum Europaeum*). Schmitt presented its replacement as a false god that would possibly instantiate a new spatial order based on United States postwar hegemony operating in the guise of liberal internationalism.[64] Giorgio Agamben continued the critique of the democratic state as a transubstantiated vehicle for totalitarian rule.[65] In a broadside against the "elevated aspirations" of the civilizing, liberal mindset, Samuel Moyn reduced much of the history of human rights discourse to the antiquarian need to create a "usable past" for the prior utopia of the Enlightenment and the ideology borne of the

60 *See* Brett Bowden, *The Colonial Origins of International Law—European Expansion and the Classical Standard of Civilization* 7 J. Hist. Int'l L. 1, 23 (2005).

61 Martti Koskenniemi, *Legal Cosmopolitanism: Tom Franck's Messianic World*, 35 N.Y.U. J. Int'l L. & Pol. 471, 484 (false universal), 486 (messianic argument) (2003).

62 *See* Judith Grbich, *Secrets of the Fetish in International Law's Messianism, in* International Law and its Others 197–220 (Anne Orford ed., 2006) (presenting the theme of international law as having a messianic logic); Anne Orford, *Beyond Harmonization: Trade, Human Rights and the Economy of Sacrifice*, 18 Leiden J Int'l L. 179 (2005) (exploring the troubled encounter between forms of multilateral messianism and its relationship to Christian theology and its forms of sacrifice and abandonment); Jennifer Beard, *Understanding International Development Programs as a Modern Phenomenon of Early and Medieval Christian Theology*, 18 Australian Feminist L.J. 27 (2003) (linking Christian practices to rule of law narratives of international development).

63 *See generally* Herbert Butterfield, Christianity, Diplomacy, and War (1953) [hereinafter Butterfield, Christianity, Diplomacy, and War]; Herbert Butterfield, Christianity and History (1949); Herbert Butterfield, Liberty in the Modern World (1952); Ian Hall & Martin Wight, *Western Values, and the Whig Tradition of International Thought*, 36 Int'l Hist. Rev. 961 (2014) (noting Butterfield's influence on Wight and on Wight's interest in reviving a natural law ethic).

64 *See* Carl Schmitt, Nomos of the Earth in the International Law of the Jus Publicum Europaeum 354–55 (1979) (contemplating future *Großräumen*).

65 *See generally* Giorgio Agamben, Homo Sacer: Sovereign Power and Bare Life (1998).

collapsing internationalist ethos it purported to advance.[66] Various perspectives and critiques of international law incorporate these corruptions of liberalism into their grander narratives of modernity's challenges and failures. And certainly the standard of civilization thesis is a target for critical appraisals of international law and the *mission civilisatrice*. However, the standard hardly has remained static. Its diachronic complexity defies convenient ideological abridgment.

2 The Evolving Logic of the Standard of Civilization in the Americas

An endogenous Eurocentric logic of immanence supported this civilization thesis. Historian Robert Kagan interpreted this logic within a North American context, assigning this vanguard ethos to John Winthrop (1587–1649) and seventeenth century New England settlers—"the First Imperialists"—who constructed their own puritanical theocracy in pursuit of a "City upon a Hill."[67] An English-inspired manifest destiny then spread across the frontier, representing the North Americans' unselfconscious embrace of Anglo-Saxon destiny, exceptionalism and "civilizationism."[68] Frederick Jackson Turner's influential thesis, *The Significance of the Frontier in American History* (1893),[69] noted how the closing of the frontier molded the nation's character. The mastery of the wilderness by the civilized, the natural by the institutional, and the boundless by the land hungry, created a new public domain that exceeded inputs from the Old World—inputs that created "a composite nationality for the American people."[70] Brooks Adams (1848–1927), grandson of John Quincy Adams and brother to Henry and Charles Francis Adams Jr., projected this thesis in terms of his passive, scientifically observed universal law that framed human history as a sine curve "oscillating between barbarism and civilization."[71] Spurred by the

66 Samuel Moyn, The Last Utopia: Human Rights in History (2010).

67 Robert Kagan, Dangerous Nation 7 (2006).

68 *Id.* at 5 (lack of self-awareness), 13 (English-inspired manifest destiny as civilizationism).

69 *See generally* Frederick Jackson Turner, The Significance of the Frontier in American History (Harold P. Simonson ed., 1963). Turner presented his thesis in an address at the Chicago meeting of the American Historical Society in 1893. *See* The Turner Thesis: Concerning the Role of the Frontier in American History, at v (George Rogers Taylor ed., 1956).

70 *Id.* at 44.

71 Brooks Adams, The Law of Civilization and Decay: An Essay on History, at v ("scientific observer"), ix ("of universal application"), viii ("oscillation between barbarism and civilization") (1897).

cultural, political, and security expressions of Manifest Destiny,[72] Turner described this sense of immanence as a coarse but acute inquisitiveness channeling a "restless, nervous energy" into an artless but expedient frontier spirit.[73] Historian Ricardo Salvatore noted the emergence of "othering" narratives in European travel literature of South America, which struggled to homogenize, and then necessarily had to normalize institutional and social landscapes with pre-existing imagery commonly associated with the North American West.[74]

Clay sensed this immanence in 1818. He pointed to the vigorous doubling of the United States population every twenty-five years, a national "income outstripping all our estimates," and the jealousies of the United States' rising importance.[75] Kagan dated Anglo-American immanence thinking to "the extraordinary economic success of the colonies."[76] Between 1650 and 1770, colonial gross national product increased by a multiple of 25, resulting in an American standard of living that exceeded any European country or world measurement up to that time. Kagan's point focused on the colonial sense of "ingenuity and industriousness" independent of export ties to England and Europe, and a triumphalism and burgeoning sense that "Americans saw their economy as the essential engine of the British Empire and its future progress."[77]

Root tapped into this continental frontier spirit, reminding São Paulistas during his 1906 tour that their country also exhibited the free spirit to "conquer the wilderness" and "subdue" Brazil's vast and savage interior.[78] In sermon-like fashion, he told his audience in Argentina: "Like you, we have had to develop the resources of a vast unpeopled land; like you, we have had to fight for a foothold against the savage Indians; like you, we have had conflicts of races for the possession of territory; like you, we have had to suffer war; like you, he

---

72 Weinberg summarized Manifest Destiny as follows: "It is the doctrine that by the destiny manifest in geography America's natural right to territory essential to its security must override the right of self-determination claimed by its inhabitants." Albert K. Weinberg, Manifest Destiny: A Study of Nationalist Expansionism In American History 35 (1935).

73 Turner, *supra* note 69.

74 *See* Ricardo D. Salvatore, *North American Travel Narratives and the Ordering/Othering of South America (c. 1810–1860)*, 9 J. Hist. Soc. 85, 106 (1996). *See also* Ricardo D. Salvatore, *Re-Discovering Spanish America: Uses of Travel Literature about South America in Britain*, 8 J. Latin Am. Cultural Stud. 199, 200 (1999) (contrasting "dark" Spanish America and "enlightened" Europe in tensions between South American travel literature and scientific expedition).

75 1 Henry Clay, *On the Emancipation of South America* [March 24, 1818], *in* The Life and Speeches of the Hon. Henry Clay 377, 378 (1857).

76 Kagan, *supra* note 67, at 34.

77 *Id.*

78 Elihu Root, Latin America and the United States: Addresses by Elihu Root 39 (R. Bacon & J.B. Scott eds., 1917).

have conquered nature, and like you, we have been holding out hands to the people of all the world, inviting them to come and add to our development and share our riches."[79] In Chile, he spoke of hemispheric maturation, predicting, like the United States in the century before, that "the twentieth century will be the century of phenomenal development in South America."[80] In Peru, he emphasized "the majestic progress of national development," the achievement in South America of "self-control" and the attainment of "the collective character competent for self-government."[81] The material greatness of the United States resulted from "that majestic progress of civilization," which Root claimed South America was experiencing, as well.[82] In whiggish fashion, Root emphasized the historical likenesses or "*past commonalities* among countries of the Western Hemisphere," that ineluctably inclined toward the establishment of republican virtues, such as "self-governance, democracy, peace, the adherence to the Monroe Doctrine, and similar constitutional models."[83]

Although the standard of civilization thesis commonly attached to international law's inglorious, imperial nineteenth century past, it arose in the twentieth century during the 1920 Advisory Committee of Jurists' discussions to craft the sources of law to be applied by the Permanent Court of International Justice.[84] It now forms part of the general principles of law clause of Statute of the International Court of Justice (ICJ).[85] It arose again at Versailles (1920) and in creating the Mandates system of the League of Nations (which established a form of tutelage of non-advanced nations based on "a sacred trust of civilization"),[86] and in other great settlement conferences, such as Lausanne (1923) and Yalta (1945).[87]

79 *Id.* at 85.

80 *Id.* at 111.

81 *Id.* at 125.

82 *Id.*

83 Juan Pablo Scarfi, The Hidden History of International Law in the Americas 21–22 (2017).

84 *See Speech by Baron Descamps on the Rules of Law to be applied, in* Procès-Verbaux of the Proceedings of the Committee, June 16th-July 24th, 1920, With Annexes, Annex 1, 322, 324 (1920). Root represented the United States in those discussions (accompanied by James Brown Scott), and concentrated his efforts on crafting a tight draft statute of the Court that bolstered compulsory jurisdiction. *See* Christopher R. Rossi, Equity and International Law: A Legal Realist Approach to International Decisionmaking 101–04 (1993).

85 *See* Statute of the International Court of Justice art. 38(1)(c) (holding: "The Court, whose function is to decide in accordance with international law such disputes as are submitted to it, shall apply: ...(d). the general principles of law recognized by civilized nations").

86 Nele Matz, *Civilization and the Mandate System Under the League of Nations as Origin of Trusteeship*, 9 Max Planck Y.B.U.N.L. 47, 55 (2005).

87 *See* North Sea Continental Shelf cases (Den. v. F.R.G.; Neth. v. F.R.G.), Judgment, 1969 I.C.J. 101, 133–35 (Feb. 20) (separate opinon by Ammoun, J.).

Frédéric Mégret encapsulated its ethos in the rise of the enlightened international bureaucracy—the International Man of civil service—who lived during the interwar period, disproportionately populated the League of Nations' intergovernmental bodies, reflected the social, ethnic, and gender homogeneity of the age, and accepted the European burdens of "humaniz[ing] international rule."[88] In the *North Sea Continental Shelf Cases* (1969), Lebanese Judge, Fouad Ammoun, proclaimed its time had "passed away," burying with it the "anachronistic" and "unjustified" legal forms that gave it expression.[89] Nigerian jurist (and later ICJ Judge), Taslim O. Elias regarded it as an embarrassing and irrelevant appendage of colonial thinking, which is now best ignored.[90]

However, textured interpretations maintain its continuing significance.[91] Like philosophy itself, the standard of civilization thesis tends to bury its undertakers.[92] Viewed as a static imperial product, the standard exuded racial, religious, and antiquated affiliations. Viewed as a socially constructed entity, the standard formed a "loosely integrated, pluralistic, and heterogenic *communities of practice*" domain,[93] with significance beyond a Eurocentric mindset. Hobson turned the standard of civilization discourse on its head, noting that the non-European civilizing process made an impress on Europe in ways

---

88 Frédéric Mégret, *The Rise and Fall of "International Man,"* in Critical International Law: Postrealism, Postcolonialism, and Transnationalism 223, 234–35 (Prabhakar Singh & Benoît Mayer eds., 2014). Mégret noted that men employees of the League vastly outnumber women and no woman ever made it to the League Council or Permanent Court of International Justice. *See id.* at 233. Europeans, primarily from Britain and France, initially outnumbered non-European League staff by a ratio of 7:1 (declining in the 1930s to 5:1), with but six officials from Latin America and no representatives from Africa. *See id.* at 235.

89 *See* North Sea Continental Shelf Cases, 1969 I.C.J. at 133.

90 T.O. Elias, The International Court of Justice and Some Contemporary Problems 14 (1983). *See also* David P. Fidler, *The Return of the Standard of Civilization*, 2 Chi. J. Int'l L. 137, 139 (2001) (calling international law's late nineteenth and early twentieth century treatment of the standard of civilization an "embarrassing piece of international legal history [that] has been forgotten" by later twentieth century students of international law.). *See also* Ignacio de la Rasilla del Moral, *La alianza entre la civilización y el derecho internacional entre Escila y Carbiddis* (*o de la brevísima historia de un anacronismo jurídico*), *in* El discurso civilizador en derecho internacional 39, 56 (Y. Gamarra ed., 2011) (calling art. 38's reference to civilized nations "*este embarazoso adjetivo*"; furthermore: "En su explicación docente del Artículo 38 1. (c), los profesores de Derecho Internacional en España suelen (si acaso) despachar esta referencia a las "naciones civilizadas" como, a lo sumo, un "anacronismo jurídico.")".

91 *See* Patrick Thaddeus Jackson, *How to Think About Civilizations, in* Civilizations in World Politics: Plural and Pluralist Perspectives 176 (Peter J. Katzenstein ed., 2010).

92 The phrase comes from Étienne Gilson's The Unity of Philosophical Experience 306 (1937) ("Philosophy always buries its undertakers").

93 Emanuel Adler, *Europe as a Civilizational Community of Practice, in* Civilizations in World Politics: Plural and Pluralistic Perspectives 67, 68 (Peter J. Katzenstein ed., 2010).

the unwitting West has yet to appreciate.[94] Becker Lorca identified a "strategic" practice among semi-peripheral intellectuals, who internalized the standard of civilization to "justify the recognition of their countries as sovereign states."[95] This appropriation of the Western standard meant to "overcome its legal consequences" by providing non-Western jurists greater agency—eventually resulting in "justifications for holding Western residents accountable under the law governing the territory, rather than the foreigner's national law applied by the counsel."[96] Obregón noted the appropriation of civilizing discourse by creole elites to stimulate immigration, land reform, and to avoid continental exclusion from the emerging European-controlled globalized system.[97] Important contributors to the civilizing discourse in Latin America were the Venezuelan/Chilean Andrés Bello (1781–1865),[98] the Argentines, Domingo Faustino Sarmiento and Carlos Calvo,[99] the prolific Peruvian writer, Manuel Atanasio Fuentes (1820–1889),[100] and the Colombian writer, José María Samper (1828–1888). According to Obregón their effects on the emerging creole legal consciousness would shape a distinctive Latin American approach to international law that partly underscored the continental connection to Europe through Roman law.[101] Within the lexicon of this European patrimony, the CACJ would reframe this community interest standard to reflect regional values of transcendental importance, while maintaining allegiance to the language of sovereign equality. The CACJ nevertheless forwarded the project of denaturing the hegemonic components of the Monroe Doctrine on which the Root Doctrine centrally depended. At the same time, it attempted, but not without inflicting a fatal self-wound, to denature its connection to the Monroe Doctrine.

94 John M. Hobson, The Eastern Origins of Western Civilization (2004). *See also* Andrew Linklater, *Civilizations and International Society*, *in* System, Society & the World: Exploring the English School of International Relations 25, 27 (Robert W. Murray ed., 2013) (acknowledging Hobson's thesis about the non-European civilizing process on the West).

95 Becker Lorca, *supra* note 50, at 66.

96 *Id.* at 67–68.

97 Liliana Obregón, *Completing Civilization: Creole Consciousness and International Law in Nineteenth-Century Latin America*, *in* International Law and Its Others 247, 248 (Anne Orford ed., 2006).

98 *See id.* at 253 n.16.

99 *See id.* at 254–56.

100 *See id.* at 257.

101 *See id.* at 250.

3 The English School and the Standard of Civilization

Butterfield's critique in *The Whig Interpretation of History* can be credited with a revival of civilization analysis within the English School. Borne of a belief in the autonomous, auto-generating, and exceptional development of rational institutions and social structure, the standard of civilization would spin off in liberal as well as anti-imperial directions, the former finding modern expression in the theoretical works of Hedley Bull and Adam Watson,[102] Martin Wight,[103] Robert Jackson,[104] Linklater,[105] Hidemi Suganami,[106] and other liberal pluralists of the English School. Indeed, the civilization thesis found a home in the English School with its projection of shared rules.[107]

The English School focused on the idea of an international society.[108] This society engaged various actors in regularized interactions based on shared interests, rules, and institutional practices.[109] Bull and Watson defined international society as "a group of states (or, more generally, a group of independent political communities) which not merely form a system, in the sense that the behavior of each is a necessary factor in the calculations of the others, but also have established by dialogue and consent common rules and institutions for the conduct of their relations, and recognize their common interest in maintaining these arrangements."[110] With elements owing to realism's fear of anarchy, and liberalism's embrace of cooperation and rational self-interest (expressed in terms of the Grotian Tradition), English School advocates engineered an understanding of international society that recognized balance of

102 *See* Hobson, *supra* note 59, at 224. *See generally* The Expansion of International Society (Hedley Bull & Adam Watson eds., 1984); Adam Watson, The Evolution of International Society (1992).

103 Martin Wight, *Western Values in International Relations*, *in* Diplomatic Investigations 89–131 (Herbert Butterfield & Martin Wight eds., 1966); Martin Wight, Systems of States (1977); Martin Wight, Power Politics (1946).

104 Robert H. Jackson, The Global Covenant: Human Conduct in a World of States (2000).

105 *See generally* Andrew Linklater, *International Society and the Civilizing Process*, 9 Ritsumeikan Int'l Aff. 1 (2011).

106 *See generally* Hidemi Suganami, The Domestic Analogy and World Order Proposals (1989).

107 *See* Andrew Linklater, *Process Sociology and International Relations*, 59 Soc. Rev. 48 (2011).

108 Tonny Brems Knudsen, *The English School: Sovereignty and International Law*, *in* Making Sense of International Relations Theory 311, 312 (Jennifer Sterling-Folker ed., 2006).

109 *Id.*

110 Hedley Bull & Adam Watson, *Introduction* to Expansion of International Society 1 (Hedley Bull & Adam Watson eds., 1985).

power considerations and "a shared subscription to" universal norms.[111] These rules allowed for the operation of Bull's famous turn of phrase—the anarchical society—where, at a minimal level, international society constrained force (the *jus ad bellum* and the *jus in bello*), honored commitments (*pacta sunt servanda*), and acknowledged property in terms of ownership (*dominium*) and control (*imperium*). For these pluralists, international society upheld rules of coexistence that states accepted to maintain a functional, operational order.[112] Butterfield located an important component of agency in the civilizing practice of diplomats, who not only represented disparate interests of sovereign states but also reflected the accumulated historical experiences of sovereign states.[113] This diplomatic theory of international relations drew from Butterfield's philosophy of history, influenced by the German historical school, which found meaning in the life experiences of those separated from us by time and space notwithstanding refractions and distortions magnified by time. The study of diplomacy and diplomatic sociabilities would deeply inform the writings of English School advocates,[114] elevating practioners' of international relations such as Elihu Root to a central position of study.[115]

At the helm of the British Committee on the Theory of International Relations, which developed into the English School in the late 1950s,[116] Butterfield,

111 Jennifer Sterling-Folker, *The English School, in* Making Sense of International Relations Theory 303, 305 (Jennifer Sterling-Folker ed., 2006) (discussing Hedley Bull's The Anarchical Society: A Study of Order in World Politics (1977)).

112 *See* Tim Dunne, *The English School and Humanitarian Intervention,* E-Int'l Rel. (Feb. 17, 2016), http://www.e-ir.info/2016/02/17/the-english-school-and-humanitarian-intervention/.

113 Paul Sharp & Herbert Butterfield, *The English School and the Civilizing Virtures of Diplomacy,* 79 Int'l Aff. 855, 858 (2003). Linklater attributed the English School's interest in diplomacy to its emphasis on the evolution of the concept of civilization. *See* Linklater, *supra* note 107, at 56.

114 *See* Hidemi Suganami, *The English School in a Nutshell,* 9 Ritsumeikan Annual Rev. Int'l Stud. 15, 24 (2010).

115 Sharp & Butterfield, *supra* note 113, at 857. On the English School interest in diplomacy, see generally Diplomatic Investigations: Essays in the Theory of International Politics (Herbert Butterfield & Martin Wight eds., 1968); Iver B. Neumann, Diplomatic Sites: A Critical Enquiry (2013); Iver B. Neumann, *The English School and Diplomacy: Scholarly Promis Unfulfilled,* 17 Int'l Rel. 341 (2003); James Der Derian, *Hedley Bull and the Idea of Diplomatic Culture, in* International Society After the Cold War: Anarchy and Order Reconsidered 84 (Rick Fawn & Jeremy Larkins eds., 1996); James Der Derian, Diplomacy: A Genealogy of Western Estrangement (1987); Adam Watson, Diplomacy: The Dialogue between States (1983); Martin Wight, Systems of States (1977).

116 For an excellent historical presentation of the work of the British Committee, which met regularly between 1959 and 1984, see Brunello Vigezzi, The British Committee on the Theory of International Politics (1954–1985); The Rediscovery of History (Ian Harvey trans., 2005). Butterfield served as the inaugural chair of the group until 1968, followed by Martin

like George Kennan and Adam Watson, concentrated on the failure of diplomacy that became the catastrophe of World War I,[117] invigorating the study of diplomatic history framed on Woodrow Wilson's new diplomacy.[118] Broader interpretations validated human agency to enlarge the boundaries of international society.[119] Broadest interpretations affirmed Kantian ideals of solidarism, establishing a normative basis for international society[120] to counter pluralism's toleration/acceptance of multiple or conflicting pathways of international society.[121]

The English School emphasized the transnational study of foreign policy and the role played by international law.[122] It paid tribute to Hugo Grotius (1583–1645) and the eponymous Grotian Tradition. Martin Wight's influential description framed the Grotian Traditon as an interchange between the Machiavellian world of political realism and the utopian world of Kantian idealism, occupying a "broad middle road" that established the rational complementarity of passions and interests.[123] At this intersection, international society established a world that is neither in perpetual conflict nor peace, yet capable of peaceful coexistence while maintaining parameters that control violence through international society's stable centerpiece—sovereignty.[124]

The English School construed the standard of civilization as an organic, subaltern component of sovereignty. Barry Buzan noted that discourse relating to the postcolonial international society came "a long way from the period in which international society was largely a globalized expression of the

Wight until 1972, then Adam Watson until 1978, and then Hedley Bull until his death in 1984.

117 *See* Watson, *supra* note 115, at 10–12.

118 Butterfield & Wight, *supra* note 115.

119 *See generally* Matthew S. Weinert, *From Cinderalla to Beauty and the Beast: (De)Humanising World Socity, in* System, Society & the World: Exploring the English School of International Relations 90 (Robert W. Murray ed., 2015). *See also* Andrew Hurrell, Global Order: Power, Values, and the Constitution of International Society 314 (2007).

120 *See generally* Nicholas Wheeler, Saving Strangers: Humanitarian Intervention in International Society (2000); Andrew Linklater, The Transformation of Political Community (1998).

121 *See generally* Matthew S. Weinert, *Reframing the Pluralist-Solidarist Debate,* 40 Millennium 33 (2011).

122 *See* Alan James, *Law and Order in International Society, in* The Bases of International Order: Essays in Honour of C.A.W. Manning 68 (Alan James ed., 1973) (noting that international law stands at the center of international society's normative framework).

123 Martin Wight, International Theory: The Three Traditions 15 (1991).

124 *See* John H. Jackson, *Sovereignty—Modern: A New Approach To An Outdated Concept,* 97 Am J. Int'l L. 782, 782 (2003) (noting the concept of sovereignty remains central despite criticisms).

European [G]*emeinschaft*, from which most non-European cultures and peoples were excluded by their colonial or unequal status."[125] It radiated concentric circles representing "lesser degrees of commitment as one moves outward from the center"—its western core.[126] The English School seemed to take "as a matter of historical fact" that a cohesive international society developed within the "accumulated experience" of the classical European state system.[127] Bull embraced the temporal development of the concept, as well:

> the demand of Asian and African peoples for equality of rights in international law was one that [they] did not put forward until they had first absorbed ideas of the equal rights of states to sovereignty, of peoples to self-determination, and of persons of different race to individual rights, which before their contact with Europe played little or no part in their experience.[128]

Critical scholars targeted Bull's absorption thesis, his openness to the moral possibility of international society,[129] and by implication, the English School's counter construction of a value-oriented—not simply a materially and hegemonically-oriented—"civilized" international society. Some critical theorists acknowledged the contributions of the English School and grounded their work within the sphere of international society,[130] however their structuration of imperialism discourse warranted an emphasis on praxis and forward-leaning strategies to counter hegemony, not the substitution of a doctrinal or ideological imperialism draped in the form of messianic universalism.[131] Laden with historicist leanings and liberalism's pretention of progress, the English School offered appeals to rationalism and solidarism,[132] supported by an academic nod in the direction of interdisciplinarity. The nineteenth century standard

125 Barry Buzan, *From International System to International Society: Structural Realism and Regime Theory Meet the English School*, 47 Int'l Org. 327, 349 (1993).

126 *Id.* at 327.

127 Hedley Bull on International Society 4, 5 (Kai Alderson & Andrew Hurrell eds., 2000).

128 *Id.* at ix.

129 Dunne, *supra* note 112.

130 Robert W. Murray, *An Introduction to the English School of International Relations*, E-Int'l Rel. (Jan. 5, 2016), http://www.e-ir.info/2016/01/05/an-introduction-to-the-english-school-of-international-relations/ (noting, emancipation theory, globalization theory, neo- or poscolonial theory, and postmodernism).

131 *See* Weinert, *supra* note 119, at 91.

132 *See* Andrew Linklater & Hidemi Suganami, The English School of International Relations: A Contemporary Reassessment 259–61 (2002).

emphasized the primacy of the European viewpoint,[133] which connected to the Latin Church and Roman law,[134] and the "binary distinction" between the emerging members of international society and those states received into the European "club."[135]

English School associate, Gerrit Gong, noted that the possibility of enforcing international club membership norms globally "became a reality for the first time during the nineteenth century as the European international system expanded."[136] Despite its "bad name," which included for Hedley Bull descriptions of domination, exploitation, unjust treatment, and arrogance,[137] the European standard of civilization imparted processual complexities beyond the litany of criticisms characterizing it as a presumptuous and insulting condition. Membership in this club, according to Bull and Gong, required satisfaction of performance standards—the protection of basic rights, transparency and efficiency in administration, adherence to international law and judicial administration, conformity to the practices of diplomatic exchange, and avoidance of odious and gross violations of human rights.[138]

English School adherents recognized civilization's transcendent, human quality, "which seem[s] to operate on human affairs by a species of chemistry."[139] Jackson argued it was possible for culturally diverse European and non-European political communities to come together as at least notionally in the first universal society of state.[140] Turgot (1727–1781), Saint-Simon (1760–1825), Hegel (1770–1831), and Savigny (1779–1861) had forged history's directional path of progress. Linklater noted that European expansion of the idea of international order could not have taken place without recognition of its treatment of colonial peoples.[141] Discussions of this standard of civilization also would carry into the twentieth century with the writings of Max Weber (1864–1924), and his conclusion that modern legal thought passed through earlier

133 *See* Alexander Orakhelashvili, *The Idea of European International Law*, 17 Eur. J. Int'l L. 316 (2006).

134 Wilhelm G. Grewe, Epochen der Völkerrechtsgeschichte 520–21 (1984). *See also* Herbert Butterfield, Christianity, Diplomacy, and War, *supra* note 63, at 81.

135 Carsten-Andreas Schulz, *Civilisation, Barbarism and the Making of Latin America's Place in 19th Century International Society*, 42 Millennium 837, 838 (2014).

136 Gong, *supra* note 48, at xi.

137 Hedley Bull, *Foreward* to Gerrit W. Gong, The Standard of "Civilization" in International Society, at vii (1984).

138 *See id.* at viii. For Gong's more detailed expression of the five requirements establishing the standard of civilization, see Gong, *supra* note 48, at 14–15f.

139 Butterfield, Christianity, Diplomacy and War, *supra* note 63, at 79.

140 Jackson, *supra* note 104.

141 *See generally* Linklater, *supra* note 105.

phases of oracular and "magically conditioned formalism and irrationality into increasingly specialized juridical and logical rationalization and systematization."[142] Norbert Elias' sociological analysis of the globalized civilizing *process* noted socially instilled (or sociogenic) constraints on cruel behavior,[143] invigorating the concept of civilization as detachable from simplistic conditions of "Western triumphalism"[144] or paternalism.[145] Linkletter argued that members of the English School—principally Herbert Butterfield and Martin Wight—separated the civilizing process of improvement from its Eurocentric intonations and pejorative connotations in ways "broadly similar to Elias' use."[146] Indeed, Butterfield emphasized that the historical process resulted from a "continual interplay and perpetual collision" of interests.[147] Similarly, Linklater noted members of the English School separated the notion of civilization in world politics from the nineteenth century "derogatory connotations" about which they were well aware. Their project was to "describe shared understandings about the need for constraints on force and for sensitivity to the cultural preferences and political interests of others."[148] Unlike Huntington's general thesis, which portrayed civilizations as coherent and monolithic, oriented around the dispositional tendency to clash,[149] Peter Katzenstein and others focused on the civilization standard's discrete, pluralistic, weakly institutionalized make-up, even questioning the coherence of the concept, marked as it is by multiple actors, traditions, and processes.[150] If Huntington's dispositional analysis "succeeded brilliantly" in securing a new paradigm for world politics, Katzenstein cautioned that his analysis was factually wrong and empirically unsupported: "most of the world's violent clashes occur[] within rather than between different civilizaitions."[151]

142 1 Max Weber, Economy and Society 34 (1968).

143 *See generally* Norbert Elias, The Civilizing Process: Sociogenetic and Psychogenetic Investigations (2000).

144 Andrew Linklater, *Norbert Elias, The "Civilizing Process" and the Sociology of International Relations*, 41 Int'l Pol. 3, 11 (2004) [hereinafter Linklater, *Norbert Elias*]; Linklater, *supra* note 107, at 49 (noting that "[l]eading English School theorists have pointed to success in creating a level of 'civility' that spans the differences between the former colonial powers and the colonised peoples.").

145 *See* Hobson, *supra* note 59, at 6.

146 *See generally* Linklater, *Norbert Elias*, *supra* note 144, at 5.

147 Herbert Butterfield, The Whig Interpretation of History 41 (1931).

148 Linklater, *Norbert Elias*, *supra* note 144, at 6.

149 *See* Peter J. Katzenstein, *A World of Plural and Pluralist Civilizations: Multiple Actors, Traditions, and Practices*, *in* Civilizations in World Politics: Plural and Pluralist Perspectives 6–7 (2009).

150 *See id.* at 7, 24 (multiple actors), 29 (multiple traditions), 32 (multiple processes).

151 *See id.* at 7 ("succeeded brilliantly"), 8 (lack of empirical support).

Varied diachronic treatments of the standard of civilization thesis made it prone to historical abridgment. Onuf, with his brother, Peter, recounted that the "*civilized* nation[] became one of the nineteenth century's most familiar turns of phrase," coruscating first across the Enlightenment philosophies of mid-eighteenth century thinkers such as Adam Smith (1723–1790), David Hume (1711–1776), and Jean-Jacques Rousseau (1712–1778), then continuing its genealogical spread with the nineteenth century writings of Auguste Comte (1798–1857) and John Stuart Mill (1806–1873), and entering the landscape of international law principally through Emmerich Vattel (1714–1767) and Francis Lieber (1800–1872), with his military instructions to officers in the field of battle, and with the validating intervening influence of Henry Wheaton (1785–1848).[152] Wheaton elaborated on Vattel's separation of internal and external sovereignty, holding that "European nations constituted a society, and thus a moral world, within which nations are equally free to pursue their interests within the limits set by international law." As the author of the immensely influential *Elements of International Law*,[153] he reinforced United States membership in this European international law as a "nation[] of European descent."[154] This relativism was expressed in his defining text. "Is there a uniform law of nations?" wrote Wheaton, "There certainly is not the same one for all the nations and states of the world. The public law ... is limited to the civilized and Christian people of Europe or to those of European origin."[155] To Wheaton, civilization and Christianity provided the dual pathways integrating the Americas into the European international legal order.

152 *See* Nicholas Onuf & Peter Onuf, Nations, Markets, and War: Modern History and the American Civil War 79–84 (2006).

153 Wheaton's treatise was the first tome devoted entirely to international law in the English language. It went through twelve English language editions and was translated into French, Spanish, Italian, Chinese, and Japanese. The Chinese translation, facilitated by the Qing Government, was the first known published Chinese translation of a western work on international law. Jianming Shen, *The Relativity and Historical Perspective of the Golden Age of International Law*, 6 Int'l Legal Theory 15, 30 (2000). Onuf noted no "writer exceeded [Wheaton] in influence for at least three decades" and his treatise "is famous for being the first translation of any international legal treatise into a non-European language." Onuf, *supra* note 41, at 4.

154 Henry Wheaton, *Preface to the Third Edition* of Elements of International Law, at xx (1846).

155 Henry Wheaton, Elements of International Law 57 (1836). Onuf and Onuf note the phrase *civilized nations* dates from the mid-eighteenth century and that Wheaton's usages of "terms such as *Christian* and *civilized* is, at least in some measure, an incidental effect of the way he corroborated the specifically European ancestry and reach of international law" with ties to the Latin Church and to Roman law, not that Wheaton "was entirely free of Eurocentric pretensions." Onuf & Onuf, *supra* note 152, at 66.

Although admired as an important catalyst for the spread of liberal internationalism, Wheaton's attitude encapsulated a sentiment of North American superintendency over Latin American that would grow over the course of the nineteenth century. Elements of virility masculinized civilization discourse, as embodied by Roosevelt's requirement of the "strenuous life" to advance civilization.[156] Roosevelt's challenge for individuals and for nations was to rise to meet the hazards of the "great game," or in Root's summary of Roosevelt's diplomatic perspective, to "view[] each international question against the background ... along which particular civilizations advance or decline."[157] By the end of the nineteenth century, the prevalence of superiority marked a commonplace attitude among North Americans. Root expressed the racial stereotypes, which Jessup noted comprised "the typical attitude of official Washington toward the Latin Americans when Root became Secretary of State."[158] In his famous dispatch, "A Vindication of Cuba" (1889),[159] written while in exile in New York City, Cuban poet and patriot, José Martí complained against the "vulgar jingoism" and "rampant ignorance" of the United States that had spilled across the pages of popular North American presses.[160] Animated by the call to annex Cuba, as presented on the pages of the influential *Manufacturer* of Philadelphia, Martí objected to aspersions cast against the "helpless" "idle" "effeminate" Cuban character.[161] These disparaging remarks supported the self-fulfilling conclusion that Latinos were "[u]nfitted by nature ... to discharge the obligations of citizenship in a great and free country." Moreover, Martí cautioned that "honorable motives" of some Cubans themselves, spellbound by the narrative of progress and liberty espoused by the United States—which Martí himself openly admired[162]—must not affirm the rhetorical allure of equality that troubling hemispheric developments did not support.

156 Gail Bederman, Manliness & Civilization: A Cultural History of Gender and Race in the United States, 1880–1917, at 171 (1995).

157 *Id.* at 196 (quoting Root's view of Roosevelt's diplomatic objectives).

158 1 Philip C. Jessup, Elihu Root, 1845–1909, at 468 (1938) (referring to Latins as "those Dagos").

159 José Martí, *A Vindication of Cuba* [letter to the editor of the Evening Post (Mar. 23, 1889)], *in* The Latino Reader: An American Literary Tradition from 1542 to the Present 99–104 (Harold Augenbraum & Margarite Fernández Olmos eds., 1997).

160 *Id.* at 99 (vulgar jingoism/rampant ignorance).

161 *Id.* at 101.

162 *See id.* at 100 (calling the United States "the greatest [nation] ever built by liberty").

4 The Early Twentieth-Century Change in Nomos and Its Effect on the Language of International Law

Ending Spain's colonial empire in the Americas not only guaranteed for the United States long-sought-after interests in Cuba, hence much of the Caribbean, it projected the United States as an immediate Pacific power with its control over assorted Spanish Pacific colonial islanders. Secretary of State John Hay (1838–1905) issued a series of "Open Door" notes,[163] putting European powers and Japan on notice of the United States' insinuation into China, using the Grotian-inspired rubric of free trade and open ports to create possibilities for commercial ventures over which it had no established claim.

In Latin America, the Hay Pauncefote Treaty (1901) with Great Britain ceded control over any transoceanic canal to the United States, thereby functionally ending British nineteenth century designs over the isthmus. Applying a "Big Stick" foreign policy as the hemispheric power, Roosevelt articulated his eponymous corollary (1904) to the Monroe Doctrine. No longer complicated by shadings of ambivalence, purely defensive characterizations, or perceptions of military weakness, the Monroe Doctrine directed Europeans to recognize an American hemispheric sphere of influence among the newly independent American republics. It warned against European revanchism and forewarned of belligerent consequences of ever again intervening in the affairs of the Americas. The Roosevelt Corollary ensured that the unfolding late nineteenth century/early twentieth-century turmoil relating to the recovery of outstanding contract debt, mostly owed to European creditors, would resolve under hemispheric management. Evidence suggests the United States threatened to use force against Germany or Great Britain to end the Venezuelan claims crisis of 1902,[164] the incident that immediately gave rise to the articulation of the Roosevelt Corollary. The United States deputized itself as the guarantor that American states would fulfil obligations to international creditors through the exercise of the United States' international police power. However, the new *nomos* of the world precluded European hemispheric interference while

163 Hay's first Open Door Note was issued on September 6, 1899. His second note of July 3, 1900, urged foreign powers to respect China's "territorial and administrative integrity" as a means of preventing reprisals against the Boxer Rebellion. *See generally* Raymond A. Esthus, *The Changing Concept of the Open Door, 1899–1910*, 46 Miss. Valley Hist. Rev. 435 (1959) (discussing the notes and the changing interpretations attached to policy by Elihu Root and other United States policy-makers, principally over Japanese involvement in Manchuria).

164 Theodore Roosevelt, The Letters of Theodore Roosevelt (Elting E. Morison ed., 1954).

changing both the vocabulary and geographic rootedness of international law. Early nineteenth century integrationist and universalist themes, patterned after Henry Clay-inspired emphases on fraternity and federation, gave way within United States imperialist circles to more unilateralist orientations. The Root Doctrine attempted to harmonize the vocabulary of Clay and the geospatial *nomos* of Theodore Roosevelt into a new *Jus Publicum Americanum*.

Carl Schmitt famously wrote that a perfected form of imperialism required more than military and economic might. It required an application of international law that was capable of determining the content of political and legal concepts.[165] According to Schmitt: "A people is only conquered when it subordinates itself to the foreign vocabulary, the foreign construction [*Vorstellung*] of what law, especially international law, is."[166] Schmitt clearly identified the Monroe Doctrine and its attendant corollaries with the evolving subordination of the language of international law to United States hegemonic constructions. Indeed, speeches across the geographical spectrum during Root's 1906 tour embraced unifying aspects of that vocabulary, particularly ascriptions affirming the defensive purpose of the Monroe Doctrine. However, they could not completely dispel darker intonations. Schmitt would later write of the distortion of the Monroe Doctrine into an imperialistic principle of world trade, placing Schmitt at the forefront of a critical discussion that noted the "transformation of a spatially conceived principle of non-interference into a spatially undifferentiated general system of interference."[167]

In the hands of United States President Woodrow Wilson and his League of Nations proposal, Schmitt claimed the Monroe Doctrine would transpose again into a transnational and trans-ethnic world doctrine of political liberalism, Anglo-Saxon capital, and intervention; "a spatially undifferentiated [*raumlose*] and borderless extension of liberal democratic principles to the entire Earth."[168] By 1906, however, its distinctiveness remained bounded mostly by the Americas with the practice of intervention treaties such as the Platt Amendment.[169] However, its impact on world geography and politics was well in the making, and it required a reworking of the language of imperialism.

165 Carl Schmitt, *Forms of Modern Imperialism in International Law, in* Spatiality, Sovereignty and Carl Schmitt: Geographies of the Nomos 44–45 (Stephen. Legg ed., 2011).

166 *Id.* at 45.

167 Carl Schmitt, *Großraum versus Universalism: The International Legal Struggle over the Monroe Doctrine, in* Spatiality, Sovereignty and Carl Schmitt: Geographies of the Nomos 47–48 (Stephen Legg ed., 2011).

168 *Id.*

169 *See* Schmitt, *supra* note 165, at 39.

Recent scholarship has highlighted Latin America's multi-dimensional embrace of the Monroe Doctrine,[170] liberalism's complicity in the construction of empire,[171] the United States' imperial history as a settler society and a conqueror of vast continental territory,[172] along with and the practice of imperial anticolonialism that would result in at least thirty-four military interventions in the Caribbean and Central America over the course of the first three decades of the twentieth century.[173] This multi-dimensionalism formed, in part, because the language of the Monroe Doctrine, its geographic reach and application, as well as its expression as a defensive or interventionist policy, never coalesced in a uniformly understood or applicable way.

To Schmitt, the Greek word *nomos* referred to the physical world and its bounded, enclosed surface space.[174] Physical imageries of *nomos* pervade his writings; indeed, they are metaphorically *grounded* in his work, with references to location, soil, land, and terrain.[175] However, he associated the Monroe Doctrine with a new *nomos*. He labeled the Monroe Doctrine the most important example of the "global linear thinking of Occidental rationalism,"[176] and his reconceptualization of the geospatial regime of the Monroe Doctrine and international law broke free of its grounded hemispheric mooring lines and suggested the rhetoric and practices of unbounded space, which now has obvious applications to the boundless modern war on terror.[177] However, Schmitt concentrated at the time on reworking the landscape of imperium that had previously been tethered to the *rayas geográficas* of Alexander VI's fourth papal bull (1494). The resulting Treaty of Tordesillas between Spain and Portugal divided the Atlantic midway between the Azores and the West Indies along a meridian three hundred and seventy leagues west of the Cape Verde Islands. Newfound discoveries west and south of the meridian became

---

170 *See, e.g.*, Scarfi, *supra* note 83.

171 Andrew Fitzmaurice, *Liberalism and Empire in Nineteenth-Century International Law*, 117 Am. Hist. Rev. 122 (2012); Anghie, *supra* note 47 ; Koskkeniemi, *supra* note 1; Uday Mehta, Liberalism and Empire: A Study in Nineteenth-Century British Liberal Thought (1999); Jennifer Pitts, A Turn To Empire; Karuna Mantena, Alibis of Empire (2010) Duncan Bell, Reordering the World (2016).

172 J. Pitts, *Political Theory of Empire and Imperialism*, 12 Annual Rev. Pol. Sci. 212 (2010).

173 Greg Grandin, Empire's Workshop: Latin America, the United States, and the Rise of the New Imperialism 20 (2006).

174 François Debrix, *The Virtual Nomos?*, *in* Spatiality, Sovereignty and Carl Schmitt: Geographies of the Nomos 220 (Stephen Legg ed., 2011).

175 *Id.*

176 Schmitt, *supra* note 64, at 286.

177 Peter Stirk, *No Peace Beyond the Line*, *in* Spatiality, Sovereignty and Carl Schmitt: Geographies of the Nomos, 277 (Stephen Legg ed., 2011).

the property of Spain; territory to the east would belong to Portugal. The rootedness of possessing the earth's geo-space would remain in subsequent formulations,[178] but Schmitt regarded the political inauguration of the Monroe Doctrine (not simply its rhetorical expression in 1823), as an example of epochal change; a turning point in the continuum of global linear thinking. He wrote:

> No sooner had the contours of the earth emerged as a real globe—not just sensed as myth but apprehensible as fact and measurable as space—than there arose a wholly new and hitherto unimaginable problem: the spatial ordering of the earth in terms of international law.[179]

5 The Monroe Doctrine's Rhetorical Inversion

Within this context of epochal change, an inversion of the language of imperialism took place. Historian Jay Sexton attributed this inversion to the rhetorical practices of "so-called large policy men"—turn of the twentieth century United States imperialist statesmen such as Roosevelt, Henry Cabot Lodge, and naval strategist, Alfred Thayer Mahan.[180] Others included Leonard Wood, commander of Roosevelt's mounted rifle regiment, the Rough-Riders, who also served as Military Governor of Cuba and Governor General of the Philippines. Richard Immerman added to the list of America's "first imperialists": Stephen Luce (1827–1917), Henry Adams (1838–1918), John Hay, and Elihu Root.[181] They steered clear of the Monroe Doctrine term because it contradicted their rationale for colonial expansion. They romanticized the near history of the United States' rise to primacy, employing their own variant of whiggish thinking—the directional and progressive logic of exceptionalism, cosmopolitanism, obligation, and administrative efficiency.[182]

Invokers of the Monroe Doctrine, however, tended to be the older generation of anti-imperialists, for whom "the Monroe Doctrine symbolized an imagined tradition of nonentanglement and unalloyed anticolonialism."[183] These

178 *See id.* at 276.

179 Schmitt, *supra* note 64, at 286.

180 Jay Sexton, The Monroe Doctrine: Empire and Nation in Nineteenth-Century America, 212–13 (2011).

181 Richard H. Immerman, Empire for Liberty: A History of American Imperialism from Benjamin Franklin to Paul Wolfowitz 134 (2010).

182 *See* Sexton, *supra* note 180, at 212.

183 *Id.* at 214.

older advocates embraced core, Progressive era domestic objectives, which between the 1890s and 1920s promoted labor and civil service reform, "Free Silver" instead of the fixed money supply of the gold standard, and universal suffrage. Michigan Governor Hazen Pingree (1840–1901), reformer and Nobel laureate, Jane Addams (1860–1935), and South Dakota Senator Richard Pettigrew (1848–1926) supported the Progressive banner and anti-imperialist views, but their movement did not influence foreign policy,[184] due to important points of contact between progressivism's principles an imperialism's objectives.[185] William Leuchtenburg argued "the Progressive movement suffered from a contradiction between humanistic values and nationalist aspirations."[186] It supported Roosevelt's big navy initiative,[187] stood silent in the face of Taft's Dollar Diplomacy,[188] and generally aligned with the results achieved rather than the means employed to secure foreign policy.[189] The spirit of David Croly's New Nationalism, as expressed in his influential book, *The Promise of American Life* (1909), elevated the national interest over sectarian or interest group politics during this time. For Croly, political community had to be a recast on a national scale.[190] Croly applied Comtean scientific principles over Jefferson's "unlimited faith in the American people,"[191] advocated strong institutional government in the Hamiltonian tradition, and greatly informed Roosevelt's worldview.[192] The receptive audiences of South American elite embraced this latter view for the republican ideals it harbored, for the elusive federation sentiments it

184 William E. Leuchtenburg, *Progressivism and Imperialism: The Progressive Movement and American Foreign Policy, 1898–1916*, 39 Miss. Valley Hist. Rev. 483, 485–87 (1952).

185 *Id.* at 500 ("imperialism and progressivism flourished together because they were both expressions of the same philosophy of government, a tendency to judge any action not by the means employed but by the results achieved.").

186 Leuchtenburg, *supra* note 184, at 503.

187 *Id.* at 488, 495. Roosevelt aggressively invigorated United States naval power during his presidency, emphasizing its "prime importance" and the need to build up sea power in his speech to the graduating class of the Naval Academy on May 2, 1902. *See* Theodore Roosevelt, *To the Graduating Class of the Naval Academy, Annapolis, Maryland, May 2, 1902*, Almanac Theodore Roosevelt, http://www.theodore-roosevelt.com/images/research/txtspeeches/4.txt.

188 Leuchtenburg, *supra* note 184, at 490–91, 492.

189 *Id.* at 500.

190 Michael J. Sandel, *The Procedural Republic and the Unencumbered Self*, 12 Pol. Theory 81, 92 (1984).

191 *See* Eric F. Goldman, Rendezvous with Destiny 201, 202 (1972) (on Comte); *see also* Edward A. Stettner, Shaping Modern Liberalism: Herbert Croly and Progressive Thought 40 (1993) (on devaluing Jefferson and his "unlimited faith in the American people.").

192 According to Leuctenburg: "Roosevelt was more deeply moved by Croly's book than by anything he had read since the early Alfred T. Mahan." Leuchtenburg, *supra* note 184, at 501.

projected, and for the fortified emphases on sovereign equality it referenced. Diverging interpretations of the Monroe Doctrine began to take shape.

Sexton argued that Root became the "point man" for Roosevelt's large policy formulation because he could walk the Monroe Doctrine's "tightrope." He could also speak "loudly enough so that European governments could hear, but not so loudly as to provoke critics at home."[193] Different interpretations of the Monroe Doctrine would also form among Latin Americans. The diverging descriptions of the Monroe Doctrine and its spatial reorientation as a rational trope for liberal internationalism (more critically assessed as imperial anticolonialism)—as opposed to a geospatial border construct promoting defensive hemispheric security—produced an outcome for international law that understandably conflated legal terminology and geospace, particularly with regard to the concept of shared sovereignty.

This conflation is not easily maintained in international law, nor is it well understood. Root's unreconciled embrace of imperial and fraternal orientations of the Monroe Doctrine naturally contributed to the problem but elliptically also served as the fount for a Central American solution to a sovereignty dispute involving the Gulf of Fonseca. Here, Central American jurists refused to subordinate usages to the foreign vocabulary of the Monroe Doctrine, as implied by North American large policy men and as idealized by Pan-Americanists. They forwarded another construction principally influenced by El Salvadoran diplomats and international legal scholars – using the condominium argument as the vehicle to advance their claim.

193 *Id.* at 231.

CHAPTER 5

The Central American Court of Justice and the Monroe Doctrine

Divergent understandings of the Monroe Doctrine revealed international law's uncomfortable association with dual aspects of sovereignty—*dominium* (ownership) and *imperium* (the power to rule)—elements not easlily reconciled. A forced cohabitation of the concepts arose in the shared sovereignty judgment of the CACJ in its 1917 treatment of the ownership of the Gulf of Fonseca, which fronts the coasts of El Salvador, Honduras, and Nicaragua. Here, the CACJ historically validated the concept of condominium and applied it over the objection of Nicaragua. Its judgment meant to forestall the imperial attempt by United States large policy men to secure the geospatial reordering of the transisthmian politics of Central America. However, the CACJ judgment reshaped the idea of common ownership to checkmate rising United States hegemonic manipulations of the doctrine of sovereign equality. It distorted condominium's meaning in international law to secure an outcome that outpaced the intentions of the parties and contributed to the early death of the CACJ, the world's first international court. Today, condominium's devalued and doctrinally maligned legal identity reflects the significance of its early twentieth century juridical treatment. Whiggish international legal history overlooks this one episode involving the spatial (re)ordering of the earth. The 1917 CACJ judgment regarding the ownership of the Gulf of Fonseca indirectly involved a Central American construct of the Monroe Doctrine and serves to this day as an unusual example of a shared sovereignty or condominium solution to problems residing at the intersection of land-sea disputes.

In ways underexplored and underappreciated, the case also highlights the non-linearity of international law's development in the Americas. While it may provide an interesting template for future coparcener arrangements, the CACJ's crafted solution depended on laws and facts that did not exist. The CACJ re-worked the good old story of hemispheric unity, with added progressive references to patrimonial and community of interest standards in an attempt to dress up sovereign equality in the manaquin of enlightened anti-imperialism. Its judgment subordinated the established language of shared sovereignty to a new *nomos* of geospatial thinking that extended condominium's application to pelagic space. The CACJ altered the rhetoric and practice of international law in this newly rationalized application, creating its own counter-narrative to defensive or triumphal applications of the Monroe and Root Doctrines.

 | DOI:10.1163/9789004379510_006

1 The Idea of Condominium

Debates about sovereignty in international law range from its permeability,[1] genealogy,[2] and construction,[3] to its continuing relevance as a unitary concept.[4] Grotius recognized divisible sovereignty in his unpublished manuscript, *De Jure Praedae Commentarius*[5] while elaborating Just War doctrine, and again in *De Jure Belli ac Pacis* (1625) to distinguish private and public war.[6] Discussions continue to this day on sovereignty's situationally specific context.[7]

Conjoined sovereignty—condominium—however, is much less discussed, although it makes appearances in conversations about the global commons,[8] common pool resource theory,[9] the law of the sea,[10] and the unfolding world of cyberspace.[11] Oppenheim,[12] Verzijl,[13] Kelsen,[14] and Lauterpacht[15] noted its

1 *See, e.g.*, Larry Catá Backer, *The Structural Characteristics of Global Law for the 21st Century: Fracture, Fluidity, Permeability, and Polycentricity*, 17 Tilburg L. Rev. 177 (2012).

2 Jens Bartelson, A Genealogy of Sovereignty (1995).

3 Nicholas Greenwood Onuf, World of Our Making: Rules and Rule in Social Theory and International Relations (1989).

4 Eelco Nicolaas van Kleffens, *Sovereignty in International Law Five Lectures*, 82 Recueil des Cours 128 (1953).

5 1 Hugo Grotius, De Iure Praedae Commentarius [Commentary on the Law of Prize and Booty] Ch. 7, at 68 (Gwladys L. Williams trans., 1950) (1604) (distinguishing public and private war). The *Commentarius* was never published during Grotius' lifetime. It came to light in 1864 and was published in 1868. Its famous twelfth chapter was reworked and published as *Mare* Liberum in 1609. In Mare Liberum's final pages, Grotius discussed divided sovereignty through the use of auxiliaries. *See* Hugo Grotius, Mare Liberum 1609–2009, at 153–55 (2009) (1609). Historian Robert Fruin made the connection between the reworked chapter and the unpublished manuscript. *See* Robert Fruin, An unpublished work of Hugo Grotius's (1925).

6 Hugo Grotius, The Rights of War and Peace in Three Books 53–54 (J. Barbeyrac trans., 1738) (1625).

7 Edward Keene, Beyond the Anarchical Society: Grotius, Colonialism and Order in World Politics (2002).

8 Garrett Hardin, *The Tragedy of the Commons*, 162 Science 1243 (1968).

9 *See, e.g.*, Elinor Ostrom, Governing the Commons: The Evolution of Institutions for Collective Action (1990).

10 Nico Schrijver, *Managing the Global Commons: Common Good or Common Sink?*, 37 Third World Q. 1252, 1256–57 (2016), (discussing the high seas and the deep seabed).

11 *See, e.g.*, Sean Kanuck, *Sovereign Discourse on Cyber Conflict under International Law*, 88 Texas L. Rev. 1571 (2009–2010).

12 1 Lasa Oppenheim, International Law: A Treatise (Peace) 220 (1905).

13 6 J.H.W. Verzijl, International Law in Historical Perspective 69 (1973).

14 Hans Kelsen, *The Legal Status of Germany According to the Declaration of Berlin*, 39 Am. J. Int'l L. 524 (1945).

15 1 Elihu Lauterpacht, International Law: Being the Collected Papers of Hersch Lauterpacht: the General Works 271–72 (Elihu Lauterpatch ed., 1970).

peculiar place in international law.[16] Historical but faded examples include Austria's and Prussia's joint rule over Schleswig-Holstein and Lauenburg (1864–66), Great Britain's and Egypt's condominium over Sudan (beginning in 1898), British and French joint rule over New Hebrides (beginning in 1906), Hungary's condominium over Bosnia and Hercegovinia (1909–1918), and the 715 year joint administration of Andorra by France and the Catalan Bishop of Urgell. Kelsen referenced the concept to present an *a contrario* argument. The sustaining dogma of sovereignty dominated the story of international law, not obscure counter instances of shared territorial title.[17]

Condominium-like associations have arisen among rivals, stimulating disputes as to whether the term appropriately applies. As we have seen, the United States and Great Britain jointly occupied the Oregon Territory northwest of the Rocky Mountains between 1818 and 1846. While each state retained equal rights of trade and settlement, the "vital question of sovereignty remained unsettled"[18] until pioneers, Manifest Destiny, and impending war with Mexico forced the resolution of this issue. Condominium discussions concerning Spitzbergen (later renamed Svalbard) took place in 1910, 1912, and 1914 in Christiania (now Oslo). Joint administration proposals circulated, including a 1912 idea establishing the territory as neutral and open to all, but administered by Sweden, Norway, and Russia. World War I interrupted discussions and new political circumstances following the 1919 Paris Peace Conference produced an agreement that problematically conferred "full and absolute sovereignty" on Norway and equal enjoyment and liberty of access provisions on all states parties to the agreement.[19] The legal meaning of these conjoined articles remains in dispute, as is indicated by Norway's increasingly isolated position relating

16 The CACJ recognized that condominium "is not common in the relations among nations," but it also recognized that "it is not an inconceivable or an isolated fact." It cited in support of this proposition publicists such as Bluntschli, Perels, Rivier, Nys, and Díaz Medina. It canvassed several historical examples to underscore the strong mutuality of state interest required for co-sovereignty to work and, oddly, included the 1876 condominium arrangement between Chile and Bolivia, which devolved into war three years later. *See El Sal. v. Nicar.*, CACJ, *Judgment of 9 March 1917*, 11 Am. J. Int'l L. 674, 712–13 (1917).

17 Hans Kelsen, *Absolutism and Relativism in Philosophy*, 42 Am. Pol. Sci. Rev. 906, 910 (1948).

18 Walter N. Sage, *The Oregon Treaty of 1846*, 27 Can. Hist. Rev. 353 (1946).

19 Treaty between Norway, The United States of America, Denmark, France, Italy, Japan, the Netherlands, Great Britain and Ireland and the British Overseas Dominions and Sweden Concerning Spitsbergen arts. 1–3, Feb. 9, 1920. The most obvious change in political circumstance affecting Spitzbergen's fate related to the absence of Russia and Germany from Paris Peace Conference discussions.

to the waters adjacent to the archipelago's territorial sea.[20] Condominium also retains significance in the international law of transboundary watercourses.[21] Here it has been analogized from the private law of Rome to express the community of interest standard, where the interests of *socii* (associates) created servitudes *pro indiviso communis*.[22]

Aside from riparian law, as noted, scholars tend to dismiss condominium as an historical relic.[23] This characterization may be unduly harsh. Shared sovereignty is fundamental to the idea of the global commons despite the dysfunctional tragedy of the commons famously presented by Garrett Hardin in the journal, *Science*.[24] Hardin's article remains among the most cited works in the social science canon.[25] Although skeptical of its sustainability as an economic concept, Hardin's thesis serves as a negative testament to the enduring currency of the condominium concept (framed in the vocabulary of the common heritage principle), which also has found expression beyond earth's terrestrial boundaries, as well.[26] However, condominium's reception into international law has never been complete and its identity and constitutive elements remain in dispute.

Given its historical treatment, and whatever future promise the concept may hold for the diminishing global commons, *the basis* for condominium's

---

20 *See generally* Christopher R. Rossi, *Norway's Imperiled Sovereingty Claim over Svalbard's Adjacent Waters*, 18 German L.J. 1497 (2017); Rachel Tiller & Elizabeth Nyman, *The Clear and Present Danger to the Norwegian Sovereignty of the Svalbard Fisheries Protection Zone: Enter the Snow Crab*, 137 Ocean & Coastal Management 24 (2017); Atle Staalesen, *Norway Takes Tough Line Against EU in Svalbard Waters*, Barents Observer (Jan. 25, 2017), https://thebarentsobserver.com/en/industry-and-energy/2017/01/norway-takes-tough-line-against-eu-svalbard-waters.

21 *See, e.g.*, Pulp Mills on the River Uruguay (Arg. v. Uru.), Judgment, 2010 I.C.J. Rep. 14, ¶ 281 (Apr. 20).

22 P. Van Warmelo, *Aspects of Joint Ownership in Roman Law*, 25 Tijdschrift voor Rechtsgeschiedenis 125 (1957).

23 *See, e.g.*, P. Schneider, *Condominium, in* 10 Encyclopedia of Public International Law 734 (R.L. Bernhardt ed., 1992).

24 *See* Garrett Hardin, *The Tragedy of the Commons*, 162 Science 1243 (1968).

25 *See In Memoriam: Garrett James Hardin*, U. Ca. Senate (noting the work was perhaps the most often cited paper about a biological principle and appeared in more than 100 anthologies). The article became one of the most requested in the subsequent history of Science, where it first appeared, http://www.sciencemag.org/site/feature/misc/webfeat/sotp/commons.xhtml.

26 *See generally* Carol R. Buxton, *Property in Outer Space: The Common Heritage of Mankind Principle vs. the "First in Time, First in Right" Rule of Property*, 69 J. Air L. & Com. 689 (2004) (discussing, inter alia, the common heritage principle within the frameworks of the Moon Treaty and Outer Space Treaty).

curious revival by the Chamber of the ICJ in the 1992 *Gulf of Fonseca* case[27] is worth reconsidering. In that case, the Chamber held that a condominium arrangement existed among three Central American countries over the waters of the Gulf of Fonseca adjacent to their Pacific Ocean coasts.[28] Except for the three-mile territorial sea, which remained under the exclusive sovereignty of El Salvador, Honduras, and Nicaragua,[29] the waters of the Gulf formed a joint inheritance[30] which was to be shared as a historic bay.[31] Each country enjoyed a single and undivided co-ownership interest,[32] which could not be divided unless there "[was] agreement to do so."[33] This *jus prohibendi* provision secured the status of the waters and their conjoined maritime ownership.

In dissent, the ICJ's most accomplished law of the sea scholar, Judge Shigeru Oda, thought that this idea of a pluri-State bay had no legal meaning.[34] Moreover, he argued that the description of the Gulf of Fonseca as a historic bay anachronistically created a legal identity three hundred years before the first legal usage of the term historic bay, around 1910.[35] According to Judge Oda, not until the 1917 Judgment had the Gulf of Fonseca ever been described as a historic bay.[36] The majority ruled, however, that the Crown of Castile handed down this coparcener arrangement after a three hundred year uninterrupted possession, passing title to the three Pacific coast states following the end of Spanish colonial rule in the Americas in the early nineteenth century.[37] The ICJ Chamber based its ruling on conclusions reached by the CACJ in 1917,[38]

27 Land, Island and Maritime Frontier Dispute (El Sal. v. Hond.: Nicar. Intervening), Judgment of Sept. 11, 1992, 1992 I.C.J. Rep. 4 (Gulf of Fonseca case).

28 *Id.* ¶ 418.

29 *Id.* ¶ 432.

30 *Id.*

31 *Id.* ¶ 432.

32 *Id.* ¶¶ 399–400.

33 *Id.* ¶ 409.

34 *Id.* ¶¶ 1, 733 (Dissenting opinion by Oda, J.). Oda's main area of emphasis as a scholar of international law is the law of the sea, beginning with his doctoral dissertation on "The Riches of the Sea and International Law." *See Judge Shigeru Oda: Bibliographical Note*, and *Judge Shigeru Oda: Select Bibliography*, *in* 1 Liber Amicorum: Judge Shigeru Oda, at xvii, xix (Nisuke Ando et al. eds., 2002).

35 Land, Island and Maritime Frontier Dispute, 1992 I.C.J. Rep. ¶ 11 (Dissenting opinion by Oda, J.).

36 *Id.* ¶ 27 (Dissenting opinion by Oda, J.).

37 *Id.* ¶ 400 (holding that the waters "had been under the single sway of the State from which [El Salvador, Honduras, and Nicaragua] were the heirs").

38 El Sal. v. Nicar., *supra* note 16, at 674.

the court Elihu Root's advocacy helped to create.[39] Uncritically, the ICJ dutifully affirmed the historical bay status of the Gulf of Fonseca established by the CACJ, whiggishly echoing an impressive litany of doctrinal authorities who had "never presented any justification for this lable outside the fact that the 1917 Judgment had so styled the Gulf."[40] One historical abridgment begat another, according to Judge Oda, leading to his whiggish lament that the juridical disregard of context created a spatial illusion of condominium in the Gulf of Fonseca both in terms of law and fact.[41]

Accounts disputing the serenity of the waters of the Spanish South Sea (Pacific Ocean) during the Crown's imperial rule call into question conclusions reached by the CACJ and the Chamber.[42] Indeed, *testigo ocular* (eye witness) accounts of the Spanish encounter with Mesoamerica generally require a healthy application of skepticism and suspicion.[43] As an example, the engraved title page to Bernal Díaz' acclaimed *Història verdadera de la conquista de la nueva España* (1632) portrays this abridgment of serenity. The cartouche depicting Spain's first encounter with the emperor of the Aztecs depicted Cortés, the Spanish conquistador, removing Montezuma's crown with one hand while manacling the compliant king of the Americas with the other.[44] Was it truly so? The narrative of Bartolomé de las Casas achieves its historical significance for presenting an early account of brutal terrestrial domination that successive juridical treatments whiggishly assumed had no connection to pelagic space.[45]

39 *See* Charles Ripley, *The Central American Court of Justice: Rethinking the World's First Court (1907–1908)*, 19 Diálogos: Revista Electrónica de Historia 47, 52 (2018) (quoting Root's 1907 letter to Costa Rica's Foreign Affairs Minister, Louis Anderson).

40 Land, Island and Maritime Frontier Dispute, 1992 I.C.J. Rep. ¶ 28 (Dissenting opinion Oda, J.).

41 *Id.* ¶ 39 (Dissenting opinion by Oda, J.).

42 *See, e.g.*, J. Esquemeling, Bucaniers of America: Or, True Account of the Most Remarkable Assaults Committed of late Years upon the Coasts of The West Indies, By the Bucaniers of Jamaica and Tortuga, Both English and French (1684) (canvassing the freebooting activities of Montauban, Sawkins, Coxon, Henry Morgan, and Basil Ringrose, among others; volume II, pt. iv additionally details the devastation wrought by Bartholomew Sharp, and others, in the South Sea); Raveneau de Lussan, A journal of a voyage made into the South Sea, by the bucaniers or freebooters of America, from the year 1684 to 1689 written by the Sieur Raveneau de Lussan; to which is Added, The voyage of the Sieur de Montauban, captain of the free-booters on the coast of Guiney, in the year 1695 (1698) (detailing his campaign against the Spaniards).

43 Matthew Restall, When Montezuma Met Cortés: The True Story of the Meeting that Changed History, at xxvii (2018).

44 *See id.* at xxiv (image), xxv–vi (discussion).

45 *See generally* Bartolomé de las Casas, Brevísima relación de la destrucción de las Indias (1552). De las Casas, moreso than any other Spanish colonial writer, became the object

The rationale supporting the application of condominium in that earlier case also presents an underreported example whiggish international law. It appears the judges resorted to triumphal straight-line analysis to cloak an anti-Monroe Doctrine judgment in a vocabulary at least rhetorically familiar and digestible to United States policy-makers. The CACJ thus adapted international legal concepts and conformed international law's hemispheric history to the overriding hemispheric concern of the time—a transisthmian oceanic canal. Using history with a mindset squarely focused on presentist circumstances, including United States intentions to militarize Central American waters, spelled disaster for the court. It also created a troubling challenge for condominium arguments as an alternative to the enduring dogma of sovereignty.

Condominium in the early-modern age of sovereignty presented an ambiguous if not paradoxical twinning of ideas. The idea of sharing sovereignty seems incongruous even today. Historian Jay Sexton noted a similar twinning of concepts with the Monroe Doctrine. The United States unilaterally asserted the shared sovereignty interests of the American continents by declaring that the Western Hemisphere was no longer open to European colonization and political interference.[46] Sexton noted, however, that the doctrine's elasticity and embedded vagueness contained lurking additives or "corollaries." These corollaries made its extension a never-ending building process, not of hemispheric solidarity *per se*, but of something less formed.[47] The Monroe Doctrine's pliability would impart multiple understandings throughout the nineteenth century. These understandings would appeal simultaneously to internationalists and imperialists, Pan-American federalists and United States isolationists, and international legal reformers and revanchists.[48] Borrowing from the revisionist view of William Appleman Williams,[49] Sexton detailed that the Monroe Doctrine's contribution to statecraft and international lawmaking could, in turn, support anticolonialism or imperialism. Fused, it simultaneously created another kind of incongruity: imperial anticolonialism—a nonintervention strategy that would grow into a policy of consistent intervention.[50] The hegemonic side-effect of coordinated opposition to European hemispheric meddling

of derision and attention in Juderías' attempt (almost four hundred years later) to dispel falsehoods pertaining de las Casas' depictions of the *leyenda negra*.

46 Jay Sexton, The Monroe Doctrine: Empire and Nation in Nineteenth-Century America 3 (2011).

47 *Id.* at 4.

48 *See id.* at 8.

49 *See infra.*

50 *See* Sexton, *supra* note 46, at 7.

resulted in the United States emerging as the imperial replacement for Old World colonial interests in the Americas.

Could the concept of condominium have developed politically and juridically as a prophylactic expedient against the rising imperial anticolonialism of the United States? A review of the CACJ's interesting but historically obscure treatment of condominium uncovers evidence suggesting this possibility. According to the rulings of the CACJ and the ICJ Chamber, the condominium concept arose in early nineteenth century relations in the Americas, alongside if not counter to the Monroe Doctrine and its emerging corollaries. Even if the two international judicial decisions express unwitting anachronistic thinking, in terms of applying non-chronological historical facts to the idea of condominium (as complained about by Judge Oda), multiple usages of condominium leading up to the 1917 CACJ judgment reveal politically expedient and divergent legal intentions, as well. Drawing conclusions about condominium's curious juridical appearance in the early twentieth century should take into account these multiple usages, as they counter the atmosphere of cooperation necessary to give highest legal expression to the idea and intertwine interventionist legal intentions that masqueraded in the form of interdependence. However, the case also validated a judicial construction of condominium that has imperfect and certainly sustaining whiggish appeal despite the circumstances behind its judicial validation.

2 The Deeper History: The Scramble for Honduras

Interest in the waters of the Gulf of Fonseca have a deep history. The waters drew the attention of Spanish conquerors relatively quickly, however first efforts centered on Atlantic coastal exploration. Christopher Columbus first identified Central America on his fourth New World voyage in 1502,[51] claiming it for the Crown of Castile. The prospect of an interoceanic route across the landmass was a matter of speculation, but it immediately came to Columbus' mind and he searched for it.[52] In 1513, Vasco Núñez Balboa "discovered" the

51 Linda A. Newson, Indian Survival in Colonial Nicaragua 92 (1987). He reconnoitered the Gulf of Honduras, Nicaragua, Costa Rica and as far south as the Isthmus. *See* F.A. Kirkpatrick, The Spanish Conquistadors 36 (1934).

52 *See* James Gustavus Whiteley, *The Diplomacy of the United States in Regard to Central American Canals*, 165 N. Am. Rev. 364 (1897). Columbus mapped the isthmus from Cape Gracias a Dios, in northeast Nicaragua to the Panamanian isthmus. *See* Thos. B. Atkins, The Inter-Oceanic Canal Across Nicaragua and the Attitude Toward It of the Government of the United States 4 (1890).

Pacific Ocean.[53] With indigenous guides showing him the way, he hacked his way across the cordilleras and jungles of modern-day Panama, setting his eyes on the Pacific Ocean and claiming it and all adjoining lands for Spain.[54] Within two decades, conquistadors had spread across the region in rivalrous pursuit of wealth, territory and the elusive waterway or land route coupling the two oceans.

By 1523, Charles v (reign: 1516–1556) began thinking about a canal, doubting the existence of a strait.[55] Overland routes were constructed at Tehuantepec in Mexico and in Panama (Darién) and Nicaragua.[56] By 1540, Sebastian Münster's woodcut of the first atlas of the Americas projected enticing and certainly imprecise pathways to Cathay, but they charted no navigable transcontinental route.[57] A Portuguese historian, António Galvão, published in 1550 plans to convert the Mexican, Darién and Nicaraguan land routes into canals,[58] and numerous accounts focused on making use of the Atrato and San Juan Rivers.[59] So began the Spanish occupation of Mesoamerica. Its three hundred year reign created across the New World administrative territories (viceroyalties and captaincies-general), administrative courts (*audiencias*), and a system of land and labor colonization (the *encomienda*) that granted the holders of title (*encomenderos*) tremendous regional power. It also created the *camino real*—the patchwork transport network of paths, roads, mule-trains, rivers, bridges, and ultimately oceans that would link the imperium north to south and east to west, convey imperial tribute, and commercialize the means of Spanish domination: gold and silver exports.[60]

---

53 *See* Robert J. Miller, *The International Law of Colonialism: A Comparative Analysis*, 12 Lewis & Clark L. Rev. 865 (2011). Aborigines showed him the way in a twenty-five day trek across the Isthmus of Darien. John T. Sullivan, Report of the Historical and Technical Information Relating to the Problem of Interoceanic Communication by way of the American Isthmus 8 (1883).

54 Miller, *supra* note 53, at 865.

55 E. Taylor Parks, Colombia and the United States, 1765–1934, at 178 (1935).

56 Hugh Gordon Miller, The Isthmian Highway 7 (1929).

57 Sebastian Münster, *Tabula Novarum Insularum*, Woodcut, 255 x 345 mm, Geographia Universalis (1540).

58 *See* Parks, *supra* note 55, at 179.

59 *See id.*

60 *See generally* Christian Strassnig, *Rediscovering the Camino Real of Panama: Archaeology and Heritage Tourism Potentials*, 9 J. Latin Am. Geo. 159 (2010); Gabrielle G. Palmer, *El Camino Real de Tierra Adentro*, vi S. N.M. Hist. Rev. 1 (1999). The conquistadors also unleashed the world's first pandemic. *See generally* Alfred W. Crosby, *Conquistador y Pestilencia: The First New World Pandemic and the Fall of the Great Indian Empires*, 47 Hisp. Am. Hist. Rev. 312 (1967).

The Spanish conquest spread quickly, following Hernán Cortes' landward entry in Veracruz on the Gulf of Mexico in 1519.[61] Historians dispute the reasons, but not that fact.[62] The Governor of Castilla del Oro (consisting of Nicaragua, Costa Rica, Panama and the northern part of Colombia), Pedrarias Dávila, orchestrated multiple expeditions to claim territory and peoples.[63] Gil González Dávila and Andrés Niño, set out from Panama in 1522 to chart the western coast of Nicaragua,[64] prompting Pedrarias to create obstacles "to gain Nicaragua for himself."[65] Cortés dispatched Pedro de Alvarado south from Mexico in 1523 to subjugate Guatemala,[66] while others, such as Alonso de Ojeca, Juan de la Cosa, and Francisco Pizarro came across the Caribbean Sea from Española (Santo Domingo) slightly earlier (1509), tending southward toward Peru.[67] Phenomenal Incan gold and silver lodes[68] would soon spur the enslavement and deportation of Mesoamericans southward to satisfy labor demands of the Spanish South American mining industry.[69]

---

61 The most famous first person accounts are provided by Cortés famous letters to Emperor Charles v (c. 1591–26); the recordings of his confessor and secretary, Francisco López de Gómara, in Historia general de las Indias (1552), and the retrospective but most highly acclaimed account of Bernal Díaz del Castillo, Historia verdadera de la conquista de la Nueva España (1632). *See also* Matthew Restall, When Montezuma met Cortés: The True Story of the Meeting that Changed History (2018) (emphasizing that Díaz was not an eyewitness to much that he described).

62 Intense discussion attaches to the genre of Spanish conquest studies, with disputes centering on William Hickling Prescott's "Great Man" thesis, which focused on the "commanding genius" of Hernán Cortés' subjugation of the Aztecs. *See* 2 William H. Prescott, History of the Conquest of Mexico with a Preliminary View of the Ancient Mexican Civilization, and the Life of the Conqueror, Hernando Cortés 17 (8th ed, 1843). For more on the debate, see Laura E. Matthew & Michel R. Oudijk, Indian Conquistadors: Indigenous Allies in the Conquest of Mesoamerica (1998); Matthew Restall, Seven Myths of the Spanish Conquest (2003).

63 *See generally* Pablo Álvarez Rubiano, Pedrarias Dávila: Contribución al studio de la figura del "Gran justador," gobernador de Castilla del Oro y Nicaragua (1944). *See also* Robert S. Chamberlain, The Conquest and Colonization of Honduras: 1502–1550, at 10 (1953).

64 Chamberlain, *supra* note 63, at 10.

65 *Id.*

66 *See* 2 Bernal Díaz del Castillo, Historia verdadera de la conquista de la Nueva España 348–49 (1939); An Account of the Conquest of Guatemala in 1524 by Pedro de Alvarado with a facsimile of the Spanish original 1525 (Sedley J. Mackie ed., 1924).

67 *See* Pablo Álvarez Rubiano, Pedrarias Dávila: Contribución al Estudio de la Figura del "Gran Justador," Gobernador de Castilla del Oro y Nicaragua Oviedo 15 (1944).

68 The account is famous, but worthy of recall: Pizarro captured the Incan Emperor, Atahualpa in 1532, who pledged and delivered upon a ransom to fill a large room with gold and two more with silver. *See* Ulrich Petersen, César E. Vidal & Donald C. Noble, *Preface to A Special Issue Devoted to the Mineral Deposits of Peru*, 85 Econ. Geo. 1287, 1287 (1990).

69 *See generally* Bartolomé de las Casas, Breve relación de la destrucción de las Indias Occidentales (1957) (providing among the earliest accounts of aboriginal mistreatment).

The economics of this colonization hinged on commercial transport, which would bring the geographic region of the isthmus clearly into focus. Writing to Emperor Charles V in 1524, Cortés detailed the logic and necessity of bridging the two oceans. He had established a ship building enterprise on the South Sea. The cost totaled more than eight thousand pesos of gold. He lamented the effort of portaging every sail, cordage, nail, and anchor over steep mountains and across great rivers at a distance of two hundred leagues or more from ports on the North Sea (Atlantic Ocean).[70] And then he had to do it all over again when a fire at the South Sea port destroyed all but the anchors.[71] The desire to find the best connection between the two oceans was one of the earliest objectives of Spanish domination. Cortés attached utmost importance to this venture because perfecting this passageway over the inhospitable terrain would open up new worlds, and he promised success would make Charles V "Sovereign of the World."[72]

By 1524, Cortés had ventured to Honduras[73] from his landward entry in Veracruz on the Gulf of Mexico in 1519.[74] Hernández de Córdoba (1475–1517) began moving from colonies established on the western shore of Lake Nicaragua northward into Honduras.[75] The functionally unworkable landscapes farther south and east of Nicaragua's Pacific coast made port access on Honduras' Caribbean littoral the earliest, most likely gateway to the West Indies and the Court of Castile.[76] Moving westward from the Caribbean, the Gulf of Fonseca seemed the obvious launching point to Asian emporia. Already, Cortés' Andalusian counterpart, Andrés Niño, had reconnoitered the Gulf of Fonseca in 1522,[77] searching the Pacific littoral for a waterway connection between the

70 The shipbuilding venture is found in Cortés' famous fourth letter to Charles V. *See* 2 Francis Augustus MacNutt, Letters of Cortés: The Five Letters of Relation from Fernando Cortes to the Emperor Charles 199–200 (1908).

71 *Id.* at 200 (fourth letter).

72 *Id. See also* Juan Antonio Márquez Domínguez & José Díaz-Diego, *The Nicaragua Interoceanic Grand Canal in the Central American Regional Development Context: Considerations for the Debate*, 66 Investigaciones Geográficas 27, 31 (2016).

73 An account of his disastrous expedition is found in his final, fifth letter to Charles V. *See* Herbert Cerwin, Bernal Díaz: Historian of the Conquest Ch. 5 (1963).

74 *See* Juan Ortiz Escamilla, *Presentación*, *in* Juan Ortiz Escamilla, El Veracruz de Hernán Cortés 16 (2015).

75 *See* Francisco Hernández de Córdoba, Biografías y Vidas, La Enciclopedia Biográfica en Línea, http://www.biografiasyvidas.com/biografia/h/hernandez_de_cordoba_2.htm; Chamberlain, *supra* note 63, at 11.

76 *Id.* at 10–11.

77 6 Hubert Howe Bancroft, The Works of Hubert Howe Bancroft: History of Central America, Vol. I: 1501–1530, at 139–40 (1883).

oceans; he named the basin for his patron, Don Juan Rodríguez de Fonseca, overseer of Spain's colonial interests in the New World.[78]

"The thrusts of Spanish expansion from several directions (over from Santo Domingo, down from Mexico, and up from Panama [and Nicaragua])," converged on Honduras, making it "one of the most perpetually turbulent provinces of the Indies."[79] Honduran historian Antonio Vallejo wrote that the disproportionate ambitions of the mandarins of Spanish conquest turned Honduras (and Nicaragua) into a land of complete anarchy.[80] Fifteenth and sixteenth century transport maps from Juan García de Hermosilla, Diego García de Palacio, Alonso Duarte and others confirmed Spanish plans for an interoceanic route from the Bay of Honduras to the Bay of Fonseca.[81] The first prospects of an artificial waterway across the isthmus appeared in 1529, but soon, Spain's monopoly over all land routes made consideration of an all-water route (however unachievable at the time) "strategically unwise because of its temptation to other powers from whose interference the overland routes were free."[82] Under Philip II (reign, 1556–1598), Spain began to safeguard its geographical knowledge of the isthmus. Philip feared that knowledge of a viable transisthmian watercourse would spur belligerent competition.[83] Mostly, he "feared that a canal might prove advantageous to the British, whose rising sea power already appeared a menace to Spanish dominance in the New World."[84] He forbade future searches under penalty of death, turning inward to the development of the *camino real*,[85] which Spain patrolled. This route cut through Honduras and linked the imperium from the viceroyalties of La Plata in South America to the continental portion of New Spain that spread across the Gulf of Mexico to California.

An intense intramural scramble for Honduras began, with rival Spanish expeditions converging simultaneously.[86] Competing Spanish *encomenderos*

78 Felipe Fernádez-Armesto, Columbus 101 (1991).

79 Chamberlain, *supra* note 63, at 1.

80 1 Antonio R. Vallejo, Historia Documentada de los límites entre la República de Honduras y las de Nicaragua, El Salvador y Guatemala 11 (1938), ("Las ambiciones desmesuradas de tales mandarins, llevaban a estos dos países [Honduras and Nicaragua] a la anarquía más completa").

81 *See* Charles L. Stansifer, *E. George Squier and the Honduras Interoceanic Railroad Project*, 46 Hisp. Am. Hist. Rev. 1, 2 n.4 and accompanying text (1966).

82 Miller, *supra* note 56, at 7 (first artificial waterway plan), and 8 ("strategically unwise…").

83 Sullivan, *supra* note 53, at 12.

84 Parks, *supra* note 55, at 139.

85 Sullivan, *supra* note 53.

86 Chamberlain, *supra* note 63.

contested colonial regulation and each other for decades.[87] The region's relatively high population density fed the Crown's enslavement needs for mining operations elsewhere, fomenting rebellion as well among Fonseca's Lenca-speaking island dwellers.[88] Three hundred years later, Honduras would still be "the political center of gravity," making its neutrality a major focus and result of the 1907 Central American Peace Conference,[89] and resulting Treaty of Peace and Amity.[90]

Imperial competition followed, however. By 1523, Portugal, England, and France had dispatched expeditions to the New World.[91] Welsh and English buccaneers, Dutch sea beggars, French corsairs, and later Scotsmen,[92] penetrated and plundered the isthmus in search of wealth and the best connection to a port on the South Sea.[93] In 1614, Dutch East India corporate vessels cruised the Pacific coast of the Americas, including the Gulf of Fonseca (Amapala Bay), plundering in hope of abducting the Viceroy of Peru.[94] Henry Morgan (1635–1688), the Welsh buccaneer, established a base of operations on the isthmus in 1671; William Patterson formed a Scottish colony of New Caledonia on Darién in

87 *See* Christopher M. White, The History of El Salvador 32 (2009) (citing competition among factions loyal to Dávila, Cortés and de Alvarado); Esteban Montes Gómez, Archaeology of the Colonial Period, Gulf of Fonseca, Eastern El Salvador 42 (2010) (unpublished Ph.D. dissertation, University of California, Berkeley) (on measures taken to avoid royal taxes).

88 Christopher R. Rossi, *Jura Novit Curia? Condominium in the Gulf of Fonseca and the "Local Illusion" of a Pluri-State Bay*, 37 Hous. J. Int'l L. 793, 806 (2015).

89 *Id.* at 817. For conventions and agreements pertaining to the work product of the Conference, which convened in Washington, D.C., Dec. 13–20, 1907, see 2 W.M. Malloy, *Treaties and Conventions Concluded at the Central American Peace Conference, held in Washington 1907, Between the Governments of Costa Rica, Guatemala, Honduras, Nicaragua and Salvador*, Treaties and Conventions of the United States 2391–2420 (1910).

90 *See* General Treaty of Peace and Amity Concluded at the Central American Peace Conference, of 1907 between Costa Rica, Guatemala, Honduras, Nicaragua, and Salvador, 20 December 1907, *in* 2 Treaties and Conventions of the United States, art. 3, 2393–94 (W.M. Malloy ed., 1910) (noting Honduras' "central geographical position" has made it "most often the theater of Central American conflicts" and declaring "from now on its absolute neutrality in event of any conflict between the other Republics"). *Id.* at 2393–94.

91 Atkins, *supra* note 52, at 5–6.

92 Sullivan, *supra* note 53, at 14–15.

93 Harold Mitchell, Europe in the Caribbean: The Policies of Great Britain, France and the Netherlands Towards their West Indian Territories in the Twentieth Century 1 (1963) (on Dutch Sea Beggars); The Caribbean: British, Dutch, French, United States (A. Curtis Wilgus ed., 1958) (presenting essays on respective areas of European control over the Caribbean).

94 Kris E. Lane, Pillaging the Empire: Piracy in the Americas 1500–1750, at 62 (Robert M. Levine ed., 1967).

1698;[95] various reports detail the 1680 crossing of the isthmus by a party of 400 filibusters portaging 18 large canoes.[96] European corsairs seriously degraded the Spanish colonial empire and forced costly defensive expenditures, disrupting Spanish commercial lanes by the second half of the sixteenth century.[97] Predation on the South Sea and the Spanish Main (the Central American coast to the northern coast of South America) extended well into to eighteen century, and included violent encounters around the Gulf of Fonseca.[98] And yet the abridged conclusion of the CACJ was that the waters of the Pacific South Sea avoided the terrestrial and Caribbean turmoil of conquest. In the midst of internecine warfare, the CACJ concluded a placid condition of condominium prevailed in the garden spot of Fonseca's littoral.

3 Nineteenth Century Developments

The first third of the nineteenth century produced a cautious balance between the promotion of unimpeded navigation (*mare liberum*, free sea)—construed politically as a hemispheric hedge against the dominance of the British navy—and the non-interference that the Monroe Doctrine projected. In 1835, the United States Senate resolved to make the right of navigation across any transcontinental canal "free and equal" to all nations.[99] However, Britain's colony at Greytown, meant that the object of North American diplomacy intended to neutralize this British threat. The illogic of rivals forming a joint protectorate over a neutralized commercial and strategic waterway raised "serious and unwelcome questions,"[100] with United States voices forewarning that such an enterprise "would be a source of future trouble."[101] Invoking the universal principle of freedom of the seas as ideological support for unilateralist expression

95 Parks, *supra* note 55, at 179; Richard Cavendish, *Founding of the Darien Colony*, 48 Hist. Today (Nov. 11, 1998), https://www.historytoday.com/richard-cavendish/founding-darien-colony.

96 Anthony de Gogorza, *Problem of Interoceanic Communication by Way of the American Isthmus, Before the American Geographical Society*, 21 J. Am. Geo. Soc'y of N.Y. 526, 537 (1889) (citing original reports at the Hydrographic Depot of Madrid, memoirs of the missionary, Rev. F. Jacobo Nalburger, S.J., and History of the Buccaneers (London)).

97 Horst Pietschmann, *Spanish Expansion in America, 1492 to c. 1580*, *in* 2 General History of the Caribbean, New Societies: The Caribbean in the Long Sixteenth Century 79, 97 (Peter C. Emmer & German Carrera Damas, eds., 1999).

98 *See* Kris E. Lane, Pillaging the Empire: Piracy in the Americas 1500–1750, at 78–83 (1976).

99 *U.S. Interest in an Interoceanic Canal 1835–1881*, GlobalSecurity.org, http://www.globalsecurity.org/military/facility/panama-canal-us.htm.

100 Miller, *supra* note 56, at 153.

101 *Id.* at 153–54 (quoting United States Secretary of State Hamilton Fish and others).

of the Monroe Doctrine marked the logic of imperial anticolonialism. It also created additional tensions by turning the principle into a hemispheric shibboleth while casting serious doubt on the character of neutralized guardianship.

However, this policy of *mare liberum*, as applied to free and equal access to a transisthmian canal, suited United States interests; it had no alternative at the time. The uneasy condominium arrangement with Great Britain over the Oregon Territory stirred larger concerns about British interests in California, perhaps resulting in its sale by Mexico to relive Mexico's indebtedness to Britsh bondholders.[102] Other rumors hinted that Britain was conspiring with Mexico to block Washington's annexation of Texas, as well.[103] Furthermore, the British had established a settlement, later the colony of British Honduras, on the Mosquito Coast beginning in the seventeenth century.[104] It would establish itself as a Caribbean power with the possessions of Bermuda, the Bahamas, Jamaica, Trinidad, and British Guiana. As Elihu Root observed: "when the United States turned its attention toward joining [its] coasts by a canal … it found Great Britain in possession of the eastern end of the route."[105] The convergence of interests in the isthmus brought the United States and Great Britain into potential conflict, as respective diplomats found themselves "diligently fishing in the murky waters of Latin American politics for a controlling position in respect to any possible Isthmian canal."[106] The Jackson (1829–1837) and Polk (1845–1849) administrations paid rhetorical tribute to the principle of free and equal right of navigation, however Manifest Destiny imparted a special meaning to transit through the canal. Root would later encapsulate the ethos of exceptionalism that unreflectingly attached to imperial anticolonialism. Although unconvincing to some in Honduras,[107] he held that "the nations of Central America had

---

102 Ephraim D. Adams, *English Interest in the Annexation of California*, 14 Am. Hist. Rev. 744 (1909); Lester G. Engelson, *Proposals for the Colonizaiton of California By England: In Con nection with the Mexican Debt to British Bondholders, 1837–1846*, 18 Cal. Hist. Soc'y Q. 136 (1939).

103 *See* Sam W. Haynes, *Manifest Destiny,* U.S. Mexican War: Prelude to War, http://www.pbs.org/kera/usmexicanwar/prelude/md_manifest_destiny.html; Lyon Rathbun, *The Debate over Annexing Texas and the Emergence of Manifest Destiny*, 4 Rhetoric & Pub. Aff. 476 (2001) (involving messages sent to the Tyler administration on the rumor Britain wanted to purchase Texas and emancipate its slaves).

104 *See* William David Setzekorn, Formerly British Honduras: A Profile of the New Nation of Belize 128 (1975) (discussing the first English settlement).

105 *See Senator Root Earnestly Advocates Arbitration: Extracts from Speech Before the U.S. Senate, January 21, 1913*, 10 Pac. Marine Rev. 7 (1912).

106 William Archibald Dunning, The British Empire and the United States 155 (1914).

107 Root was attacked on the pages of the Honduran daily, *El Cronista*, on October 26, 1912, accused of claiming the United States was "the greater and nobler Rome" intent on placing beneath [the United States'] flag all of Mexico, Central America and the Caribbean

no right to debar the world from its right of passage across the Isthmus ... We could not have taken it for our selfish interest ... it was only because civilization had its rights to passage across the Isthmus and because we made ourselves the mandatory of civilization to assert those rights that we are entitled to be there at all."[108] By century's end, the United States had assigned to itself the right of priority in terms of serving as the canal's mandatory power. This designation became increasingly clear after the United States Civil War (1861–1865),[109] and with the gradual decline of British hemispheric influence in the second half of the nineteenth century.

In 1848, the British had seized the Nicaraguan port of San Juan de Nicaragua, renaming the likely terminus of any canal Greytown. The indignant Nicaraguan government granted the United States an exclusive right to construct a canal or railway through Nicaragua. A United States agreement with Honduras then secured Tigre Island in the Gulf of Fonseca, prompting Britain to take possession first.[110] The Clayton-Bulwer Treaty (1850) between the United States and Great Britain responded to this growing competition by agreeing that any canal had to remain neutral as between the two.[111] Challenges to the Treaty arose almost immediately, as predicted, with vociferous complaints by Senator Stephen A. Douglas that that the Polk and Buchanan (1857–1861) administrations had abjured application of the Monroe Doctrine in view of Great Britain's encroachments on the Mosquito Coast.[112] John Bassett Moore noted these

---

islands. Root responded that the claims were "impudent forgeries," a view seconded by the editors of the *American Journal of International Law*. *See Elihu Root Before Latin America*, 7 Am. J. Int'l L. 144 (1913).

108 Miller, *supra* note 56, at vii (quoting Root).

109 Whiteley, *supra* note 52, at 365.

110 *See* Dunning, *supra* note 106, at 155–57 (discussing the political maneuvering between Britain and the United States leading to the conclusion of the 1850 Clayton-Bulwar Treaty).

111 *Convention for Facilitating and Protecting the Construction of a Ship Canal Between the Atlantic and Pacific Oceans, and for Other Purposes, Apr. 19, 1850, in* 5 Treaties and Other International Acts of the United States of America, 1776–1863, at art. 1, 671–75 (H. Miller ed., 1931–1948) (the Clayton-Bulwer Treaty). It was superseded by the The Hay-Pauncefote Treaty (1901), which also guaranteed open passage for all countries "on terms of entire equality." *See Ship Canal (Hay-Pauncefote Treaty)*, *in* 12 Treaties and Other International Agreements of the United States of America: United Kingdom and Zanzibar, 1776–1949, at arts. I, 258 (superseded), and III, 259 (equality) (C. Bevans ed., 1974) (reprint of the Treaty between the United States and Great Britain to Facilitate the Construction of a Ship Canal, signed in Washington D.C. on November 18, 1901).

112 *See* Stephen A. Douglas, *On the Clayton Bulwer Treaty, delivered in the Senate of the United States, March 10 and 17, 1853, in* Henry Martyn Fling, The Life and Speeches of Stephen A. Douglas 31ff (Martyn Fling ed., 1860) (debate with Senator Clayton).

complaints persisted throughout the Treaty's lifespan, and were then recast against the Hay-Pauncefote Treaty (1900), which provided for United States control over the canal but preserved the canal's neutrality.[113]

The mid-nineteenth century also brought new hegemonic interests—banana men, railroad and steamer-carriage tycoons, and North American filibusters,[114] none more reviled than the Tennessee insurrectionist, William Walker, who, briefly, assumed the Presidency of Nicaragua[115] before his ousting and later execution by firing squad in Honduras.[116] Proposals appeared to establish Nicaraguan or Honduran interoceanic connections along the general routes that Spanish explorers had surmised more than two centuries before.[117] American geographer and diplomat, George Squier, extensively surveyed the area. He discovered a route between the bays of Fonseca and Honduras that split between the Humuya and Goascoran Rivers and the "great chain of the [c]ordilleras."[118] Elsewhere he reported that the Gulf of Fonseca was "beyond dispute the finest port, or rather 'Constellation of Ports,' on the entire Pacific Coast of America" and the logical "western terminus" of a proposed interoceanic road.[119] Inter-coastal speculation had already drawn Nicaragua's attention to the transport baron, Cornelius Vanderbilt and a competing railroad venture

113 *Nicaraguan Neutrality in Light of History*, XX (No. 11) Literary Digest 327–28 (Mar. 17, 1900) (discussing John Bassett Moore's views).

114 The term filibuster, prior to 1900, most frequently applied to American mercenaries (adventurers) who participated in private military forces to unseat foreign governments with which the United States was at peace. The practice involved thousands of Americans before the Civil War and impacted Mexico and Nicaragua, and also Cuba, Ecuador, Canada, Honduras, and Hawaii. *See* Robert E. May, *Young American Males and Filibustering in the Age of Manifest Destiny: The United States Army as a Cultural Mirror*, 78 J. Am. Hist. 857, 875 (1991). *See generally* Lester D. Langley & Thomas Schoonover, The Banana Men: American Mercenaries and Entrepreneurs in Central America, 1880–1930 (1995).

115 *See* Charles H. Brown, Agents of Manifest Destiny: The Lives and Times of the Filibusters 346 (1980); T.J. Stiles, *The Filibuster King: The Strange Career of William Walker, the Most Dangerous International Criminal of the Nineteenth Century*, Gilder Lehrman Instit. Am Hist.: Hist. Now, https://www.gilderlehrman.org/history-by-era/jackson-lincoln/essays/filibuster-king-strange-career-william-walker-most-dangerous-i.

116 Robert E. May, Manifest Destiny's Underworld: Filibustering in Antebellum America 51 (2002).

117 *See, e.g.*, E.G. Squier, Preliminary Notes to a Report on the Proposed Honduras Interoceanic Railway (1854), *reprinted in* Hathi Trust Digital Libr., https://babel.hathitrust.org/cgi/pt?id=hvd.32044012941688;view=1up;seq=9.

118 *Id.* ("Letter from Mr. Squier to Mr. Edwards," May 1, 1833). *See also id.* ([Letter from] "Mr. Squier to Mr. Edwards," Apr. 10, 1853 (confirming a traversable pass through the cordilleras)).

119 E.G. Squier, Honduras Interoceanic Railway: With Maps of the Line and Ports; and An Appendix 12 (1857).

across Panama.[120] He secured a charter from the government for a monopoly transit route from San Juan del Norte (Greytown) to the Gulf of Fonseca.[121] Vanderbilt's land route across Nicaragua included an option to dig a canal at his personal expense, but the plan proved impractical.[122] In the mid-1850s, his Accessory Transit Company transported twenty-four thousand so-called "49ers of the California gold rush from New York to San Francisco across Central America. His route followed the San Juan River to Lake Nicaragua (by steamship) and then to the Pacific coast by stagecoach, short-circuiting the longer route around South America's Cape Horn.[123] When Frenchman Ferdinand de Lesseps' counter-conventional plan to establish a canal through Panama failed in 1889,[124] the United States moved in, securing protocols for canals with Costa Rica, Nicaragua, and Colombia; the 1903 Hay-Bunau-Varilla Treaty,[125] written by United States Secretary of State John Hay, secured the fate of United States dominance and the construction of the Panama Canal.[126]

4 The Immediate Background

In the CACJ case, El Salvador secured a favorable judgment against Nicaragua, which prohibited Nicaragua from implementing an agreement with the United States, the so-called Bryan-Chamorro Treaty (1914).[127] That Treaty granted

120 *See* Aims McGuinness, Path of Empire: Panama and the California Gold Rush 57–69 (2008).

121 Langley & Schoonover, *supra* note 114, at 6. *See also* Stiles, The First Tycoon: The Epic Life of Cornelius Vanderbilt 176 (2010).

122 William Oscar Scroggs, *William Walker and the Steamship Corporation in Nicaragua*, 19 Am. Hist. Rev. 792, 793 (1905). Scroggs also detailed the intrigues between rival interoceanic transport companies that helped dismantle, with Vanderbilt's involvement, the filibusters' political hold on Nicaragua. *Id.* at 805–07.

123 Frank McNeil, War and Peace in Central America 47 (1988).

124 *See* Sexton, *supra* note 46, at 179 (noting his scheme bucked conventional wisdom when he started digging in Panama rather than Nicaragua).

125 *See Convention for the Construction of a Ship Canal, Nov. 18, 1903, reprinted in* 2 Treaties and Conventions of the United States 1349–57 (W.M. Malloy ed., 1910) (Hay-Bunau-Varilla Treaty).

126 *See* Thomas M. Leonard, Panama, The Canal and the United States: A Guide to Issues and References 59–66 (1993).

127 *El Salvador v. Nicaragua*, CACJ, *Judgment of 9 March 1917*, *supra* note 38, at 730 (holding, in part, that "the Government of Nicaragua is under the obligation ... to reestablish and maintain the legal status that existed prior to the Bryan-Chamorro Treaty between the litigant Republics"). In a separate case, Costa Rica sued Nicaragua, and the CACJ ruled Nicaragua violated a prior consultation agreement when it concluded the Bryan-Chamorro

to the United States options to build an interoceanic canal and a naval base in the Gulf of Fonseca. It also granted to the United States a renewable ninety-nine year lease on islands in the Caribbean.[128]

The United States had no interest in exercising a Nicaraguan canal option. It had already secured treaty rights to build and control the Panama Canal in 1904,[129] which opened merely days after the countries signed the Bryan-Chamorro Treaty.[130] These rights had been obtained at Colombia's expense, from which Panama seceded with United States support.[131] Having secured control of the Panamanian isthmus,[132] the United States intended to block foreign powers, principally Japan[133] and Germany,[134] from building a competing inter-oceanic

---

Treaty. *See Costa Rica v. Nicaragua, CACJ, Judgement of 30 September 1916*, 11 Am. J. Int'l L. 181 (1917).

128 *Id.* Ch. VI (holding that Nicaragua had been bound by a preceding General Treaty of Peace and Amity with El Salvador and "could not, without authorization and consent of El Salvador grant a naval base in the Gulf of Fonseca" because the CACJ "was impressed ... with the common ownership pertaining to the three co-sovereigns, since none of them could properly dispose of its rights independently without affecting those of the other sovereigns, in view of the status of community in which the Gulf has been and is held"). Fonseca's base was never built; Little Corn and Great Corn islands were to serve as ports in the Caribbean.

129 John Major, Prize Possession: The United States and the Panama Canal, 1903–1979, at 9 (1993).

130 The Bryan-Chamorro Treaty was signed on August 5, 1914; the Panama Canal opened August 15, 1914. The United States Senate ratified the treaty on February 18, 1916, after the treaty had been renegotiated and replaced due to concerns about conferring protectorate status on Nicaragua. *See Proposed interoceanic canal treaty between the United States and Nicaragua, and protests of Salvador and Costa Rica in relation thereto*, Off. Historian, https://history.state.gov/historicaldocuments/frus1913/ch94.

131 Leonard, *supra* note 126, at 2.

132 The 1901 Hay Pauncefote Treaty between the United States and Great Britain abrogated an 1850 agreement (the Clayton-Bulwer Treaty) to end competition over a proposed canal through Central America. The 1901 Treaty granted the United States the right to pursue an isthmian canal. In June 1902, the United States Senate approved a canal option through Colombia (Panama; the Hay-Herrán Treaty), but Colombia's senate rejected it. Panama declared independence on November 3, 1903 and negotiated with the United States the 1903 Hay-Bunau-Varilla Treaty, which secured for the United States rights to build the canal. *See* Building the Panama Canal, 1903–1914, Off. Historian, https://history.state.gov/milestones/1899-1913/panama-canal.

133 *See* C. Harvey Gardiner, *The Japanese and Central America*, 14 J. Interamerican. Stud. & World. Aff. 15, 16 (1972), (noting rumors of Colombia's overture to enter into a canal treaty with Japan).

134 *See* Robert F. Smith, *A Note on the Bryan-Chamorro Treaty and German Interest in a Nicaraguan Canal*, 9 Caribbean Stud. 63–66 (1969); Melvin Small, *The United States and the German "Threat" to the Hemisphere, 1905–1914*, 28 Americas 252, 267 (1972), (noting "American sensitivity to German activities in countries near the Panama Canal").

route. The Bryan-Chamorro Treaty served this purpose, with provisions to militarize the waters on both sides of the isthmus to protect the Panama Canal and turn Nicaragua into a quasi-protectorate. Already, the Taft administration (1909–1913) had dispatched warships to Nicaragua's port at Bluefields to protect nationals and support the conservative uprising against the government of José Santos Zelaya (1853–1919).[135] In 1909, Nicaragua had made overtures to rival powers suggesting canal construction rights in exchange for loan guarantees.[136] Following Japanese corporate land ventures surrounding Magdalena Bay in Baja, Mexico,[137] suspicions mounted over foreign hemispheric intrusions. The United States Senate responded with the Lodge Corollary (1912). If the Monroe Doctrine made the European re-conquest of the Americas a *casus belli*,[138] the Lodge Corollary made non-American port ownership in the Americas a matter of grave concern to the United States.[139] This pronouncement caught the attention of European and Central American states because the United States' stature as a world power had coalesced following the Spanish American War.[140] As a newborn, two ocean power, the Lodge Corollary clearly brought into focus the strategic importance of the Gulf of Fonseca. A Honduran route would necessarily involve a Pacific terminus at the Gulf of Fonseca; a Nicaraguan route held out that prospect, but more likely would involve traversing the San Juan River Basin shared with Costa Rica, which runs from the Atlantic and connects to Lake Nicaragua, itself about twelve miles inland from

135 *See generally* Benjamin Harrison, *The United States and the 1909 Nicaragua Revolution*, 41 Caribbean Q. 46–63 (1995).

136 *See* Philip W. Travis, Reagan's War on Terrorism in Nicaragua: The Outlaw State 11 (2017).

137 *Land at Magdalena bay, Mexico, etc.*, 48 Cong. Rec. 9923 (1912).

138 *Transcript of the Monroe Doctrine (1823)*, Our Documents, https://www.ourdocuments.gov/doc.php?doc=23&page=transcript ("…the American … are henceforth not to be considered as subjects for future colonization by any European powers").

139 48 Cong. Rec. 10045 (1912) ("That when any harbor or other place in the American continent is so situated that the occupation thereof for naval or military purposes might threaten the communications or the safety of the United States, the Government of the United States could not see without grave concern the possession of such harbor or other place by any corporation or association which has such a relation to another Government, not American, as to give that Government practical power of control for national purposes.").

140 Nicholas John Spykman, America's Strategy in World Politics: The United States and the Balance of World Power 81–82 (1942) (noting that the Spanish-American War marked a turning point in U.S.–British relations and the recognition of the United States' hegemonic position in the Americas).

the Pacific Ocean.[141] Both possibilities placed the region at the epicenter of future, indeed ongoing international judicial proceedings.[142]

The Bryan-Chamorro Treaty foreclosed both Honduran and Nicaraguan canal prospects while providing an additional security guarantee—a Pacific coast naval port to defend the Panama Canal. The canal's Caribbean terminus was well protected, with United States naval bases located on its eastern seaboard, at Guantánamo Bay, Cuba, and later, at Roosevelt Roads, Puerto Rico.[143] For added security, the Treaty secured for the United States a ninety-nine year renewable lease for the construction of naval bases on Great Corn Island and Little Corn Island in the Caribbean. Fortifying the canal's perimeter also meant preventing a blockading power from controlling the canal's approaches.[144] However, the Pacific coast of Mesoamerica remained almost as wide-open and unsecure as the Spanish fleet had left it.[145] The establishment of a naval presence in the Gulf of Fonseca satisfied an important hemispheric military concern of the United States,[146] as much as the Panama Canal promoted United States commercial interests. Nicaragua also benefitted. Unlike El Salvador's port at La Unión, or Honduras' outlet at Ampala, Nicaragua had no safe anchorage in the Gulf of Fonseca, therefore no commercially viable outlet to the ocean other than what the United States proposed to build. The Treaty provided more than a pelagic corrective to Nicaragua's impoverished geo-political station within the Gulf of Fonseca; it tilted the Gulf of Fonseca's balance of

141 American transport baron, Cornelius Vanderbilt and his Accessory Transit Company utilized this route to supply east coast labor to California during the California gold rush. T.J. Stiles, The First Tycoon: The Epic Life of Cornelius Vanderbilt 176 (2010).

142 Six border dispute cases involving Central American states are currently before the I.C.J. *See* Pending Cases, International Court of Justice, http://www.icj-cij.org/docket/index.php?p1=3&p2=1.

143 *See Roosevelt Roads Naval Station*, Global Security.org, http://www.globalsecurity.org/military/facility/roosevelt-roads.htm (conceived of by Asst. Sec. of Navy Franklin D. Roosevelt in 1919, eventually becoming one of the largest in the world).

144 *See* John Major, Prize Possession: The United States and the Panama Canal 1903–1979, 156 (1993) (noting United States Admiral George Dewey's concern of securing approaches to the canal).

145 The U.S. Navy considered purchasing Cocos Island, one hundred miles south of the Panama Canal, but found it unsatisfactory. *See* Edward S. Kaplan, U.S. Imperialism in Latin America: Bryan's Challenges and Contributions, 1900–1920 (1998).

146 *See* U.S. Navy Department Memorandum, Dec. 3, 1913, portion *reprinted in* United States Department of State Bureau of Intelligence and Research, Appendix II, ¶ 11 (Report 668-AR, Aug. 17, 1983, declassified Nov. 28, 2012), *available at*: https://www.cia.gov/library/readingroom/docs/CIA-RDP08C01297R000400140013-1.pdf) (suggesting the "desirability of securing rights to use" the Gulf of Fonseca as naval bases "in view of the possibility of a canal being dug across Nicaragua at some future day").

power decidedly in Nicaragua's favor.[147] This prospect deeply troubled El Salvador, and condominium became its unlikely legal and political antidote.

5 Outcomes from the 1914 CACJ Judgment

The CACJ rendered its 1914 judgment against the backdrop of this deeply politicized history. Panama Canal political machinations impacted the decision as much as the intramural foreign relations of the Gulf of Fonseca disputants. The CACJ penned its own obituary by precluding Nicaragua from perfecting the Bryan-Chamorro Treaty with the United States. The ruling proved ruinous for the first international court in modern history. Nicaragua refused to honor the *jus prohibendi* decision, declared it null and void, and denounced the CACJ.[148] The progressive interwar jurist, Manley O. Hudson (1886–1960) noted in all but name that Nicaragua's exodus from the birth of modern adjudicative dispute settlement involved the "overshadowing" influence of the United States.[149] The CACJ, formed to represent "the national conscience of Central America,"[150] collapsed due to the influence of the state that played a key role in establishing it,[151] ending its brief, ten year existence.[152]

Two other outcomes are particularly noteworthy. The ruling fractured the forestalled but persistent idea of a Pan-American approach to international law. And it produced a condominium solution based on an atmosphere of hostility, quite the opposite sentiment of close cooperation stipulated by

147 Philip Marshall Brown, *Costa Rica v. Nicaragua*, 11 Am. J. Int'l L. 158 (1917) (noting "any naval base within [the Gulf of Fonseca's] limits would necessarily control the whole body of water.").

148 *See* Rosa Riquelme, *Latin America and the Central American Court of Justice*, *in* Latin America and the International Court of Justice: Contributions to International Law 39, 46 (Paula Wojcikiewicz Almeida & Jean-Marc Sorel eds., 2017) (discussing Nicaragua's denunciation of the CACJ).

149 M.O. Hudson, *The Central American Court of Justice*, 26 Am. J. Int'l L. 777–81 (1932).

150 Convention for the Establishment of a Central American Court of Justice, Dec. 20, 1907, *reprinted in* 2 Am J. Int'l L. (Supp.) 231–43 (1908) (art. XIII).

151 Thomas J. Dodd, *La corte de Justicia centroamericana, 1907–1918: Su legado, la defensa de derechos individuales*, 12–13 Revista de Historia 67, 77 (1986) ("La ironía suprema en la historia de la Corte es que aunque Estados Unidos jugó un papel clave en la fundación del Tribunal, también contribuyó a su destrucción en 1918.").

152 The 1991 Protocol of Tegucigalpa invigorated the movement to reconstitute the Court through the creation of the Central American Integration System (SICA-Sistema de Integración Centroamericana). *See* CACJ/CCJ: Central American Court of Justice, PICT (Project on International Courts and Tribunals), *available at*: http://www.pict-pcti.org/courts/CACJ.html.

Lauterpacht for the successful operation of shared sovereignty. These considerations are taken up in turn, although they are intimately conjoined.

6 The Fracturing of the Pan-American Consciousness

The CACJ ruling reworked the Lodge Corollary, but from a Central American, not North American, perspective. The CACJ held that the attempt to cede to a foreign power a military station in the waters of the Gulf menaced the regional peace, violated obligations established by the 1907 Central American Peace Conference held in Washington, D.C., and constituted a "most serious and transcendental" alteration of constitutional order.[153] The CACJ concluded: "The exercise of the public *auctoritas*, of *imperium*, or of jurisdiction, on the part of the [United States] fundamentally alter[ed] the normal life of the nation [El Salvador], because national territory and its exclusive possession are indispensable elements of sovereignty."[154] This rationale adapted the logic and language of the Lodge Corollary, but ironically turned it against its progenitor. The Lodge Corollary intended to thwart European revanchism but the CACJ reinterpreted it as a conspicuous obstacle to Central American regional aspiration.

This ruling marked an important break with rising Pan-Americanism and its converging association with the *Pax Americana*, or the worldwide predominance of the United States beginning early in the twentieth century, with antecedents tracing to the mid-nineteenth century. The *Pax Americana* focused in part on the Gulf of Fonseca as a means to secure the trade route across Central America. The North American concern against European encroachment catalyzed an incipient Central American legal movement, which had germinated in fits and starts beginning with emancipation from Spain and early attempts to create the Federation of the Center of America.[155] Important points of contact existed between the United States' *Pax Americana* and a burgeoning Pan-Americanism, particularly the characterization of European interests as predicated on old-order balance of power calculations. Powerful liberal voices in Latin America also sounded in support of the Monroe Doctrine. John Bassett Moore described its intent as a bulwark against "commercial monopoly

153 El Sal. v. Nicar., *supra* note 38, at 726.

154 *Id.*

155 Juan Carlos Puig, Les Principes du Droit International Public Américain 14 (Paris: Éditions A. Pedone, 1954) ("On puet dire qu'à partir de l'instant même de leur emancipation, les Nations américaines ont commence à proclaimer des principes du Droit des gens qui étaient différents et même opposes à ceux en viguer jusque là").

and political absolutism on the American continents," noting in this sense that "it found an enthusiastic response in popular opinion."[156] The influential Mexican minister to the United States, Matiás Romero, construed it as a safeguard against French intrusions in Mexico and as a means of promoting his government's liberal agenda of linking hemispheric economies (*La Reforma*); Argentina's Domingo Faustino Sarmiento embraced it as a catalyst for technology and knowledge exchange; Costa Rica's foreign minister interpreted it as a hedge against further territorial annexations;[157] and the influential Cuban politician and Judge of the Permanent Court of International Justice, Antonio Sánchez de Bustamante y Sirven surveyed its implications *vis-à-vis* a transmithian route,[158] and ultimately became associated with advocates of its hemispheric appeal.[159] However, any nascent sense of *communitas* or continental solidarity bore important qualitative differences as between the two, and also as distinguished from an awakening, indigenous sense of Latin Americanism.

Latin Americanism as a movement developed in the mid-eighteenth century and imparted a much more circumspect interpretation of the United States' hemispheric presence based on lessons of the annexation of Texas, the Mexican-American War,[160] and in terms of primordial distinctions of national character. Latin Americanism matured in literary and intellectual circles, with principal contributions from José Martí, José Enrique Rodó, and Rubén Darío.[161] Rodó, in *Ariel* (1900), noted North American virtues as identified by Tocqueville.[162] However, he recast historian Frederick Jackson Turner's frontier thesis of the independent American character[163] as a provincial, insatiable will to dominate.[164] Manfred Lachs (1914–1993) identified strains of this Latin American sensitivity in treatments of "extra-territorial privilege" in the international legal writings of the distinguished Venezuelan contemporary of Simón

156 Samuel Guy Inman, *The Monroe Doctrine and Hispanic America*, 4 Hisp. Am. Hist. Rev. 644 (1921), (quoting Moore).

157 *See* Sexton, *supra* note 46, at 145–47.

158 Antoine S. de Bustamante, *Le canal de panama et le droit international*, 27 *Revue de Droit International et de legislation comparée* 223–53 (1895).

159 Juan Pablo Scarfi, The Hidden History of International Law in the Americas: Empire and Legal Networks 176 (2017), (noting de Bustamante held a strong belief and faith in the Monroe Doctrine).

160 *Id.* at 6–7 (referring to Latin Americanism as the antithesis of Pan-Americanism).

161 *Id.* at 61.

162 José Enrique Rodó, Ariel 49 (2011) (1900).

163 *See generally* Frederick Jackson Turner, *The Significance of the Frontier in American History*, Annual Report of the American Historical Association 119–227 (1894).

164 Rodó, *supra* note 162, at 49 ("y obligados por su aspiración insaciable de dominio a cultivar la energía de todas las actividades humanas").

Bolívar, Andrés Bello.[165] His treatise of international law, written in 1832,[166] was "particularly severe" on the practice of intervention,[167] and it gave rise thirty-six years later to Carlos Calvo's hemispheric emphasis on state responsibility and national treatment, which attempted to restrict the settlement of investment disputes to the locale in which the investment was located.[168] Amancio Alcorta advanced this view, suggesting as well the distinct character of Latin American international law.[169] Juan Pablo Scarfi noted that Vicente Quesada was the first to make such a case,[170] but that Alcorta was its most prominent proponent.[171] Argentine diplomat Luis Drago worked to forbid recourse to war to recover contract debt, which had precipitated many interventions, most recently the European blockade and bombardment of Venezuela in 1902–1903.[172] He fêted Root during Root's 1906 tour of Latin America, recalling the "thrilling utterances of Henry Clay" in defense of Latin American liberty while underscoring the traditional United States policy of hemispheric "intercommunion of thought and purpose," but he ambivalently tethered his praise to the rising concern about the forcible collection of public debts.[173] The principle of sovereign equality had been at the basis of Pan-American international law. Root made reference to it during his famous 1906 tour; former United States Secretary of State, Robert Bacon repeated the emphasis during his similar tour in 1913; James Brown Scott noted the same in terms of Article 3 of the American

165 Manfred Lachs, The Teacher in International Law: Teachings and Teaching 87 (2d rev. ed., 1987).

166 *See generally* Andrés Bello, Principios de derecho de gentes (1832).

167 Lachs, *supra* note 165, at 85.

168 Charles Calvo, Le Droit International Théorique et Pratique Précédé d'un Exposé Historique des Progrès de la Science du Droit des Gens 257 (1870) ("La consequence générale qui découle directement de l'indépendance du pouvoir législatif et du pouvoir judiciaire reconnue á tous le États souverains, c'est que ceux-ci ont le droit, sans ingérence étrangère d'acune sorte, de punir comme de récompenser, en d'autres termes de placer sous l'action de leurs lois et de leurs tribunaux les sujets nationaux qui se trouvent dans les limites de leur territoire juridictionnel").

169 Lachs, *supra* note 165, at 87 (referencing Amancio Alcorta's *Tratado de Derecho Internacional* (1878)).

170 *See* Scarfi, *supra* note 159, at 65 (citing Quesada's 1882 article, *Derecho internacional latinoamericano: del principio conservador de las nacionalidades en nuestro continente*).

171 *See id.* at 75.

172 *See generally* Nancy Mitchell, The Danger of Dreams: German and American Imperialism in Latin America Ch. 2 (1999) (on the Venezuelan claims crisis of 1902–1903).

173 *Speech of Dr. Luis M. Drago, 17 Aug. 1906, in* Latin America and the United States: Addresses by Elihu Root 93–94 (R. Bacon & J.B. Scott eds., 1917).

Institute of International Law Declaration, which enshrined the principle.[174] Drago's invocation of Clay's name carried symbolic weight across South America: Clay had defended South America in the trying times of colonial emancipation, making "the United States … the first to receive us with open arms as their equals in the community of sovereign nations."[175]

Drago had reformulated the "Calvo Clause"[176] in a long, 1902 memorandum to the United States, giving uncomfortable pause to United States diplomats by invoking the Monroe Doctrine as against all interventions to reclaim debt, which naturally made it applicable as against United States Gunboat Diplomacy in Latin America.[177] Drago's tightly formed restriction on the previously unfettered right to use war as an instrument of national policy attained conventional status at the Second Hague Peace Conference in 1907.[178] The Roosevelt administration (1901–1909) had made good use of it as a means of substituting international arbitration to defuse an impending hemispheric war with Europe stemming from the Venezuelan Claims Crisis (1902–1903), and the incident led to the modification of the Monroe Doctrine with the Roosevelt Corollary, which granted to the United States the right to intervene in Europe's stead in matters involving Latin American claims.[179] However, the anticolonial rhetoric that sought to strengthen hemispheric unity through emphasis of Pan-American sovereign equality and exceptionalism took on more caustic, imperial characteristics. To paraphrase Scarfi, the sameness of sovereign

174 *See* Scarfi, *supra* note 159, at 49–50.

175 Drago, *supra* note 173, at 94.

176 The Calvo Clause attempted to deny aliens doing business in Latin American the right of diplomatic protection in matters involving contractual disputes. It asserted that resolution of such disputes should be achieved through local courts and the application of local law. *See generally* Mauel R. García-Mora, *The Calvo Clause in Latin American Constitutions and International Law*, 33 Marq. L. Rev. 205 (1950).

177 Lars Schoultz, Beneath the United States: A History of U.S. Policy Toward Latin America 179–80 (1998).

178 *See* Convention Respecting the Limitations of the Employment of Force for the Recovery of Contract Debts, art. 1, *reprinted in* The Reports to the Hague Conferences of 1899 and 1907, 489 (James B. Scott ed., 1917) [the Drago Doctrine]. The Convention also is called the "Porter Convention," owing to a proposal formulating Drago's doctrine and submitted at the second plenary session, June 19, 1907, and at the first meeting of Commission 1, June 22, 1907, by United States delegate, Horace Porter. *See* William I. Hull, The Two Hague Conferences and their Contributions to International Law 352–53 (1908).

179 Theodore Roosevelt, *Fourth Annual Message 6 December 1904*, The American Presidency Project, *available at*: http://www.presidency.ucsb.edu/ws/?pid=29545; Theodore Roosevelt, *Fifth Annual Message, 5 December 1905*, The American Presidency Project, *available at*: http://www.presidency.ucsb.edu/ws/?pid=29546 (detailing and expanding on the Roosevelt Corollary).

equality in the eyes of Pan-Americanists became a solvent of sovereignty for advocates of an imperial, United States hemispheric leadership.[180] Opposition to this viewpoint spread across the continent, nowhere more prevalent than in the *Autonomista* (self-government) movement in Cuba, as evidenced by the writings of Eliseo Giberga, and reframed more explicitly in anti-imperial depictions by Francisco Caraballo and Raúl de Cárdenas.[181]

The Bryan-Chamorro Treaty contributed to the caustic reassessment of United States exceptionalism by Latin Americanists. Tainted by its connection to discussions involving protectorates, the Treaty posed an irrevocable threat to a long-desired pluralistic ideal of Central American unity[182] and sparked a revival of regionalist solidarity. If the Bryan-Chamorro Treaty altered the "normal" life of the nations in the region, as noted by the CACJ, the idea of normalcy in the contested space of Central America presented a confused amalgam of overlapping if not competing interests.

7 Overlapping Interests

In the early twentieth century, a "coterie" of United States imperialists—Roosevelt, Mahan, Senators Henry Cabot Lodge and Cushman Davis—maneuvered to establish the United States as the undisputed hemispheric hegemon.[183] United States diplomat and historian, Warren Zimmermann added John Hay and Root to his list of "the fathers of American imperialism."[184] They asserted a new, expanded, frontier thesis[185] that challenged dysfunctional balance of power arrangements. As an example, Davis chaired the United States Senate Foreign Relations Committee (1897–1900), during the period of the

180 *See* Scarfi, *supra* note 159, at 51.

181 *See* Carlos M. Trelles, *Study of Cuban Bibliography Relative to the Monroe Doctrine [Translation]*, 5 Hisp. Am. Hist. Rev. 113–14 (1922) (referencing Giberga's *Apuntes sobre la cuestión de Cuba* and anti-imperial works of Caraballo and Cárdenas, among others). For more on the *Autonomista* movement, see generally Marta Bizcarrondo, *El Autonomismo Cubano 1878–1898: Las Ideas y Los Hechos*, 19 Historia Contemporánea 69–94 (1999).

182 *See* Theodore Roosevelt, Fourth Annual Message 6 December 1904, *supra* note 179. "Salvador also claimed that the naval station would interfere with the reestablishment of a Central American Union." Isaac Joslin Cox, *Nicaragua and the United States, 1909–1927*, 726 (World Peace Foundation Pamphlet, Vol. X, No. 7, 1927).

183 Leonard, *supra* note 126, at 60.

184 Zimmermann, First Great Triumph: How Five Americans Made Their Country a World Power 8 (2002) (listing Hay, Mahan, Root, Cabot Lodge, and Theodore Roosevelt as the five who can "faily be called the fathers of modern American imperialism.").

185 *See generally* Turner, *supra* note 163.

Spanish-American War, participated as a United States Commissioner in the Peace Treaty discussions, and authored a treatise on international law that explicitly linked the vulnerability of the western coast of the United States to the need of annexing Hawaii in partial pursuit of strategic interests connected to the proposed Nicaraguan canal.[186] In contrast to this view, a sentiment within the Pan-American movement encapsulated an epistemic rapprochement arising in juridical and diplomatic circles to promote liberal rule-orientation. This movement attempted to institutionalize third party dispute settlement and the rule of law as substitutes for war. Many jurists across the Americas embraced this undifferentiated amalgam of Manifest Destiny's ethos of United States exceptionalism as an alternative to European intervention. This ethos actually reflected multiple meanings of Manifest Destiny, dualities that expressed isolationist and internationalist perspectives, expansionist and anti-annexatioinist views, ideological and self-interested intentions, and Anglo-Saxonist and Pan-American frameworks.[187] More affirming views crystallized within the American Institute of International Law (AIIL) with the promotion of an American voice for the progressive development of international law.[188] Uruguayan foreign minister Baltasar Brum (1883–1933), citing the Monroe Doctrine, molded this affirming view of hemispheric solidarity into a proposal to establish a League of American Nations to supplement Wilson's grander proposal for a League of Nations.[189]

However, cracks in the Pan-American profile of solidarity began to appear. James Brown Scott directly criticized Brum's proposal for infringing on the exclusive right of the United States to invoke the Monroe Doctrine.[190] More critical appraisals took on the generic character of "imperial anticolonialism."[191] The AIIL was never able to shed itself of its contradictory multilateral and imperial impulses. In the 1920s, the liberal internationalist and multilateral aspirations of the AIIL would come into contact with "imperial anxieties"

---

186 *See* Cushman K. Davis, A Treatise on International Law including American Diplomacy 130–34 (1901).

187 *See* Sexton, *supra* note 46, at 246–47.

188 *Id.* at 59–85. *See also* Paolo Amorosa, The American Project and the Politics of History: James Brown Scott and the Origins of International Law 90 (noting the elevation of prominent Cuban international lawyers within the AIIL, including Antonio Sánchez de Bustamante y Sirvén and Cosme de la Torriente y Peraza).

189 Inman, *supra* note 156, at 674 (quoting Brum during his presidency of Uruguay). *See also* Baltasar Brum, *Fraternal Future of America*, 4 The World Court 540 (1915) (writing as Uruguay's foreign minister).

190 Scarfi, *supra* note 159, at 83.

191 William Appleman Williams, The Tragedy of American Diplomacy Ch. 1 (1959) [Imperial Anticolonialism].

embedded in "US-led governmental and hemispheric organizations, such as the Pan-American Union," and in State Department policies focusing on Cuba.[192] The codification process to establish an international law of the Americas would flag; indeed, relations between Scott and Álvarez would sour, and the work of the AIIL eventually gave way to the hemispheric network of the Inter-American movement.[193] An important branch of the Inter-American movement developed a decidedly critical approach to international law as the structural support of hemispheric inequality and dependency, spawning in the late 1940s the work of the Economic Commission for Latin America and the UNCTAD movement under Argentine economist, Raúl Prebisch (1901–1986).[194]

Álvarez had framed the basis for this Pan-American initiative in terms of the triple bond of unity springing from colonialization and emancipation, the nineteenth century fear of re-conquest by European powers, and a new, twentieth spirit of hemispheric community, which sounded the arrival of his novel theoretical contribution – an American International Law.[195] However, the study of Fonseca's deep-water port and its fortuitous and relatively proximate location to the transcontinental waterway, impart deeper meaning to the legal construction of *communitas*, reframed as condominium, and the operational difficulties that awaited its application.

8 The CACJ's Judgment and Impact on Pan-Americanism

The CACJ's judgment brought a turbulent period of United States-Central American international legal relations to a close, although not on a good note. Turbulence began with the revelation in 1913 that the United States and Nicaragua were deep into negotiations to conclude the Chamorro-Weitzel Treaty, later revised and renamed the Bryan-Chamorro Treaty. Already, United States marines had been dispatched to Managua to support the faltering, debt-ridden conservative regime of newly-installed President Adolfo Díaz. They would remain for more than two decades.[196] The Treaty, negotiated in secret, leaked to

192 Scarfi, *supra* note 159, at 87.

193 *See id.* Chs. 4 and 5.

194 *See generally* André Gunder Frank, *Latin American Development Theories Revisited: A Participant Review Essay*, 3 Eur. J. Dev. Res. 146–59 (1991); Karin Mickelson, *Rhetoric and Rage: Third World Voices in International Legal Discourse*, 16 Wisc. Int'l L.J. 353–419 (1997).

195 Alejandro Álvarez, *Latin America and International Law*, 3 Am. J. Int'l L. 269, 347 (1909).

196 Withdrawing in 1933. *See* Dana Gardner Munro, The United States and the Caribbean Republics, 1921–1933 Ch. 6 (1974).

Central American neighbors, prompting immediate protests as its provisions became known.

Costa Rica's Legation to the United States was the first to register "great surprise," having learned "in an informal way" of the intended Nicaraguan canal and militarization of the Gulf.[197] Criticizing the United States for fully understanding the consequences of this agreement, its foreign minister protested formally that "it was impossible from every point of view to build an interoceanic canal in Nicaragua without affecting Costa Rica."[198] United States President Grover Cleveland, presiding as sole arbitrator in an 1888 dispute between the two countries, had upheld the validity of an 1858 boundary treaty between Nicaragua and Costa Rica (the Cañas-Jerez Treaty).[199] Cleveland ruled "[t]he Republic of Nicaragua remains bound not to make any grants for canal purposes across her territory without first asking the opinion of the Republic of Costa Rica."[200] Regardless of whether Cleveland intended this provision as a *pactum de contrahendo* or *pactum de negotiando* (an agreement to agree in the future, or an agreement to negotiate in the future), the lack of any consultation indicated to Costa Rica that an interoceanic *fait accompli* involving the Gulf of Fonseca was in the making. El Salvador accused the United States of acting in bad faith.[201] Nicaragua's campaign against Honduras in 1907, which directly lead to the Washington Peace Conference, convinced El Salvador of Nicaragua's intention to turn Honduras into a dependency.[202] These suspicions carried over into El Salvador's interpretation of the Bryan-Chamorro Treaty, and raised concerns in Guatemala as well.[203] Moreover, the 1858 treaty, and Cleveland's award, had recognized the condominium status of the bays on the Atlantic and Pacific littorals (the Bay of San Juan del Norte on the Atlantic,

197 Letter from the Minister of Costa Rica to the Secretary of State, Washington, Apr. 17, 1913 [translation], Papers Relating to the Foreign Relations of the United States, File No. 817.812/22.

198 *Id.*

199 *See* Award in Regard to the Validity of the Treaty of Limits between Costa Rica and Nicaragua of 15 July 1858, XXVIII Reports of International Arbitral Awards 189–236 [2006].

200 *Id.* pt. 10, 210.

201 *See* Letter of the Secretary of State [Bryan] to the American Minister to Salvador, Sept. 26, 1913, Papers Relating to the Foreign Relations of the United States, File No. 711.13/34 [Telegram-Paraphrase] (instructing the American Minister to Salvador to express deep regret to the President of Salvador regarding insinuations questioning the good faith and friendliness of the United States).

202 Robert L. Scheina, Latin America's Wars Volume I: The Age of the Caudillo, 1791–1899, at 1819 (2003).

203 *See* Letter of the Secretary of State [Bryan] to the American Minister to Guatemala, Aug. 2, 1913, Papers Relating to the Foreign Relations of the United States, File No. 711.15 [Telegram-Paraphrase].

and Salinas Bay on the Pacific),[204] which the Costa Rican legation recognized and strenuously protested as a violation intended by perfection of the secret agreement.[205]

Word of Nicaragua's deal-in-the-making spread across Central America, provoking public demonstrations, inflammatory media responses, and plans for repressive responses.[206] El Salvador proposed a summit meeting with Guatemala, Honduras, and Costa Rica to coordinate opposition but the initiative degenerated due to Central American infighting: Honduras feared that El Salvador wanted to use the meeting to foment revolution in Nicaragua.[207] The precursor to the Bryan-Chamorro Treaty (the Chamorro-Weitzel Treaty) sought to secure through Dollar Diplomacy[208] an additional concession from cash-strapped Nicaragua, although no persuasion was needed. Unable to meet its public payroll,[209] deeply in debt to German, British, and Italian interests, and beset by "continual revolution," Nicaragua proposed becoming a protectorate

204 *See* Award in Regard to the Validity of the Treaty of Limits between Costa Rica and Nicaragua of 15 July 1858, *supra* n.199, 199 (holding the bays of San Juan del Norte and Salinas "shall be common to both Republics").

205 *See* Letter of the Minister of Costa Rica [J.B. Calvo] to the Secretary of State, Apr. 17, 1913, Papers Relating to the Foreign Relations of the United States, File No. 817.812/22 [Translation].

206 *See, e.g.*, Letter from the Secretary of State [Bryan] to the American Minister to Guatemala, Aug. 2, 1914, Papers Relating to the Foreign Relations of the United States, File No. 711.13/15 [Telegram-Paraphrase] (noting diplomatic reports of demonstrations at San Jose and San Salvador); Letter from the Secretary of State [from John Bassett Moore for the Secretary of State] to the American Minister to Salvador, Washington, Aug. 5, 1913, Papers Relating to the Foreign Relations of the United States, File No. 711.12/18 (reporting of hostile sentiment in Salvador and possible measures the Mélendez government would take to repress hostility for the establishment of a U.S. naval station in the Gulf of Fonseca).

207 See Telegram, undated, handed to the Department of State, Oct. 10, 1913 – Translation, Minister for Foreign Affairs of Nicaragua to the Nicaraguan Minister at Washington, Papers Relating to the Foreign Relations of the United States, File No 711.13/37.

208 "Dollar Diplomacy" characterized the foreign policy of United States President William Howard Taft and his Secretary of State, Philander Knox from 1909–1913; the plan corporatized diplomatic relations, using private finance capital to facilitate U.S. overseas interests with the intent of creating stability. The policy was pursued principally in the Caribbean and Central America and China. *See generally* Emily S. Rosenberg, Financial Missionaries to the World: The Politics and Culture of Dollar Diplomacy, 1900–1930 (1999). In exchange for the concessions, the United States forgave three million dollars in debt owed by Nicaragua to foreign creditors. *See* Harold Eugene Davis, John J. Finan & F. Taylor Peck, Latin American Diplomatic History 161 (1977).

209 *See* Message of the President, Adolfo Díaz, to the Congress, Managua, 17 December 1913, (noting the need to secure loans to pay deferred salaries), extracts enclosed and translated in the letter from The American Minister [Benjamin L. Jefferson] to the Secretary of State, Managua, 17 December 1913, Papers Relating to the Foreign Relations of the United

of the United States through the extension of the Platt Amendment that had conferred such status on Cuba.[210] Opposition was widespread but no more influential than the protests encountered in the United States Senate, which forced a renegotiation that excised that provision with the incoming Wilson administration and changed the treaty's name to the Bryan-Chamorro Treaty.[211] Elihu Root, then a senator from New York, authored the Platt Amendment's key provision, Article III, which granted the United States the right to intervene to preserve Cuba's independence,[212] and he crafted the Foraker Act (1900),[213] which incorporated Puerto Rico as a United States territory. And yet even he questioned the basis for establishing a protectorate in a territory "with a President of whom we have good reason to believe ... does not represent more than one-fourth of the subjects of the country."[214] His colleague, William Borah (1865–1940), expressed a different view: "We made a treaty with ourselves. We made a treaty with a government that represented us from the other side of the negotiating table."

9 El Salvador's "Perfect Lawsuit"

However, the damage was done and the virulent association of the Bryan-Chamorro Treaty with the undermining of Central American sovereign equality had spread. El Salvador's response combined a diplomatic formulation

States, File No. 817.032/8, available at: https://history.state.gov/historicaldocuments/frus1913/d1309.

210 Letter from the Minister of Nicaragua to the Secretary of State, Washington, Feb. 12, 1914, *reprinted in* Cox, *supra* note 182, at 827–28.

211 *See* Letter of the Minister of Costa Rica [J.B. Calvo] to the Secretary of State [W.J. Bryan] [trans], Jul. 7, 1914, *reprinted in* Cox, *supra* note 182, at 828. The Chamorro-Weitzel Treaty had been negotiated with Taft's Secretary of State, Philader C. Knox, and his Envoy Extraordinary and Minister Plenipotentiary to Nicaragua, George T. Weitzel; Knox was replaced by Wilson's representative, William Jennings Bryan, with the administration change in March 1913. The new treaty was re-presented, minus the protectorate provision, as the Bryan-Chamorro Treaty.

212 I William M. Malloy, Treaties, Conventions, International Acts, Protocols, and Agreements between the United States of America and other Powers, 1776–1909, (Washington: Government Printing Office, 1910) Relations with Cuba, concluded May 22, 1903, (Article III: "The Government of Cuba consents that the United Sates may exercise the right to intervene for the preservation of Cuban independence") [Platt Amendment], 362, 364.

213 Pub. L. 56–191, 31 Stat. 77 (1900) [Organic Act of 1900].

214 Rodolfo Cerdaz-Cruz, The Communist International in Central America, 1920–36, 31 (1993) (quoting Root's letter to Paul Fuller).

produced by Francisco Martínez Suárez, and Reyes Arrieta Rossi,[215] and reframed doctrinally by Salvador Rodríguez González in an article published by the *American Journal of International Law*.[216] Martínez and Arrieta, seasoned diplomats, had intimate knowledge of the political context and crafted what later would be described, perhaps self-servingly, as "one of the most perfect lawsuits ever presented before an international tribunal."[217] Martínez would later serve on the CACJ and Rodríguez (along with Salvador Gallegos and Federico Mejía) had represented El Salvador at the 1907 Washington Peace Conference.[218] With connections to El Salvador's modernist International Theosophical Society,[219] they crafted what became known as the Meléndez Doctrine,[220] named after El Salvador president, Carlos Meléndez (terms of office: 1913–1914; 1915–1918).

Within the diplomatic correspondence leading up to the lawsuit, El Salvador's Chargé d'Affaires implied that "the interests and progress of all and every one of the [Central American states] are one and the same,"[221] and that "they form a common patrimony" that the Treaty would destroy.[222] Arguments also stressed that the militarization of the Gulf of Fonseca would "menace" the region, make Central America a potential target of the war in Europe, and violate the neutrality of Honduras, which had been secured by the 1907 Washington Conference.[223] Both Costa Rica and El Salvador protested and

---

215 *See* Historia de la diplomacia, Ministerio de Relaciones Exteriores de El Salvador, *available at*: http://www.rree.gob.sv/index.php?option=com_content&view=article&id=260&Itemid=234.

216 Salvador Rodríguez González, *The Neutrality of Honduras and the Question of the Gulf of Fonseca*, 10 Am. J. Int'l L. 509–42 (1916).

217 Gilberto Aguilar Avilés, Historia de la Corte Suprema de Justicia de El Salvador 175 (San Salvador, El Salvador: Sección de la Corte Suprema de Justicia, 2000) (quoting Alfredo Martínez Moreno: "…no vacilamos en calificar como una de las demandas más perfectas que se hayan presentado ante Tribunal Internacional alguno, por la hondura de su argumentación convincente y la riqueza doctrinaria de su contenido.").

218 *See id.* at 173–74.

219 *See* Raúl Ernesto Moreno Campos, Reframing Salvadoran Modernity: A Political and Cultural History of Power and the Dialectics of the Hegemonic Bloc in El Salvador, ca. 1850–1944 (2015) (Ph.D. dissertation, University of California, Los Angeles).

220 See Aguilar, *supra* note 217, at 175; Rodríguez, *supra* note 216, at 509. *See also* El Golfo De Fonseca y El Tratado Bryan-Chamorro: Celebrado entre Los Estados Unidos de Norte América y Nicaragua: Doctrina Meléndez: Documentos Oficiales (San Salvador: República de El Salvador, 1917).

221 Letter of the Chargé d' Affaires of Salvador [Carlos A. Meza] to the Secretary of State [Bryan] [trans], Jul. 8, 1914, *reprinted in* Cox, *supra* note 182, at 830–31.

222 Letter of the Chargé d' Affaires of Salvador [Carlos A. Meza] to the Secretary of State [Bryan] [trans], Jul. 21, 1914, *reprinted in* Cox, *supra* note 182, at 831.

223 *See* El Salvador v. Nicaragua, *supra* note 38, at 681.

eventually brought cases before the CACJ.[224] For its part, Nicaragua denied that any such condominium arrangement existed in the Gulf of Fonseca or that El Salvador's opinion represented Nicaragua's.[225]

Central to El Salvador's claim was the right of a state in its sovereign capacity to negotiate as a free agent with another sovereign state concerning matters of vital interest to other neighboring states.[226] Although the United States was not named in the suits, and not subject to the jurisdiction of the Court, it found itself in the embarrassing situation of having become party to an agreement made in violation of the rights of other Nicaragua and Costa Rica as defined by President Cleveland in his 1888 award.[227] The Meléndez Doctrine conflated the 1888 award with status of the Gulf of Fonseca, which it asserted, largely through reliance on the geographic and historical exposition of Rodríguez, constituted an indivisible or communal bay. El Salvador relied on the geographic and historical characterization of the Gulf as *inter fauces terrae*.[228] Interestingly, the entire rationale of the CACJ seemed to embrace El Salvador's argument. The judgment mirrors El Salvador's *note verbale*, as written by its Minister to the United States, Francisco Dueñas, on October 21, 1913 in protest of Nicaragua's planned treaty with the United States.[229]

Other political and economic factors certainly motivated articulation of the Meléndez Doctrine. El Salvador's economy depended in large scale on coffee exports to Europe. German investments had deeply penetrated into neighboring Guatemala's coffee market; German interests controlled 60 percent of its coffee plantations.[230] El Salvador's common front with Guatemala *vis-à-vis* Nicaragua (prompting the 1907 Peace Conference) was put at risk by the Bryan-Chamorro's proposal to militarize the Gulf of Fonseca. Some European states had pursued a qualified neutrality to preserve commercial ties but keep out of the European war theatre. The Central American region's close identification

224 Cox, *supra note 182*, at 724–25.

225 *Id.* 726.

226 Philip Marshall Brown, *Costa Rica v. Nicaragua*, 11 Am. J. Int'l L. 156, 158 (1917).

227 *Id.* 157.

228 Aguilar, *supra* note 217, at 175 ("El punto central de la tesis salvadoreña fue el criterio de que el Golfo de Fonseca, geográfica y históricamente, es una bahía territorial definida por el doctor Rodríguez González en los siguientes términos: 'Siempre que un espacio de mar interyacente en las costas de dos o más Estados, tenga el carácter de mar territorial, el conjunto de sus aguas en todo el espacio de la superficie comprendida inter fauces terrae es, necesariamente un golfo o bahía común e indiviso'").

229 *See* Letter of the Minister of Salvador [Dueñas] to the Secretary of State, Oct. 21, 1913, Papers Relating to the Foreign Relations of the United States, File No. 817.812/49 [Translation].

230 Thomas Schoonover, *Germany in Central America, 1820s to 1929: An Overview*, *in* 33 Jahrbuch für Geschichte Lateinamerikas – Anuario de Historia de América Latina 50 (2016).

with the interests of the United States threatened El Salvador's autonomy, although its concerns were also recast to include Honduras. In addition to the condominium argument, Martínez forwarded the doctrine of benevolent neutrality, which directly aimed at avoiding European market share loss of coffee exports.[231]

10 Condominium

The Bryan-Chamorro Treaty exposed the weakness of an awakening of Mesoamerican internationalism that had been invigorated along lines of liberal international rule making and federalism. Costa Rica construed the pact as the end to the "special nature of the relations" between the Central American states.[232] This fitful attempt to recreate the short-lived Federal Republic of Central America was most immediately put at risk. Although disunion marked the history of Central American identity following the Spanish conquest, "the ideal of federation" had never been lost.[233] Following Spain's retreat from the New World, and declarations of independence in 1821, the newly formed isthmian republics pursued a Mesoamerican or Central American Federation. The Federation of the Center of America, as it also was called, consisted of Costa Rica, El Salvador, Guatemala, Honduras, and Nicaragua. It formed in 1823, the same year United States President James Monroe announced his eponymous doctrine in a speech before Congress. By 1838, however, the Federation began to fracture due to civil war, and periodic attempts to revive it into the twentieth century failed. However, the federation had been supported by the Monroe administration (1817–1825) at the outset,[234] and a proto-Pan-Americanism had

231 *See* Francisco Martínez Suárez, ChalatenangoSV.com, *available at*: http://www.chalatenangosv.com/francisco-martinez-suarez (noting he: "elaboró la 'Doctrina de la Neutralidad Benévola,' una figura jurídica dirigida a evitar el involucramiento directo de El Salvador en la Primera Guerra Mundial, y así evitar perder los mercados europeos los cuales eran muy importantes para las exportaciones nacionales del café.").

232 Letter of the Minister of Costa Rica, in Cox, *supra* note 182, at 828–29.

233 William F. Slade, *The Federation of Central America*, 8 J. of Race Dev. 79, 79 (1917); Juan Antonio Márques Domínguez & José Díaz-Diego, *The Nicaragua Interoceanic Grand Canal in the Central American Regional Development Context: Considerations for the Debate*, 66 Investigaciones Geográficas 27, 29 (2016), ("Even today, the idea of a United States of Central America endures in the yearning of many intellectuals who see in the union a possible solution to the underdevelopment of the region.").

234 The United States recognized the Federation on August 4, 1824, receiving Antonio José Cañas as Envoy Extraordinary and Minister Plenipotentiary. *See A Guide to the United States' History of Recognition, Diplomatic, and Consular Relations, by Country, since 1776: Central*

influenced Monroe's Secretary of State, Henry Clay, to forge hemispheric connections.[235] Separation from Spanish rule prompted *El gran libertador*, Simón Bolívar to advocate in favor of the Panama Congress, a Pan-American meeting to solidify a new order of hemispheric relations.[236] Clay also had discussed with the Federation's Washington representative a joint venture to capitalize construction of a canal.[237] Clay wrote: "If the work should ever be executed, the benefits of it ought not to be exclusively appropriated to any one nation, but should be extended to all parts of the globe upon payment of just compensation or reasonable tolls."[238]

The Federation idea found expression in El Salvador's condominium argument over Fonseca's waters, but had little appeal nor had made much landward impression. Indeed the ICJ only applied the doctrine to Fonseca's waters, noting the land history of the region was different.[239] Most Central American states ended up supporting the Allies in World War I—save for El Salvador—which maintained its neutral status. The war deflected emphasis on the practical application of the ruling, which in important respects, Fonseca's littoral powers attempt to refine to this day. If not the most perfect lawsuit, El Salvador's position proved persuasive both in terms of its presentation before the CACJ and in terms of its portrayal of fraternal history across the isthmus as the basis for condominium.

However, the Bryan-Chamorro Treaty exposed deep fissures in the Pan-American legal attempt to substitute the rule of law for geo-politics across the isthmus. This attempt had been at the heart of the 1907 Central American Peace Conference organized by the United States and Mexico, and the Central American response to the treaty tarnished severely Root's efforts. The conference's considerable work product, a treaty of peace and eight conventions including a framework for continued hemispheric engagement and integration,[240] nevertheless burnished his reputation as a pragmatic conciliator, and an advocate

American Federation, Office of the Historian, United States Department of State, https://history.state.gov/countries/central-american-federation.

235 *See* John Barrett, *Pan-Americanism and Its Inspiration in History*, 19 Records of the Columb. Hist. Soct'y 19, 156, 157 (1916).

236 Joseph M. Rogers, The True Henry Clay 139 (1904).

237 See Sheldon B. Liss, The Canal: Aspects of United States Panamanian Relations 13 (1967).

238 Whiteley, *supra* note 52, at 365 (quoting Clay's letter to Commissioners of United States to Panama Congress).

239 Gulf of Fonseca Case ¶ 386 ("No evidence has been presented to the Chamber suggesting that there was for these waters ... anything analogous to those boundaries of provincial sway, which have been so much discussed in respect of the land.").

240 James Brown Scott, *The Central American Peace Conference of 1907*, 2 Am J. Int'l L. 121, 133 (1908).

for the quotidian, unspectacular structuration of international legal procedures and institutions that would build the foundation for dispute settlement and keep nations, principally his own, out of trouble.[241] One year before, Root had received the Nobel Peace Prize[242] and the selection committee specifically cited Root's "strenuous efforts to improve relations between the small Central American countries"[243] as a basis for conferring onto him the prize. Indeed, Root had instructed the United States delegation at the 1907 Conference to seek mechanisms for strengthening regional bonds, for instance through the professionalization and independence of the judges of the CACJ.[244] Historian and statesman Thomas Dodd noted that objective had been achieved. The jurists and diplomats assigned to the CACJ were highly respected and experienced within the legal profession.[245] Root would go on to play an important role in the 1920 Advisory Committee of Jurists' meeting to craft the Statute of the Permanent Court of International Justice,[246] but he was waning in age and stature. Caught between the unreconciled ethos of exceptionalism and rule-abidance, or, imperial anticolonialism, he became an early exemplar of international law's turbulent twentieth century history in the Americas.

The ruling also confirmed a quixotic condominium arrangement, based on the conveyance of sovereignty belonging to the single political entity of the Spanish Crown and passing undivided to the Central American Federation.[247] The CACJ glossed over the fact that Honduras and Nicaragua attempted to divide the waters of the Gulf in 1900 as between themselves, as had El Salvador and Honduras in 1884;[248] and that Honduras had attempted to sell Tigre island in the Gulf of Fonseca to a United States citizen in 1854,[249] the same year

---

241 *See* James B. Morrow, *Life of Elihu Root, Statesman and Peace-Worker*, Wash. Herald (Jan. 11, 1914) (praising Root as "logical instead of rhetorical; cultural rather than imaginative").

242 Root was awarded the Nobel Peace Prize in 1912, but he received the award in 1913. *See* The *Nobel Peace Prize 1912*, Nobelprize.org, *available at*: http://www.nobelprize.org/nobel_prizes/peace/laureates/1912/.

243 *Id.*

244 *The Court: History*, International Court of Justice, http://www.icj-cij.org/court/index.php?p1=1&p2=1.

245 Dodd, *supra* note 151, at 73 ("…las personas asignadas a la Corte eran abogados de formación, juristas y diplomáticos de experiencia. Eran sumamente respetados en la profesión legal.").

246 *See generally*, Procès-Verbaux of the Proceedings of the Committee, June 16th–July 24th 1920 with Annexes (1920).

247 El Sal. v. Nicar., *supra* note 38, at 677.

248 *Id.* at 678.

249 U.S. Navy Department Memorandum, Dec. 3 1913, Appendix I, ¶ 4 (noting Guatemala, Costa Rica, and El Salvador lodged formal complaints with Honduras protesting the proposed sale of Tigre Island to a U.S. citizen).

leading Honduran historian Antonio Vallejo argued that Honduras held undisputed title ("*sin contradicción ninguna*") to all islands in the Gulf of Fonseca.[250] The CACJ's employment of condominium as an antidote to the Lodge Corollary belied widespread contextual problems. The region's imperiled financial condition, latent intramural hostility between Honduras and Guatemala/El Salvador,[251] recent military interventions by the United States in Honduras (1903, 1907, 1911, and 1912) and Panama (1903), and its occupation of Nicaragua (1912–1933),[252] undercut the unity of purpose implied by condominium. In effect, the CACJ attempted to force a cohabitation, supported principally by El Salvador, which years later brought the disputants again before the ICJ. The ICJ Chamber reaffirmed the coparcener agreement, which arose in the waters of the Gulf of Fonseca centuries before the CACJ's judgment.

11 Conclusion

El Salvador's adroit employment of condominium as a legal argument to frustrate application of the imperial anticolonial Lodge Corollary stands as a historical reminder of the politicized adaptation of the shared sovereignty concept—an adaptation of the standard of civilization concept as applied by Central American jurists in defense of non-intervention. A declassified United States State Department report written in the early 1980s noted numerous and serious disputes among the littoral powers surrounding the Gulf of Fonseca.[253] Those disputes carry over to the present day.[254] As among themselves, sharing sovereignty over the Gulf of Fonseca presents serious and sustaining problems—however not in terms of holding opposable to the world the shared sovereignty status of the Gulf. In this sense, the condominium concept secured a viable expression because the littoral states united in trumping competing

---

250 *Id.* at Appendix I, ¶ 5 (referencing Vallejo's *Limites de Honduras* (1926)). On Vallejo's stature, see Rolando Sierra Fonseca, Antonio R. Vallejo y la historiografía fundante en Honduras, *La Tribuna* (Mar. 30, 2014), *available at*: http://www.latribuna.hn/2014/03/30/antonio-r-vallejo-y-la-historiografia-fundante-en-honduras/.

251 *See Honduras v. Salvador and Guatemala, CACJ, Judgment,* Dec. 19, 1908, Dec. 19, 1908, 3 Am J. Int'l L. 729–36 (1909) (concerning Honduran claims of meddling and regime change initiatives orchestrated by Guatemala and El Salvador).

252 *See generally* Lester D. Langley, The Banana Wars: United States Intervention in the Caribbean, 1898–1934 (rev. ed., 2002).

253 *See* Procès-Verbaux , *supra* note 146.

254 *See* Gustavo Adolfo González Bermúdez, Victor Emilio Jara Calderón, & Jeffry Alejandro Garro Fallas, *El Golfo de Fonseca, más que un conflicto político. La perspectiva desde los actores locales y pobladores costeros*, 16 Revista Pensamiento Actual 147–61 (2016).

claims or interests before they arose to threaten the resource rich waters of the Gulf. It was not always this way, but the much disputed CACJ decision in 1914 developed into this incontrovertible tripartite relation.

Lauterpacht may have correctly noted the fundamental common denominator to successful application of shared sovereignty is an atmosphere of close cooperation. While such a condition may be lacking among Fonseca's littoral states, nothing obviates that prospect from one day taking hold. However, a review of the four hundred year history of the Gulf of Fonseca provides a muted appreciation for shared sovereignty's future given the political uses to which it has been put, notwithstanding validation by the CACJ and the Chamber of the ICJ. Condominium's positive contribution to international law diminishes within the context of the history of the Gulf of Fonseca. In the waters enclosed by El Salvador, Honduras, and Nicaragua, condominium's expression owes more to the search for a legal antidote to imperial anticolonialism than to the embrace of the shared values that give highest legal expression to its name. One of the small ironies associated with the troubled history of the idea of condominium in international law is that the meaning of condominium in the Gulf of Fonseca is still much disputed among the three littoral powers adjacent to its shore, and yet the constructed condominium arrangement, however flawed, remains respected and opposable to the world.

CHAPTER 6

Conclusion

A directional turn in the history of international law places new emphasis on the Americas. This emphasis revisits and reframes overarching narratives of progress, with emphasis on emerging voices, indigenous storylines, and contextual critiques. The directional turn extends beyond particular hemispheric or disciplinary orientations. Fields of political science and international relations have become "much more hospitable to history and historical investigation than behavioralism ever was."[1] Revisionist histories continue to play an important role in attacking traditional assumptions that historically have accompanied the straightforward grand narration leading to falsely progressive and moralizing—whiggish—outcomes and conclusions.[2]

This book adds a cautionary note to the revisionist critique. The same cautionary note applies to the sustaining mythologies of the liberal approach, and in fact to all synthetic overviews, which necessarily must reduce contextual nuance. Critical assessments of method should not unduly foster an estrangement from contextualism, which critics associate with the hyper-rationalizations of the Cambridge School, Quentin Skinner, and others. English School adherents never relinquished their high regard for the role of history in framing the understanding of international relations, although they often have been criticized for failing to connect the "pretension[s] of cumulative knowledge" to a more dispassionate scientific theory, or to a "mechanistic view of history that lends itself to the prediction of future events."[3] Part of this estrangement traces to a tension between theorists and historians of international law and relations. Theorists resist historians' penchant for particularism; historians resist theorists' inclination toward abstraction. Diplomacy offers something of a middle ground, where doctrine and policy intermix with the staked out positions of theorists and historians. The arena of the political represents the

1 Nicolas Guilhot, *Portrait of the Realist as a Historian: On Anti-Whiggism in the History of International Relations*, 21 Eur. J. Int'l Rel. 4 (2015) (quoting J. Farr, J.G. Gunnell and R. Seidelman).

2 *See generally* Deborah Z. Cass, *Navigating the Newstream: Recent Critical Scholarship in International Law*, 65 Nordic J. Int'l L. 341 (1996).

3 William Bain, *Are There Any Lessons of History? The English School and the Activity of Being an Historian*, 44 Int'l Pol. 513, 514 (2007).

 | DOI:10.1163/9789004379510_007

proving ground. It underscores the intimate connection between theory, history, and the study of both.[4]

Butterfield recognized that indelibly human qualities also acted like a species of chemistry on the construction of history. More than simply a discreet subset of political science, the English School view of international relations conformed to a more interdisciplinary perspective, melding inputs from diplomacy, history, politics, and international law. These inputs add disciplinary complexity to tired whiggish narratives[5] and to seemingly well understood tropes such as the Monroe Doctrine. The whiggish critique stands as an invaluable reminder of the witting care needed to situate new or emerging voices in the stream of international legal discourse involving the Americas.

Root once said "The twentieth century will be the century of South America."[6] International law's current turn to the history of Latin America seemingly agrees with the sentiment, while transporting its expression into the twenty-first century, or perhaps the next. Regardless of timing, the reclamation of history as a construct of future pathways in international law will benefit from the keen awareness of methodological abridgment. Anti-whiggish movements through history highlight complexity, disillusion assumptions, and challenge continuity. These are welcome disruptions. Historiography's wisdom keeps these disruptive doors unlocked. Awareness of history's bumptious twists and turns ultimately leads to contextual refinement—not to be confused with a smoothing over of the temporal path, which always lead forwards.

Hiram Bingham correctly noted more than one century ago that the Monroe Doctrine turned into a shibboleth. Bingham's only mischaracterization was to label it "obsolete." His description meant to underscore that it no longer served an outdated defensive purpose, and that it displayed imperial applications. However, whiggish depictions of the shibboleth also abridged deep-seated complexities that informed of hemispheric nuances relating to federation and union. They downplayed the significance of civilization discourse, but not without reason given the term's associations with racism and colonialism. They treated as *passé* the anxieties of geo-strategic station and fears of encirclement, as if hemispheric security issues described a *nomos* far removed from today's structure of globalized relations. They nominalized juridical and

4 For more on the tensions between historians and theorists, see George Rodrigo Bandeira Galindo, *Martti Koskenniemi and the Historiographical Turn in International Law*, 16 Eur. J. Int'l L. 539, 547–48 (2005).

5 Duncan Bell, *Writing the World: Disciplinary History and Beyond*, 85 Int'l Aff. 7 (2009).

6 *Speech at the Moneda, Sept. 2, 1906*, in Latin American and the United States: Addresses by Elihu Root 110–111 (R. Bacon & J.B. Scott eds., 1917).

diplomatic permutations from the peripheral mestizo, creole and Pan-American attempts to conform inherited vocabularies to statecraft and state-building enterprises of weak republics with strong *caudillo* traditions. These traditions emerged in the shadows of Spain's receding and the United States' emerging empires. New discussions of the history of international law in the hemisphere should unveil these histories, as well.

Whiggish depictions promoted cross-purpose characterizations of the Monroe Doctrine in the encoded language of competing ideological perspectives. International lawyers and diplomats relied on the semiotics inherited from this discourse within hierarchical arrangements of handed down Roman law, Common law, and Canon law traditions. Whiggish exemplars in this legalist vocabulary arose from reductive and abridged expressions of free trade, freedom of the seas, and sovereign equality. Normative expressions of exceptionalism and entitlement conformed interpretations of the Monroe Doctrine to stilted reflections of rule-orientation by the large policy men predisposed to see things that way. The English School captured the elements of these broad-based depictions by adding dimensions of social content to theorizing about international relations. From this review of its influence on the historiography of international law and Latin America, and on resurgent questions relating to both, broader implications of whiggish thinking challenge international law today.

Compartmentalizations of methodology into simplified competing paradigms (for instance realism, idealism, institutionalism) or great ideological debates (for instance freedom versus security, order versus anarchy, individualism versus universalism) begin to embrace global, spatial, colonial, or imperial histories. This widening of perspectives introduces the growing body of literature to expressions other than, or in addition to the "hegemonic global order radiating outwards from Europe and North America towards the ex-colonial world."[7] These histories erode the mythologies of standard historiographical presentations, regardless of liberal or revisionist varieties. Historians historically have borne the lion's share of concern about whiggish thinking. It hovers like an intramural pox over their methodological house. However, whiggish perspectives present challenges beyond the historians' domain.

---

7 Hilary Charlesworth & David Kennedy, *Afterword: and Forward—There Remains So Much We Do Not Know, in* International Law and Its Others 403 (Anne Orford ed., 2006). *See also* Non-Western International Relations Theory: Perspectives on and Beyond Asia (Amitav Acharya & Barry Buzan eds., 2010); Pinar Bilgin, *Looking for "the International" Beyond the West,* 31 Third World Q. 817 (2010) (reviewing literature).

Legal scholars, foreign policy analysts, court decisions and the judges who construct them, diplomats and academics who apply and interpret them, contribute to the articulation of whiggish straight-line analysis and the attending abridgments of factual or contextual circumstance. As Duncan Bell has noted, sometimes the discipline-defining stories meant to ascribe fixed, coherent, and legitimating meaning instead project mythologies through "highly simplified narratives."[8]

Earlier we noted that Butterfield's usage of the term whiggish now applies to all oversimplified narratives of progress that seek moral clarity by interpreting past events in light of present politics. How true, but how misleading. Butterfield constructed his argument as a complaint against liberalism's adoration of progress. This devotional perspective bore false witness to liberalism's providentialism and optimism, which detracted from Butterfield's project of reclaiming Christian Realism from modernity's rationalisms.[9]

Butterfield's connection of whiggish history to a purposeful but false moral trajectory overshadows the whig interpretation's sustaining contribution. Whiggish history is really about historical abridgment in pursuit of any ideological outcome or outlook, not simply the impalement of liberalism's parochial objectives on its triumphal path of progress. This conclusion implicates any historiographic enterprise, and certainly could be applied against its progenitor.

Perhaps Butterfield hoisted himself by his own petard by imbuing his critique of liberal historians with a methodological standard of review that he whiggisly abridged as applied to his own Christian conservatism. The all-too-human plight of historiography, at best, promotes an ever-present awareness of abridgment, not the eradication of unavoidable generalizations. All counterpoising paradigmatic formulations fashion an outcome that professes to be the best-of-all-possible prescriptive, predictive, descriptive, or explanatory pathways. Butterfield's important point about the fungibility of liberalism's moral certainty, and the teleological backtracking from liberalism's presumed progressive outcome—also regarded as the anachronistic inversion of history's ineluctable march *forwards*—applies across the methodological spectrum. Undue concentration on Butterfield's focus on liberalism downplays whiggism's problematic appearance across the methodological spectrum.

---

8 Bell, *supra* note 5, at 5.

9 Nicolas Guilhot, *Portrait of the Realist as a Historian: On Anti-Whiggism in the History of International Relations*, 21 Eur. J. Int'l L. 9 (providentialism), 10 (critique of rationalist modernity) (2015).

1 Whiggish Thinking Alive and Well

Although this book has concentrated on the refreshment of Butterfield's methodological approach in terms of international law's (re)turn to history in Latin America, the (re)telling of complexities and multiple meanings associated with the development of the Monroe Doctrine has taken on added life in international law. The recovery of the complex meaning of the Monroe Doctrine and the whiggish formulations that conform the antecedent doctrine to presentist manipulations of ideology make it susceptible to a new application, and certainly within a new hemispheric context. The Monroe Doctrine's pelagic expression rendered the Caribbean Sea a catalyst for United States control over the Atlantic and Pacific Oceans' commercial corridors, which led in 1899 to China's doorstep and the Open Door policy. Might another sea now serve another country's pelagic intention to springboard into another ocean for purposes of securing commercial rule?

The recent *South China Sea Arbitration*[10] foretells of a new Monroe Doctrine-like corollary with whiggish implications. The South China Sea is the fifth largest body of water in the world. It accounts for five trillion dollars in annual commercial activity involving one-third of maritime traffic worldwide.[11] Although resoundingly defeated in the arbitral case it refuses to acknowledge, China still claims wide-ranging sovereign rights over upwards of ninety percent of this sea, via a controversial U-shaped line. China claims its sovereign authority predates the 1982 United Nations Convention on the Law of the Sea,[12] to which it belongs, by millennia.[13] Critics date China's ambiguous sovereignty claim, first indicated in response to domestic political crises affecting the Qing Dynasty in 1909, to 1947, when a founder of the China Geographical Society added the controversial U-shaped dotted line enclosing the South China Sea to a map generated by Chiang Kai-shek's Kuomintang Government.[14] This

10 *See* In the Matter of the South China Sea Arbitration (Phil. v. China), Award on Jurisdiction and Admissibility, PCA Case Repository 2013–19 (Perm Ct. Arb. 2015).

11 Christopher R. Rossi, *Treaty of Tordesillas Syndrome: Sovereignty ad Absurdum and the South China Sea Arbitration*, 20 Cornell Int'l L.J. 231, 245 (2017).

12 United Nations Convention on the Law of the Sea, Dec. 10, 1982, 1833 U.N.T.S. 397.

13 The Tribunal rejected this point as irrelevant given China's accession to the convention. The Tribunal ruled against China on all of the substantive issues and circumvented jurisdictional objections by China that the case involved a sea boundary delimitation (a jurisdictional exception from the compulsory dispute settlement provision of the convention), addressing instead the question of historic rights as opposed to historic title in terms of China's U-shaped line.

14 *See generally* Bill Hayton, The South China Sea: The Struggle for Power in Asia (2014). In fact, China did not actually present its claim in the form of the U-shaped map until 2009, when

cartographic revision responded to simmering French imperial claims over six of the misnamed Spratly Islands,[15] located in the South China Sea.

The vagueness of China's claim, alternatively expressed in terms of its defense of its "historic rights," "historic title," and "historic waters," nevertheless indicates a Monroe Doctrine-like attempt to create a Great Wall—a Great Pelagic Wall—around China's access to blue water. Perhaps China's latent insecurities following its Century of Humiliation by western powers account for this defensive posturing.[16] And yet China's unformed explanation bears increasing resemblance to an expansive and foreboding foreign policy.

Construed as the antechamber to the greater Indian Ocean, the South China Sea may become China's naval footprint in a possibly decades-long drama for dominance with the United States, much like how the Greater Caribbean provided the United States and its large policy men with a seafaring foothold for hemispheric control followed by rapid expansion into the Pacific Ocean as against Old Europe interests—movements that established for the United States hemispheric and soon thereafter world dominance.[17]

Perhaps China is asserting that a power to rule over the South China Sea nevertheless established a trans-historical right of ownership, a Sinicized version of Manifest Destiny. If China thinks time is on its side, it may be seeking to re-establish tributary relationships which would substitute the authoritarian Chinese political regime for the mythologized folklore of China as the Middle

---

the map was appended to two *notes verbales* submitted to the U.N. Secretary-General. *See Note Verbale of the People's Republic of China to the U.N. to the Secretary-General of the U.N.* (May 7, 2009), http://www.un.org/depts/los/clcs_new/submissions_files/mysvnm33_09/chn_2009re_mys_vnm_e.pdf [https://perma.cc/4488-YP9B].

15 As the Tribunal concluded, the Spratlys are not islands, nor do they appropriately form an archipelago. *See* In the Matter of the South China Sea Arbitration (Award), *supra* note 10, ¶ 7.

16 China suffered a series of humiliations at the hands of western imperial powers beginning with the Opium War (1840–1842), the Sino-French War (1883–1885), Japan's defeat of the Qing Dynasty in the Sino-Japanese War (1894–1895), and the resulting independence of tributary states, Korea and Taiwan, along with the suppression of the Boxer Rebellion (by the Eight-Nation Alliance: Austria-Hungary, British Empire, France, Italy, Japan, Russia, and the U.S.). *See* George P. Jan, *The Doctrine of Nationalism and the Chinese Revolution*, *in* Sun Yat-Sen's Doctrine in the Modern World 138, 140–42 (Chu-yuan Cheng ed., 1989) (discussing the emergence of modern Chinese nationalism); *see also* Dong Wong, China's Unequal Treaties: Narrating National History (2005) (on the mid-nineteenth century emergence of the polemical use of the phrase "unequal treaties" in the formation and expression of Chinese nationalism).

17 *See generally* Rossi, *supra* note 11.

Kingdom—the center of the East and South Asian universe.[18] The prospect of a Sinocentric Age of Empire arises,[19] akin to that created by nineteenth century European probes to "find the peripheries" of ideological and economic domination in Africa, Asia, and the Pacific.[20] Employing a so-called "cabbage strategy" of wrapping individual features of the South China Sea in layers of incremental appropriation,[21] China's attempt to "further consolidate claims" now intensifies through law enforcement patrols within the U-shaped line,[22] military-capable airstrips fabricated on top of underwater shoals elevated by the ecologically catastrophic dredging up of sea bottom, and the militarization of the surrounding sea space, all intended to establish Sinocentric corollaries to its U-shaped version of the Monroe Doctrine.

China's emphasis on historic rights to the South China Sea bears the imprimatur of a whiggish use of history. It resembles the sense of entitlement exhibited by early twentieth century United States large policy men in their assertive control over the Caribbean and the Pacific coasts of the isthmus. China's emerging large policy men abridge the historical narratives in an area so rich in dynastic tradition—the Funan and Khmer in Cambodia, the spread of the Sanskrit cosmopolis, the Champa in the Mekong, and the Mac in northern Vietnam, the sultanates of Malacca and Indonesia, and, of course, the Han and the Ming dynasties in China.[23] According to Victor Lieberman, the dynastic character infusing the area of the South China Sea contributed to "South Asia's luxuriant cultural polymorphism,"[24] more so than a definitive, indivisible, and uninterrupted claim of *dominium* over the pelagic highway that contributed to such polymorphism.[25] Chinese historical narratives, however, accentuate the activity on the maritime Silk Road dating to the Qin (221–206 B.C.E.) and

18 *See generally* Mohan Malik, *Historical Fiction: China's South China Sea Claims*, World Aff. (May/June 2013), http://www.worldaffairsjournal.org/article/historical-fiction-china%E2%80%99s-south-china-sea-claims; Martin Jacques, When China Rules the World: The End of the Western World and the Birth of A New Global Order Ch. 8 (2009) (discussing Middle Kingdom mentality).

19 The term is borrowed from Eric Hobsbawm's The Age of Empire: 1875–1914 (1987), which details the period of European worldwide colonial expansion.

20 *See* Antony Anghie, *Finding the Peripheries: Sovereignty and Colonialism in Nineteenth-Century International Law*, 40 Harv. Int'l L.J. 1 (1999).

21 *See* Harry Kazianis, *China's Expanding Cabbage Strategy*, Diplomat (Oct. 29, 2013), http://thediplomat.com/2013/10/chinas-expanding-cabbage-strategy/.

22 Keyuan Zou, *The South China Sea*, *in* The Oxford Handbook of the Law of the Sea 626, 636 (Donald R. Rothwell et al., eds., 2015).

23 Rossi, *supra* note 11, at 259.

24 Victor Lieberman, Strange Parallels: Southeast Asia in Global Context, c. 800–1830: Volume 2, Mainland Mirrors: Europe, Japan, China, South Asia, and the Islands 680 (2009).

25 Rossi, *supra* note 11, at 259.

Admiral Zheng He's (1371–1433) seven fabled voyages while in route to Champa (southern Vietnam), Malacca, India, and East Africa, as if general commercial and military trawling necessarily constituted a desire to exercise *dominium*.[26] These accounts seem to abridge the sudden recall of these voyages by the Confucian controllers of the Ming Court and China's centuries-long inward turn.

Taking a page from the Chinese playbook, Vietnam now has reframed formerly "marginal" islands in the South China Sea as the center of a "reimagined map of the nation's territory ... a figurative cartographic navel of the national geo-body" that projects "Vietnamese sovereignty claims over portions of the South China Sea."[27] South China Sea coastal states have their own versions of history, but "no one state seems to have actually exercised dominant authority to the exclusion of all others."[28]

However, China's display of entitlement derives from a claim of historic right although doubtless reinforced by its naval modernization campaign.[29] Contested sovereignty claims generate appeals to the historical record, where *effectivités*[30] buttress and counter narratives to establish better title among disputants.[31] Rather than ending such disputes, *effectivités* often fall prey to selective interpretation—as evidenced by the CACJ in its 1914 decision—making wholesale reliance on them susceptible to the whiggish complaint. The *South China Sea Arbitration* has generated a debate over the Tribunal's rejection of *effectivités* supporting Chinese *dominium* over the South China Sea. A more turbulent discussion awaits consideration, one that has long weakened the international project to secure the open, rule-based, reciprocal (cooperative),

26 *See* Robert Finlay, *The Treasure-Ships of Zheng He: Chinese Maritime Imperialism in the Age of Discovery*, 23 Terrae Incognitae 4 (1991).

27 Edyta Roszko, *Geographies of Connection and Disconnection: Narratives of Seafaring in Lý So'n* , *in* Connected and Disconnected in Vietnam: Remaking Social Relations in a Post-Socialist Nation 347, 349 (Philip Taylor ed., 2016).

28 Peter A. Dutton, An Analysis of China's Claim to Historic Rights in the South China Sea, in Major Law and Policy Issues in the South China Sea: European and American Perspectives 57, 73 (Yann-Huei Song & Keyuan Zou eds., 2014).

29 Officially named the People's Liberation Army Navy (PLAN), which has notable expanded since 2005. *See* Alex Hempel, *The Rise of the People's Liberation Army Navy: Chinese Naval Modernization from 1990 to 2018*, White Fleet.net (Mar. 25, 2018), https://whitefleet.net/2018/03/25/the-rise-of-chinas-peoples-liberation-army-navy-modernization-from-1990-to-2018/.

30 *See generally* Charles de Visscher, Les *Effectivités* du Droit International Public (1967). *See also* Frontier Dispute (Burk. Faso/Mali), Judgment, 1986 I.C.J. Rep. 554, ¶ 63 (Dec. 22) (defining *effectivités* as "the conduct of the administrative authorities as proof of the effective exercise of territorial jurisdiction in the region during the colonial period").

31 *See, e.g.*, Frontier Dispute (Burk. Faso/Mali), *supra* note 30, ¶ 63 (discussing the purpose of *effectivités*).

institutional liberal order on which is based freedom of the seas.[32] This discussion involves the less than complete embrace of freedom of the seas even among some of liberal internationalism's ardent supporters—a syndromic consequence of Treaty of Tordesillas thinking, now undergoing Sinicized interpretation.

2 Extrapolated Colonial *Effectivités*

Does China's claim to the South China Sea date from the Han Dynasty over two thousand years ago, or to a repurposed mid-1940s Kuomintang map created to dispute French colonial intrusions? Situated within the mix of discussions among politicians, jurists, diplomats, and international bureaucrats about which date prevails is a tale of historical abridgment, with extrapolated interpretations of relevant historical circumstances and colonial *effectivités* to enliven applications of whiggish debates for decades to come. A trans-historical sense of parochialism abounds in whiggish thinking. The history of the South China Sea and is reminiscent of the Portuguese claim that they were the first navigators of the sea leading to the Indians (East Asian trade routes)—a claim Hugo Grotius labeled "absurd" in *Mare Liberum* more than four hundred years ago.[33]

We have looked at elements of whiggish interpretation within the periodized and geo-spatial frameworks of the new American republics, western expansion, nineteenth century imperial jockeying over control of the Caribbean and its isthmus, civilization discourse, and the mindsets of the CACJ and (to a lesser extent the Chamber of the ICJ) as it dealt with legal implications of large-policy machinations. In that latter context, third party adjudicators fell prey to whiggish temptation. Now, we could append to this discussion the statist adaptation of the whig interpretation of history, where international lawyers, diplomats, and third party arbitrators seemingly fall victim to it. This turn to problems of historiography as encountered by international courts and tribunals underscores the global implications of whiggish thinking, its ongoing challenges within the framework of international relations, the currency of Butterfield's capacious lament about the misuses of history, and the vitality of English School teachings as a means, not of avoiding or defeating abridgements

32 *See* G. John Ikenberry, Liberal Leviathan: The Origins, Crisis, and Transformation of the American World Order 18 (2011) (describing attributes of the distinctive liberal international order).

33 Hugo Grotius, Mare Liberum 1609–2009, at 85 (Robert Feenstra ed., 2009) (1609).

of history, but of inculcating an ever-present awareness that such pitfalls await any disciplinary approach that wittingly or unwittingly turns both eyes away from the past.

3 The Whiggish Problem of Historical Recall

A whiggish problem of historical recall threatens whenever title to territory is disputed. A modern dispute suffices to make the point: Who owns Svalbard? That question was settled by a 1920 Treaty, which grants to Norway "full and absolute sovereignty" over the archipelago (then called Spitzbergen). That same treaty granted to all high contracting parties "equal enjoyment" rights over the territories specified in the treaty. When crafted, the Svalbard Treaty knew of only two such applicable territories: the rights pertaining to Spitzbergen's *terra firma*, and the rights pertaining to its territorial sea. Since that time, the Law of the Sea has extended the breadth of the territorial sea, added the contiguous zone, crafted the continental shelf doctrine, extended continental shelf doctrine, and subjected the superjacent water column to sovereign-like control of the coastal state over the Exclusive Economic Zone. Norway claims no ambulatory significance attaches to the 1920 Treaty's extension of equal access and enjoyment rights to signatories, as these new regimes were not within the contemplation of parties at the time of the treaty's creation. In Norway's view, the teeming resources of the water adjacent and subjacent to the archipelago's territorial sea belong to Norway. Not so, according to a host of other high contracting parties (now including North Korea) and the European Union. They argue the term is a generic term that incorporates the intervening development of the Law of the Sea. As Norway's sovereignty over the adjacent waters grew over time, so too did the signatories' rights of equal enjoyment and access to the same expanding areas.

The ascertainment of good title often involves a reliance on historical circumstances concerning disputed facts. International law has relied on appeals to factual circumstances to quiet title. Judges and arbitrators can rely on factual circumstances to help validate sovereignty, although under no circumstances can reliance prevail where good title already exists.[34] The acquisition of historic title in international law now requires satisfaction of three conditions. The state must exercise the necessary jurisdiction; it must exercise that authority continuously for a long period (evidencing *possesio longi temporis*); and it

34 *See* Frontier Dispute (Burk. Faso/Mali), *supra* note 30, ¶ 63.

must do so without opposition from other states.[35] In the hermeneutics of international legal problem solving, *effectivités* compliment, supplement, or confirm assertions of sovereignty, but they do not function to create sovereignty. *Effectivités* have played an essential role in showing how title is interpreted in practice, and such proofs have extended to colonial administration.[36] However, judges and arbitrators, like historians, have encountered problems interpreting the record. Consequently, proof of ownership redounds to historical recall and competing national narratives. Russians tout Spitzbergen's discovery by Pomor hunters who migrated north from the White Sea, naming the archipelago Grumant. Norwegians highlight Viking claims as contained in Icelandic sagas. English title traces to Sir Hugh Willougby's discovery before he perished in a tempest. Danes attach first finder rights owing to Danish King Christian IV's general assertion of sovereignty over all of the Northern Sea. Dutch accounts note that Willem Barents named the archipelago in 1596 despite mistaking it for part of Greenland. Thereafter an assortment of Dutch, English, French, and Scandinavian whaling fleets competed and battled for control over its waters.

We have reviewed the whiggish resort to *effectivités* in relation to the CACJ's questionable declaration of a long-standing condominium arrangement governing the waters of the Gulf of Fonseca. A false conclusion from this review would minimize the importance of *effectivités* in juridical calculations. A more nuanced conclusion would stimulate an awareness of the anachronisms that attend unwitting juridical abridgments and fanciful recreations of *effectivités*. The Chamber in *El Salvador/Honduras* sounded an alarm, treating *effectivités*, especially colonial *effectiviés* as a type of realistic fiction: they tell a story that attempts to detail life as it was, but often presents a plot line that is "confused and contradictory."[37] Similarly, the Chamber in *Burkina Faso/Mali* approached the application of colonial *effectivités* with circumspection, referencing the careful weight to be given to their complexity.[38] In *Eritrea v. Yemen*, arbitrators deemed the factual record "voluminous in quantity" yet "sparse in useful

35 Fisheries Case (U.K. v. Norway), 1951 I.C.J. Rep. 116, 130 (Dec. 18). *See also Juridical Regime of Historic Waters, Including Historic Bays-Study Prepared by the Secretariat*, at ¶¶ 80, 185, [1962] 2 Y.B. Int'l L. Comm'n, U.N. Doc No. A/CN.4/143 (1962). *Cf.* Island of Palmas (Neth. v. U.S.), 2 R.I.A.A. 829, 840 (1928) (establishing territorial sovereignty "by the continuous and peaceful display of the functions of state within a given region").

36 *Id.*

37 *See* Malcolm D. Evans, *Case Concerning the Land, Island and Maritime Frontier Dispute (El Salvador/Honduras: Nicaragua Intervening), Judgment of 11 September 1992*, 42 Int'l & Comp. L.Q. 929, 934 (1993).

38 *See* Frontier Dispute (Burk. Faso/Mali), *supra* note 30, ¶ 63.

content."[39] Here, the Tribunal's search for *effectivités* stalled in deciding a territorial dispute over islands in the Red Sea.[40] Both sides presented extensive evidence—Eritrea tracing its claim to the chain of title beginning with the Italian colonization of its mainland in the latter nineteenth century;[41] Yemen to maps of the *Bilad el-Yemen* (realm of Yemen) rule dating to the sixth century, and declarations of the Imam of Yemen and third states.[42] The Tribunal rejected the idea that the uninhabited islands were within historic waters: as long as the colonial situation prevailed, neither party "was in a position to demonstrate any kind of historic title that could serve as a sufficient basis to confirm sovereignty over any of the disputed islands."[43] In the end, neither party was "able to persuade the Tribunal that the history of the matter reveals the juridical existence of an historic title, or of historic titles, of such long-established, continuous and definitive lineage to these particular islands, islets and rocks as would be sufficient basis for the Tribunal's decision."[44]

Instead, the openness of the Red Sea for fishing and "unrestricted traffic from one side to the other" created "a sort of '*servitude internationale*' falling short of territorial sovereignty" but providing a "legal basis for maintaining certain aspects of a *res communis* that has existed for centuries for the benefit of the populations on both sides of the Red Sea." In this sense, *Eritrea v. Yemen* and the *Gulf of Fonseca* case discounted historical arguments that tended toward the establishment of a modern day *imperium*, almost as if the juridical mindset orients toward a wishful avoidance of that outcome. We have seen how a juridically imposed counter-solution—condominium—creates problems of its own. However, the whiggish mindset can work on the diplomatic and statist level as well. Proof of historic title, or for that matter a right of self-determination of peoples over a particular geo-space, forever tempts controversies associated with the application of history—from the Malvinas/Falkland dispute, to Palestine, Nagorno-Karabakh, Svalbard and numerous places elsewhere.

The use of history to support whiggish perspectives is alive and well. The problem of whiggish thinking cannot be eradicated from judicial practices, from the pitfalls and selective remembrances of yesteryear, from the parochial and statist prejudices of diplomacy, or from the predispositions of scholarly pursuits. Butterfield's concern is embedded in doctrine and policy, and in the

39 Territorial Sovereignty and Scope of the Dispute (Eri. v. Yemen), Award of the Arbitral Tribunal in the First Stage of the Proceedings, 22 R.I.A.A. 268, ¶ 241 (Perm. Ct. Arb. 1998).

40 *Id.*

41 *Id.* ¶¶ 13–14.

42 *Id.* ¶ 31.

43 *Id.* ¶ 125.

44 *Id.* ¶ 449.

historical study and presentation of revisionist and controlling presentations of international law. As international law's metaphoric wheel turns again to the study of its development in the Americas, the renewed challenge among rising voices will be to write its history and review its totemic expressions as historiography has always demanded—mindful of its complexities, assumptions, and abridgments and with one eye on the present and one eye on the past.

Selected Bibliography

Internet Sources

"A Guide to the United States' History of Recognition, Diplomatic, and Consular Relations, by Country, since 1776: Central American Federation." *U.S. Department of State: Office of the Historian*, https://history.state.gov/countries/central-american-federation.

Adams, John Quincy. "Special Message to the House of Representatives of the United States, March 15, 1826." *The American Presidency Project*, http://www.presidency.ucsb.edu/ws/index.php?pid=66632.

Adams, John Quincy. "July 4, 1821: Speech to the U.S. House of Representatives on Foreign Policy." University of Virginia Miller Center: Presidential Speeches, https://millercenter.org/the-presidency/presidential-speeches/july-4-1821-speech-us-house-representatives-foreign-policy.

Alihusain, C. *Interview: A Historical Look at Latin-American Contributions in the early Years of The Hague Academy*, Peace Palace Library, August 30, 2017, https://www.peacepalacelibrary.nl/2017/08/interview-a-historical-look-at-latin-american-contributions-in-the-early-years-of-the-hague-academy/. "The Nobel Peace Prize 1912 – Presentation Speech". *Nobelprize.org*. Nobel Media AB 2014. Web. 10 Nov 2017, http://www.nobelprize.org/nobel_prizes/peace/laureates/1912/press.html.

"An Ordinance for the Government of the Territory of the United States North-West of the River Ohio," §13, July 13, 1787, National Archives Microfilm Publication M332, roll 9, *reprinted in Our Documents*, https://www.ourdocuments.gov/doc.php?flash=true&doc=8.

"Application of Missouri for Admission into the Union as a State (Dec. 29, 1819)." *Library of Congress: American State Papers* 557, https://memory.loc.gov/cgi-bin/ampage?collId=llsp&fileName=038/llsp038.db&recNum=570.

Abello-Galvis, Ricardo and Walter Arévalo-Ramírez. "Jesús María Yepes (1892–1962)." *Société française pour le droit international*, 2017, http://www.sfdi.org/internationalistes/yepes/.

Biografías y Vidas. La Enciclopedia Biográfica en Línea, Francisco Hernández de Córdoba, http://www.biografiasyvidas.com/biografia/h/hernandez_de_cordoba_2.htm.

"Biographies of the Secretaries of State: Elihu Root (1845–1937)." *U.S. Department of State, Office of the Historian*, U.S. Department of State, history.state.gov/departmenthistory/people/root-elihu.

"Blaine and Pan Americanism, 1880s/1890s." *U.S. Department of State, Office of the Historian*, https://history.state.gov/milestones/1866-1898/blaine.

Bolívar, Simón. *La "Carta de Jamaica:" Contestación de un Americano meridional a un caballero de esta isla, el 6 de Septiembre de 1815*, http://cw.routledge.com/textbooks/dawson/data/Carta_de_Jamaica_by_de_Simon_Bolivar.pdf.

Bolívar, Simón. "Letter from Jamaica (1815)." Brown University Library Center for Digital Scholarship: Modern Latin America, https://library.brown.edu/create/modernlatinamerica/chapters/chapter-2-the-colonial-foundations/primary-documents-with-accompanying-discussion-questions/document-2-simon-bolivar-letter-from-jamaica-september-6-1815/.

"Building the Panama Canal, 1903–1914." *U.S. Department of State, Office of the Historian,* https://history.state.gov/milestones/1899-1913/panama-canal.

Caplan, Lincoln. "The Root Room." *Harvard Law Bulletin*, 2017, https://today.law.harvard.edu/feature/the-root-room/.

Cavendish, Richard. "Founding of the Darien Colony," 48 *History Today*. November 11, 1998, https://www.historytoday.com/richard-cavendish/founding-darien-colony.

Cronon, William. "Two Cheers for the Whig Interpretation of History | AHA." *Perspective on History*, American Historical Association, Sept. 2012, www.historians.org/publications-and-directories/perspectives-on-history/september-2012/two-cheers-for-the-whig-interpretation-of-history.

David, Saul, *Slavery and the "Scramble for Africa,"* BBC (Feb. 17, 2011), http://www.bbc.co.uk/ history/british/abolition/scramble_for_africa_article_01.shtml.

"Diplomatic Failure at Tampico: The 'Dolphin Incident'." Library of Congress: Mexican Revolution, *U.S. Collections Library of Congress*, http://www.loc.gov/exhibits/mexican-revolution-and-the-united-states/wilson-to-veracruz.html#obj011.

Dunne, Tim. "The English School and Humanitarian Intervention." *E-International Relations*, February 17, 2016, http://www.e-ir.info/2016/02/17/the-english-school-and-humanitarian-intervention/.

"Enabling Act of 1802." *Ohio History Central*, www.ohiohistorycentral.org/w/Enabling_Act_of_1802.

ESIL Lecture Series, "Anne Orford-Histories of International Law and Empire.", *YouTube*, January 23, 2013, https://www.youtube.com/watch?v=b5UzlTLEMko.

Fulton, Robert A. *The Legend of the Colt .45 Caliber Semi-Automatic Pistol and the Moros*. 2009, www.morolandhistory.com/related%20articles/legend%20of%20.45.htm.

"Francisco Martínez Suárez." *ChalatenangoSV.com*, https://www.chalatenangosv.com/francisco-martinez-suarez.

"From Thomas Jefferson to George Rogers Clark, 25 December 1780." *National Archives: Founders Online*, https://founders.archives.gov/documents/Jefferson/01-04-02-0295.

Gallatin, Albert. "To Thomas Jefferson from Albert Gallatin, January 13, 1803." *National Archives: Founders Online*, https://founders.archives.gov/documents/Jefferson/01-39-02-0281.

Garrity, Patrick J. "Debating the Monroe Doctrine." *CRB Digital*, August 15, 2012, http://www.claremont.org/crb/basicpage/debating-the-monroe-doctrine/.

Garrity, Patrick. "She Goes Not Abroad, In Search of Monsters to Destroy: The Dispute Between John Quincy Adams and Henry Clay Over the South American Revolutions." *Classics of Strategy*, March 2009, http://www.classicsofstrategy.com/She%20Goes%20Not%20Abroad.pdf.

Giaimo, Cara. "When the Western World Ran on Guano." *Atlas Obscura*. October 14, 2015, https://www.atlasobscura.com/articles/when-the-western-world-ran-on-guano.

Glaser, Bonnie S. "Conflict in the South China Sea." *Council on Foreign Relations*, October 2016, http://www.cfr.org/asia-and-pacific/conflict-south-china-sea/p36377.

Hamilton, Alexander. "Federalist Paper No. 22," December 14, 1787, *Avalon Project*, http://avalon.law.yale.edu/18th_century/fed22.asp.

Hamilton, Alexander. "Federalist Paper No. 11," *Avalon Project*, http://avalon.law.yale.edu/18th_century/fed11.asp.

Haynes, Sam W. "Manifest Destiny, Prelude to War." *PBS*, http://www.pbs.org/kera/usmexicanwar/prelude/md_manifest_destiny.html.

Hempel, Alex. "The Rise of the People's Liberation Army Navy: Chinese Naval Modernization from 1990 to 2018." WhiteFleet.net, March 25, 2018, https://whitefleet.net/2018/03/25/the-rise-of-chinas-peoples-liberation-army-navy-modernization-from-1990-to-2018/.

Historia de la diplomacia, Ministerio de Relaciones Exteriores de El Salvador, http://www.rree.gob.sv/index.php?option=com_content&view=article&id=260&Itemid=234.

"In Memoriam, Garrett James Hardin." *University of California*, 2003, https://senate.universityofcalifornia.edu/_files/inmemoriam/html/garretthardin.htm.

"Interview—Walter D. Mignolo." *E-International Relations*, June 1, 2017, http://www.e-ir.info/2017/06/01/interview-walter-d-mignolo/.

Jefferson, Thomas. "Letter to the President of the United States (James Monroe), Monticello, October 24, 1823." *American History*, http://www.let.rug.nl/usa/presidents/thomas-jefferson/letters-of-thomas-jefferson/jefl275.php.

Jefferson, Thomas. "Letter to Alexander von Humboldt, December 6, 1813." *American History*, http://www.let.rug.nl/usa/presidents/thomas-jefferson/letters-of-thomas-jefferson/jefl224.php.

Jefferson, Thomas. "To John C. Breckinridge, Monticello, August 12, 1803." *American History*, http://www.let.rug.nl/usa/presidents/thomas-jefferson/letters-of-thomas-jefferson/jefl159.php.

Jefferson, Thomas. "To the Governor of Virginia (James Monroe), Washington, November 24, 1801." *American History*, http://www.let.rug.nl/usa/presidents/thomas-jefferson/letters-of-thomas-jefferson/jefl142.php.

Krauze Enrique, "The April Invasion of Veracruz." *N.Y. Times: Opinion*, April 20, 2014, https://www.nytimes.com/2014/04/21/opinion/krauze-the-april-invasion-of-veracruz.html.

Kazianis, Harry. "China's Expanding Cabbage Strategy." *The Diplomat*, October 29, 2013, http://thediplomat.com/2013/10/chinas-expanding-cabbage-strategy/.

"Letter from the American Minister [Benjamin L. Jefferson] to the Secretary of State, Managua, 17 December 1913." *Papers Relating to the Foreign Relations of the United States*, File No. 817.032/8, available at: https://history.state.gov/historicaldocuments/frus1913/d1309.

"Letter of Mr. Blaine to Mr. Osborn." *Foreign Relations of the United States*, Volume 14, November 29, 1881 http://images.library.wisc.edu/FRUS/EFacs2/1881-82v01/reference/frus.frus188182v01.i0008.pdf.

Lindsay, James. M. "TWE Remembers: The U.S. Invasion of Veracruz Mexico, Council on Foreign Relations." *Council on Foreign Relations: The Water's Edge*, April 21, 2014, https://www.cfr.org/blog/twe-remembers-us-invasion-veracruz-mexico.

Little, Richard. "Reassessing 'The Expansion of International Society'." *E-International Relations*, January 28, 2016, http://www.e-ir.info/2016/01/28/reassessing-the-expansion-of-international-society/.

"Louisiana Purchase 1803." *U.S. Department of State: Office of the Historian*, https://history.state.gov/milestones/1801-1829/louisiana-purchase.

Madison, James. "Federalist Paper No. 51." The Structure of the Government Must Furnish the Proper Checks and Balances Between the Different Departments, February 8, 1788. *Avalon Project*, http://avalon.law.yale.edu/18th_century/fed51.asp.

Malik, Mohan. "Historical Fiction: China's South China Sea Claims." *World Affairs*, May/June 2013, http://www.worldaffairsjournal.org/article/historical-fiction-china%E2%80%99s-south-china-sea-claims.

"Message of President James Monroe at the Commencement of the First Session of the 18th Congress, December 2, 1823 [the Monroe Doctrine]." *National Archives*, https://www.ourdocuments.gov/doc.php?doc=23&page=transcript.

"Message of the President, Adolfo Díaz, to the Congress, Managua, 17 December 1913, extracts enclosed and translated in the letter from The American Minister [Benjamin L. Jefferson] to the Secretary of State, Managua, 17 December 1913," *Papers Relating to the Foreign Relations of the United States*, File No. 817.032/8, available at: https://history.state.gov/historicaldocuments/frus1913/d1309

"Mexico Must Wipe Out Insult to Flag." Library of Congress: Mexican Revolution U.S. Collections, *Library of Congress, Henry T. Mayo Papers (1836–1937)* (photo. Reprint 1991), http://www.loc.gov/exhibits/mexican-revolution-and-the-united-states/wilson-to-veracruz.html#obj010.

Morrow, James B. "Life of Elihu Root, Statesman and Peace-Worker." *The Washington Herald*, January 11, 1914, http://chroniclingamerica.loc.gov/lccn/sn83045433/1914-01-11/ed-1/seq-32/.

"Motion Regarding the Western Lands, [6 September] 1780, Editorial Note." *National Archives: Founders Online*, https://founders.archives.gov/documents/Madison/01-02-02-0051.

Murray, Robert W. "An Introduction to the English School of International Relations." *E-International Relations*, January 5, 2016, http://www.e-ir.info/2016/01/05/an-introduction-to-the-english-school-of-international-relations/.

"New States Clause." *The Heritage Guide to the Constitution*, https://www.heritage.org/constitution/#!/articles/4/essays/125/new-states-clause.

"Presentation speech by Ragnvald Moe, Nobel Committee, 10 Dec. 1913," *Nobel prize.org*, https://www.nobelprize.org/nobel_prizes/peace/laureates/1912/press.html.

"Proposed Interoceanic Canal Treaty Between the United States and Nicaragua, and Protests of Salvador and Costa Rica in Relation Thereto." December 2, 1913. *U.S. Department of State, Office of the Historian*, https://history.state.gov/historicaldocuments/frus1913/ch94.

Roosevelt, Theodore. "Fourth Annual Message to the Senate and the House of Representatives, December 6, 1904," *The American Presidency Project*, http://www.presidency.ucsb.edu/ws/?pid=29545.

Roosevelt, Theodore. "Sixth Annual Message," December 3, 1906. *The American Presidency Project*. http://www.presidency.ucsb.edu/ws/?pid=29547.

Roosevelt, Theodore. "To the Graduating Class of the Naval Academy, Annapolis, Maryland, May 2, 1902." *Almanac of Theodore Roosevelt*, http://www.theodore-roosevelt.com/images/research/txtspeeches/4.txt.

"Roosevelt Roads Naval Station." *Global Security.org*, http://www.globalsecurity.org/military/facility/roosevelt-roads.htm.

Rush, Cynthia R. *The War of the Pacific: The Empire Crushes Peru's American System Project*, EIR History 56 (Feb. 3, 2013) http://www.larouchepub.com/eiw/public/2013/eirv40n06-20130208/54-60_4006.pdf.

Schoonover, Bruce. "Acquisition of the Danish West Indies by the United States," *St. John Historical Society*, March 8, 2005, https://stjohnhistoricalsociety.org/vol-vi-no-5-march-2005-acquisition-of-the-danish-west-indies-by-the-united-states-by-bruce-schoonover/.

Sierra Fonseca, Rolando, "Antonio R. Vallejo y la historiografía fundante en Honduras." *La Tribuna*, March 30, 2014, http://www.latribuna.hn/2014/03/30/antonio-r-vallejo-y-la-historiografia-fundante-en-honduras/.

Smith, George H. "Lord Acton and the History of Liberty, Part 2." *Libertarianism.org*., March 12, 2013, https://www.libertarianism.org/publications/essays/lord-acton-history-liberty-part-2.

Song, Yann-huie. "Taiwan's Response to the Philippines-PRC South China Sea Arbitration." *Asia Maritime Transparency Initiative*, July 15, 2015, https://amti.csis.org/taiwans-response-to-the-philippines-prc-south-china-sea-arbitration/

"Spratly Islands." *CIA World Factbook*, https://www.cia.gov/library/publications/the-world-factbook/geos/pg.html.

Staalesen, Atle. "Norway Takes Tough Line Against EU in Svalbard Waters." *Barents Observer*, January 25, 2017, https://thebarentsobserver.com/en/industry-and-energy/2017/01/norway-takes-tough-line-against-eu-svalbard-waters.

"Stalemate: Treaty of Ghent Ends War of 1812 in a Draw." *United States Naval Institute*, Dec. 24, 2014, https://www.usni.org/naval-history-blog/9644.

Steinhauer, Jason. "The Forgotten Senator, Statesman, and Nobel Laureate Elihu Root," with Charles Laderman. Podcast from John W. Kluge Center, August 11, 2016. http://www.loc.gov/loc/kluge/podcasts/laderman.html.

Stiles, T.J. "The Filibuster King: The Strange Career of William Walker, the Most Dangerous International Criminal of the Nineteenth Century." *History Now*, https://www.gilderlehrman.org/history-by-era/jackson-lincoln/essays/filibuster-king-strange-career-william-walker-most-dangerous-i.

"The Court: History." *International Court of Justice*, http://www.icj-cij.org/court/index.php?p1=1&p2=1.

"The Danish West-Indies." *Rigsarkivet*, https://www.virgin-islands-history.org/en/history/sale-of-the-danish-west-indian-islands-to-the-usa/the-sales-treaty-1902/.

"The Federalist Papers No. 11." *Avalon Project – Documents in Law, History and Diplomacy*, avalon.law.yale.edu/18th_century/fed11.asp.

"The Forgotten Senator, Statesman, and Nobel Laureate Elihu Root," with Charles Laderman (Podcast, Aug. 11, 2016), The John W. Kluge Center, Library of Congress, http://www.loc.gov/loc/kluge/podcasts/laderman.html.

"The Nobel Peace Prize 1912." *Nobelprize.org*, http://www.nobelprize.org/nobel_prizes/peace/laureates/1912/.

"The Philippine-American War, 1899–1902." *U.S. Department of State, Office of the Historian*, https://history.state.gov/milestones/1899-1913/war.

"The Senate Approves the Treaty of Ghent for Ratification, Feb. 16, 1815." *U.S. Senate*, https://www.senate.gov/artandhistory/history/minute/Senate_Approves_Treaty_of_Ghent.htm.

"The United States, Cuba, and the Platt Amendment, 1901." *U.S. Department of State Archive*, https://2001-2009.state.gov/r/pa/ho/time/ip/86557.htm.

"United States Department of State Bureau of Intelligence and Research, Appendix II," (Report 668-AR, August 17, 1983, declassified November 28, 2012), https://www.cia.gov/library/readingroom/docs/CIA-RDP08C01297R000400140013-1.pdf.

"U.S. Debt and Foreign Loans, 1775–1795." *U.S. Department of State, Office of the Historian*, https://history.state.gov/milestones/1784-1800/loans.

"U.S. Interest in an Interoceanic Canal 1835–1881." *GlobalSecurity.org*, http://www.globalsecurity.org/military/facility/panama-canal-us.htm.

Washington, George. "Farewell Address 1796." *Avalon Project*, http://avalon.law.yale.edu/18th_century/washing.asp.

Wilson, Woodrow. "Address to a Joint Session of Congress on the Tampico Incident" (April 20, 1914). *The American Presidency Project*, http://www.presidency.ucsb.edu/ws/?pid=65376.

Yoder, Edwin M. Jr. "A Gentleman and a Scholar." *Washington Post*, June 21, 1986, https://www.washingtonpost.com/archive/lifestyle/1986/06/21/a-gentleman-and-a-scholar/84870ef7-8382-4a58-9977-f2f7dc19b739/?utm_term=.ce0181eb5f54.

Articles and Books

Aalberts, Tanja and Ingo Venzke. "Moving Beyond Interdisciplinary Wars: Towards an Understanding of International Law as Practice." In *International Law as a Profession*, 287–310. Edited by Jean d'Aspremont, Tarcisio Gazzini, André Nollkaemper, and Wouter Werner. Cambridge: Cambridge University Press, 2017.

Abello-Galvis, Ricardo and Walter Arévalo-Ramírez. "The Influence of the Latin American Doctrine on International Law: The Rise of Latin American Doctrines at The Hague Academy During the Early Twentieth Century." In *Latin America and the International Court of Justice: Contributions to International Law*, 15–28. Edited by Paula Wojcikiewicz Almeida and Jean-Marc Sorel. London: Routeledge, 2016.

Abente, Diego. "The War of the Triple Alliance: Three Explanatory Models." 22(2) *Latin American Research Review* 47–69, 1987.

Acharya, Amitav and Barry Buzan, eds. *Non-Western International Relations Theory: Perspectives on and Beyond Asia*. London: Routledge, 2010.

Acosta Alvarado, Paola Andrea. "REDIAL e Imperialismo y derecho internacional. Oportunidad para la reflexión." 39 *Revista Derecho Del Estado Nueva Serie* 3–16, 2017.

Adams, Brooks. *The Law of Civilization and Decay: An Essay on History*. New York: MacMillan Co., 1897.

Adams, Ephraim D. "English Interest in the Annexation of California." 14(4) *The American Historical Review* 744–763, 1909.

Adams, John Quincy. *Memoirs of John Quincy Adams, Comprising Portions of His Diary from 1795 to 1848*. Edited by Charles Francis Adams. Volume v. Philadelphia: J.B. Lippincott & Co., 1875.

"Address by Col. Henry L. Stimson." In *Elihu Root: President of the Century Association, 1918–1927; Addresses Made in His Honor, at the Club House, April 27, 1937*, 19–38. New York, N.Y.: Century Association, 1937.

Adler, Emanuel. "Europe as a Civilizational Community of Practice." In *Civilizations in World Politics: Plural and Pluralistic Perspectives*, 67–90. Edited by Peter J. Katzenstein. London and New York: Routledge, 2010.

Agamben, Giorgio. *Homo Sacer: Sovereign Power and Bare Life*. Stanford: Stanford University Press, 1998.

Aguilar Avilés, Gilberto. *Historia de la Corte Suprema de Justicia de El Salvador*. San Salvador: El Salvador, 2000.

Akinwumi, Olayemi. "Political or Spiritual Partition: The Impact of the 1884/85 Berlin Conference on Christian Missions in Africa." In *Christianity in Africa and the African Diaspora: The Appropriation of a Scattered Heritage*. Edited by Afe Adogame et al. London: Continuum International Publishing Group, 2008.

Alderson, Kai and Andrew Hurrell, eds. *Hedley Bull on International Society*. London: Macmillan, 2000.

Alexandrowicz, C.H. *An Introduction to the History of the Law of Nations in the East Indies '(16th, 17th and 18th Centuries)'*. Oxford: Clarendon Press, 1967.

Alexandrowicz, C.H. *History and Theory of International Law: The Law of Nations in Global History*. Oxford University Press, 2017.

Alexandrowicz, C.H., "Introduction." In *Alberico Gentili and the Development of International Law: His Life, Work, and Times*, vii–ix. Edited by Gesina H.J. van der Molen. 2nd rev. edn. Leyden: A.W. Sijhoff, 1968. JX

Allot, Philip. "International Law and the American Mind." 97 *Proceedings of the American Society of International Law* 129–31, 2003.

Álvarez, Alejandro. *The Monroe Doctrine: Its Importance in the International Life of the States of the New World*. Oxford University Press, 1924.

Álvarez, Alejandro. *Le droit international américain*. Paris: A. Pedone, 1910.

Álvarez, Alejandro. "Latin America and International Law." 3(2) *American Journal of International Law* 269–253, 1909.

Álvarez Rubiano, Pablo. *Pedrarias Dávila: Contribución al studio de la figure del "Gran justador", gobernador de Castilla de Oro y Nicaragua*. Madrid: Instituto Gonzalo Fernández de Oviedo, 1944.

Amorosa, Paolo. *The American Project and the Politics of History: James Brown Scott and the Origins of International Law*. Dissertation, University of Helsinki, 2018.

Anaya, S. James. *Indigenous Peoples in International Law*. New York: Oxford University Press, 1990.

Ando, Nisuke, Edward McWhinney and Rüdiger Wolfrum, eds., Betsy Baker Röben, asst. gen. ed. *Liber Amicorum: Judge Shigeru Oda*. Volume 1. The Hague, London, New York: Kluwer Law International, 2002.

Anghie, Antony. "The Evolution of International Law: Colonial and Postcolonial Realities." 27(5) *Third World Quarterly* 739–753, 2006.

Anghie, Antony. *Imperialism, Sovereignty and the Making of International Law*. New York: Cambridge University Press, 2005.

Anghie, Antony. *Colonialism, Sovereignty, and the Making of International Law*. Cambridge University Press, 2004.

Anghie, Antony. "Finding the Peripheries: Sovereignty and Colonialism in Nineteenth-Century International Law." 40(1) *Harvard International Law Journal* 1–80, 1999.

Anghie, Antony and B.S. Chimni. "Third World Approaches to International Law and Individual Responsibility in Internal Conflicts." 2(1) *Chinese Journal of International Law* 77–103, 2003.

Anghie, Antony, Martti Koskenniemi and Anne Orford, *Imperialismo y Derecho Internacional*. Bogotá: Nuevo Pensamiento Jurídico, 2017.

"Arbitration and Peace Treaties." 8 (1) *American Journal of International Law* 341–343, 1914.

Archarya, Amitav and Barry Buzan. "Why Is There No Non-Western International Relations Theory? An Introduction." 7(3) *International Relations of the Asia-Pacific* 287–312, 2007.

Atkins, Thos. B. *The Inter-Oceanic Canal Across Nicaragua and the Attitude Toward It of the Government of the United States*. New York: The New York Printing Company, 1890.

Avilés, Gilberto Aguilar. *Historia de la Corte Suprema de Justicia de El Salvador*. San Salvador, El Salv.: Sección de la Corte Suprema de Justicia, 2000.

Backer, Larry Catá. "The Structural Characteristics of Global Law for the 21st Century: Fracture, Fluidity, Permeability, and Polycentricity." 17(2) *Tilburg Law Review* 177–199, 2012.

Backgrounder. "Understanding China's Position on the South China Sea Disputes." *Institute Security & Development Policy* 1–8, 2016.

Bain, William. "The English School and the Activity of Being an Historian." In *Theorising International Society: English School Methods*, 146–166. Edited by Cornelia Navari. New York: Palgrame Macmillan, 2009.

Bain, William. "Are There Any Lessons of History? The English School and the Activity of Being an Historian." 44(5) *International Politics* 513–530, 2007.

Ballagh, James Curtis. "The Monroe Doctrine: An Interpretation." 12(1) *American Journal of International Law* 214–220, 1918.

Bancroft, Hubert Howe.*The Works of Hubert Howe Bancroft. Volume VI: History of Central America: Volume 1: 1501–1530*. San Francisco: A.L. Bancroft & Company, Publishers, 1883.

Bandeira Galindo, George Rodrigo. "Martti Koskenniemi and the Historiographical Turn in International Law," 16(3) *European Journal of International Law* 539–559, 2005.

Barbosa, Ruy, "Speech of Senatory Ruy Barbosa." In *Latin America and the United States: Addresses by Elihu Root*, 19–27. Edited by Robert Bacon and James Brown Scott. Cambridge: Harvard University Press; London: Humphrey Milford, 1917.

Barreto, Jóse-Manuel. "Imperialism and Decolonization as Scenarios of Human Rights History." In *Human Rights from a Third World Perspective: Critique, History, and International Law*, 140–171. Edited by José-Manuel Barreto. Newcastle upon Tyne: Cambridge Scholars Publishing, 2013.

Barreto, Jóse-Manuel. "Cerberus: Rethinking Grotius and the Westphalian System." In *International Law and Empire: Historical Explorations*, 149–176. Edited by Martti

Koskenniemi, Walter Rech and Manuel Jiménez Fonseca. Oxford: Oxford University Press, 2017.

Barrett, John. "Pan-americanism and Its Inspiration in History." 19 *Records of the Columbia Historical Society* 156–159, 1916.

Barrett, John. *The Pan American Union: Peace, Friendship, Commerce*. Washington, D.C.: Pan American Union, 1911.

Bartelson, Jens. *Sovereignty as Symbolic Form*. London: Routledge, 2014

Bartelson, Jens. *A Genealogy of Sovereignty*. New York: Cambridge University Press, 1995.

Bartlett, Levi. "Guano, Hen Manure, and Some Other Things." In *The Cultivator Ser. No. 3*, 177–178. Albany: Luther Tucker and Son, 1858.

Bartlett, Ruhl J. *The League to Enforce Peace*. Chapel Hill: University of North Carolina Press, 1944.

Bauer, K. Jack. *The Mexican War, 1846–1848*. New York: Macmillan, 1974.

Baxter, Maurice G., *Henry Clay and the American System*. Lexington: University Press of Kentucky, 2000.

Beard, Jennifer. "Understanding International Development Programs as a Modern Phenomenon of Early and Medieval Christian Theology." 18 *Australian Feminist Law Journal* 27–54, 2003.

Becker Lorca, Arnulf. *Mestizo International Law: A Global Intellectual History 1842–1933*. Cambridge: Cambridge University Press, 2014.

Becker Lorca, Arnulf. "Universal International Law: Nineteenth-Century Histories of Imposition and Appropriation." 51(2) *Harvard International Law Journal* 475–552, 2010.

Becker Lorca, Arnulf. "International Law in Latin America or Latin America International Law—Rise, Fall, and Retrieval of a Tradition of Legal Thinking and Political Imagination." 47(1) *Harvard International Law Journal* 283–305, 2006.

Bederman, David J. "Appraising a Century of Scholarship in the American Journal of International Law." 100(1) *American Journal of International Law* 20–63, 2006.

Bederman, Gail. *Manliness & Civilization: A Cultural History of Gender and Race in the United States, 1880–1917*. Chicago and London: University of Chicago Press, 1995.

Bell, Duncan. *Reordering the World: Essays on Liberalism and Empire*. Princeton: Princeton University Press, 2016.

Bell, Duncan. "Writing the World: Disciplinary History and Beyond." 85(1) *International Affairs* 3–22, 2009.

Bello, Andrés, *Principios de derecho de gentes*, Santiago: Chile, 1832.

Bemis, Samuel Flagg. *John Quincy Adams and the Foundations of American Foreign Policy*. New York: A.A. Knopf, 1949.

Benevenutto Murrieta, Pedro M. *La Doctrina Monroe. Sus Antecedentes historicos. Principales Aplicaciones*. Lima: La Revista de la Universidad Católica , 1935.

Beneyto, José Maria and Justo Corti Varela, eds. *At the Origins of Modernity: Francisco de Vitoria and the Discovery of International Law*. Springer International Publishing AG, 2017.

Beneyto, José Maria and David Kennedy, eds. *New Approaches to International Law: The European and the American Experiences*. The Hague: T.M.C. Asser Press, 2012.

Benn, Carl. *The Iroquois in the War of 1812*. Buffalo: University of Toronto Press, 1998.

Bentley, Michael. *The Life and Thought of Herbert Butterfield: History, Science and God*. Cambridge: Cambridge University Press, 2011.

Berkhofer, Jr., F. Robert "Americans versus Indians: The Northwest Ordinance, Territory Making, and Native Americans." 84(1) *Indiana Magazine of History* 90–108, March 1988.

Berkhofer, Jr., F. Robert "Jefferson, the Ordinance of 1784, and the Origins of the American Territorial System." 29(2) *William & Mary Quarterly* 231–262, 1972.

Bevans, C. *Treaties and Other International Agreements of the United States of America, 1776–1949*. Washington, D.C.: Government Printing Office, 1968–1976.

Bevir, Mark. "The Errors of Linguistic Contextualism." 31(3) *History and Theory* 276–298, 1992.

Bilgin, Pinar. "Looking for 'the International' Beyond the West." 31(5) *Third World Quarterly* 817–828, 2010.

Billington, Ray Allen and Martin Ridge. *Westward Expansion: A History of the American Frontier*. Albuquerque: University of New Mexico Press, 1949.

Bingham, Hiram. *Across South America: An Account of a Journey from Buenos Aires to Lima by way of Potosí with Notes on Brazil, Argentina, Bolivia, Chile, and Peru*. Boston: Houghton Mifflin, 1911.

Bingham, Hiram, *Lost City of the Incas: the Story of Machu Picchu and its Builders*. New York: Atheneum, 1948.

Bingham, Hiram. "The Latin American Attitude Toward the Monroe Doctrine." 8 *Proceedings of the American Society of International Law* 180–201, 1914.

Bingham, Hiram. *The Monroe Doctrine: An Obsolete Shibboleth*. Oxford: Oxford University Press, 1913.

Bizcarrondo, Marta, "El Autonomismo Cubano 1878–1898: Las Ideas y Los Hechos." 19 *Historia Contemporánea* 69–94, 1999.

Blakeslee, George H. "Should the Monroe Doctrine Continue to be a Policy of the United States?" Address, April 24–25, 1914. 8 *Proceedings of the American Society of International Law* 217–230, 1914.

Bolívar, Simón. Doctrina del libertador. 3rd edition, Manuel Pérez Vila, editor. Biblioteca Ayacucho, 2009.

Bonilla, Heraclio. "The War of the Pacific and the National and Colonial Problem in Peru." 81(1) *Past & Present*, 92–118, 1978.

Borschberg, Peter. *Hugo Grotius, The Portuguese and Free Trade in the East Indies*. Singapore: NUS Press, 2010.

Boutros-Ghali, Boutros. "The Role of International Law in the Twenty-First Century: A Grotian Moment." 18(5) *Fordham International Law Journal* 1609–1616, 1995.

Boutwell, George S. *The Venezuelan Question and the Monroe Doctrine*. Washington, D.C.: Gibson Brother, 1896.

Bowden, Brett. "The Colonial Origins of International Law. European Expansion and the Classical Standard of Civilization." 7(1) *Journal of the History of International Law*, 1–23, 2005.

Bowman, Jr., Charles "Manuel Torres, A Spanish Patriot in Philadelphia, 1796–1822." 94(1) *The Pennsylvania Magazine of History and Biography* 26–53, 1970.

Boxer, C.R. *The Dutch Seaborne Empire, 1600–1800*. New York: Alfred A. Knopf, 1965.

Brown, Charles H. *Agents of Manifest Destiny: The Lives and Times of the Filibusters*. Chapel Hill: University of North Carolina Press, 1980.

Brown, Philip Marshall. "Costa Rica v. Nicaragua." 11(1) *American Journal of International Law* 158–160, 1917.

Brum, Baltasar, "Fraternal Future of America." 4 *The World Court* 540–542, 1915.

Bull, Hedley. *The Anarchical Society: A Study of Order in World Politics*. New York: Palgrave Macmillian, 1977.

Bull, Hedley, "The State's Positive Role in World Affairs." 108(4) *Daedalus* 111–123, 1979.

Bull, Hedley, and Adam Watson, editors. *The Expansion of International Society*. Oxford: Clarendon Press, 1984.

Burr, Robert N. *By Reason or Force: Chile and the Balancing of Power in South America, 1830–1905*. Oakland: University of California Press, 1965.

Burrow, John. *A History of Histories: Epics, Chronicles, Romances and Inquiries from Herodotus and Thucydides to the Twentieth Century*. New York: Knopf, 2008.

Buszynski, Leszek. "The South China Sea: Oil, Maritime Claims, and U.S.-China Strategic Rivalry" 35(2) *Washington Quarterly* 139–156, 2012.

Buszynski, Leszek. *The Development of the South China Sea Maritime Dispute*. New York: Boutledge, 2013.

Buszynski, Leszek and Christopher B. Roberts. *The South China Sea Maritime Dispute: Political, Legal and Regional Perspectives*. New York: Rutledge, 2015.

Butterfield, Herbert. *Liberty in the Modern World*. Toronto: Ryerson Press, 1952.

Butterfield, Herbert. *Christianity and History*. London: G. Bell and Sons, Ltd., 1949.

Butterfield, Herbert. *The Whig Interpretation of History*. London: G. Bell and Sons, Ltd., 1968 [1931].

Butterfield, Herbert. *Christianity, Diplomacy and War*. Nashville: Abingdon Press, 1953.

Butterfield, Herbert and Martin Wight eds. *Diplomatic Investigations: Essays in the Theory of International Politics*. Cambridge: Harvard University Press, 1968.

Buxton, Carol R. "Property in Outer Space: The Common Heritage of Mankind Principle vs. the "First in Time, First in Right" Rule of Property Law." 69(4) *Journal of Air Law and Commerce* 689–707, 2004.

Buzan, Barry, "From International System to International Society: Structural Realism and Regime Theory Meet the English School." 47(3) *International Organization* 327–352, 1993.

Calderón, Francisco García. "A Latin-American Criticism of the Monroe Doctrine." 29(4) *Current History* 548–553, January 1, 1929.

Calvo, Charles. *Le Droit International Théorique et Pratique Précédé d'un Exposé Historique des Progrès de la Science du Droit des Gens.* Paris; Amyot: A. Durand et Perdone-Lauriel; Cuillaumin et C(ie), 1870.

Cass, Deborah Z. "Navigating the Newstream: Recent Critical Scholarship in International Law." 65 *Nordic Journal of International Law* 341–383, 1996.

Cavallar, Georg. "Vitoria, Grotius, Pufendorf, Wolff and Vattel: Accomplices of European Colonialism and Exploitation or True Cosmopolitans?" 10(2) *Journal of the History of International Law* 181–209, 2008.

Cayton, Andrew R.L. *The Frontier Republic: Ideology and Politics in the Ohio Country, 1780–1825*. Kent and London: The Kent State University Press, 1987.

Cayton, Andrew R.L. "The Northwest Ordinance from the Perspective of the Frontier." In *The Northwest Ordinance 1787: A Bicentennial Handbook*, 1–24. Edited by Robert M. Taylor Jr. Indianapolis: Indiana Historical Society, 1987.

Cayton, Andrew R.L. "The Debate Over the Panama Congress and the Origins of the Second American Party System." 74(2) *The Historian* 219–238, 1985.

Central American Court of Justice. *Costa Rica v. Nicaragua*. Judgment, 30 Sep. 1916. 11 *American Journal of International Law* 181–229, 1917.

Central American Court of Justice. *El Salvador v. Nicaragua*. Judgment, 9 Mar. 1917. 11 *American Journal of International Law* 674–730, 1917.

Cerdaz-Cruz, Rodolfo. *The Communist International in Central America, 1920–36*. London: Macmillan, 1993.

Cerwin, Herbert. *Bernal Díaz: Historian of the Conquest*. Norman: University of Norman Press, 1963.

Chakrabarty, Dipesh, *Provincializing Europe: Postcolonial Thought and Historical Difference*. Princeton: Princeton University Press, 2000.

Chamberlain, Robert S. *The Conquest and Colonization of Honduras: 1502–1550*. Washington, D.C.: Carnegie Institution of Washington, 1953.

Charlesworth, Hilary and David Kennedy. "Afterword: and Forward—There Remains So Much We Do Not Know." In *International Law and Its Others*, 401–408. Edited by Anne Orford. Cambridge: Cambridge University Press, 2006.

Chimni, B.S. "The Self, Modern Civilization, and International Law: Learning from Mohandas Karamchand Gandhi's Hind Swaraj or Indian Home Rule." 23(4) *European Journal of International Law* 1159–1173, 2012.

Chimni, B.S. "Third World Approaches to International Law: A Manifesto." 8(1) *International Community Law Review* 3–27, 2006.

Chinese Society of International Law. "The Tribunal's Award in the "South China Sea Arbitration" Initiated by The Philippines Is Null And Void." 15(2) *Chinese Journal of International Law* 457– 458, 2016.

Clay, Henry. "On the Emancipation of South America." In *The Life and Speeches of the Hon. Henry Clay*, 377–419. Edited by Daniel Mallory. Hartford: S. Andrus & Son, 1854.

Coates, Benjamin Allen. *Legalist Empire: International Law and American Foreign Relations in the Early Twentieth Century*. New York: Oxford University Press, 2016.

Cogliano, Francis D. *Thomas Jefferson: Reputation and Legacy*. Edinburgh: Edinburgh University Press, 2006.

Coker, William S. "The Panama Canal Tolls Controversy: A Different Perspective." 55(3) *Journal of American History* 555–564, 1968.

Collin, Richard H. *Theodore Roosevelt's Caribbean: The Panama Canal, The Monroe Doctrine, and the Latin American Context*. Baton Rouge: Louisiana State University Press, 1990.

Coolidge, Archibald Carey, *The United States As A World Power*. New York: Macmillan, 1918 [1908].

Cox, Isaac Joslin. "Nicaragua and the United States, 1909–1927." 10(7) *World Peace Foundation Pamphlet* 703–887, 1927.

Crosby, Alfred W. "Conquistador y Pestilencia: The First New World Pandemic and the Fall of the Great Indian Empires." 47(3) *Hispanic American Historical Review* 321–337, 1967.

Croxton, Derek. "The Peace of Westphalia of 1648 and the Origins of Sovereignty." 21(3) *International History Review* 569–591, 1999.

Curzon, Lord George. "Frontiers." In *The Romanes Lectures*, Oxford: Clarendon Press, 1907.

D'Aspremont, Jean. *Epistemic Forces in International Law: Foundational Doctrines and Techniques of International Legal Argumentation*. Cheltenham: Edward Elgar Publishing Ltd., 2015.

Davis, Cushman K. *A Treatise on International Law including American Diplomacy*. St. Paul: Keefe-Davidson Law Book Co., 1901.

Davis, Harold Eugene, John J. Finan, and F. Taylor Peck, eds. *Latin American Diplomatic History*. Baton Rouge: Louisiana State University Press, 1977.

Debrix, François. "The Virtual Nomos?" In *Spatiality, Sovereignty and Carl Schmitt: Geographies of the Nomos*, 220–226. Edited by Stephen Legg. New York: Routledge, 2011.

De Bustamante, Antoine S. "Le canal de panama et le droit international." 27 *Revue de Droit International et de legislation comparée* 223–253, 1895.

De Gandia, Enrique. *Mariano Moreno Su Pensamiento Politico*. Editorial Pleamar, 1968.

De Gorgoza, Anthony. "Problem of Interoceanic Communication by Way of the American Isthmus, Before the American Geographical Society." 21 *Journal of the American Geographical Society of New York* 526–529, 1889.

Delabie, Lucie. "Les nouvelles approaches du droit international." *Revue québécoise de droit international* 57–80, 2016.

Delabie, Lucie. *Approches Américaines du droit International: Entre unité et diversité*. Paris: Editions Pedone, 2011.

De Lapradelle, A.G., and Ellery C. Stowell. "Latin America at The Hague Conference." 17(4) *The Yale Law Journal* 270–280, 1908.

De la Rasilla del Moral, Ignacio. *In the Shadow of Vitoria: A History of International Law in Spain (1770–1953)*. Leiden: Brill/Nijhoff, 2017.

De la Rasilla del Moral, Ignacio. "La alianza entre la civilización y el derecho internacional entre Escila y Carbiddis (o de la brevísima historia de un anacronismo jurídico)." In *El discurso civilzador en derecho internacional*, 41–60. Edited by Yolanda Gamarra. Zaragoza: Institucion Fernando El Catolico, 2011.

De la Rasilla del Moral, Ignacio. "A Propósito del giro historiográfico en Derecho internacional." In *La idea de América en el pensamiento ius internacionalista del siglo XXI*, 33–42. Edited by Yoland Gamarra Chopo. Institución Fernando el Católico, 2010.

De Lapradelle, A.G. and Ellery C. Stowell. "Latin America at The Hague Conference." 17(4) *The Yale Law Journal* 270–280, 1908.

De las Cacas, Bartolomé, *Brevísima relación de la destrucción de las Indias Occidentales*. Mexico: Romerovargas y Blasco, 1957 [1552].

Der Derian, James. "Hedley Bull and the Idea of Diplomatic Culture." In *International Society After the Cold War: Anarchy and Order Reconsidered*, 84–100. Edited by Rick Fawn and Jeremy Larkins, 1996.

Der Derian, James. *On Diplomacy: A Genealogy of Western Estrangement*. Oxford: Basil Blackwell, 1987.

Derrida, Jacques. *Specters of Marx: the State of the Debt, the Work of Mourning, and the New International*. New York: Routledge, 1994.

De Visscher, Charles. *Les Effectivités Du Droit International Public*. Paris: A. Pedone, 1967.

Dierksmeier, Claus. "Krausism." In *A Companion to Latin American Philosophy*, 110–127. Edited by Susana Nuccetelli, Ofelia Schutte and Otávio Bueno. West Sussex, UK: Blackwell Publishing Ltd., 2010.

Díaz del Castillo, Bernal. *Historia verdadera de la conquista de la Nueva España*. Madrid: Imprenta del Reyno, 1632.

Díaz del Castillo, Bernal. *Historia verdadera de la conquista de la Nueva España*. Tomo II. Introducción y notas por Joaquín Ramírez Cabañas. Mexico, D.F.: Editorial Pedro Robredo, 1939 [1632].

Dodd, Thomas J. "La corte de Justicia centroamericana, 1907–1918: Su legado, la defensa de derechos Individuales." 12–13 *Revista de Historia* 67–82, 1986.

Dolinger, Jacob. "The Influence of American Constitutional Law on the Brazilian Legal System." 38(4) *The American Journal of Comparative Law* 803–838, 1990.

Dorais, Geneviève. "Missionary Critiques of Empire, 1920–1932: Between Interventionism and Anti-Imperialism." 39(3) *International History Review*, 337–403, 2016.

Douglas, Stephen A. "On the Clayton Bulwer Treaty." In *The Life and Speeches of Stephen A. Douglas*, 31–70. Edited by Henry Martyn Flint. Philadelphia: John E. Potter and Company, 1860.

Drago, Luis M. "Speech of Dr. Luis M. Drago (Aug. 17, 1906)." In *Latin America and the United States: Addresses by Elihu Root*, 6–11. Edited by Robert Bacon and James Brown Scott. Cambridge: Harvard University Press; London: Humphrey Milford, 1917.

Drago, Luis M. and H. Edward Nettles. "The Drago Doctrine in International Law and Politics." 8(2) *Hispanic American Historical Review*, 204–223, 1928.

Dryzek, John S. and Stephen T. Leonard. "History and Discipline in Political Science." 82(4) *American Political Science Review* 1245–1260, 1988.

Dubin, Martin David. "Elihu Root and the Advocacy of a League of Nations, 1914–1917." 19(3) *Western Political Quarterly* 439–455, 1966.

Dunn, John. "The Identity of the History of Ideas." 43(164) *Philosophy* 85–104, 1968.

Dunne, Gerald T. Grenville Clark, *Public Citizen*. New York: Farrar, Straus, Giroux, 1986.

Dunne, Tim. "The English School." In *The Oxford Handbook of Political Science*, 730–747. Edited by Robert E. Goodin. Oxford: Oxford University Press, 2009.

Dunne, Tim. *Inventing International Society: A History of the English School*. Edited by Eugene Rogan. New York: St. Martin's Press, Inc., 1998.

Dunning, William Archibald. *The British Empire and the United States*. New York: Charles Scribner's Sons, 1914.

Dutton, Peter A. "An Analysis of China's Claim to Historic Rights in the South China Sea." In *Major Law and Policy Issues in the South China Sea: European and American Perspectives*, 57–74. Edited by Yann-Huei Song and Keyuan Zou. New York: Routledge, 2014.

Duve, Thomas. "European Legal History—Concepts, Methods, Challenges." In *Entanglements in Legal History: Conceptual Approaches*, 29–66. Edited by Thomas Duve. Max Planck Institute for European Legal History, 2014.

Elderkin, John, Chester Sanders Lord and Horatio Nelson Fraser, eds. *Speeches at the Lotos Club*. New York: Private Print, 1901.

Elderkin, John. *A Brief History of the Lotos Club*. New York: Press of Macgowan & Slipper, 1895.

El Golfo De Fonseca y El Tratado Bryan-Chamorro: Celebrado entre Los Estados Unidos de Norte América y Nicaragua: Doctrina Meléndez: Documentos Oficiales. San Salvador: República de El Salvador, 1917.

Elias, Norbert, *The Civilizing Process: Sociogenetic and Psychogenetic Investigations*. Translated by Edmund Jephcott. Revised Edition edited by Eric Dunning, Johan Goudsblom and Stephen Mennell. Oxford: Blackwell Publishers Ltd., 2000.

Elias, Taslim O. *The International Court of Justice and Some Contemporary Problems*. Leiden: M. Nijhoff Publishers, 1983.

Ellis, L. Ethan. *Frank B. Kellogg and American Foreign Relations, 1925–1929*. New Brunswick: Rutgers University Press, 1961.

Elton, Geoffrey R. *The Practice of History*. Malden, MA: Blackwell, 1967.

Engelson, Lester G. "Proposals for the Colonization of California By England: In Connection with the Mexican Debt to British Bondholders, 1837–1846." 18(2) *California Historical Society Quarterly* 136–148 (1939).

Epp, Roger. "The British Committee on the Theory of International Politics and Its Central Figures." In *Guide to the English School in International Studies*, 25–36. Edited by Cornelia Navari and Daniel Green. Oxford: John Wiley & Sons, 2014.

Esquemeling, John. *Bucaniers of America: Or, True Account of the Most Remarkable Assaults Committed of late Years upon the Coasts of The West Indies, By the Bucaniers of Jamaica and Tortuga, Both English and French*. London: William Crooke, at the Green Dragon without Temple-bar, 1684.

Esthus, Raymond A. "The Changing Concept of the Open Door, 1899–1910." 46(3) *Mississippi Valley Historical Review* 435–454, 1959.

Evans, Malcolm D. "Case Concerning the Land, Island and Maritime Frontier Dispute (El Salvador/Honduras: Nicaragua Intervening), Judgment of 11 September 1992." 42(4) *International and Comparative Law Quarterly* 929–937, 1993.

Falk, Richard. "Some Thoughts on the Decline of International Law and Future Prospects." 9(1) *Hofstra Law Review*, 399–410, 1980.

Farrand, Max, ed. *Records of the Federal Convention of 1781*. Volume 2. New Haven: Yale University Press, 1911.

Fasolt, Constantine. *The Limits of History*. Chicago: University of Chicago Press, 2004.

Fassbender, Bardo and Anne Peters, eds. *The Oxford Handbook of the History of International Law*. Oxford: Oxford University Press, 2013.

Ferguson, Niall. *Colossus: The Rise and Fall of American Power*. London: Penguin Books, 2004.

Ferguson, William Scott, C.H. Haskins, E.F. Gay and R.B. Meriman, "Archibald Cary Coolidge (1866–1928)." 64 *Proceedings of the American Academy of Arts and Sciences* 514–518, 1930.

Fernádez-Armesto, Felipe. *Columbus*. New York: Oxford University Press, 1991.

Fidler, David P. "The Return of the Standard of Civilization." 2(1) *Chicago Journal of International Law* 135–157, 2001.

Finch, George A. "James Brown Scott, 1866–1943." 38(1) *American Journal of International Law* 183–217, 1944.

Finkelman, Paul. "Jefferson and Slavery: 'Treason Against the Hopes of the World'." In *Jeffersonian Legacies*, 1–18. Edited by Peter S. Onuf. Charlottesville: University of Virginia, 1993.

Finkelman, Paul. "The Northwest Ordinance: A Constitution for an Empire of Liberty." In *Pathways to the Old Northwest: An Observance of the Bicentennial of the Northwest Ordinance* 1–18. Edited by Lloyd A. Hunter. Indianapolis: Indiana Historical Society Press, 1988.

Finlay, Robert. "The Treasure-Ships of Zheng He: Chinese Maritime Imperialism in the Age of Discovery." 23 *Terrae Incognitae* 1–12, 1991.

Fitzmaurice, Andrew. "Context in the History of International Law." 20(1) *Journal of the History of International Law* 5–30, 2018.

Fitzmaurice, Andrew. "The Problem of Eurocentrism in the Thought of Francisco de Vitoria." In *At the Origins of Modernity: Francisco de Vitoria and the Discovery of International Law*, 77–95. Edited by José María Beneyto and Justo Corti Varela. Springer International Publishing AG, 2017.

Fitzmaurice, Andrew. "Liberalism and Empire in Nineteenth-Century International Law." 17(1) *The American Historical Review* 122–140, 2012.

Fitzmaurice, Andrew. "The Justification of King Leopold II's Congo Enterprise by Sir Travers Twiss." In *Law and Politics in British Colonial Thought: Transpositions of Empire*. Edited by Shaunnagh Dorsett & Ian Hunter. London: Palgrave Macmillan, 2011.

Foner, Philip S. and Richard C. Winchester, eds. *The Anti-Imperialist Reader: A Documentary History of Anti-Imperialism in the United States, Volume I: From The Mexican War to the Election of 1900*. New York: Holmes & Meyer, 1984.

Forbes, Duncan. *The Liberal Anglican Idea of History*. Cambridge: Cambridge University Press, 1952.

Ford, Worthinton Chauncy. "John Quincy Adams and the Monroe Doctrine." 8(1) *The American Historical Review* 28–52, 1902.

Förster, Stig, Wolfgang J. Mommsen and Ronald Robinson *Bismarck, Europe, and Africa: The Berlin Africa Conference 1884–1885 and the Onset of Partition*. Edited by Stig Förster et al. London: Oxford University Press, 1988.

Foster, John W. "Misconceptions and Limitations of the Monroe Doctrine." 8 *Proceedings of the American Society of International Law* 119–126, 1914.

Foucault, Michel. *The Archaeology of Knowledge*. A.M. Sheridan Smith trans. New York: Pantheon Book, 1972.

Frank, André Gunder. "Latin American Development Theories Revisited: A Participant Review Essay." 3(2) *The European Journal of Development Research* 146–159 (2007).

Fruin, Robert. "An Unpublished Work of Hugo Grotius's." 5(1) *Bibliotheca Visseriana* 13–26, 1925.

Fukuyama, Francis, *The End of History and the Last Man*. New York: Avon Books, Inc., 1992.

Gaastra, Femme S. "War, Competition and Collaboration: Relations between the English and Dutch East Indian Company in the Seventeenth and Eighteenth Centuries." In *The Worlds of the East India Company*, 49–68. Edited by H.V. Bowen, Margarette Lincoln, and Nigel Rigby. Boydell Press, 2002.

Gadamer, Hans-Georg. *Truth and Method*. New York: Seabury Press, 1975.

Gamarra, Yolanda. "Rafael Altamira y Crevea (1866–1951). The International Judge as 'Gentle Civilizer'" 14(1) *Journal of the History of International Law* 1–49, 2012.

García Calderón, Francisco. "A Latin-American Criticism of the Monroe Doctrine." 29(4) *Current History* 548–553, 1929.

García-Mora, Mauel R. "The Calvo Clause in Latin American Constitutions and International Law." 33(4) *Marquette Law Review* 205–219, 1950.

Gardiner, C. Harvey. "The Japanese and Central America." 14(1) *Journal of Interamerican Studies and World Affairs* 15–47 1972.

Garwood, Ellen. *The Undying Flame: Mariano Moreno of Buenos Aires*. Washington, D.C.: American Studies Center, 1986.

Gibson, Charles. *Spain in America*. New York: Harper Colophon Books, 1966.

Gidel, Gilbert. *Le Droit International Public De La Mer: Le Temps De Paix* (*La Mer Territoriale Et La Zone Contigue*'). Méllotée, Châteauroux, Paris, 1934.

Gil, Henry. "The Point of View of Latin-America on the Inter-American Policy of the United States." 6(1) *American Political Science Review* 164–172, 1912.

Gilderhus, Mark T. "The Monroe Doctrine: Meanings and Implications." 36(1) *Presidential Studies Quarterly* 5–16, 2006.

Gilson, Étienne. *The Unity of Philosophical Experience*. San Francisco: Ignatius Press, 1937.

Ginio, Ruth. "Negotiating Legal Authority in French West Africa: The Colonial Administration and African Assessors, 1903–1918." In *Intermediaries, Interpreters, and Clerks: African Employees in the Making of Colonial Africa*. Edited by Benjamin N. Lawrance et al. Madison: University of Wisconsin Press, 2006.

Golder, Ben. "Foucault and the Incompletion of Law." 21(3) *Leiden Journal of International Law* 747–763. 2008.

Goldman, Eric F. *Rendezvous with Destiny*. New York: Alfred A. Knopf, 1972.

Gong, Gerrit W. *The Standard of 'Civilization' in the International Society*. New York: Clarendon Press, 1984.

González, Salvador Rodríguez. "The Neutrality of Honduras and the Question of the Gulf of Fonseca." 10(3) *American Journal of International Law* 509–542, 1916.

González Bermúdez, Gustavo Adolfo, Victor Emilio Jara Calderón, and Jeffry Alejandro Garro Fallas, "El Golfo de Fonseca, más que un conflicto político. La perspectiva desde los actores locales y pobladores costeros." 16(26) *Revista Pensamiento Actual* 147–61, 2016.

Gordon, Robert W. "Historicism in Legal Scholarship." 90(5) *Yale Law Journal* 1017–1056, 2005.

Gordon-Reed, Annette, and Peter S. Onuf. *"Most Blessed of the Patriarchs": Thomas Jefferson and the Empire of the Imagination*. Liveright Publishing Corporation, 2016.

Gott, Richard. "Karl Krause and the Ideological Origins of the Cuban Revolution." Occasional Paper No. 28, University of London Institute of Latin American Studies, 2002.

Grandin, Greg. "The Liberal Traditions in the Americas: Rights, Sovereignty, and the Origins of Liberal Multilateralism." 117(1) *American Historical Review* 68–91, 2012.

Grandin, Greg. *Empires Workshop: Latin America, the United States, and the Rise of the New Imperialism*. New York: Metropolitan Books, 2006.

Granger, Henry G. "The Stain on Our Flag." *The New York Independent*, August 17, 1911.

Grbich, Judith. "Secrets of the Fetish in International Law's Messianism." In *International Law and its Others*. Edited by Anne Orford. Cambridge: Cambridge University Press, 2006.

Green, Daniel M. "Introduction to the English School in International Studies." In *Guide to the English School in International Studies*, 1–6. Edited by Cornelia Navari and Daniel Green. Oxford: John Wiley & Sons, 2014.

Grewe, Wilhelm G., *Epochen der Völkerrechtsgeschichte*. Baden-Banden: Nomos Verlagsgesellschaft, 1984.

Grotius, Hugo. *De Iure Praedae Commentarius. Commentary on the Law of Prize and Booty*. Volume 1. Translated by Gwladys L. Williams with the collaboration of Walter H. Zeydel. Oxford: Clarendon Press, 1950 [1604].

Grotius, Hugo. *Mare Liberum 1609–2009*. Edited by Robert Feenstra. Leiden: Brill, 2009 [1609].

Grotius, Hugo. *The Freedom of the Seas, or the Right Which Belongs to the Dutch to take part in the East Indian Trade*. Translated by Ralph Van Deman Magoffin, with an introduction by James Brown Scott. New York: Oxford University Press, [1609].

Grotius, Hugo. *The Rights of War and Peace in three books: Wherein are explained, the law of nature and nations, and the principle points relating to government*. Translated by Jean Barbeyrac. London: W. Innys and R. Manby, J. and P. Knapton, D. Brown, T. Osborn, and E. Wicksteed, 1738 [1625].

Grovogui, Siba N. "Regimes of Sovereignty: Rethinking International Morality and the African Condition." 8(3) *Journal of International Relations* 315–338, 2002.

Grovogui, Siba N'zatioula. *Sovereigns, Quasi Sovereigns, and Africans: Race and Self-Determination in International Law*. Minneapolis: University of Minnesota Press, 1996.

Guani, Albert. "La solidarité international dans l'Amérique Latine." 8(III) *Recueil des Cours* 203–340, 1925.

Guilhot, Nicolas. "Portrait of the Realist as a Historian: On Anti-Whiggism in the History of International Relations." 21(1) *European Journal of International Law* 3–26, 2015.

Hackett, Charles Wilson. "The Development of John Quincy Adams's Policy with Respect to an American Confederation and the Panama Congress, 1822–1825." 8(4) *Hispanic American Historical Review* 496–526, 1928.

Hagedorn, Hermann. *Leonard Wood: A Biography, Volume 1*. New York: Harper & Brothers, 1931.

Haggenmacher, Peter. "La place de Francisco de Vitoria parmi les fondateurs du droit international." In *Actualité de la pensée juridique de Francisco de Vitoria*, 27–80. Edited by Antonio Truyol Serra, Henry Mechoulan, Peter Haggenmacher, Antonio Ortiz-Arce, Primitivo Marino and Joe Verhoeven. Bruxelles: Bruylant, 1998.

"Haiti's Trouble with Germany." 26 *The Chautauquan* 439 (1897–1898).

Hall, A. Rupert. "On Whiggism." 21(1) *History of Science* 45–59, 1983.

Hall, Ian. "Martin Wight, Western Values, and the Whig Tradition of International Thought." 36(5) *The International History Review* 961–981, 2014.

Hall, M., and P. Jackson, editors. *Civilization Identity* The Production and Reproduction of "Civilizations" in International Relations. New York: Palgrave Macmillan, 2007.

Hamil, Hugh M. "Introduction." In *Caudillos: Dictators in Spanish America*, 3–26. Edited by Hugh M. Hamil. Norma: University of Oklahoma Press, 1967.

Hamilton, Richard F. *America's New Empire: The 1890s and Beyond*. New Brunswick: Transaction Publishers, 2010.

Hammer, Leonard M. *A Foucauldian Approach to International Law: Descriptive Thoughts for Normative Issues*. London: Routledge, 2007.

Hardin, Garrett. "The Tragedy of the Commons." 162 (3859) *Science* 1243–1248, 1968.

Hardy, Osgood. "The Itata Incident." 5(2) *Hispanic American Historical Review* 195–226 (1922).

Haring, C.H. *The Spanish Empire in America*. San Diego: Harcourt, 1947.

Harper, John Lamberton. *American Machiavelli: Alexander Hamilton and the Origins of U.S. Foreign Policy*. New York: Cambridge University Press, 2004.

Harrison, Benjamin. "The United States and the 1909 Nicaragua Revolution." 41(3–4) *Caribbean Quarterly* 46–63, 1995.

Hart, Albert Bushnell. *The Monroe Doctrine: An Interpretation*. Boston: Little, Brown, and Company, 1916.

Hartley, L.P. *The Go-Between*. New York: Stein and Day, 1967 [1953].

Hathaway, Oona A. and Scott J. Shapiro, *The Internationalists: How a Radical Plan to Outlaw War Remade the World*. New York: Simon & Schuster, 2017.

Hawthorne, Julian. *History of the United States from 1492 to 1910*. Volume 3. Neuilly sur Seine: Ulan Press, 2012.

Hayton, Bill. *The South China Sea—The Struggle for Power in Asia*. New Haven: Yale University Press, 2014.

Healy, David. *James G. Blaine and Latin America*. Columbia and London: University of Missouri Press, 2001.

Hendrick, Burton J. "Great American Fortunes and Their Making." *McClure's Magazine*, November, 1907.

Hendrickson, David C. *Union, Nation, or Empire: the American Debate over International Relations, 1789–1941*. Lawrence, KA: University Press of Kansas, 2009.

Herrick, Charles. "Statement." 8 *Proceedings of the American Society of International Law* 96–104, 1948.

Hertslet, Edward. *The Map of Africa by Treaty*. Edited by Edward Hertslet 3rd edn. London: Harrison and Sons, 1894.

Herwig, Holger H. *Germany's Vision of Empire in Venezuela 1871–1914*. Princeton: Princeton University Press, 1986.

Hill, Howard C. *Roosevelt and the Caribbean*. New York: Russell & Russell, 1965.

Hinderaker, Eric. *Elusive Empires: Constructing Colonialism in the Ohio Valley, 1673–1800*. New York: Cambridge University Press, 1997.

Hirsch, H.N. *The Enigma of Felix Frankfurther*. New York: Basic Books, 1981.

Hiscox, Michael J. "The Magic Bullet? The RTAA, Institutional Reform, and Trade Liberalization." 53(4) *International Organization* 669–698, 1999.

Hobsbawm, Eric. *The Age of Empire: 1875–1914*. London: Weidenfeld & Nicholson, 1987.

Hobson, John M. *The Eastern Origins of Western Civilisation*. Cambridge: Cambridge University Press, 2004.

Hobson, John M. *The Eurocentric Conception of World Politics: Western International Theory, 1760–2010*. Cambridge: Cambridge University Press, 1992.

Hochschild, Adam. *King Leopold's Ghost: A Story of Greed, Terror, and Heroism in Colonial Africa*. Boston: Houghton Mifflin Harcourt, 1998.

Hudson, Manley O. "The Central American Court of Justice." 26(4) *American Journal of International Law* 759–786, 1932.

Hughes, Charles E. "Observations on the Monroe Doctrine." 17(4) *American Journal of International Law* 611–628, 1923.

Hughes, Charles E., Henry Cabot Lodge, Oscar W. Underwood, and Elihu Root. "Conference on the Limitation of Armament: Report of the American Delegation." 16(1) *American Journal of International Law* 159–233, 1922.

Hull, William I. *The Two Hague Conferences and their Contributions to International Law*. Boston: Ginn & Company, 1908.

Hunt, Michael H. *The American Ascendancy: How the United States Gained and Wielded Global Dominance*. Chapel Hill: University of North Carolina Press, 2007.

Hunter, Ian. "Global Justice and Regional Metaphysics: On the Critical History of the Law of Nature and Nations." In *Law and Politics in British Colonial Thought: Transpositions of Empire*, 11–30. Edited by Shannaugh Dorsett and Ian Hunter. New York: Palgrave Macmillan, 2010.

Huntington, Samuel P. *The Clash of Civilizations and the Remaking of World Order*. New York: Simon and Schuster, 1996.

Hurrell, Andrew. *On Global Order: Power, Values, and the Constitution of International Society*. New York: Oxford University Press, 2007.

Ikenberry, John. *Liberal Leviathan: The Origins, Crisis, and Transformation of the American World Order*, 18. Princeton: Princeton University Press, 2011.

Immerman, Richard H. *Empire for Liberty: A History of American Imperialism from Benjamin Franklin to Paul Wolfowitz*. Princeton and Oxford: Princeton University Press, 2010.

Ingram, Alton Earl. *The Root Mission to Russia, 1917*. Dissertation, LSU Historical Dissertations and Theses, 1970.

Inman, Samuel Guy. "The Monroe Doctrine and Hispanic America." 4(4) *The Hispanic American Historical Review* 635–676, 1921.

Jackson, John H. "Sovereignty—Modern: A New Approach To An Outdated Concept." 97(4) *American Journal of International Law* 782–802 (2003).

Jackson, Patrick Thaddeus. "How to Think About Civilizations." In *Civilizations in World Politics: Plural and Pluralist Perspectives*, 176–200. Edited by Peter J. Katzenstein. London and New York: Routledge, 2010.

Jackson, Robert H. *The Global Covenant: Human Conduct in a World of States*. New York: Oxford University Press, 2000.

Jacques, Martin. *When China Rules the World: The End of the Western World and the Birth of A New Global Order*. 2nd edn. New York: Penguin, 2009.

James, Alan. *Sovereign Statehood: Basis of International Society*. New York: Harper Collins Publishers Ltd., 1986.

James, Alan. "Law and Order in International Society." In *The Bases of International Order: Essays in Honour of C.A.W. Manning*, 60–84. Edited by Alan James. London: Oxford University Press, 1973.

Jan, George P. "The Doctrine of Nationalism and the Chinese Revolution." In *Sun Yat-Sen's Doctrine in The Modern World*, 138–159. Edited by Chu-yuan Cheng. Boulder: Westview Press, 1989.

Janis, Mark Weston. *The American Tradition of International Law: Great Expectations 1789–1914*. Oxford: Clarendon Press, 2004.

Jessup, Philip Caryl. *Elihu Root*. Volume I. Dodd, Mead & Company, 1938.

Jessup, Philip Caryl. *Elihu Root*. Volume II. Dodd, Mead & Company, 1938.

Johns, Fleur, Thomas Skouteris and Wouter Werner. "Editors' Introduction: Alejandro Álvarez and the Launch of the Periphery Series" 19(4) *Leiden International Law Journal* 875–77, 2006.

Johnson, D.H.N. "Artificial Islands" 4(2) *International Law Quarterly* 203–215, 1951.

Jones, Henry. "Lines in The Ocean: Thinking with the Sea About Territory and International Law." 4(2) *London Review of International Law* 307-343, 2016.

Jones, Howard. *Crucible of Power: A History of U.S. Foreign Relations Since 1892*. Lanham: Rowman and Littlefield Publishing Group, Inc., 2001.

Jouannet, Emmanuelle. "Universalism and Imperialism: The True-False Paradox of International Law?" 18(3) *European Journal of International Law* 379–407, 207.

Juderías, Julián. *La Leyenda Negra: [por] Julián Juderías; Estudios Acerca Del Concepto De España En El Extranjero*. Editorial Araluce, 1917.

Kalmo, Hent and Quentin Skinner, eds. *Sovereignty in Fragments: The Past, Present and Future of a Contested Concept*. New York: Cambridge University Press, 2010.

Kagan, Robert. *Dangerous Nation*. New York: Vintage Books, 2006.

Kane, John. *Between Virtue and Power: The Persistent Moral Dilemma of U.S. Foreign Policy*. New Haven: Yale University Press, 2008.

Kanuck, Sean. "Sovereign Discourse on Cyber Conflict Under International Law." 88(7) *Texas Law Review* 1571–1598 (2009–2010).

Kaplan, Edward S. *U.S. Imperialism in Latin America: Bryan's Challenges and Contributions, 1900–1920*. Westport: Greenwood Press, 1998.

Karnes, Thomas L. "Hiram Bingham and His Obsolete Shibboleth." 3(1) *Diplomatic History* 39–57, 1979.

Katzenstein, Peter J. "A World of Plural and Pluralist Civilizations: Multiple Actors, Traditions, and Practices." In *Civilizations in World Politics: Plural and Pluralist Perspectives*, 1–41. London and New York: Routledge, 2010.

Kayaoğlu, Turan. *Legal Imperialism: Sovereignty and Extraterritoriality in Japan, the Ottoman Empire, and China*. Cambridge: Cambridge University Press, 2010.

Keene, Edward. *Beyond the Anarchical Society: Grotius, Colonialism and Order in World Politics*. Cambridge: Cambridge University Press, 2002.

Kelsen, Hans. "Absolutism and Relativism in Philosophy." 42(5) *American Political Science Review* 906–914, 1948.

Kelsen, Hans. "The Legal Status of Germany According to the Declaration of Berlin." 39(3) *American Journal of International Law* 518–526, 1945.

Kendall, Lane Carter. "Andres Santa Cruz and the Peru-Bolivian Confederation." 16(1) *The Hispanic American Historical Review* 29–48, 1936.

Kennedy, David. *International Legal Structures*. Baden-Baden: Nomos Verlagsgesellschaft, 1987.

Kennedy, David M. and Thomas Bailey. The American Spirit: United States History as Seed by Contemporaries. Belmont: Cengage Learning, 2009.

Kinsella, Helen, *The Image Before the Weapon: A Critical History of the Distinction Between Combatant and Civilian*. Ithaca and London: Cornell University Press, 2011.

Kirgis, Frederic L. *The American Society of International Law's First Century: 1906–2006*. Leiden and Boston: Martinus Nijhoff Publishers, 2006.

Kirkpatrick, J.A. *The Spanish Conquistadors*. London: A&C Black Ltd., 1934.

Klabbers, Jan. "The Relative Autonomy of International Law and the Forgotten Politics of Interdisciplinarity." 1(1–2) *Journal of International Law and International Relations* 35–48, 2004.

Knudsen, Tonny Brems. "The English School: Sovereignty and International Law." In *Making Sense of International Relations Theory*, 311–326. Edited by Jennifer Sterling-Folker. Boulder: Lynne Rienner Publishers, 2006.

Koselleck, Reinhart, *Futures Past: On the Semantics of Historical Time*. Translated by Keith Tribe. New York: Columbia University Press, 2004.

Koskenniemi, Martti. "Expanding Histories of International Law." 56(1) *American Journal of Legal History* 104–112, 2016.

Koskenniemi, Martti. "Diplomats, Professors, and Then Some: Notes for a History of International Law in 20th Century Finland." 85(4) *Nordic Journal of International Law* 322–333, 2016.

Koskenniemi, Martti. "Vitoria and Us." 22(1) *Journal of the Max Planck Institute for European Legal History* 199–138, 2014.

Koskenniemi, Martti. "Histories of International Law: Significance and Problems for a Critical View." 27(2) *Temple International and Comparative Law Journal* 215–40, 2013.

Koskenniemi, Martti. "The Mystery of Legal Obligation." 3(2) *International Theory* 319–325, 2011.

Koskenniemi, Martti. "Legal Cosmopolitanism: Tom Franck's Messianic World." 35 *New York University Journal of International Law & Politics* 471–486, 2003.

Koskenniemi, Martti. "International Law in Europe: Between Tradition and Renewal." 16 *European Journal of International Law* 113–124, 2005.

Koskenniemi, Martti. *Gentle Civilizer of Nations: The Rise and Fall of International Law 1870–1960* (*Hersch Lauterpacht memorial lectures*). Cambridge University Press, 2001.

Koskenniemi, Martti, Walter Rech and Manuel Jiménez Fonseca, eds. *International Law and Empire: Historical Explorations*. New York: Oxford University Press, 2017.

Krasner, Stephen D. *Sovereignty: Organized Hypocrisy*. Princeton University Press, 1999.

Kratochwil, Friedrich. *"Sovereignty as Dominium: Is There a Right to Humanitarian Intervention?"* In *Beyond Westphalia? State Sovereignty and International Intervention*, 21–42. Edited by Gene M. Lyons and Michael Mastanduno. Baltimore: John Hopkins University Press, 1995.

Kuhn Thomas, S. *The Structure of Scientific Revolutions*. Chicago: University of Chicago Press, 1962.

Lachs, Manfred. *The Teacher in International Law: Teachings and Teaching*. 2nd. rev. edn. Leiden: Martinus Nijhoff Publishers, 1987.

LaFeber, Walter. "Jefferson and an American Foreign Policy." In *Jeffersonian Legacies*, 370–394. Edited by Peter S. Onuf. Charlottesville: University of Virginia Press, 1993.

Lai To, Lee. *China and The South China Sea Dialogues*, 9. Westport: Greenwood, 2009.

Lamb, Robert. "Quentin Skinner's Revised Historical Contextualism: A Critique." 22(3) *History of the Human Sciences* 51–73, 2009.

Lamb, Robert. "Feature Book Review: Quentin Skinner's 'Post-modern' History of Ideas." 89(295) *History* 424–433, 2004.

Landauer, Carl. "The Ambivalences of Power: Launching the American Journal of International Law in an Era of Empire and Globalization." 20(2) *Leiden Journal of International Law* 325–358, 2007.

Lane, Jack C. *Armed Progressive: General Leonard Wood*. San Rafael: Presidio Press, 1978.

Lane, Kris E. *Pillaging the Empire: Piracy in the Americas*, 1500–1750. Armonk: M.E. Sharpe, 1976.

Langfur, Hal. *"Colonial Brazil (1500–1822)."* In *A Companion to Latin American History*, 89–105. Edited by Thomas H. Holloway. West Sussex: Blackwell, 2008.

Langley, Lester D. *America and the Americans: The United States in the Western Hemisphere*. 2nd edn. Athens & London: The University of Georgia Press, 2010.

Langley, Lester D. *The Banana Wars: United States Intervention in the Caribbean, 1898–1934*. Rev. edn. Lanham: Scholarly Resources Inc., 2002.

Langley, Lester D. and Thomas Schoonover, *The Banana Men: American Mercenaries and Entrepreneurs in Central America, 1880–1930*. Lexington: University of Kentucky Press, 1995.

Lash, Joseph P. *From the Diaries of Felix Frankfurther: With a Biographical Essay and Notes*. New York: W.W. Norton and Co., 1974.

Laslett, Peter. *The World We Have Lost*. London: Methuen, 1965.

Lauterpacht, Elihu, ed. *International Law: Being the Collected Papers of Hersch Lauterpacht. Volume 1. The General Works*. Cambridge: Cambridge University Press, 1970.

Lauterpacht, Hersch. "Sovereignty Over Submarine Areas." 27(1) *British Yearbook of International Law* 376–433, 1950.

Lauterpacht, Hersch. "The Grotian Tradition in International Law." 23(1) *British Yearbook of International Law* 1–53, 1946.

Lawrance, Benjamin N. and et al. "African Intermediaries and the "Bargain" of Collaboration." In *Intermediaries, Interpreters, and Clerks: African Employees in the Making of Colonial Africa*. Edited by Benjamin N. Lawrance et al. Madison: University of Wisconsin Press, 2006.

Leng, Lee Yong. "Offshore Boundary Disputes in Southeast Asia." 10(1) *Journal of Southeast Asian Studies* 175–189, 1979.

León de la Barra, Fr[ancisco]. "La mediation et la conciliation internals." 1(1) *Recueil des Cours* 553–568, 1923.

Leonard, Thomas M. *Panama, the Canal, and the United States: A Guide to Issues and References*. Claremont: Regina Books, 1993.

Leopold, Richard W. *Elihu Root and the Conservative Tradition*. New York: Little Brown, 1954.

Lesaffer, Randall. "International Law and its History: The Story of An Unrerequited Love." In *Time, History and International Law*, 27–41. Edited by Matthew Craven, Malgosia Fitzmaurice and Maria Vogiatzi. Leiden: Martinus Nijhoff Publishers, 2006.

Lesaffer, Randall. "The Temple of Peace: The Hague Peace Conferences, Andrew Carnegie and the Building of the Peace Palace (1898–1913)." 140 *Mededelingen van de Koninklijke Netherlandse Vereniging voor Internationaal Recht* 1–38, 2013.

Lesaffer, Randall. "Law and History: Law Between Past and Present." *In Law and Method*, 133–152. Edited by Bart Van Klink and Sanne Taekema. Tübingen: Mohr Siebeck (2011).

"Letter from Charles Francis Adams to Hiram Bingham," April 29, 1914. Bingham Family Papers, Box 22, Manuscripts and Archives Division, Sterling Memorial Library, Yale University.

"Letter of Francisco Dueñas, Minister of Salvador." Received by United States Secretary of State, *Papers Relating to the Foreign Relations of the United States 1912–1915*, October 21, 1913.

"Letter of the Minister of Costa Rica [J.B. Calvo] to the Secretary of State, April 17, 1913 [translation]." *Papers Relating to the Foreign Relations of the United States*, File No. 817.812/22.

"Letter of the Minister of Salvador [Dueñas] to the Secretary of State, October 21, 1913 [translation]." *Papers Relating to the Foreign Relations of the United States*, File No. 817.812/49.

"Letter of the Secretary of State [Bryan] to the American Minister to Guatemala." August 2, 1913, *Papers Relating to the Foreign Relations of the United States*, File No. 711.15.

"Letter of the Secretary of State [Bryan] to the American Minister to Salvador." September 26, 1913, *Papers Relating to the Foreign Relations of the United States*, File No. 711.13/34.

Leuchtenburg, William E. "Progressivism and Imperialism: The Progressive Movement and American Foreign Policy, 1898–1916." 39(3) *The Mississippi Valley Historical Review* 483–504 (1952).

Lieberman, Victor. *Strange Parallels, Volume 2: Mainland Mirrors: Europe, Japan, China, South Asia, and the Islands*. Cambridge: Cambridge University Press, 2009.

Lieberman, Victor. *Strange Parallels: Southeast Asia in Global Context, C. 800–1830: Volume 2, Mainland Mirrors: Europe, Japan, China, South Asia, and the Islands*, 680. New York: Cambridge University Press, 2009.

Lihr, Tuomas. "Elihu Root and International Legalism: Legalist Remarks on Collective Security and American Realism." 1 *Helsinki Law Review* 63–92, 2014.

Lillich, Richard B. "The Jay Treaty Commissions." 37(2) *St. John's Law Review* 260–283, 1962–1963.

Linklater, Andrew. "Civilizations and International Society." In *System, Society & the World: Exploring the English School of International Relations*, 25–28. Edited by Robert W. Murray. Bristol: e-International Relations, 2013.

Linklater, Andrew. "International Society and the Civilizing Process." 9(1) *Ritsumeikan International Affairs* 1–26, 2011.

Linklater, Andrew. "Process Sociology and International Relations." 59(1) *The Sociological Review* 48–64 (2011).

Linklater, Andrew. "Norbert Elias, The 'Civilizing Process' and the Sociology of International Relations." 41(1) *International Politics* 3–35, 2004.

Linklater, Andrew and Hidemi Suganami, *The English School of International Relations: A Contemporary Reassessment*. Cambridge: Cambridge University Press, 2006.

Liss, Sheldon B. *The Canal: Aspects of United States Panamanian Relations*. Notre Dame: University of Notre Dame Press, 1967.

Lockey, Joseph Byrne, *Pan-Americanism: Its Beginnings*. New York: The Macmillan Co., 1920.

López de Gómara, Francisco. *Historia General De Las Indias*. Con una introducción y notas por D. Joaquín Ramírez Cabañas. I–II. Mexico, D.F. Editorial Pedro Robredo, 1943 [1552].

López Morillas, Juan. *El Krausismo Español: Perfil de Una Aventura Intelectual*. Fondo de Cultura Económica, 1956.

Lyftogt, Kenneth L. *Iowa and the Civil War. Volume 1: Free Child of the Missouri Compromise, 1850–1862*. Iowa City, Iowa: Camp Pope Publishing, 2018.

Lyons, Gene M. and Michael Mastanduno, eds. *Beyond Westphalia: State Sovereignty and International Intervention*. Baltimore: Johns Hopkins University Press, 1995.

Macaulay, Thomas Babington, *History of England*. Sheridan: Heron Books, 1967 [1848].

Mackie, Sedley M., ed. *An Account of the Conquest of Guatemala in 1524 by Pedro de Alvarado with a Facsimile of the Spanish Original*. New York: Cortes Society, 1924.

MacNutt, Augustus. *Letters of Cortes: The Five Letters of Relation from Fernando Cortes to the Emperor Charles*. Volume. II. New York and London: G.P. Putnam's Sons, The Knickerbocker Press, 1908.

Major, John. Prize Possession: *The United States and the Panama Canal, 1903–1979*. New York: Cambridge University Press, 1993.

Malloy, William M. *Treaties and Conventions of the United States*. Volume I. Washington, D.C.: United States Government Printing Office, 1910.

Malloy, William M. *Treaties and Conventions of the United States*. Volume II. Washington, D.C.: United States Government Printing Office, 1910.

Mamolea, Andrei. The Myth of Legalism in US Foreign Relations. Dissertation, Graduate Institute of International and Development Studies, Geneva, 2018.

Manela, Ezra. "The United States in the World." In *American History Now*, 202–221. Edited by Eric Foner and Lisa McGirr. Philadelphia, PA: Temple University Press, 2011.

Mantena, Karuna. *Alibis of Empire: Henry Maine and the Ends of Liberal Imperialism*. Princeton: Princeton University Press, 2010.

Manning, C.A.W. *The Nature of International Society*. London: London School of Economics, 1962.

Maisch, Christian J. "The Falkland/Malvinas Islands Clash of 1831–32: U.S. and British Diplomacy in the South Atlantic." 24(2) *Diplomatic History* 185–209, 2000.

Major, John. *Prize Possession: The United States and the Panama Canal, 1903–1979*. Cambridge: Cambridge University Press, 1993.

Marcosson, Isaac Frederick. *Leonard Wood: Prophet of Preparedness*. New York: John Lane Company, 1917.

Marks III, Frederick W. *Velvet on Iron: The Diplomacy of Theodore Roosevelt*. Lincoln: University of Nebraska Press, 1979.

Márquez Domínguez, Juan Antonio and José Díaz-Diego. "The Nicaragua Interoceanic Grand Canal in the Central American Regional Development Context: Considerations for the Debate." 66 *Investigaciones Geográficas* 27–41, 2016.

Marti, José. "A Vindication of Cuba [Letter to the Editor of the Evening Post Mar. 23, 1889]." In *The Latino Reader: An American Literary Tradition from 1542 to the Present*, 99–104. Edited by Harold Augenbraum and Margarite Fernandez Olmos. Boston: Houghton Mifflin Company, 1997.

Matos, José. "L'Amérique et la Société des Nations." 28(III) *Recueil des Cours* 1–104, 1929.

Matthew, Laura E. and Michel R. Oudijk, *Indian Conquistadors: Indigenous Allies in the Conquest of Mesoamerica*. Norman: University of Oklahoma Press, 1998.

Matua, Makau. "What Is Twail?" 94 *Proceedings of the American Society of International Law Annual Meeting* 31–38, 2000.

Matz, Nele. "Civilization and the Mandate System Under the League of Nations as Origin of Trusteeship." 9 *Max Planck United Nations Year Book* 47–95, 2005.

Matthewson, Tim. "Jefferson and the Nonrecognition of Haiti." 140 *Proceedings of the American Philosophical Society* 22–48, 2013.

Maurer, Noel. *The Empire Trap: The Rise and Fall of the U.S. Intervention to Protect American Property Overseas, 1893–2013*. Princeton University Press, 2013.

May, Robert E. *Manifest Destiny's Underworld: Filibustering in Antebellum America*. Chapel Hill: University of North Carolina Press, 2002.

May, Robert E. "Young American Males and Filibustering in the Age of Manifest Destiny: The United States Army as a Cultural Mirror." 78(3) *The Journal of American History* 857–886. 1991.

Mayr, Ernst. "When is Historiography Whiggish?" 51(2) *Journal of the History of Ideas* 301–309, 1990.

Mazower, Mark. "An International Civilization? Empire, Internationalism and the Crisis of the Mid-Twentieth Century" 82(3) *International Affairs* 553–566, 2006.

Mbembe, Achille. *Sortir de la grande nuit: Essai sur l'Afrique décolonisée*. London: Routledge, 2013.

McCallum, Jack. *Leonard Wood: Rough Rider, Surgeon, Architect of American Imperialism*. New York: NYU Press, 2006.

McGuinness, Aims, *Path of Empire: Panama and the California Gold Rush*. Ithaca and London: Cornell University Press, 2008.

McIntire, C.T. *Herbert Butterfield: Historian As Dissenter*. New Haven: Yale University Press, 2004.

McIntyre, Kenneth B.. *Herbert Butterfield: History, Providence, and Skeptical Politics*. Wilmington: Intercollegiate Studies Institute Books, 2011.

Mecham, J. Lloyd. *The United States and Inter-American Security*, 1889–1960. Austin: University of Texas Press, 1961.

Mechoulan, Henry, "Vitoria, père du droit international?" In *Actualité de la pensée juridique de Francisco de Vitoria*, 11–27. Edited by Antonio Truyol Serra, Henry Mechoulan, Peter Haggenmacher, Antonio Ortiz-Arce, Primitivo Marino and Joe Verhoeven. Bruxelles: Bruylant, 1988.

Mégret, Frédéric. "The Rise and Fall of "International Man" In *Critical International Law: Postrealism, Postcolonialism, and Transnationalism*. Edited by Prabhakar Singh, and Benoît Mayer. Oxford: Oxford University Press, 2014.

Mehta, Uday. *Liberalism and Empire: A Study in Nineteenth-Century British Liberal Thought*. Chicago: University of Chicago Press, 1999.

Mickelson, Karin. "Rhetoric and Rage: Third World Voices in International Legal Discourse." 16(2) *Wisconsin International Law Journal* 353–419, 1997.

Mignolo, Walter D. "The Making and Closing of Eurocentric International Law: The Opening of a Multipolar World Order." 36(1), *Comparative Studies of South Asia, Africa and the Middle East* 182–195, 2016.

Milkis, Sidney M., and Michael Nelson. *The American Presidency: Origins and Development*, 1776–2014. 7th edn. Los Angeles: Sage/CQ Press, 2016.

Mill, John Stuart. *On Liberty*. London: John W. Parker and Son, 1859.

Miller, Hugh Gordon. *The Isthmian Highway*. New York: The Macmillan Company, 1929.

Miller, David Hunter. *Treaties and Other International Acts of the United States of America, 1776–1863*. 8 Volumes. Washington, D.C.: Government Printing Office, 1931–1948.

Miller, Hunter. "The Hague Codification Conference" 24(4) *American Journal of International Law* 674–693, 1930.

Miller, Robert J. "The International Law of Colonialism: A Comparative Analysis." 12(4) *Lewis and Clark Law Review* 847–922, 2011.

Milne, David. *Worldmaking: The Art and Science of American Diplomacy*. New York: Farrar, Straus, and Giroux, 2015.

Mitchell, Harold. *Europe in the Caribbean: The Policies of Great Britain, France and the Netherlands Towards their West Indian Territories in the Twentieth Century*. Stanford: Hispanic American Society, 1963.

Mitchell, Nancy, *The Danger of Dreams: German and American Imperialism in Latin America*. Chapel Hill, London: University of North Carolina Press, 1999.

Montes Gómez, Esteban. *Archaeology of the Colonial Period, Gulf of Fonseca, Eastern El Salvador*. Dissertation, Graduate Division of the University of California, Berkeley, 2010.

Moore, John Bassett. *History and Digest of the International Arbitrations to Which the United States Has Been a Party*. Washington, D.C.: Government Printing Office, 1898.

Morison, Elting E., ed. *The Letters of Theodore Roosevelt. Volume 7*. Cambridge: Harvard University Press, 1954.

Moreno, Mariano. *Doctrina Democrática*. Edited by Ricardo Rojas. Buenos Aires: Librería La Facultad, 1915.

Moreno, Campos, Raúl Ernesto. *Reframing Salvadoran Modernity: A Political and Cultural History of Power and the Dialectics of the Hegemonic Bloc in El Salvador, ca. 1850–1944*. Dissertation, University of California, Los Angeles, 2015.

Morrow, James B. "Life of Elihu Root, Statesman and Peace-Worker." *Washington Herald*, January 11, 1914.

Moyn, Samuel. "Martti Koskenniemi and the Historiography of International Law in the Age of the War on Terror." In *The Law of International Lawyers: Reading Martti Koskenniemi*, 340–359. Edited by Wouter Werner, Marieke de Hoon and Alexis Galán. Cambridge: Cambridge University Press, 2017.

Moyn, Samuel. *The Last Utopia: Human Rights in History*. Cambridge: Harvard University Press, 2010.

Moynihan, Daniel Patrick. *On the Law of Nations*. Cambridge, MA: Harvard University Press, 1990.

Munro, Dana Gardner, *The United States and the Caribbean Republics, 1921–1933*. Princeton: Princeton University Press, 1974.

Münster, Sebastian. *Geographia Universalis*. Basle: Henri Petri, 1540.

Nabuco, Joaquim, "Speech of His Excellency Joaquim Nabuco (July 31, 1906)." In *Latin America and the United States: Addresses by Elihu Root*, 3–5. Edited by Robert Bacon and James Brown Scott. Cambridge: Harvard University Press; London: Humphrey Milford, 1917.

Naish, Paul D. *Slavery and Silence: Latin America and the U.S. Slave Debate*. Philadelphia: University of Pennsylvania Press, 2017.

Neary, Peter F. "The Panama Canal Tolls Dispute 1912–1914." 7(3) *Journal of Transportation History* 173–179, 1966.

Nietzsche, Friedrich. *The Use and Abuse of History*. Translated by Adrian Collins with an Introduction by Julius Kraft. Indianapolis: Bobbs-Merrill Educational Publishing, 1980 [1874].

Nesi, Giuseppe. *L'Uti Possidetis Iuris Nel Diritto Internazionale*. Verona: Casa Editrice Dott. Antonio Milani, 1996.

Neuner, Thomas. *Karl Krause (1781–1832) in der Spanischsprachigen Welt: Spanien, Argentinien, Kuba*. Leipziger Universitätsverlag, 2004.

Neumann, Iver B. "*Diplomatic Sites: A Critical Enquiry*." Oxford: Oxford University Press, 2013.

Neumann, Iver B. "The English School on Diplomacy: Scholarly Promise Unfulfilled." 17(3) *International Relations* 341–369, 2003.

Newbold, Stephanie P. "Statesmanship and Ethics: The Case of Thomas Jefferson's Dirty Hands." 65(5) *Public Administration Review* 669–677, 2005.

Newson, Linda A. *Indian Survival in Colonial Nicaragua*. Norman: University of Oklahoma Press, 1987.

"Nicaraguan Neutrality in Light of History." 20(11) *The Literary Digest* 327–328, March 17, 1900.

Nijman, Janne E. *Seeking Change by Doing History*. Amsterdam: Amsterdam University Press, 2018.

Nissel, Alan Tzvika. *A History of State Responsibility: The Struggle for International Standards (1870–1960)*. Dissertation, University of Helsinki, Faculty of Law, 2016.

Nussbaum, Arthur. *A Concise History of the Law of Nations*. London: Macmillan, 1954.

Nye, Joseph S. Jr. *The Paradox of American Power*. New York: Oxford University Press, 2002.

O'Connell, Mary Ellen. "Elihu Root and Crisis Prevention." 95 *Proceedings of the American Society of International Law* 115–118, 2001.

Obiora, Leslye. "Book review: Antony Anghie, Imperialism, Sovereignty and the Making of International Law." 40(3) *Law and Society Review* 729–730, 2006.

Obregón, Liliana. "Identity Formation, Theorization and Decline of a Latin American International Law." In *Latin America and the International Court of Justice: Contributions to International Law*, 3–14. Edited by Paula Wojcikiewicz Almeida and Jean-Marc Sorel, New York: Routledge, 2017.

Obregón, Liliana. "The Non-Recognition of Haiti and the Cosmopolitan Imagination." In *Cosmopolitanisms in Enlightenment Europe and Beyond*, 159–180. Edited by Mónica García-Salmones and Pamela Slotte. Pieterlen: Peter Lang, 2013.

Obregón, Liliana. "Construyendo la region Americana: Andrés Bello y el Derecho Internacional." In *Andrés Bello y los Estudios Latinoamericanos*, 189–218. Edited by Beatriz González Stephan and Juan Poblete, 2009.

Obregón, Liliana. "Latin American International Law." In *Routledge Handbook of International Law*, 154–64. Edited by David Armstrong. New York: Routledge, 2009.

Obregón, Liliana. "Between Civilisation and Barbarism: Creole Interventions in International Law." 27(5) *Third World Quarterly* 815–832, 2006.

Obregón, Liliana. "Noted for Dissent: The International Life of Alejandro Álvarez." 19(4) *Leiden Journal of International Law* 983–1016, 2006.

Obregón, Liliana. "Completing Civilization: Creole Consciousness and International Law in Nineteenth-Century Latin America." In *International Law and Its Others*, 247–264. Edited by Anne Orford. Cambridge: Cambridge University Press, 2006.

Octavio, Rodrigo. "Les sauvages américains devant le droit." 31(1) *Recueil des Cours* 177–292, 1930.

Okafor, Obiora Chinedu. "Critical Third World Approaches to International Law (TWAIL): Theory, Methodology, or Both?" 10(4) *International Community Law Review* 371–378, 2008.

Onuf, Nicholas Greenwood. *'The Mightie Frame': Epochal Change and the Modern World*. Oxford: Oxford University Press, 2018.

Onuf, Nicholas. "'Tainted by Contingence': Retelling the Story of International Law." In *International Legal Theory: Essays and Engagements, 1966–2006*, 359–380. London and New York: Routledge-Cavendish, 2008.

Onuf, Nicholas. "Henry Wheaton and the 'Golden Age of International Law.'" 6(1) *International Legal Theory* 2–9, 2001.

Onuf, Nicholas Greenwood. "Sovereignty: Outline of a Conceptual History." 16(4) *Alternatives* 425–446, 1991.

Onuf, Nicholas Greenwood. *World of Our Making: Rules and Rule in Social Theory and International Relations*. Columbia: University of South Carolina Press, 1989.

Onuf, Peter. *Statehood and Union: A History of the Northwest Ordinance*. Bloomington: Indiana University Press, 1987.

Onuf, Nicholas, and Peter Onuf. *Nations, Markets, and War: Modern History and the American Civil War*. University of Virginia Press, 2006.

Onuf, Peter, and Nicholas Onuf. *Federal Union Modern World: The Law of Nations in an Age of Revolutions 1776–1914*. 1993.

Onuma, Yasuaki. "When Was the Law of International Society Born? An Inquiry of the History of International Law from an Intercivilisation Perspective." 2(1) *Journal of the History of International Law* 1–66, 2000.

Onuma, Yasuaki. "Introduction." In *A Normative Approach to War: Peace, War, and Justice in Hugo Grotius*, 1–10. Edited by Yasuaki Onuma. Oxford: Clarendon, 1993.

Oosterveld, Willem Theo. *The Law of Nations in Early American Foreign Policy: Theory and Practice from the Revolution to the Monroe Doctrine*. Boston: Brill Nijhof, 2015.

"Opening Remarks of Mr. Elihu Root." *Proceedings of the American Society of International Law at Its Annual Meeting*, Volume. 8, 1914.

Oppenheim, Lasa. *International Law: A Treatise*. Volume 1. Edited by Ronald F. Roxburgh. 3rd edn. London: Longman, 1920–1921.

Oppenheim, Lasa. *International Law: A Treatise*. Vol. 1. New York and Bombay: Longmans, Green, and Co., 1905.

Orakhelashvili, A. "The Idea of European International Law." 17(2) *European Journal of International Law* 315–347, 2006.

Orford, Anne. "International Law and the Limits of History." In *The Law of International Lawyers: Reading Martti Koskenniemi*, 297–320. Edited by Wouter Werner, Marieke De Hoon, and Alexis Galán. Cambridge: Cambridge University Press, 2017.

Orford, Anne. "On International Legal Method." 1(1) *London Review of International Law* 166–197, 2013.

Orford, Anne, "The Past as Law or History? The Relevance of Imperialism for Modern International Law." IILJ Working Paper 2012/2. History and Theory of International Law Series; University of Melbourne Legal Studies Research Paper No. 600, September 9, 2011.

Orford, Anne. "Beyond Harmonization: Trade, Human Rights and the Economy of Sacrifice." 18 *Leiden Journal of International Law* 179–213, 2005.

Orford, Anne, ed. *International Law and Its Others*. Cambridge: Cambridge University Press, 2003.

Ortiz Escamilla, Juan. *El Veracruz de Hernán Cortés*. Veracruz, Mexico: Gobierno del Estado de Veracruz, Secretaría de Educación del Estado de Veracruz, Universidad Veracruzana, 2015.

Osgood, Robert. *Ideals and Self-Interest in America's Foreign Policy*. Chicago: University of Chicago Press, 1953.

Ostrom, Elinor. *Governing the Commons: The Evolution of Institutions for Collective Action*. Cambridge: Cambridge University Press, 1990.

Owens, Robert M. *Red Dreams, White Nightmares Pan-Indian Alliances in the Anglo-American Mind*, 1763–1815. University of Oklahoma Press, 2015.

Oxman, Bernard H. "The Territorial Temptation: A Siren Song at Sea." 100 (4) *American Journal of International Law* 830–851, 2006.

Özsu Umut. *Formalizing Displacement: International Law and Population Transfer*. Oxford: Oxford University Press, 2015

Packeiser, Matthias. Full Sovereign Equality: A Historical Study of Latin American Countries Under International Law. Paper presented at the *Repensando y renovando el derecho internacional dentro, desde y sobre la América Latina* conference, sponsored by the Latin American Society of International Law, the Universidad de Los Andes, Universidad del Rosario, and Universidad Externado, Bogotá, Colombia (Sept. 26–28, 2017).

Pagden, Anthony. *The Uncertainties of Empire: Essays in Iberian and Ibero-American History*. London: Variorum, 1994.

Pagden, Anthony. *The Fall of Natural Man: The American Indian and the Origins of Comparative Ethnology*. Cambridge: Cambridge University Press, 1982.

Palmer, Gabirelle G. *"El Camino Real de Tierra Adentro."* 6 *Southern New Mexico Historical Review* 1–6, 1999.

Parks, E. Taylor. *Colombia and the United States, 1765–1934*. Durham: Duke University Press, 1935.

Pedrozo, Raúl. *China Versus Vietnam: An Analysis of the Competing Claims in the South China Sea*. CNA Analysis & Solutions, 2014.

Perrone, Sean. "Spanish Consuls and Trade Newtorks between Spain and the United States, 1795–1820." 38(1) *Bulletin for Spanish and Portuguese Historical Studies* 75–94, 2013.

Petersen, Ulrich, César E. Vidal and Donald C. Noble. "Preface to A Special Issue Devoted to the Mineral Deposits of Peru." 85(7) *Economic Geology* 1287–1295, 1990.

Pham, Hung. "Philippines v. China: The South China Sea Finally Meets International Law." 16(2) *Chicago Kent Journal for International and Comparative Law* 1–12, 2016.

Pharand, Donat. *The Northwest Passage: Arctic Straits*. Leiden: Brill, 1984.

Philpott, Daniel. "Ideas and the Evolution of Sovereignty." In *State Sovereignty: Change and Persistence in International Relations*, 15–48. Edited by Sohail H. Hashmi. University Park: Penn State University Press, 1997.

Pietschmann, Horst, "Spanish Expansions in America, 1492 to c. 1580." In *General History of the Caribbean, Volume II, New Societies: The Caribbean in the Long Sixteenth Century*, 79–113. Edited by Peter C. Emmer and German Carrera Damas. New York: Palgrave Macmillan, 1999.

Pitts, Jennifer. "Political Theory of Empire and Imperialism." 13(1) *Annual Review of Political Science* 211–235 (2010).

Pitts, Jennifer. *A Turn To Empire: The Rise of Imperial Liberalism in Britain and France*. Princeton: Princeton University Press, 2006.

Planas-Suárez, Simón. "L'extension de la doctrine de Monroe en Amérique du Sud." 5(IV) *Recueil des Cours* 267–365, 1924.

Pocock, J.G.A. *Politics, Language, and Time: Essays on Political Thought and History*. Chicago: University of Chicago Press, 1971.

Poe, Marshall. "Butterfield's Sociology of Whig History: A Contribution to the Study of Anachronism in Modern Historical Thought." 25(4) *Clio: A Journal of Literature, History and the Philosophy of History* 345–63, 1996.

Pocock, J.G.A. *The Machiavellian Moment: Florentine Political Thought and the Atlantic Republican Tradition*. New York: Princeton University Press, 2016 [1975].

Pollock, Heldon. *The Language of the Gods in the World of Men: Sanskrit, Culture, And Power in Premodern India*. London: University of California Press, 2006.

Powell, Michael J. *From Patrician to Professional Elite: The Transformation of the New York City Bar Association*. New York: Russell Sage Foundation, 1988.

Prado y Ugarteche, Javier. "Speech of His Excellency Javier Prodo y Ugarteche." In *Latin America and the United States: Addresses by Elihu Root*, 6–11. Edited by Bacon, Robert and James Brown Scott. Cambridge: Harvard University Press; London: Humphrey Milford, 1917.

Prescott, William H. *History of the Conquest of Mexico with a Preliminary View of the Ancient Mexican Civilization, and the Life of the Conqueror, Hernando Cortés*, Volume II. 8th edn. New York: Harper and Brothers, 1843.

Procès-Verbaux of the Proceedings of the Committee, June 16th–July 24th, 1920, with Annexes. League of Nations Advisory Committee of Jurists. Van Langenhuysen: The Hague, 1920.

Puig, Juan Carlos. *Les Principes du Droit International Public Américain*. Paris: Éditions A. Pedone, 1954.

Quince, Charles. *Resistance to the Spanish-American and Philippine Wars: Anti-Imperialism and the Role of the Press, 1895–1902*. Jefferson: McFarland & Company, Inc., 2017.

Quirk, Robert E. *An Affair of Honor: Woodrow Wilson and the Occupation of Veracruz*. New York: W.W. Norton Company, 1982.

Rajagopal, Balakrishnan. *International Law From Below: Development, Social Movements and Third World Resistance*. New York: Cambridge University Press, 2003.

Ralston, Jackson H., and W.T. Sherman Doyle. *Venezuelan Arbitrations of 1903*. Washington, D.C.: General Printing Office, 1904.

Rathbun, Lyon. "The Debate over Annexing Texas and the Emergence of Manifest Destiny." 4(3) *Rhetoric and Public Affairs* 459–494 (2001).

Raveneau de Lussan, *A journal of a voyage made into the South Sea, by the bucaniers or freebooters of America, from the year 1684 to 1689 written by the Sieur Raveneau de Lussan; to which is Added, The voyage of the Sieur de Montauban, captain of the freebooters on the coast of Guiney, in the year 1695*. London: Printed for The. Newborough at the Golden Ball in St. Paul's Church-yard, Iohn Nicholson at the King's Arms in Little Britain, and Benj. Tooke at the Temple-Gate Near Temple-Bar, 1698.

Remini, Robert V. *Henry Clay: Statesman for the Union*. New York, London: W.W. Norton & Company, 1991.

Restall, Matthew. *When Montezuma Met Cortés: The True Story of the Meeting that Changed History*. New York: HarperCollins Publishers, 2018.

Restall, Matthew. *Seven Myths of the Spanish Conquest*. Oxford: Oxford University Press, 2003.

Reus-Smit, Christian. "Imagining Society: Constructivism and the English School." 4(3) *British Journal of Politics and International Relations* 487–509, 2002.

Rhoads, Edward J.M. *China's Republican Revolution: The Case of Kwangtung 1895– 1913*. Cambridge: Harvard University Press, 1975.

Riddell-Dixon, Elizabeth. "Canada and Arctic Politics: The Continental Shelf Extension." 39(4) *Ocean Development & International Law* 343–359, 2008.

Rimini, R.V. "The Treaty of Ghent: The American Perspective." 44(1) *Handeligen Der Maatschappij Voor Geschiedenis en Oudheidkunde te Gent*, 1990.

Ripley, Charles. "The Central American Court of Justice (1907–1908)." 19(1) *Diálogos: Revista Electrónica de Historia* 47–68, 2018.

Riquelme, Rosa. "Latin America and the Central American Court of Justice." In *Latin America and the International Court of Justice: Contributions to International Law*, 39–49. Edited by Paula Wojcikiewicz Almeida and Jean-Marc Sorel. New York: Routledge, 2017.

Ritter, Stephen K. "Cold Fusion Died 25 Years Ago, but the Research Lives On." 94(44) *Chemical & Engineering News* 34–39, 2016.

Roberts, Anthea, Stephan B. Paul, Pierre-Hugues Verdier and Mila Versteeg. "Comparative International Law: Framing the Field." 109(3) *American Journal of International Law* 467–474 (2015).

Robertson, William Spence. "The Monroe Doctrine Abroad in 1823–1824." 6(4) *American Political Science Review* 546–563, 1912.

Rodríguez González, Salvador. "Doctrina Meléndez." In *Las Tres Doctrinas: La Doctrina Monroe, La Doctrina Drago, La Doctrina Meléndez*, 106–114. San Salvador, El Salvador: C.Z.: Ediciones del Ministerio de Cultura, 1949.

Rodríguez González, Salvador. "The Neutrality of Honduras and the Question of the Gulf of Fonseca." 10 *American Journal of International Law* 509–542, 1916.

Rodó, José Enrique. *Ariel*. Red ediciones S.L., 2011 [1900].

Roelofsen, C.G. "Grotius and International Law." In *Grotius Reader: A Reader for Students of International Law and Legal History*, 3–23. Edited by L.E. van Holk and C.G. Roelofsen. The Hague: T.M.C. Asser Instituut, 1983.

Rogers, Joseph M. *The True Henry Clay*. London: J.B. Lippencott Company, 1904.

Roosevelt, Theodore *The Letters of Theodore Roosevelt*. Edited by Elting E. Morison. Cambridge: Harvard University Press; Oxford University Press, 1954.

Roosevelt, Theodore, *An Autobiography*. New York: Charles Scribner's Sons, 1920.

Root, Elihu, "Address to the Third Conference of the American Republics, Rio de Janeiro [July 31, 1906]." In *Latin America and the United States: Addresses by Elihu Root*, 6–11. Edited by Robert Bacon and James Brown Scott. Cambridge: Harvard University Press; London: Humphrey Milford, 1917.

Root, Elihu. "Annual Banquet (April 25, 1914)." 8 *Proceedings of the American Society of International Law* 325–341, 1914.

Root, Elihu, et al. "Latin America and the United States: Addresses by Elihu Root." *Latin America and the United States: Addresses by Elihu Root*. 1917.

Root, Elihu. "Reply of Mr. Root (Montevideo, Aug. 10, 1906)." In *Latin America and the United States: Addresses by Elihu Root*, 6–11. Edited by Robert Bacon and James Brown Scott. Cambridge: Harvard University Press; London: Humphrey Milford, 1917

Root, Elihu. "The Real Monroe Doctrine." 8 *Proceedings of the American Society of International Law* 6–22 (1914).

Rosenberg, Emily S. *Financial Missionaries to the World: The Politics and Culture of Dollar Diplomacy, 1900–1930*. Cambridge: Harvard University Press, 1999.

Rossi, Christopher R. *Sovereignty and Territorial Temptation: The Grotian Tendency*. New York: Cambridge University Press, 2017.

Rossi, Christopher R. "The Migingo Island Dispute Between Kenya and Uganda." 42(2) *Brooklyn Journal of International Law* 659–693, 2017.

Rossi, Christopher R. "Treaty of Tordesillas Syndrome: Sovereignty ad Absurdum and the South China Sea Arbitration." 20 *Cornell International Law Journal* 231–283, 2017.

Rossi, Christopher R. "Norway's Imperiled Sovereignty Claim over Svalbard's Adjacent Waters." 18(6) *German Law Journal* 1497–1530, 2017.

Rossi, Christopher R. "*Jura Novit Curia*? Condominium in the Gulf of Fonseca and the "Local Illusion" of a Pluri-State Bay." 37(3) *Houston Journal of International Law* 793–840, 2015.

Rossi, Christopher R. "A Particular Kind of Dominium: The Grotian 'Tendency' and the Global Commons in a Time of High Arctic Change." 11(1) *Journal of International Law and International Relations* 1–60, 2015.

Rossi, Christopher R. "The Northern Sea Route and the Seaward Extension of Uti Possidetis (Juris)." 83(4) *Nordic Journal of International Law* 476–508, 2014.

Rossi, Christopher R. *Broken Chain of Being: James Brown Scott and the Origins of Modern International Law*. The Hague, London, Boston: Kluwer Law International, 1998.

Rossi, Christopher R. *Equity and International Law: A Legal Realist Approach to International Decisionmaking*. Irvington-on-Hudson: Transnational Publishers, 1993.

Roszko, Edyta. *Geographies of Connection and Disconnection: Narratives of Seafaring In Lý So'n* in *Connected and Disconnected in Vietnam: Remaking Social Relations in A Post-Socialist Nation* 347, 349. Edited by Philip Taylor. Acton: ANU Press, 2016.

Ruiz-Fabri, Hélène, Mark Toufayan and Emmanuelle Tourme-Jouannet. *Droit international et nouvelles approaches sur le tiers-monde: entre repetition et renouveau/ International Law and New Approaches to the Third World: Between Repetition and Renewal*. Paris: Société de Législation Comparée, 2013.

Saffo, Paul Laurence. "The Common Heritage of Mankind: Has the General Assembly Created a Law to Govern Seabed Mining?" 53(2) *Tulane Law Review* 492–520, 1979.

Sage, Walter N. "The Oregon Treaty of 1846." 27(4) *Canadian Historical Review* 349–367, 1946.

Salvatore, Ricardo D. "North American Travel Narratives and the Ordering/Othering of South America (C. 1810–1860)." 9(1) *Journal of Historical Sociology* 85–110 (1996).

Salvatore, Ricardo D. "Re-Discovering Spanish America: Uses of Travel Literature about South America in Britain." 8(2) *Journal of Latin American Cultural Studies* 199–217 (1999).

Samelson, Franz. "Whig and Anti-Whig Histories-And Other curiosities of Social Psychology." 36(4) *Journal of the History of Behavioral Science* 499–506, 2000.

Samuels, Marwyn. *Contest for the South China Sea*. New York: Methuen, 1982.

Sandel, Michael J. "The Procedural Republic and the Unencumbered Self." 12(1) *Political Theory* 86–96, 1984.

Sarmiento, Domingo Faustino. *North and South America: A Discourse Delivered Before the Rhode-Island Historical Society*. Providence: Knowles, Anthony & Co., 1866.

Sarmiento, Jorge L. "Consolidating Power: The Making of Modern Colombia after the Panama Debacle." 93(1) *Ezra's Archives* 93–113, 2013.

Scarfi, Juan Pablo. *The Hidden History of International Law in the Americas: Empire and Legal Networks*. Oxford: Oxford University Press, 2017.

Scharf, Michael P. *Customary International Law in Times of Fundamental Change: Recognizing Grotian Moments*. New York: Cambridge, 2014.

Scheina, Robert L. *Latin America's Wars: The Age of the Caudillo, 1791–1899. Volume 1*. Washington, D.C.: Potomac Books, Inc., 2003.

Schmidt, Brian C. *The Political Discourse of Anarchy: A Disciplinary History of International Relations*. Albany: State University of New York Press, 1998.

Schmidt, Brian C. "The Historiography of Academic International Relations." 20(4) *Review of International Studies* 349–367, 1994.

Schmitt, Carl. "Forms of Modern Imperialism in International Law." In *Spatiality, Sovereignty and Carl Schmitt: Geographies of the Nomos*, 29–45. Edited by Stephen Legg, Matthew Hannah trans. New York: Routledge, 2011.

Schmitz, David F. *Henry L. Stimson, The First Wise Man*. Wilmington: Scholarly Resources Inc., 2001.

Schmitt, Carl. "Großraum versus Universalism: The International Legal Struggle over the Monroe Doctrine." In *Spatiality, Sovereignty and Carl Schmitt: Geographies of the Nomos*, 46–54. Edited by Stephen Legg. New York: Routledge, 2011.

Schmitt, Carl. *The Nomos of the Earth in the International Law of the Jus Publicum Europaeum*. New York: Telos Press, 2006.

Schneider, Peter. "*Condominium*." In 10 *Encyclopedia of Public International Law*, 732–735. Edited by Rudolf L. Bernhardt. Amsterdam: North-Holland, 1992.

Schoenbaum, Thomas J. "Symposium on the South China Sea Arbitration: The South China Sea Arbitration Decision: The Need for Clarification." 110 *AJIL Unbound* 290–295, 2016.

Schoonover, Thomas. "Germany in Central America, 1820s to 1929: An Overview." 33 *Jahrbuch für Geschichte Lateinamerikas-Anuario de Historia de América Latina*, 33–60, 2016.

Schouenborg, Laust, "The English School and Institutions: British Institutionalists?" In *Guide to The English School In International Relations*, 77–90. Edited by Cornelia Navari and Daniel Green. Oxford: John Wiley & Sons, 2014.

Schoultz, Lars. *Beneath the United States: A History of U.S. Policy Toward Latin America*. Cambridge: Harvard University Press, 1988.

Schrijver, Nico. "Managing the Global Commons: Common Good or Common Sink?" 37(7) *Third World Quarterly* 1252–1267, 2016.

Schulz, Carsten-Andreas. "Accidental Activists: Latin American Status-Seeking at The Hague." 61(3) *International Studies Quarterly* 612–622 (2017).

Schulz, Carsten-Andreas. "Civilisation, Barbarism and the Making of Latin America's Place in 19th-Century International Society." 42(3) *Millennium: Journal of International Studies* 837–859, 2014.

Schwarzenberger, Georg "The Standard of Civilization in International Law." 8(1) *Current Legal Problems* 212–234, 1955.

Scobbie, I. "The ICJ and the Gulf of Fonseca: When Two Implies Three but Entails One." 18(1) *Marine Policy* 249–262, 1994.

Scott, James Brown. *Law, the State, and the International Community*. Volume I. New York: Colombia University Press, 1939.

Scott, James Brown. Papers. Lauinger Library, Georgetown University. Washington, D.C.

Scott, James Brown. *The Spanish Origin of International Law: Francisco de Vitoria and His Law of Nations*. Oxford: Clarendon Press, 1934.

Scott, James Brown, ed. *The International Conferences of American States, 1889–1928*. New York: Oxford University Press, 1931.

Scott, James Brown, ed. *The Hague Conventions and Declarations of 1899 and 1907*. 3rd. edn. New York: Oxford University Press, 1918.

Scott, James Brown, ed. *The Reports to the Hague Conferences of 1899 and 1907*. New York: Clarendon Press, 1917.

Scott, James Brown. "The Purchase of the Danish West Indies by the United States of America." 10(3) *American Journal of International Law* 682–688, 1916.

Scott, James Brown. *The Hague Peace Conferences of 1899 and 1907. Volume I*. Baltimore: Johns Hopkins University, 1909.

Scott, James Brown. "The Central American Peace Conference of 1907." 2(1) *American Journal of International Law* 121–143, 1908.

Scott, James Brown, and Robert Bacon. "Introductory Note." In *Latin America and the United States: Addresses by Elihu Root*, ix–xii. Collected and Edited by Robert Bacon and James Brown Scott. Cambridge: Harvard University Press, 1917.

Scott, J.B., and R Bacon. "Speech of His Excellency Joaquim Naboco." In *Latin America and the United States: Addresses by Elihu Root*, 3–5. Collected and Edited by Robert Bacon and James Brown Scott. Cambridge: Harvard University Press, 1917.

Scott, J.B., and R. Bacon. "Speech of the Secretary of State [Address to the Third Conference of the American Republics, July 31, 1906]." In *Latin America and the United States: Addresses by Elihu Root*, 6–11. Collected and Edited by Robert Bacon and James Brown Scott. Cambridge: Harvard University Press, 1917.

Scott, J.B., and R. Bacon. "Speech of Dr. Luis M. Drago. August 17, 1906" In *Latin America and the United States: Addresses by Elihu Root*, 93–96. Collected and Edited by Robert Bacon and James Brown Scott. Cambridge: Harvard University Press, 1917.

Scott, J.B., and R. Bacon. "Speech of His Excellency Javier Prado y Ugarteche. September 11, 1906." In *Latin America and the United States: Addresses by Elihu Root*, 116–122. Collected and Edited by Robert Bacon and James Brown Scott. Cambridge: Harvard University Press, 1917.

Scott, J.B., and R. Bacon. "Speech of Senator Ruy Barbosa. (August 2, 1906)." In *Latin America and the United States: Addresses by Elihu Root*, 19–27. Collected and Edited by Robert Bacon and James Brown Scott. Cambridge: Harvard University Press, 1917.

Scroggs, William Oscar. "William Walker and the Steamship Corporation in Nicaragua." 19(4) *The American Historical Review* 797–811, 1905.

"Senator Root Earnestly Advocates Arbitration: Extracts from Speech Before the U.S. Senate." 10(3) *Pacific Marine Review* 7–12, 1912–1913.

Setzekorn, William David. *Formerly British Honduras: A Profile of the New Nation of Belize*. Athens: Ohio University Press, 1975.

Sewell, Keith C. *Herbert Butterfield and the Interpretation of History*. London: Palgrave Macmillan, 2005.

Sexton, Jay. *The Monroe Doctrine: Empire and Nation in Nineteenth-Century America*. Farrar, Straus and Giroux, 2011.

Sharp, Paul. "Herbert Butterfield, The English School, and the Civilizing Virtues of Diplomacy." 79(4) *International Affairs* 855–878, 2003.

Sheinin, David. "Rethinking Pan Americanism: An Introduction." In *Beyond the Ideal: Pan Americanism in Inter-American Affairs*, 1–8. Edited by David Sheinin. Westport: Greenwood Press, 2000.

Shen, Jianming. "The Relativity and Historical Perspective of the Golden Age of International Law." 6(1) *International Legal Theory* 15–34, 2000.

Singh, Prabhakar and Benoît Mayer, eds. *Critical International Law: Postrealism, Postcolonialism, and Transnationalism*. Oxford: Oxford University Press, 2014.

Simon, Joshua. *The Ideology of Creole Revolution: Imperialism and Independence in American and Latin American Political Thought*. Cambridge: Cambridge University Press, 2017.

Simon, Joshua. "The Americas' More Perfect Unions: New Institutional Insights from Comparative Political Theory." 12(4) *American Political Science Association* 808–828, 2014.

Simpson, Gerry. *Great Powers and Outlaw States: Unequal Sovereigns in the International Legal Order*. Cambridge: Cambridge University Press, 2009.

Simpson, Gerry. "Duelling Agendas: International Relations and International Law (Again)." 1(1–2) *Journal of International Law and International Relations* 61–74, 2004.

Skinner, Quentin. *Visions of Politics: Volume 1: Regarding Method.* Cambridge: Cambridge University Press, 2002.

Skinner, Quentin. "History and ideology in the English Revolution." In *Visions of Politics: Hobbes and Civil Science: Volume 3*, 238–263. Cambridge: Cambridge University Press, 2002.

Skinner, Quentin. "Meaning and Understanding in the History of Ideas." 8(1) *History and Theory* 3–53, 1969.

Skouteris, Thomas. *The Notion of Progress in International Law Discourse.* T.M.C. Asser Press, 2009.

Slade, William F. "The Federation of Central America." 8(2) *The Journal of Race Development* 79–150, 1917.

Slaughter, Anne-Marie. "An American Vision of International Law?" 97 *Proceedings of the American International Law Society* 125–129, 2003.

Small, Melvin. "The United States and the German 'Threat' to the Hemisphere, 1905–1914." 28(3) *The Americas* 252–270, 1972.

Smith, Joseph. "The First Conference of American States (1889–1890) and the Early Pan American Policy of the United States." In *Beyond the Ideal: Pan Americanism in Inter-American Affairs.* Edited by David Sheinin. Westport: Greenwood Press, 2000.

Smith, Robert F. "A Note on the Bryan-Chamorro Treaty and German Interest in a Nicaraguan Canal." 9(1) *Caribbean Studies* 63–66, 1969.

Southerland, Matthew. "China's Island Building in the South China Sea: Dam- Age to the Maritime Environment, Implications and International Law" *U.S.-China Economics & Securities Review Commission*, 2016.

"Speech by Baron Descamps on the Rules of Law to be applied." In *Procès-Verbaux of the Proceedings of the Committee, June 16th–July 24th, 1920, With Annexes, Annex 1.* The Hague: Van Langenhuysen Brothers, 1920.

Sprout, Harold, and Margaret Sprout. *The Rise of American Naval Power, 1776–1918.* Princeton University Press, 1939.

Spykman, Nicholas John. *America's Strategy in World Politics: The United States and the Balance of World Power.* New York: Harcourt, Brace and Company, 1942.

Squier, E.G. *Honduras Interoceanic Railway: With Maps of the Line and Ports; and An Appendix.* London: Trübner & Co., 1857.

Squier, E.G. *Preliminary Notes to a Report on the Proposed Honduras Interoceanic Railway.* New York: Tubbs, Nesmith, and Teall Printers, 1854.

Stansifer, Charles L. "E. George Squier and the Honduras Interoceanic Railroad Project." 46(1) *The Hispanic American Historical Review* 1–27, 1966.

Stedman's Medical Dictionary. 5th edn. Philadelphia: Lippincott Williams & Wilkins, 2005.

Steinberg Philip, E., "Lines of Division, Lines of Connection: Stewardship in the World Ocean." 89(2) *Geographical Review* 254–264, 1999.

Steinle, Stephanie. “Georg Schwarzenberger (1980–1991).” In *Jurists Uprooted: German-Speaking Emigré Lawyers in Twentieth Century Britain*. Edited by Jack Beatson & Reinhard Zimmermann. Oxford: Oxford University Press, 2004.

Sterio, Milena. “A Grotian Moment: Changes in the Legal Theory of Statehood.” 39 *Denver Journal International Law & Policy* 209, 2011.

Sterling-Folker, Jennifer. “The English School.” In *Making Sense of International Relations Theory*, 299–306. Edited by Jennifer Sterling-Folker. Boulder: Lynne Rienner Publishers, 2006.

Stettner, Edward A. *Shaping Modern Liberalism: Herbert Croly and Progressive Thought*. Lawrence: University Press of Kansas, 1993.

Stevenson John, R. and H. Oxman Bernard. “The Third United Nations Conference on the Law of the Sea: The 1974 Caracas Session.” 69(1) *American Journal of International Law* 1–30, 1975.

Steward, Richard W., ed. *American Military History, Volume 1: The United States Army and the Forging of A Nation, 1775–1917*. Washington, D.C.: Center of Military History, 2005.

Stiles, T.J. *The First Tycoon: The Epic Life of Cornelius Vanderbilt*. Vintage Books, 2010.

Stirk, P. “No Peace Beyond the Line.” In *Spatiality, Sovereignty and Carl Schmitt: Geographies of the Nomos*, 276–283. Edited by Stephen Legg. New York: Routledge, 2011.

Stoetzer, O. Carlos. *Karl Christian Friedrich Krause and His Influence in the Hispanic World*. Koln: Böhlau Verlag, 1980.

Strassnig, Christian. “Rediscovering the Camino Real of Panama: Archaeology and Heritage Tourism Potentials.” 9(2) *Journal of Latin American Geography* 159–168, 2010.

Suganami, Hidemi, “The Historical Development of the English School.” In *Guide to the English School in International Studies*, 7–24. Edited by Cornelia Navari and Daniel Green. Hoboken: Wiley Blackwell, 2014.

Suganami, Hidemi. “The English School in a Nutshell.” 9(4) *Ritsumeikan Annual Review of International Studies* 621–636, 2010.

Suganami, Hidemi. *The Domestic Analogy and World Order Proposals*. New York: Cambridge University Press, 1989.

Sullivan, John T. *Report of the Historical and Technical Information Relating to the Problem of Interoceanic Communication by way of the American Isthmus*. Washington, D.C.: Government Printing Office, 1883.

Sumner, William Graham. *Earth-Hunger and Other Essays*. Edited by Albert Galloway Keller. New Haven: Yale University Press, 1913.

Sutherland, John and Cedric Thomas Watts. *Henry v, War Criminal?: And Other Shakespeare Puzzles*. Oxford and New York: Oxford University Press, 2000.

Sweetman, Jack. “Take Veracruz At Once.” 28(2) *Naval Historical Magazine* 34–41, 2014.

Talmon, Stefan. “The South China Sea Arbitration: Is There a Case to Answer?” In *The South China Sea Arbitration: A Chinese Perspective*, 15–79. Edited by Stefan Talmon and Bing Bing Jia. Oxford: Hart, 2014.

Taylor, A.J.P. Germany's First Bid for Colonies 1884–1885: A Move in Bismarck's European Policy. Hamden, Connecticut: Archon Books, 1967.

"Telegram, undated, handed to the Department of State, October 10, 1913 [translation]." Minister for Foreign Affairs of Nicaragua to the Nicaraguan Minister at Washington. *Papers Relating to the Foreign Relations of the United States*, File No 711.13/37.

Taylor, George Rogers. *The Turner Thesis: Concerning the Role of the Frontier in American History*. Edited by George Rogers Taylor. Lexington: Heath, 1956.

"The March of Arbitration and Conciliation." 93 *Advocate of Peace Through Justice* 235–238, 1931.

Thompson, Kenneth, "Butterfield and the Theory of International Politics." In *Herbert Butterfield: The Ethics of History and Politics*, 41–54. Edited by Kenneth Thomson. Lanham: University Press of America, 1980.

Tichner, Arlene B. "Seeing IR Differently: Notes from the Third World." 32(2) *Millenium* 295–324, 2003.

Tiller, Rachael, and Elizabeth Nyman, "The Clear and Present Danger to the Norwegian Sovereignty of the Svalbard Fisheries Protection Zone: Enter the Snow Crab." 137 *Ocean & Coastal Management* 24–33, 2017.

Timmermann, Andreas. Hipólito Yrigoyen (1850–1933): "Krausism" and International Understanding. Paper delivered at the Latin America and International Law Conference, Albrecht Mendelssohn Bartholdy Graduate School of Law, University of Hamburg, February 8–9, 2018.

Tompkins, E. Berkeley. *Anti-Imperialism in the United States: The Great Debate*. Philadelphia: University of Pennsylvania Press, 1970.

Topulos, Katherine. "Book Review." 28(1) *International Journal of Legal Information* 150–153, 2000.

Toufayan, Mark. "'Suffering' the Paradox of Rights? Critical Subaltern Historiography and the Genealogy of Empathy." In *Critical International Law: Postrealism, Postcolonialism, and Transnationalism*, 167–169. Edited by Prabhakar Singh and Benoît Mayer. Oxford University Press, 2014.

Tucker, Robert W. and David C. Hendrickson. *Empire of Liberty: The Statecraft of Thomas Jefferson*. Oxford: Oxford University Press, 1990.

Tucker, Spencer C. "Elihu Root." In *A Global Chronology of Conflict: From the Ancient World to the Modern Middle East. Volume 1: ca. 3000 BCE–1499* CE., 1746–1747. Edited by Spencer C. Tucker. Santa Barbara: ABC/CLIO, 2010.

Turner, Frederick Jackson. "The Significance of the Frontier in American History." *Annual Report of the American Historical Association* 119–227, 1894.

Travis, Philip W. *Reagan's War on Terrorism in Nicaragua: The Outlaw State*. Lanham: Lexington Books, 2017.

Trelles, Carlos M. "Study of Cuban Bibliography Relative to the Monroe Doctrine." 5(1) *The Hispanic American Historical Review* 107–115, 1922.

Truyol Serra, Antonio. "Les principals étapes de la vie de Vitoria." In *Actualité de la pensée juridique de Francisco de Vitoria*, 1–10. Edited by Truyol Serra Antonio, Henry Mechoulan, Peter Haggenmacher, Antonio Ortiz-Arce, Primitivo Marino and Joe Verhoeven. Bruxelles: Bruylant, 1988.

Tryon, James L. "The Hague Conferences." 20(6) *Yale Law Journal* 470–485, 1911.

Tucker, Robert W., and David C. Hendrickson. *Empire of Liberty: the Statecraft of Thomas Jefferson*. Oxford University Press, 1990.

Tuveson, Ernest Lee. *Redeemer Nation: The Idea of America's Millennial Role*. University of Chicago Press, 1968.

Twiss, Travers. *The Oregon Territory, Its History and Discovery*. New York: D. Appleton & Co., 1846.

Ugarte, Manuel. *La Nación Latinoamericana*. Fundación Biblioteca Ayachucho, 1987.

Ulmen, G.L. "American Imperialism and International Law: Carl Schmitt on the US in World Affairs." 72(1) *Telos* 43–71, 1987.

Urrutia, F.J. "La codification du droit international en Amérique." 22(II) *Recueil des Cours* 81–231, 1928.

Vallejo, Antonio R. *Historia Documentada de los límites entre la Republica de Honduras y las de Nicaragua, el Salvador y Guatemala, Tomo 1*. S.N. New York, 1938.

Van Atta, John R. *Securing the West: Politics, Public Lands, and the Fate of the Old Republic, 1785–1850*. Baltimore: The Johns Hopkins University Press, 2014.

Van Kleffens, Eelso Nicolaas. "Sovereignty in International Law: Five Lectures." 82(I) *Recueil des Cours* 1–131, 1953.

Van Vollenhoven, Cornelis. *De Drie Treden Van Het Volkenrecht*. S-Gravenhage: Martinus Nijhoff, 1918.

Van Warmelo, P. "Aspects of Joint Ownership in Roman Law." 25(2) *Tijdschrift voor Rechtsgeschiedenis* 125–195, 1957.

Vásquez Medina, Luis E. *La Verdad Detrás de la Guerra del Pacífico: El Imperio Británico contra el systema Americano de economía en Sudamérica*. Lima: Arquitas, 2012.

Verzijl, J.H.W. *International Law in Historical Perspective*. Volume 6. Leiden: A.W. Sijthoff, 1973.

Vile, John R., ed. *Great American Lawyers: An Encyclopedia*. Vol. 2, ABC-CLIO, 2001.

Vigezzi, Brunello. *The British Committee on the Theory of International Politics (1954–1985): The Rediscovery of History*. Ian Harvey trans. Milano: Edizioni Unicopli, 2005.

Vincent, R.J. *Nonintervention and International Order*. Princeton: Princeton University Press, 1974.

Vitier, Cintio and Daisaku Ikeda. *José Martí, Cuban Apostle: A Dialogue*. New York, N.Y.: I.B. Tauris & Co. Ltd., 2013.

Warren, Christopher N. "Henry v, Anachronism, and the History of International Law." In *The Oxford Handbook to English Law and Literature, 1500–1700*, 709–727. Edited by Lorna Hutson. Oxford: Oxford University Press, 2017.

Washburn, Albert H. "The Legality of the Pacific Blockade III." 21(5) *Columbia Law Review* 442–459, 1921.

Watson, Adam. *The Evolution of International Society: A Comparative Historical Analysis*. New York: Routledge, 1992.

Watson, Adam. *Diplomacy: The Dialogue Between States*. London: Eyre Methuen, 1983.

Weber, Max. *Economy and Society: An Outline of Interpretive Sociology*. Edited by Guenther Roth and Claus Wittich. Bedminster Press, 1968.

Weeramantry, Christopher. "The Grotius Lecture Series: Opening Tribute to Hugo Grotius." 14(6) *American University of International Law Review* 1515–1569, 1999.

Weinberg, Albert K. *Manifest Destiny: A Study of Nationalist Expansionism In American History*. Baltimore: Johns Hopkins Press, 1935.

Weinert, Matthew S. "From Cinderella to Beauty and the Beast: (De)Humanising World Society." In *System, Society & the World: Exploring the English School of International Relations*, 90–97. 2nd edn. Edited by Robert W. Murray. Bristol: E-International Relations Publishing, 2015.

Weinert, Matthew S. "Reframing the Pluralist-Solidarist Debate." 40(1) *Millennium* 21–41, 2011.

Weitzel, George Thomas. *American Policy in Nicaragua. Memorandum on the Convention Between the United States and Nicaragua Relative to an Interoceanic Canal and A Naval Station in the Gulf of Fonseca, Signed At Managua, Nicaragua, On February 8, 1913*. Washington, D.C.: Government Printing Office, 1916.

Wertheim, Stephen, "The League That Wasn't: American Designs for a Legalist-Sanctionist League of Nations and the Intellectual Origins of International Organization, 1914–1920." 35(5) *Diplomatic History* 797–836, 2011.

Westlake, John. *International Law (Peace)*. Volume 1. Cambridge: Cambridge University Press, 1910.

Weststeijn, Arthur. "Provincializing Groitus: International Law and Empire in a Seventeenth-Century Malay Mirror." In *International Law and Empire: Historical Explorations*, 21–38. Edited by Martti Koskenniemi, Walter Rech and Manuel Jiménez Fonseca. Oxford: Oxford University Press, 2017.

Whatmore, Richard. "Introduction to the New Princeton Classics Edition." In J.G.A. Pocock, *The Machiavellian Moment: Florentine Political Thought and the Atlantic Republican Tradition*, vii–xxii, 2016. New Princeton Classics Edition, 2016.

Wheaton, Henry. *Elements of International Law: with a Sketch of the History of the Science*. Philadelphia: Carey, Lea & Blanchard, 1836.

Wheless, Joseph. "What Countries Benefit by the Monroe Doctrine." 8 *Proceedings of the American Society of International Law* 171–180, 1914.

Whitaker, Arthur P. *The Western Hemisphere Idea: Its Rise and Decline*. Ithaca: Cornell University Press, 1954.

White, Christopher M. *The History of El Salvador*. Westport and London: Greenwood Press, 2009.

Whiteley, James Gustavus. "The Diplomacy of the United States in Regard to Central American Canals." 165(490) *The North American Review* 364–378, 1897.

Wight, Martin. *International Theory: The Three Traditions.* Edited by Gabriele Wight and Brian Porter. London: Leicester University Press, 1991.

Wight, Martin. *Systems of States*. Leicester: Leicester University Press, 1977.

Wight, Martin. "Western Values in International Relations." In *Diplomatic Investigations*, 89–131. Edited by Herbert Butterfield and Martin Wight. London: Allen & Unwin, 1966.

Wight, Martin. *Power Politics*. "Looking Forward" Pamphlets, No.8. London: Royal Institute of International Affairs, 1946.

Wiley, Edwin. *Lectures on the Growth and Development of the United States*. Volume 10. Edited by Everett Irving Rines and Albert Hart. New York: American Educational Alliance, 1916.

Wilgus, A. Curtis, ed. *The Caribbean: British, Dutch, French, United States*. Gainesville: University of Florida Press, 1958.

Williams, Robert A. Jr. *The American Indian in Western Legal Thought: The Discourses of Conquest.* New York: Oxford University Press, 1990.

Williams, William Appleman. *The Tragedy of American Diplomacy*. New York: Dell Publishing Company, 1972.

Wilson, Adrian and T.G. Ashplant. "Whig History and Present-Centered History." 31(1) *The Historical Journal* 1–16, 1988.

Wilson, Eric Michael. *The Savage Republic: De Indis of Hugo Grotius, Republicanism and Dutch Hegemony within the Early Modern World-System* (*c. 1600–1619*). Leiden, Boston: Martinus Nijhoff Publishers, 2008.

Wilson, Peter. "The English School's Approach to International Law." In *Theorising International Society: English School Methods*, 167–188. Edited by Cornelia Navari. New York: Palgrave Macmillan, 2009.

Woodrow, Wilson. "War Messages." 65th Congress, 1st Sess. 1917, Washington, D.C., Washington, D.C. Senate Doc. No 5, Serial No. 7264.

Witt, John Fabian. "The Dismal History of the Laws of War." 1(3) *University of California Irvine Law Review* 895–911, 2011.

Wittgenstein, Ludwig. *Tractatus Logico-Philosophicus*. New York: Harcourt , 1951 [1921].

Wong, Dong. *China's Unequal Treaties: Narrating National History*. Plymouth: Rowman & Littlefield, 2005.

Woolsey, Theodore S. "An American Concert of the Powers." 45 *Scribner's Magazine* 364–368, November 19, 1898.

Wrigley, Edward Anthony. *Industrial Growth and Population Change: A Regional Study of the Coalfield Areas of North-West Europe in the Later Ninteenth Century.* Cambridge: Cambridge University Press, 2006.

Xue, Guifang (Julia). "The South China Sea: Competing Claims and Conflict Situations." In *The Limits of Maritime Jurisdiction*, 225–248. Edited by Clive H. Scholfield, Seokwoo Lee, and Moon-Sang Kwon. Leiden: Koninklijke Brill Nv, 2014.

Yearbook of the International Law Commission 1962. Volume II. New York: United Nations, 1964.

Yepes de Uprimny, Inés. *Jesús María Yepes y el derecho internacional Americano*. Bogotá: Editorial Temis Librería, 1980.

Yepes, J.M. "Les accords régionaux et le droit international." 71(II) *Recueil des Cours* 227–344, 1947.

Yepes, J.-M. "Les problèmes fondamentaux du droit des gens en Amérique." 47(I) *Recueil des Cours* 1–144, 1934.

Yepes, J.M. "La contribution de l'Amérique latine au développement du droit international public et privé." 32(II) *Recueil des Cours* 691–800, 1930.

Young, Crawford. *The African Colonial State in Comparative Perspective*. New Haven: Yale University Press, 1994.

Yu, Mincai. "China's Responses to the Compulsory Arbitration on the South China Sea Dispute: Legal Effects and Policy Options." 45(1) *Ocean Development and International Law* 1–16, 2014.

Yu, Peter Kien-Hong. "The Chinese (Broken) U-Shaped Line in the South China Sea: Points, Lines, and Zones." 25(3) *Contemporary Southeast Asia* 405–430, 2003.

Zapatero Miguel, Pablo. "Francisco de Vitoria and the Postmodern Grand Critique of International Law." In *At the Origins of Modernity: Francisco de Vitoria and the Discovery of International Law*. Edited by José María Beneyto and Justo Corti Varela, 77–95. Springer International Publishing AG, 2017.

Zapatero, Pablo. "Legal Imagination in Vitoria. The Power of Ideas." 11(2) *Journal of the History of International Law* 221–271, 2009.

Zasloff, Jonathan, "Law and the Shaping of American Foreign Policy: From the Gilded Age to the New Era." 78(1) *New York University Law Review* 239–373, 2003.

Zimmermann, Warren. *First Great Triumph: How Five Americans Made Their Country a World Power*. New York: Farrar, Straus and Giroux, 2002.

Zou, Keyuan. "The South China Sea." In *The Oxford Handbook of the Law of the Sea*, 626–646. Edited by Donald R. Rothwell, Alex G. Oude Elferink, Karen N. Scott, and Tim Stephens. New York: Oxford University Press, 2015.

Name and Author Index

Subject Index

www.ingramcontent.com/pod-product-compliance
Lightning Source LLC
Chambersburg PA
CBHW051400240926
51852CB00002B/75
9789004389182